TRANSLATING THE NEW TESTAMENT

McMaster New Testament Studies

The McMaster New Testament Studies series, edited by Stanley E. Porter, is designed to address particular themes in the New Testament that are of concern to Christians today. Written in a style easily accessible to ministers, students, and laypeople by contributors who are proven experts in their fields of study, the volumes in this series reflect the best of current biblical scholarship while also speaking directly to the pastoral needs of people in the church today.

Translating the New Testament

Text, Translation, Theology

Edited by

Stanley E. Porter and Mark J. Boda

WILLIAM B. EERDMANS PUBLISHING COMPANY
GRAND RAPIDS, MICHIGAN / CAMBRIDGE, U.K.

© 2009 Wm. B. Eerdmans Publishing Co.
All rights reserved

Published 2009 by
Wm. B. Eerdmans Publishing Co.
2140 Oak Industrial Drive N.E., Grand Rapids, Michigan 49505 /
P.O. Box 163, Cambridge CB3 9PU U.K.

Library of Congress Cataloging-in-Publication Data

Translating the New Testament: text, translation, theology /
   edited by Stanley E. Porter and Mark J. Boda.
      p.   cm.   — (McMaster New Testament studies)
   Proceedings of a colloquium held in May 2005 at
   McMaster Divinity College, Hamilton, Ont.
   Includes index.
   ISBN 978-0-8028-6377-5 (pbk.: alk. paper)
   1. Bible. N.T. — Translating — Congresses.
   I. Porter, Stanley E., 1956-   II. Boda, Mark J.

BS449.T7475   2009
220.501 — dc22

                                2009023800

www.eerdmans.com

Contents

Preface ix

Contributors xii

Abbreviations xiv

Translating the New Testament: An Introduction
to Issues of Text, Translation, and Theology 1
   Stanley E. Porter

PART 1: TEXT

New Testament Textual Research, Its Methods and Its Goals 13
   Barbara Aland

Rule 9, Isolated Variants, and the "Test-Tube" Nature
of the NA^{27}/UBS^4 Text: A Byzantine-Priority Perspective 27
   Maurice A. Robinson

The Significance of the Papyri in Revising the
New Testament Greek Text and English Translations 62
   Philip Comfort

CONTENTS

THE TEXT AND LUKE 16:19-31

The Text of Luke 16   93
  Barbara Aland

The Rich Man and Lazarus — Luke 16:19-31: Text-Critical Notes   96
  Maurice A. Robinson

Two Illustrations of Scribal Gap Filling in Luke 16:19   111
  Philip Comfort

PART 2: TRANSLATION

Assessing Translation Theory: Beyond Literal
and Dynamic Equivalence   117
  Stanley E. Porter

A Translation That Induces a Reading Experience:
Narrativity, Intratextuality, Rhetorical Performance,
and Galatians 1–2   146
  Alain Gignac

Hebrews 10:32-39 and the Agony of the Translator   167
  Luke Timothy Johnson

TRANSLATION AND LUKE 16:19-31

Comparative Discourse Analysis as a Tool in
Assessing Translations, Using Luke 16:19-31 as a Test Case   185
  Stanley E. Porter and Matthew Brook O'Donnell

Synchronic Observations on Luke 16:19-31 as Preparation
for a Translation   200
  Alain Gignac

Narrative Perspectives on Luke 16:19-31   207
  Luke Timothy Johnson

PART 3: THEOLOGY

Mistranslation and the Death of Christ: Isaiah 53 LXX
and Its Pauline Reception — 215
Francis Watson

On Probabilities, Possibilities, and Pretexts:
Fostering a Hermeneutics of Sobriety, Sympathy, and
Imagination in an Impressionistic and Suspicious Age — 251
Edith M. Humphrey

An Intertextual Reading of Moral Freedom
in the Analects and Galatians — 271
K. K. Yeo

A Latin American Rereading of Romans 7 — 290
Elsa Tamez

THEOLOGY AND LUKE 16:19-31

To Squeeze the Universe into a Ball —
Playing Fast and Loose with Lazarus? — 307
Edith M. Humphrey

A Confucianist, Cross-cultural Translation of Luke 16:19-31:
Ethics, Eschatology, and Scripture — 314
K. K. Yeo

A Rereading of Luke 16:19-31 — 319
Elsa Tamez

PART 4: TEXT, TRANSLATION, AND THEOLOGY

Quo vadis? From Whence to Where in New Testament
Text Criticism and Translation — 327
Richard N. Longenecker

CONTENTS

Index of Modern Authors 347

Index of Ancient Sources 351

Preface

Several years ago the Canadian Bible Society decided to commemorate their one hundredth anniversary (2006) by sponsoring a series of academic colloquia at Canadian educational institutions. By doing this they were seeking to show their support for biblical scholarship in a tangible way, as well as encouraging further reflection on the translation of the Bible. The first of these colloquia was held at Regent College (Vancouver) in 2003, while the second was co-sponsored with the faculties of theology and religious studies at McGill University, University of Montreal, and Acadia University in Montreal at the end of May 2004 and considered the theme of translating the Hebrew Bible.

The present volume represents the academic fruit of the third in this series of colloquia, co-sponsored with McMaster Divinity College through its yearly Bingham Colloquium and held over three days in May 2005 on our campus in Hamilton, Ontario. The purpose of this third conference was to showcase scholarship related to translating the New Testament, with various scholars invited to consider the main theme under one of three main subtopics: text, translation, and theology.

The essays in this volume are witness to the depth and breadth of knowledge of the invited speakers. Each of the three days considered one of the main subtopics, beginning with text, moving to translation, and finishing with theology. The focus of "text" was on issues related to establishing the text to be used for modern translation. The focus of "translation" was on issues related to the methodology used for the translation of these ancient texts. The focus of "theology" was on issues related to the hermeneutical framework for translating these texts for a diverse global readership.

Those who attended the conference enjoyed both plenary lectures, in which each speaker was given significant time to consider a key scholarly issue related to their sub-theme, and plenary seminars, in which all the speakers on the topic were asked to bring their own hermeneutical framework and methodological skills to bear on a particular pericope in the New Testament (Luke 16:19-31). In this way the conference tried to balance the theoretical with the practical, not only to provide insight into the conceptual framework of the speaker, but also to see how this impacts translation. Time was set aside in each session for questions from and interaction with the conference attendees, furthering one of the key goals of the conference as a creative opportunity to join together in a common project through extended conversation and dialogue. At the conference banquet on the second evening, Dr. Richard Longenecker offered his mature reflection on a lifetime of study on text and translation.

Such a conference would not have been possible without the generous support of the Canadian Bible Society. Rev. Dennis Hillis, District Director for South Central Ontario and co-chair of the planning committee, Rev. Phyllis Nesbitt, National Director, and Dr. Hart Wiens, Director of Scriptural Translation, provided consistent support for the conference through finances, personnel, and expertise. We are especially thankful to Ms. Susan Asuncion in the South Central Ontario District Office for her administrative work on the conference and Nelly Safari in the National Office for her help with publicity.

The conference was co-sponsored with McMaster Divinity College and functioned as the eleventh Bingham Colloquium. The Divinity College's president Dr. Stanley Porter not only played a key role in spearheading the colloquium but also served on the planning committee, chaired sessions, and delivered papers. Dr. Michael Knowles, associate professor of preaching at the Divinity College, also assisted by chairing sessions on the second day. Many of the logistics of the conference were administered by Jenn Bowler, conference coordinator at McMaster Divinity College. Without her help the conference would not have been possible and for her assistance we are thankful. Financial support for the Bingham Colloquium was provided through the generosity of an endowment honoring H. H. Bingham, a noted Baptist leader in Ontario. His leadership abilities were recognized by Baptists all across Canada and the world. He served as general secretary to the Baptist Convention of Ontario and Quebec and as vice-president of the Baptist World Alliance. He displayed the qualities of genuine friendship, dedicated leadership, unswerving Christian faith, tireless devotion to duty, insightful service as a preacher and pastor, and visionary direction for congregation and denomination alike. This colloquium has been endowed by his daughter, Mrs. Doris Kennedy of Calgary, Alberta, as an act of admiration and appreciation for a wonderful father and minister.

The present volume represents written forms of the various papers that were delivered over the three-day conference in May 2005. Following the conference, the speakers were given an opportunity to revise their essays in light of the discussion, and so the present essays have been impacted by the interaction that took place throughout the conference. Transforming these essays into a published volume has involved hours of editing. We are thankful to Andrew Pitts for his assistance with some of this work in the final stages of the project. To the various speakers, now authors, found within this volume, we extend our thanks for taking time out of their busy schedules for the conference as well as providing the essays in this volume. And finally we are grateful to William B. Eerdmans Publishing Company for their continued support of the McMaster New Testament Studies series.

It was our plan from the beginning that this colloquium would be an opportunity for creative dialogue around the key issues related to translating the New Testament in the twenty-first century. It is our hope that this conversation, which began in the live sessions at McMaster Divinity College, will continue as readers engage the material in the present volume and continue to refine both translation theory and translation practice.

MARK J. BODA
Translating the New Testament
Colloquium Co-Chair

Contributors

BARBARA ALAND, Professor emerita and former Director of the Institute for New Testament Textual Research, University of Münster, Germany

MARK J. BODA, Professor of Old Testament, McMaster Divinity College, Hamilton, ON, Canada

PHILIP COMFORT, Senior Editor of Bible Reference, Tyndale House Publishers, Wheaton, IL, USA; Adjunct Professor, Religion, Carolina Coastal University, Conway, SC, USA

ALAIN GIGNAC, Professor of New Testament, Faculté de théologie et de sciences des religions, Université de Montréal, Quebec, Canada

EDITH M. HUMPHREY, William F. Orr Professor of New Testament, Pittsburgh Theological Seminary, Pittsburgh, PA, USA

LUKE TIMOTHY JOHNSON, R. W. Woodruff Professor of New Testament and Christian Origins, Candler School of Theology, Emory University, Atlanta, GA, USA

RICHARD N. LONGENECKER, Professor Emeritus of New Testament, Wycliffe College, University of Toronto, ON, Canada

MATTHEW BROOK O'DONNELL, Adjunct Professor of New Testament, McMaster Divinity College, Hamilton, ON, Canada, and Partner of OpenText.org

Contributors

STANLEY E. PORTER, President, Dean and Professor of New Testament, McMaster Divinity College, Hamilton, ON, Canada

MAURICE A. ROBINSON, Senior Professor of New Testament, Southeastern Baptist Theological Seminary, Wake Forest, NC, USA

ELSA TAMEZ, Translation Consultant of the United Bible Societies and Emerita Professor of the Universidad Biblica Latinoamericana, San Jose, Costa Rica

FRANCIS WATSON, Chair of Biblical Interpretation, Department of Theology and Religion, Durham University, UK

KHIOK-KHNG (K. K.) YEO, Harry R. Kendall Professor of New Testament, Garrett-Evangelical Theological Seminary, Evanston, IL, USA

Abbreviations

AB	Anchor Bible
ANTF	Arbeiten zur neutestamentlichen Textforschung
BEThL	Bibliotheca ephemeridum theologicarum lovaniensium
BHS	*Biblia hebraica stuttgartensia*
BHTh	Beiträge zur historischen Theologie
Bib	*Biblica*
BT	*The Bible Translator*
CBQ	*Catholic Biblical Quarterly*
CBR	*Currents in Biblical Research*
CEV	Contemporary English Version
DJD	Discoveries in the Judaean Desert
ECM	Editio Critica Maior
ESV	English Standard Version
GNT	Good News Translation
HCSB	Holman Christian Standard Bible
HSB	Holman Standard Bible
HTB	Histoire du texte biblique
HTR	*Harvard Theological Review*
HTS	Harvard Theological Studies
ICC	International Critical Commentary
IGNTP	International Greek New Testament Project

Abbreviations

Int	*Interpretation*
JBL	*Journal of Biblical Literature*
JSNT	*Journal for the Study of the New Testament*
JSNTSup	Journal for the Study of the New Testament — Supplement Series
JSOTSup	Journal for the Study of the Old Testament — Supplement Series
JTS	*Journal of Theological Studies*
KJV	King James Version
mg	marginal reading
NA^{27}	B. Aland et al., eds., *Nestle-Aland Novum Testamentum Graece*, 27th ed.
NAB	New American Bible
NASB	New American Standard Bible
NEB	New English Bible
Neot	*Neotestamentica*
NET	NET Bible
NICNT	New International Commentary on the New Testament
NIGTC	New International Greek Testament Commentary
NIV	New International Version
NJB	New Jerusalem Bible
NKJV	New King James Version
NLT	New Living Translation (2nd ed.)
NovT	*Novum Testamentum*
NovTSup	Novum Testamentum Supplements
NRSV	New Revised Standard Version
NTGF	New Testament in the Greek Fathers
NTS	*New Testament Studies*
NTTS	New Testament Tools and Studies
NU	Nestle^{27}/UBS^4
REB	Revised English Bible
RSR	Recherches de science religieuse
RSV	Revised Standard Version
RTL	*Revue théologique de Louvain*
SBLDS	Society of Biblical Literature Dissertation Series
ScEs	*Science et esprit*
SD	Studies and Documents
SNTSMS	Society for New Testament Studies Monograph Series

ABBREVIATIONS

SP	Sacra Pagina
STDJ	Studies on the Texts of the Desert of Judah
TCGNT	Bruce Metzger, *A Textual Commentary on the Greek New Testament*
TDNT	*Theological Dictionary of the New Testament*
TNIV	Today's New International Version
TS	Texts and Studies
TR	Textus Receptus
TZ	*Theologische Zeitschrift*
UBS^4	United Bible Societies, *The Greek New Testament*, 4th ed.
WBC	Word Biblical Commentary
WH	Westcott & Hort
WUNT	Wissenschaftliche Untersuchungen zur Neuen Testament

Translating the New Testament: An Introduction to Issues of Text, Translation, and Theology

Stanley E. Porter

What does it mean to translate the New Testament? This is a question that has been answered in various ways for nearly two thousand years.[1] The earliest translations of the New Testament were by ancient Christians, such as those made into Syriac, Coptic, or Armenian.[2] These translations were made so that local Christians who were not functional in the Greek of the New Testament could hear and possibly even read the New Testament in their native language.[3] This tradition has been maintained up to the present day, for the same reasons. Few modern Christians are capable of reading the Greek of the New Testament, and so they are reliant upon translations to gain access to the content and meaning of the sacred text. The results, even in ancient times but especially in modern times, have been that a variety of translations has been produced. We know that there were various textual traditions of the New Testament itself, and the same was true for the translations that were made of it. As a result, in ancient times and modern times alike, there are a variety of translational traditions. However, it is in modern times that translations have become a business in their own right, with new ones being produced at a phenomenal rate. This

---

1. For a conspectus of opinions and statements from Jerome onward, see H. J. Störig, ed., *Das Problem des Übersetzens* (Darmstadt: Wissenschaftliche, 1963).
2. See, e.g., B. M. Metzger, *The Early Versions of the New Testament* (Oxford: Clarendon, 1977).
3. This is not the place to discuss levels of literacy in the ancient world, except to note that, for most people, their Scriptures were heard orally, not read.

is true of English to be sure, but there is usually a choice of translation available in most modern Western languages.[4]

When one thinks of translation, one normally thinks of interlingual translation. Interlingual translation — distinguished by Roman Jakobson from intralingual and semiotic translation[5] — occurs when one language is rendered into another language. This definition itself begs a number of questions, such as what constitutes a language and what it means to render one language into another in terms of comprehension, fidelity to the original, orality and readability, and the like. Interlingual translation continues to be one of the most important types of translation and the one that biblical scholars are most familiar with. In a very real sense, every biblical scholar who uses the original languages is a Bible translator, as it is a necessity to understand and hence to render the source text into language that is understandable by those who do not know that particular language. Putting aside the issues of intralingual and semiotic translation,[6] we must continue to ask questions regarding the nature of interlingual translation. A number of organizations and Bible societies are concerned daily with such questions.

The notion of "translating the New Testament," which forms the basis of this volume of essays, however, is designed to expand the categories with which we talk about the concept of biblical and especially New Testament translation. In order to facilitate such discussion, the topic is broken down into three (it seemed like a good biblical number) useful subcatego-

---

4. Numerous histories of Bible translation have been written. See, e.g., F. F. Bruce, *History of the Bible in English* (3rd ed.; Guildford: Lutterworth, 1979); D. Ewert, *From Ancient Tablets to Modern Translations: A General Introduction to the Bible* (Grand Rapids: Zondervan, 1983), esp. 183-266. A recent discussion is B. M. Metzger, *The Bible in Translation: Ancient and English Versions* (Grand Rapids: Baker, 2001).

5. See R. Jakobson, "On Linguistic Aspects of Translation," in *On Translation* (ed. R. Brower; Cambridge, MA: Harvard University Press, 1959), 232-39, here 233. It is worth noting that, except for the work done by such people as Eugene Nida and those specifically concerned with translation, the topic of translation is not typically discussed by linguists. For example, in the excellent work edited by N. E. Collinge, *An Encyclopaedia of Language* (London: Routledge, 1990), there are no essays devoted to translation and only three references in the index (in a book of 1,011 pages). For a recent treatment of Nida's influential work, see S. E. Porter, "Eugene Nida and Translation," *BT* 56, no. 1 (2005): 8-19.

6. Intralingual translation involves, according to Jakobson, "rewording" in the same language as the source, and semiotic translation involves the use of sign systems other than words, such as a film (Jakobson, "Linguistic Aspects," 233).

ries: text, translation, and theology. The second term seems redundant, but I will return to that issue in a moment.

The first issue is that of text. One of the first issues that a translator must confront is the general question of the text of the New Testament that one translates.[7] This broad issue involves at least two major, closely related specific issues. The first concerns the broad nature of the text-type that is translated, and the second concerns the principles by which a particular variant reading in the text is adjudicated.[8] Both of these issues are discussed in this volume, with a good bit of disagreement to be found among the contributors. Concerning the first, one realizes that in the history of discussion two major text-types have constituted the basis for translations of the New Testament. The first is the Byzantine, Textus Receptus or Majority text, sometimes called the traditional text.[9] These texts are not identical, but are close enough to be lumped together for consideration here.[10] Advocates of the so-called traditional text hypothesis believe that the text that exists in the greatest number of manuscripts and was most widely used within Christendom from the second half of the first millennium to the nineteenth century constitutes the text of the New Testament. This text is found in the largest number of manuscripts by far, and it deserves to be considered when establishing the text of the New Testament. Ever since the nineteenth century and the discovery of many new manuscripts (such as Sinaiticus and the papyri), and the consequent development of principles for textual criticism, the Alexandrian text-type, especially as known

---

7. This is a huge issue with an enormous bibliography that is beyond discussion here. I am focusing upon several more specific issues. An excellent collection of essays on various dimensions is B. D. Ehrman and M. W. Holmes, eds., *The Text of the New Testament in Contemporary Research: Essays on the Status Quaestionis* (Grand Rapids: Eerdmans, 1995).

8. The development of the Greek text and the principles of textual criticism have an interesting history. For a brief overview, see B. M. Metzger, *The Text of the New Testament: Its Transmission, Corruption, and Restoration* (2nd ed.; Oxford: Clarendon Press, 1968), 95-246, esp. 209-11.

9. At least three scholarly editions of these texts are worth noting. See F. H. A. Scrivener, *The New Testament in Greek* (Cambridge: Cambridge University Press, 1908), the so-called Textus Receptus; Z. C. Hodges and A. L. Farstad, eds., *The Greek New Testament according to the Majority Text* (2nd ed.; Nashville: Nelson, 1985); and M. A. Robinson and W. G. Pierpont, *The New Testament in the Original Greek: Byzantine Textform 2005* (Southborough, MA: Chilton, 2005).

10. See D. B. Wallace, "The Majority Text Theory: History, Methods, and Critique," in Ehrman and Holmes, eds., *Text of the New Testament*, 297-320, esp. 297n.1.

through establishment of an eclectic text, has gained prominence.[11] This volume represents an interesting mix of opinion on this issue. Some argue to retain the dominance of the Byzantine text, while others argue for the Alexandrian. There is also divided opinion over the role of the papyri in establishing this text. Some scholars have thought that the papyri have not been given their full weight in textual criticism. Another issue is how one arbitrates individual variants. In the course of discussing particular texts, not only do various scholars represent different opinions on the broad question of text-types, but when it comes to discussing individual variants there are often differences of opinion. An observer can see that it is easy to talk at cross-purposes on such an issue, because a proponent of a particular text-type might fail to recognize that another position also accepts a particular variant, or at least gives it significant weight and merit, even if finally rejecting it for another.

There are several key points that I believe should be taken away from the discussion of textual criticism. The first is that there is still much work to be done in this area. Perhaps because it has in the past been called lower criticism, there are those who think that it is less important, and hence it has been neglected. There are still many manuscripts to be collated and checked against others and against their use in the critical editions of the New Testament. A second point is that there remains misunderstanding by advocates of various positions regarding contrary opinions. The result is that sometimes it is easy to fall into a stereotype, rather than appreciating a disputatious opinion. A third is that the criteria for adjudicating a textual variant need to continue to be developed, in order to move away from an ad hoc, case-by-case determination of each textual variant and expand to more inclusive criteria that take the larger variant context into consideration. A fourth is the question of whether it is worth exploring the use of a single manuscript, rather than an eclectic text as the primary basis for New Testament studies. This is an issue not directly raised in this volume, but one that looms in the wings in such discussion.

The second major area is translation itself. In a volume on translation it might seem strange to have a subsection on the concept of translation. However, the nature of this volume lends itself to questions of translation theory in their own right. Considering the fact that interlingual

---

11. The so-called Nestle-Aland text. See K. Aland and B. Aland, *The Text of the New Testament* (trans. E. Rhodes; Grand Rapids: Eerdmans, 1988).

translation is a process that goes back thousands of years, it is perhaps somewhat surprising that theoretical reflection on its practice is a relatively recent phenomenon.[12] The result has been that the major categories for discussion of translation have become relatively fixed in terms of an opposition between a literal or formal equivalence and a dynamic or functional equivalence translational approach.[13] The perceived opposition between these two approaches is still prevalent in biblical studies, even though outside of biblical studies translation theory has taken a number of important expansive turns.[14] The variety of opinions and perspectives represented at the conference that gave rise to this volume gives evidence of the fact that important and innovative new perspectives on translation are being explored, some more successfully than others. Whereas most previous discussion of translation has revolved around an overly simplified opposition between emphasis upon the original writer and emphasis on the contemporary reader, some of these new approaches shift these variables significantly, while introducing new factors into the translational matrix. The equation now includes more factors from the ancient world than were heretofore accounted for, and with them a correspondingly more complex view of the modern context into which a translated text is brought. There has even been a heightened awareness of the social and cultural groundedness of translation, to the point of ethically questioning both its presuppositions and its effects.[15]

As a result, it has become clear that there are a number of further fac-

---

12. A good summary of the history of translation theory is found in E. A. Nida, *Toward a Science of Translating with Special Reference to Principles and Procedures Involved in Bible Translating* (Leiden: Brill, 1964), 11-29. For a competing view in terms of English literature, see L. Venuti, *The Translator's Invisibility: A History of Translation* (London: Routledge, 1995).

13. Still one of the best discussions of this opposition is found in E. A. Nida and C. R. Taber, *The Theory and Practice of Translation* (Leiden: Brill, 1969), 3-8, 12-14.

14. Two recent works that explore some of these developments are: J. Munday, *Introducing Translation Studies: Theories and Applications* (London: Routledge, 2001), and T. Wilt, ed., *Bible Translation: Frames of Reference* (Manchester: St. Jerome, 2003).

15. Some of the works that raise these questions are: L. Venuti, ed., *Rethinking Translation: Discourse, Subjectivity, Ideology* (London: Routledge, 1992); P. Zlateva, ed., *Translation as Social Action: Russian and Bulgarian Perspectives* (London: Routledge, 1993); L. Venuti, ed., *The Scandals of Translation: Towards an Ethics of Difference* (London: Routledge, 1998); S. Bassnett and H. Trivedi, eds., *Post-Colonial Translation: Theory and Practice* (London: Routledge, 1999).

tors to consider in approaching the task of translation. One is the need to explore translation in terms of various linguistic factors. A noteworthy challenge for previous translational models has been the same challenge that various linguistic models have faced, and that is the need to conceive of translation as a variable function related to the phenomena to be translated. This means that various linguistic phenomena, depending on how they are used within their source and receptor language, need to be translated in various ways. A second factor is consideration of the notion of context. Context is often invoked in biblical studies, but, though it is widely used, it is not always clearly understood. The notion of context is one that merits further exploration, both in terms of the original context in which an ancient text was composed, and in terms of the situation into which a text is introduced. A third factor is the need to incorporate a variety of extra-biblical factors into the translational equation. These include a wider perspective on usage that includes rhetorical principles of the time of composition and of reception, religious concepts and structures understood then and now, and cultural phenomena that constrain textual performance, ancient and modern.

The third and final dimension of translation treated in this conference volume is the issue of theology. This may appear to be the most surprising element to be included within the ambit of a discussion on translating the New Testament. However, theology is in some ways the silent guest in any translational exercise. It is readily admitted that the text to be translated must be established before translation can commence. It is also increasingly recognized, as noted above, that translation itself is not a theory-neutral enterprise but demands serious methodological awareness and critical reflection. The notion of theology having an impact on translation has always cast its shadow over the enterprise, and the essays included here attempt to bring this realization into the open in a tangible and explicit way. One of the major developments in recent biblical study, including that of the New Testament, is a return to serious biblical theological reflection.[16] Several of the contributors to this volume are advocates of a serious biblical theology that appreciates the Bible, often in its entirety and not simply in terms of the New Testament, as a theological document

---

16. For an older view, see G. Hasel, *New Testament Theology: Basic Issues in the Current Debate* (Grand Rapids: Eerdmans, 1978). D. O. Via, *What Is New Testament Theology?* (Minneapolis: Fortress, 2002), raises many of the major contemporary issues.

that must be read within this larger context.[17] If it must be read within this larger theological context, then it must be translated within this context as well. This biblical theological thrust constitutes a major paradigm for much recent biblical study. One of the criticisms of much previous Bible translation work has been that it has not been fully cognizant of or taken into consideration varying and diverse theological and cultural contexts of those into whose languages the Bible has been rendered. As a result, a variety of culturally relevant theological positions must be brought to bear on translational practice. With the significant expansion of and burgeoning of Christianity in Asia, Latin America, and Africa — each of these areas reflective of a complex set of theological and cultural issues — translation must take such factors into account. There is no single way that this can be done, but a variety of ways must be explored.

The issues that are brought to the fore here regarding theology and translation are several. One is the complex relation that exists between conceptual theological notions and the specific features of linguistics. Theology works best when it is grounded in texts, but texts have an uncanny way of being more complex than can be easily contained within the straitjacket of doctrine. This emerges as an issue to consider, both in the immediate sense of rendering a text for the first world, and especially in terms of how concepts are determinative or not for rendering texts for the non-first world. A second factor is the relation that exists between the Testaments. In many ways, we have examples of theological translation within the Bible itself when we consider how the Old Testament is understood and translated in the New. These relations are not themselves unproblematic, however, which makes their normative function elusive at times. A third and final factor is consideration of how the variety of pressure-point issues of the day have an effect upon theological translation. There are a number of issues that appear to demand address in the contemporary context, but many of these issues may not have been issues for the ancient world. There are also a number of issues that were relevant to the ancients that are not of direct concern to the contemporary reader. The question of how these competing demands are addressed, while being faithful to the original text

---

17. See, e.g., J. Reumann, ed., *The Promise and Practice of Biblical Theology* (Minneapolis: Fortress, 1991); S. J. Kraftchick, C. D. Myers Jr., and B. C. Ollenburger, eds., *Biblical Theology: Problems and Perspectives* (Nashville: Abingdon, 1995); and S. Hafemann, ed., *Biblical Theology: Retrospect and Prospect* (Downers Grove, IL: InterVarsity Press, 2002).

and to the contemporary context in order to create a responsible present text, becomes a major challenge.

One of the more interesting features of the original conference was that we asked each participant not only to offer their paper in their respective area, whether that was text, translation, or theology, but to apply their perspective to a common passage chosen for the conference itself. That passage was Luke 16:19-31, the story regarding the rich man and Lazarus. Part of the task of selecting the passage was to ensure that it offered a challenge for each area. There were certainly passages that stood out for one or even two of the issues, but finding a passage that raised questions for all three was not straightforward. Nevertheless, the passage in Luke's Gospel proved to be more than sufficient to provoke response and discussion. This exercise was chosen so that each area of discussion, as well as each contributor, could not select a passage that was unduly favorable to their respective position. The common passage put all interpreters on the same theoretical common ground and enabled exemplification of each perspective for the same set of data within the text. That exegetical feature of the conference has been retained in this volume, so that most contributors to the main essays have also included a treatment of the passage in Luke 16. Therefore, the treatments of this passage reflect the various approaches and principles of the participant and benefit from application of these methods.

The volume concludes with a summative essay that attempts to reflect in broad terms on the entire question of the nature of translation and transmission of the New Testament. We are pleased that we have not only the individual essays that probe methods and approaches but also one essay that steps back from the focused discussion and reflects more cumulatively upon the entire enterprise, both in its history and in its accomplishments.

The question of how one translates the New Testament involves the larger question of what factors one must take into consideration when translating the New Testament. The essays included in this volume suggest a number of answers to these questions. No doubt only time will tell which answers address the major and most important questions of translation. For many of these questions there are also other answers than those presented here, some because the answers have not yet been formulated and some because they do not seem, at least to those considering such things, to be the right answers. There are no doubt many other questions to be raised that have not been addressed in this volume but that will one way or another emerge in due course as significant and meritorious. They will demand answers at some time in the future. In any case, the concept of Bible translation is an important one for the contemporary church, because it constitutes one of the major bridges between the world of the Bible and the contemporary context. It is also a phenomenon that transcends most boundaries. It encompasses the smallest phenomena of the biblical text and the largest and most complex theological and cultural issues. On this basis alone, the topic deserves further serious discussion and debate.

PART 1
TEXT

New Testament Textual Research, Its Methods and Its Goals

Barbara Aland

Can we ever be sure that we know or ever will know the text of the New Testament as it was originally written? Does there exist an original text of the New Testament at all, or do we have only thousands of manuscripts of the New Testament, so that it may be only an arbitrary choice of one manuscript or a group of manuscripts as a zero point for text history? Readings then may be arbitrarily regarded as variants of a so-called "original" text. Furthermore, any or even all of these may have been consciously or unconsciously altered. These questions outline the main problems of textual criticism. The problems are by no means resolved by the fact that the New Testament is transmitted in more than 5,600 extant manuscripts, but it may be rather more difficult to trace them back to a so-called "original text." The question before us now is how to deal with this situation.

My essay will contain the following parts. First, I will give an overview of the Institute of New Testament Textual Research and its scholarly work. For it is in this Institute that we were able to develop our theories and methods studying together in a single building and thus able to be in direct contact with each other, encouraging and criticizing each other. Secondly, I want to introduce our material and the special problems that we were faced with by that material. We have to be aware that the more traditional methods of evaluating this material according to internal and external criteria of

---

Dr. Barbara Emmet very kindly helped me to correct my English expression.

textual criticism are not sufficient, for decisions reached by internal criteria may often be reached more or less by chance and may be reversible. Decisions reached by the internal criteria in textual criticism do not necessarily need to be discarded, but nonetheless must be supported more effectively than before by external criteria. That means our understanding of the value of the individual manuscript, particularly the early ones, must be strengthened, their reliability or their individual conspicuousness concerning errors and interpolations etc. must be improved, individually and in relation to all other manuscripts, and finally, an overall stemma of all extant New Testament manuscripts should be reached. Here we have to free ourselves from practicing textual criticism in accordance with the peculiar textual methods only, which are not reliable as a basis for decision making. But may that be enough? Of course not. Therefore we have to ask ourselves the main question before us: what goal can we reach? Can we claim to reach the very original text? And if we cannot claim that in any essential way, what is the text that we print in our editions, and what is the relationship between the printed text and the lost original? Therefore, thirdly, I will try to give an overview of the goals and methods that result from the material of the New Testament manuscripts and that we follow in our Institute. Fourthly, I will treat some points resulting from two or three still open questions: the role of the scribe in New Testament manuscripts, the influence of "orality," the communities that "commissioned" these texts, and their reaction to the completed manuscripts delivered.

The Institute of New Testament Textual Research, Its History and Its Scholarly Work

The Institute was founded more than forty-five years ago in 1959, by Kurt Aland, who was its director until December 1983. From the very beginning up to our work today his scholarly experience and spiritual authority have determined the character of the Institute. On the occasion of his seventieth birthday in 1985 he gave a lecture in the main building of our university entitled: "The Principal Document of Faith: A Report on Forty Years of Work on Its Text." The title tells you something about the main interest he took in his long-lasting text-critical work.[1]

---

1. Published in *Bericht der Hermann Kunst-Stiftung zur Förderung der neutestamentlichen Textforschung für die Jahre 1982-1984*, 9-75.

New Testament Textual Research, Its Methods and Its Goals

Kurt Aland joined Erwin Nestle in editing the Novum Testamentum Graece at the beginning of the 1950s.[2] At that time, Nestle was responsible for preparing a new edition of the work of his father, Eberhard Nestle. Aland was surprised to see that so far no manuscript, not even a facsimile, had been used for the critical apparatus. By no account could the apparatus in use be considered "bad" or unworthy, for it had been developed with careful scrutiny from the concise editions that were available in those days. But it was nonetheless only a short apparatus indicating text types and only a few manuscripts that had been referred to in the older editions.

Soon it became obvious that a thorough revision of the edition would be necessary, which culminated in the new text and apparatus of the 26th (1979) and then 27th (1993) editions. This had become a matter of urgency because of the great manuscript discoveries of the twentieth century, especially regarding papyri. Aland began with the preparations of the new Nestle already in the early fifties. When in 1955 he was invited to participate in an editorial committee with M. Black, B. M. Metzger, A. Wikgren, and first A. Vööbus and later C. M. Martini, he gladly accepted. The task of the committee was to produce the well-known UBS Greek New Testament. I consider it an honor to have joined the committee together with J. Karavidopoulos in 1982. The intensive cooperation of this international and interconfessional committee proved so fruitful and stimulating that Kurt Aland decided to contribute his preliminary work toward a new text for the Nestle Edition of the Greek New Testament. That is the reason why both editions offer the same text. The apparatus was done by the Institute in Münster and is still being revised and enlarged constantly. The 28th edition is currently in preparation and is supplemented by an electronic edition for the very first time.

From the very beginning Kurt Aland and the Münster Institute followed this principle: You cannot succeed in constituting the text of the New Testament if you know only a fraction of all extant manuscripts, which had been the case so far. But like every other editor in classical philology, you are obliged to collect all the manuscripts and then to study the

---

2. Regarding the history of the Nestle edition, see B. Aland and B. Köster, "100 Jahre Novum Testamentum Graece," in *100 Jahre Novum Testamentum Graece 1898-1998* (ed. Eberhard Nestle, Erwin Nestle, K. Aland, B. Aland; Jubiläumsausgabe, Nestle-Aland 27. Auflage, 5. korrigierter Druck; Stuttgart: Deutsche Bibelgesellschaft, 1998), v-xx.

transmission of the text in order to come back as far as possible to the text of the New Testament.

So in the beginning the members of the Institute were occupied with traveling, mostly within Europe, but also to the Middle East. If you consider the fact that New Testament manuscripts are scattered all over the continents from America to Australia (one has been found even in Japan) you can surely imagine the variety of problems that had to be solved in the beginning, especially when the budget was always very low.

In the early sixties travel from the Münster Institute began, including travel to England, Italy, France, Ireland, and Turkey; and, of course, above all, we undertook expeditions to Greece (in 1963, 1964, and 1965). We traveled from the north to the south, from the east to the west. The journeys took place under hard conditions. Our staff was confronted with a great number of difficulties and problems, for they had to overcome barriers of the church and the state as well. The monks and the directors of libraries had to be convinced of the importance of the work on the text of the New Testament and of our trustworthiness. We always promised not to give microfilms to other people but to use them only in the Institute and there and only there to provide free access to the microfilms to every interested scholar. We have never broken that promise even now to this day. The first manuscript expeditions took place even before the foundation of the Institute. All of these journeys were fascinating. The most unique experience was certainly the expedition to the monastery of Saint Catherine in the Sinai desert. We went to this place in 1982, at a time when we were the only visitors in the monastery (incredible nowadays). The story of the find of the Codex Sinaiticus by Tischendorf in the nineteenth century is well known. In 1975 another considerable find of manuscripts took place, and we were allowed not only to look at those remarkable findings but also to produce microfilms of the New Testament manuscripts.

As a result of all the expeditions we have now obtained more than 90 percent of the extant Greek New Testament manuscripts on microfilm, for a total of more than 5,600 manuscripts.

Goals of New Testament Textual Criticism

Although we cannot claim ever to have established the New Testament text in its original "Ur-text" form, our goal was to get as close to this "Ur-text" form as was humanly possible. In doing so, we distinguished between the following terms:

- The *original text* means the author's text. It is lost and cannot be reconstructed directly by tools of textual criticism.
- The *initial text* means the form of a text that stands at the beginning of the textual tradition. It is close to the "original" but cannot be identified with the "original" text.[3]
- The *established text* represents the hypothetical reconstruction of the initial text. It is the primary line text of the edition. We try as precisely as possible to reconstruct the initial text through the established text.

It is important that the users of the *Editio Critica Maior* and of the Nestle always keep in mind that the text line of our edition does not claim to be the original text. This text is lost and cannot be reconstructed. Although this may be disappointing for some of us, we have to ask methodically what is the initial text and what is its relationship to the original text. In defining this and our primary methodologies I depend on Gerd Mink and his work. I would like to express my thankfulness for Gerd's and other colleagues' steady efforts of genius, without which we could not even begin to undertake a massive work such as that of the *Editio Critica Maior*.

The initial text is a hypothetical, reconstructed text, as it presumably and hypothetically existed, before beginning its journey throughout history to be copied over and over again. The initial text corresponds to a hypothetical witness (A= *Ausgangstext*). The initial text is not identical with the original text, the text of the author. Between the autograph and the initial text considerable changes may have taken place for which there may not be a single trace in the surviving textual tradition. Even if this should not be the case, differences between the original and the initial text must be taken into account.

---

3. Cf. G. Mink, "Problems of a Highly Contaminated Tradition: The New Testament: Stemmata of Variants as a Source of a Genealogy of Witnesses," in *Studies in Stemmatology II* (ed. P. van Reenen, A. den Hollander, M. van Mulken; Amsterdam: Benjamins, 2004), 13-85, cf. 25-27; G. Mink, "Was verändert sich in der Textkritik durch die Beachtung genealogischer Kohärenz?" in *Recent Developments in Textual Criticism: New Testament, Other Early-Christian and Jewish Literature (Papers read at a NOSTER conference in Münster, January 4-6, 2001)* (ed. W. Weren and D. A. Koch; Assen: Royal Van Gorcum, 2003), 39-68.

In my view, however, those alterations that may have happened between the stage of the original text and the initial text are not overly serious ones, since we will see that the early text tradition is normally a trustworthy one. So we may cautiously conclude that the initial text differed only somewhat and not essentially from the original text.

The Material of New Testament Textual Criticism

The mass of extant witnesses to the New Testament text is larger than that of any other ancient Greek text. The first manuscripts still existing were copied only fifty to one hundred years after the New Testament writings came into being. We possess, as is well known, about eighty papyri copied before the fourth/fifth century. That is an unusually high number of early manuscripts, one not seen in any other textual tradition. The later text tradition comprises about 5,600 manuscripts, which is also an extraordinarily high number. It must be assumed that in both periods — in the early one up to the fourth/fifth century and later on in the following thousand years and more of New Testament transmission in manuscript form — much has been lost, especially in the earliest time. Therefore, we have to develop different text-critical methods according to the different character of the extant material. In my view we should apply slightly different methodologies to the early papyri than we use with the later ones. Although in those later times, too, much has been lost, nonetheless the structures of the textual tradition become more apparent. For both periods it is valid to say that the plethora of textual variants in the manuscripts has presented scholars with complex problems relating to the transmission of the text and its history. We have therefore tried to develop two similar but different methods for treating the early material (a) and the huge mass of later manuscripts (b).

Methods of Textual Criticism

Methods in Treating the Early Material

One may ask what could be the benefit of studying the earliest papyri that contain mostly only a few verses. I do not speak, of course, of the six so-called big papyri, comprising whole gospels or letters of the New Testament, which therefore can be studied by the methods described later on under (b). But what can we gain from those small fragments comprising sometimes only a few verses? I think we can gain quite a lot.

The most important issue in working with the earliest fragments is that they mostly offer a very good text. This perspective is extremely helpful in trying to imagine one kind of early text transmission. By asking why the text of the fragments is so reliable — with a lot of carelessness, of course — we have doubtless to answer that this is attributable to a good and old text, the initial or perhaps even the original text itself. There are no traces of early text families. We may conclude, therefore, that the value of these earliest texts lies precisely in their proximity to the initial text of which they are descendants. Although we cannot possibly reconstruct the oral transmission of these texts, nonetheless they are the closest thing we have to any possible initial text. That gives them a special validity despite all the minor mistakes made through carelessness that are spread throughout some of the fragments.

In contrast to the transmission of the Apocryphon of John, for example, the authority of the writing is to be derived from its reliability in relating an old written text, not from its reliability in relating the spoken word.[4] Regarding our earliest manuscripts we can only succeed in tracing the manuscripts to a written text and not to any oral transmission.

Consequently, our method comprises the following steps. First, we collate the papyrus text in full. Secondly, we compare it with the initial text, that is, the hypothesis of the initial text, the NA^{27} or GNT^4 edition. Although that may seem to be unreliable in some respects, it is more sensible to use the text of those editions based on ample demonstration of editorial labor over a period of more than one hundred years than to compare the fragments with single New Testament manuscripts. Thirdly, we look for manuscripts reading the same variants, and, fourthly, we consider the difficulties of the written *Vorlage* that significantly affect the quality of the papyrus manuscripts.

I have investigated the early papyri according to this method.[5] The

---

4. See the helpful article of K. L. King, "Approaching the Variants of the Apocryphon of John," in *The Nag Hammadi Library after Fifty Years: Proceedings of the Society of Biblical Literature Commemoration, Nov. 17-22, 1995* (ed. J. D. Turner and A. McGuire; Nag Hammadi and Manichaean Studies 44; Leiden: Brill, 1997), 105-37, cf. 115.

5. B. Aland, "Kriterien zur Beurteilung kleinerer Papyrusfragmente des Neuen Testaments," in *New Testament Textual Criticism and Exegesis. Festschrift J. Delobel* (ed. A. Denaux;

analysis results in several conclusions, the most important of which is that nearly all papyri can be traced to the initial text, which they render, however, with very different levels of care. While some of them copy their *Vorlage* with almost no mistakes, others, like P^{45}, are loaded and overloaded with mistakes and scribal blunders, but are nevertheless based on a good and old text. P^{45} in particular allows us to understand the development of variants in early times. These variants are not the result of redactional work in different places but the result of quick and careless copyists. Only sometimes may we find some manuscripts reading the same variants (P^{66} 05 01 032 038) but not, as some scholars may assume, as witnesses of a "Western" tradition, but actually the opposite, for some later manuscripts preserve elements of the early papyri sometimes carelessly copied but in principle based on the initial text.

In conclusion, the early papyri enable us to reconstruct the early transmission of the written New Testament text. They do not reflect the oral transmission, which cannot be understood through New Testament manuscripts.

Methods in Treating Later Manuscripts

The great mass of later manuscripts cannot be investigated in this way. To analyze each and every one of them individually would only be confusing. To develop a methodology for dealing with the later manuscripts, Kurt Aland with his collaborators in the Institute of New Testament Textual Research gathered nearly all of the extant New Testament manuscripts all over the world and filed them in films and photos in the Institute (which is open to every scholar who wants to study these manuscripts). The next

---

BEThL 161; Leuven: Leuven University Press/Peeters, 2002), 1-13; B. Aland, "Der textkritische und textgeschichtliche Nutzen früher Papyri, demonstriert am Johannesevangelium," in *Recent Developments in Textual Criticism: New Testament, Other Early Christian and Jewish Literature (Papers read at a NOSTER conference in Münster, January 4-6, 2001)* (ed. W. Weren and D. A. Koch; Assen: Royal Van Gorcum, 2003), 19-38; B. Aland, "The Significance of the Chester Beatty Biblical Papyri in Early Church History," in *The Earliest Gospels: The Origins and Transmission of the Earliest Christian Gospels — The Contribution of the Chester Beatty Gospel Codex P^{45}* (ed. B. Aland and C. Horton; JSNTSup 258; London: T&T Clark, 2004), 108-21. Cf. particularly K. S. Min, *Die früheste Überlieferung des Matthäusevangeliums (bis zum 3./4. Jh.), Edition und Untersuchung* (ANTF 34; Berlin: de Gruyter, 2005).

step was to analyze this mass of material. Aland therefore selected a series of test passages distributed throughout the New Testament where the textual traditions differ characteristically from each other. As a result, we gained a first impression of the textual character of all the manuscripts, significantly of those belonging to the Byzantine text. In the Catholic Epistles, for example, about 330 from a total of about 550 manuscripts belong to this group. They should not be totally eliminated from any further editorial considerations, but only a few of them need to be included to represent this group of manuscripts, which are purely or almost purely reproductions of an identical text.

The test passages provide an initial insight into the textual character of the manuscripts. They are not sufficient to reach further goals, such as making an overall genealogy of all New Testament manuscripts as a basis for the *Editio Critica Maior* of the New Testament text, for they provide only a limited number of passages, on the basis of which one cannot examine the manuscripts sufficiently. The method necessary for such a goal was developed by Gerd Mink in the Institute for New Testament Textual Research, as I have mentioned above.

This method, too, is based on the fact that all variants of the included manuscripts (only duplications of the Byzantine text are excluded) are investigated. Local stemmata (i.e., "trees") based upon just one place of variation are constructed. Very often the text critic can determine which reading has to be considered the one from which all the other variations emerged. The local stemmata comprise a first overall pattern of the average relation of all witnesses to each other. The important thing about this is that witness here does not mean the physical manuscript as a paleographical entity, but rather the text of the manuscript with its variations.[6] "The local stemmata represent a hypothesis," writes G. Mink, "about which variant arose from which. There, each source variant is prior, the one developed from it posterior."[7] The decision about that is of the utmost significance. It is based on all the reliable combinations in all local stemmata, providing a first insight into the average mutual dependence of witnesses; that is, the textual flow between them gives evidence as to from which witnesses textual forms of other witnesses may have developed. The procedure results in finding wit-

---

6. Mink, "Problems," 29.

7. Mink, "Problems," 31. Cf. also particularly the conclusion to Mink's long article (pp. 76-77).

nesses that are predominantly prior or predominantly posterior. Through this method some previously quite unknown manuscripts appear of great importance in their position in the stemma and sometimes even appear to have a direct connection to the initial text.

Local stemmata that could not be constructed at first may be revised and corrected on the basis of the material investigated thus far. The overall pattern will be more and more exact, thereby providing information about the most important connections in an overall stemma. The goal of Mink's method is to gain an overall pattern of the text transmission, which combines the results of the local stemmata in the most effective and simple way and leads to a better text criticism based on clearer external criteria. We may understand the complexity of the transmission processes better although we can only reconstruct a hypothesis of the initial text. But two things seem to be clear: (a) this hypothesis of the initial text comes close to the original text, and (b) we can reconstruct only the transmission of the written text — and to a certain degree the written preliminary stages of the canonical text. The oral transmission with its variety of audiences and their impact on the written text cannot be reconstructed by our manuscripts.

The Role of the Scribe

The preceding methodologies and especially the investigation of the early papyri result in a new understanding of the role of the scribe. He is a copyist who wants to copy the text as accurately and clearly as possible. He is not a theologian who wants to alter the text or to write an apocryphon, but he is mainly a so-called documentary scribe who makes it his ambition and task to render the texts as reliably as possible. The proof of that contention lies in the character of the earliest text transmission described above. Early New Testament papyri are not only without any serious mistakes, as we have seen, but are based on the same good and old text copied with more or less care. We may assume that scribes themselves did not arbitrarily make changes in documents, but rather strove to render their texts as exactly as possible — and perhaps, if they were Christians, even more painstakingly if they were given the chance to copy the New Testament text.

The first great shift in the New Testament transmission theory that occurred in the middle of the twentieth century had to do with the findings of that time. Scholars once believed that very early manuscripts were simply unkempt (*verwildert,* as the technical term goes), and not just loaded but overloaded with many mistakes. Only in the fourth century — so it was thought — were the texts of such excellent manuscripts as that of Vaticanus and Sinaiticus then shaped by the redactional work of gifted philologists. But then our understanding changed perforce as the evidence from new discoveries made at that time came into play, particularly with manuscripts P^{75}, P^{66}, and even P^{45} and others. Today we no longer believe that the text of the fourth-century manuscripts was shaped by redactional work.

The best proof of that fact is the famous P^{75}. It turned out to be so similar to the text of Codex Vaticanus that current text-critical scholarship could only draw the conclusion that the text of Codex Vaticanus and of P^{75} derives not from the same source but from an older, well-written text. The text of Codex Vaticanus was not, as former generations thought, established by the redactional work of some great philologist in the fourth century. This holds true for other early papyri, too. P^{66}, for example, is apparently the copy of a well-written gospel *Vorlage.* Although it contains many mistakes, these mistakes nevertheless seem to be only the result of individual acts of carelessness. That is, the carelessness does not appear across the board, but only in some sentences that show a simple syntactic structure. Difficult sentences are normally copied well and exactly. P^{45}, too, represents the kind of manuscripts one might expect from an experienced transcriber of documents. On the whole a reliable copy of the canonical gospels was thus produced despite conspicuous omissions and transpositions, which can now be explained not as changes of a theological scholar or a writer of biblical apocrypha but as the work of an intelligent scribe, that is, a scribe who grasps the text of its exemplar and in essence reproduces it exactly though liberally, because complicated expressions and repetitions are sometimes simplified and/or dropped.

To sum up, all of the above mentioned manuscripts apparently are copies of a normative text of the canonical gospels, and they aim to represent this text exactly, even though a number of accidental blunders and even deliberate changes may also have occurred.

The Influence of "Orality"

Because texts in antiquity were always transmitted both through speech and in writing, there may be a connection between oral and written transmission in our field as well, and especially through the influence of orality on what was written. A possible area of such influence is the liturgy with its common prayer, a text known to all members of a community. Parallels in the LXX or in synoptic gospel texts also known to the community and the scribes by recitation may also be a source of "oral" influence. The impact of orality on written texts is a fascinating area of study, but only to the degree it can be known. Orality may have influenced some variations, but we cannot trace our tradition back to the oral transmission period in principle. The only conclusion we may draw is this: If we do not see radical changes in the transmission of a text later on, it follows that we should not see them earlier on either, before the initial text.[8] And thus we should be able to trust the initial text as being fairly close to the original text. But we should refrain from speculations, the more so because any ideal of verbatim transmission may have been dependent on the text genera that were transmitted. The Logia Jesu, for example, were transmitted in a relatively free way, because most traditional cultures see the loci of both truth and authority primarily in persons and their utterances, not in documents and records. The transmission of the Catholic epistles, for example, happened quite differently. They were letters destined to teach the communities, and consequently it was important that they be copied as precisely as possible. But, of course, even they have a textual history, and in its reconstruction it is important not only to come as close as possible to the "author" and its text but also to take into account the influence of the reader/listener on the variations that show up in the manuscripts (i.e., to detect some reader perspectives given in the variations of the manuscripts).

The Reaction of the Community That Commissioned an Early Manuscript

I have always asked myself what would have been the reaction of a community who commissioned a manuscript such as that of, let us say, P^{45}, who paid a considerable sum for it and received the well-known codex

---

8. This does not mean that "composition is not a matter of unique creatio ex nihilo" (cf. King, "Approaching the Variants," 119). It is a matter of unique creatio ex nihilo, and since our manuscripts are in fact so similar to each other, we may cautiously trace the initial text back to the original text.

with its beautiful appearance but its many deviations from the text that we know as the normal text.

The question is whether those who commissioned the work were completely unaware of its errors and oversights, or whether they believed that its minor textual differences, which they recognized from other known manuscripts or from worship services of neighboring churches, were unimportant. The thesis I propose here is that actually for those who commissioned the work these minor differences were inconsequential because they did not alter the meaning of the text. And if this can be demonstrated it would be extraordinarily illuminating about attitudes toward the New Testament text in the third century.

To find a methodological basis for answering this question, let us observe the general usage with regard to quotations in early times. As to the first alternative, we cannot assume that communities had an official corrector appointed to supervise the production of texts. Otherwise all the codices would have been proofread better than they actually were. Any errors in a second- or third-century manuscript (nonsense readings, omissions, transpositions or even deliberately changed sentences) would have been noticed by some members of the church. If they were still not corrected, we are forced to accept the second alternative: the congregation and its ministers did not consider the "minor" deviations and errors in their manuscripts to be important. They tolerated them, the more so because we must consider the commissioning communities to have been largely illiterate.[9] Thus they would have been unable to detect the inaccuracies in their manuscripts, and any lector they employed could easily adapt the written text to the normative text known by the community.

A good example of this kind of text consciousness (or, conversely, lack of verbatim text consciousness) is found in Clement's well-known lengthy citation of Mark 10:17-31 in *Quis dives salvetur* 4:4-10. The author quite clearly intends to present the readers of his diatribe with the literal text of the parable of the Rich Young Man; otherwise he could have referred to the well-known story with a simple allusion. What he actually provides is a closely text-related but very free quotation.

The frequent changes make hardly any difference in meaning and are attested almost exclusively by Clement. We have found harmonizations

---

9. Cf. the illuminating book of H. Y. Gamble, *Books and Readers in the Early Church: A History of Early Christian Texts* (New Haven: Yale University Press, 1995).

with parallel passages of other synoptic gospels, transpositions, choice of synonyms, omissions, additions. None of these have to do with literary ambitions but rather go back to the rapid dictation of the author Clement to his stenographer, changes that were not regarded as worth correcting.

But this is important: If Clement could expect his Alexandrian audience to accept the text he gave them as the text of the New Testament, then we can infer that for him and for his readers these "minor" changes did not matter. The variations Clement allowed himself define precisely the range of what was considered insignificant. If such variations were possible for the sophisticated Clement in a passage so lengthy that it was midway between a citation and a text manuscript, they are also conceivable in manuscripts. We may also draw the inference that the readers of such manuscripts were well aware of such divergences but regarded them as trivial.[10]

In conclusion it may be said that early papyri and early quotations do reflect the situation of the New Testament in early times, both precisely and revealingly. They attest the significance of the New Testament as a most influential constant in the self-consciousness of the communities. The New Testament text has to be reconstructed according to the insight gained by studying the manuscripts and quotations alone and — more important — in relationship to each other. That will take a long time, but it is our responsibility to do so.

---

10. I have treated Clement's passage in a broader context in Aland, "Significance," 117-21.

Rule 9, Isolated Variants, and the "Test-Tube" Nature of the NA^{27}/UBS^4 Text: A Byzantine-Priority Perspective

Maurice A. Robinson

Vouloir proposer des corrections qui n'ont pour elles le témoignage d'aucun document, manuscrit, version ou écrivain ecclésiastique, c'est faire oeuvre d'imagination et non de critique.[1]

It is beyond question that the text presented in the current Nestle-Aland 27th and United Bible Societies' 4th editions[2] is regarded by many throughout the world as the closest possible approximation to the New Testament autographs, or at least the best text that can be constructed by modern methods of New Testament textual criticism.[3] Such assumptions

---

1. E. Jacquier, *Le Nouveau Testament dans L'Église Chrétienne. Tome Second: Le Text du Nouveau Testament* (3rd ed.; Paris: J. Gabalda, 1913), 314; "Wanting to propose corrections that do not have for themselves the testimony of any document, manuscript, version, or ecclesiastical writer is to make a work of inspiration and not of criticism."

2. B. Aland et al., eds., *Nestle-Aland Novum Testamentum Graece* (27th ed., 8th rev. and exp. printing; Stuttgart: Deutsche Bibelgesellschaft, 2001), hereafter cited as NA^{27}; B. Aland et al., eds., *The Greek New Testament*, 4th ed., 5th rev. and exp. printing (Stuttgart: Deutsche Bibelgesellschaft, 2001), hereafter cited as UBS^4.

3. W. Weren, "Textual Criticism: Mother of All Exegesis," in *Recent Developments in Textual Criticism, New Testament, Other Early Christian and Jewish Literature (Papers Read at a NOSTER Conference in Münster, January 4-6, 2001)* (ed. W. Weren and D. A. Koch; Studies in Theology and Religion 8; Assen: Royal Van Gorcum, 2003), 3-16, states: "Nowadays, exegetes from various Christian denominations worldwide make use of the Nestle-Aland text. . . . Because of its broad acceptance, the NA^{27} has been referred to as the new

are drawn without regard to the clear statement presented in the introduction to NA[27]: "It should naturally be understood that this text is a working text . . . : it is not to be considered as definitive, but as a stimulus to further efforts toward defining and verifying the text of the New Testament."[4]

Despite this caution, the *de facto* conclusion of most students, instructors, and scholars — including members of the Münster Institut für neutestamentliche Textforschung[5] — appears to be that this NA[27]/UBS[4] text *does* represent the epitome of New Testament text-critical scholarship:

'standard text.' . . . Faith in the reconstruction of the original text of the Greek New Testament that has so far been achieved is so great that some researchers conceive the Nestle-Aland text as the *Ausgangstext,* . . . which in its turn can be compared to the texts of actually existing manuscripts. . . . This *Ausgangstext* . . . is seen as the potential predecessor of all actually existing textual witnesses" (5, 8).

4. NA[27], 45*. In a similar manner, the UBS[4] preface declares (viii): "The text of the edition has remained unchanged. This should not be misunderstood to mean that the editors now consider the text as established. Work on the text of the Holy Scriptures continues to be a task of concern for each of the editors who will offer the results of their research in future editions."

5. See, for example, K. Aland, "The Significance of the Papyri for Progress in New Testament Research," in *The Bible in Modern Scholarship: Papers Read at the 100th Meeting of the Society of Biblical Literature, December 28-30, 1964* (ed. J. P. Hyatt; Nashville: Abingdon, 1965), 325-46: "The aim which we want to achieve . . . can be so defined: *to establish the original text of the NT,* that is, the text-form in which the NT writings were officially put into circulation" (341); K. Junack, "The Reliability of the New Testament Text from the Perspective of Textual Criticism," *BT* 29 (1978): 128-40: "The purpose of textual research is . . . *to achieve a reconstruction of the original wording of the text,* or at least the form of the text used by the scribes of the oldest surviving copies of the text" (129); B. Aland, "New Testament Textual Research, Its Method and Its Goals," in *Tell Me the Word Easy to Understand: Textual Criticism and Bible Translation, In Honor of Young Jin Min* (ed. T. Wang; 2 vols.; Seoul: Christian Literature Society of Korea, 2000), 1:63-77: "The ultimate goal of New Testament textual research . . . is *to discover the original text of the New Testament* or, to put it more modestly, *to come as close as possible to the lost autographs* of the authors" (1:63); "Do we know the original text of the New Testament? . . . I believe *we are very close to it* although we do not have it in all its details" (1:72); G. Mink, "Editing and Genealogical Studies: The New Testament," *Literary and Linguistic Computing* 15 (2000): 51-56: "The initial text [NA[27]], called A [= *Ausgangstext*] . . . is not necessarily identical to the original text . . . [but] may be hypothesized as representing *the starting point of the tradition at each passage*" (52); K. Wachtel, "Colwell Revisited: Grouping New Testament Manuscripts," in *The New Testament Text in Early Christianity: Proceedings of the Lille Colloquium, July 2000* (ed. C.-B. Amphoux and J. K. Elliott; HTB 6; Lausanne: Éditions du Zèbre, 2003), 31-43, states that one must "reduce the material to those documents which are needed for the reconstruction of a text *as close as possible to the original*" (39) [emphasis added throughout].

Rule 9, Isolated Variants, and the "Test-Tube" Nature of the NA²⁷/UBS⁴ Text

it indeed *should* be used and regarded as a quasi-"original" text unless specific (and mostly minor) alterations are suggested and accepted (such as those noted in the fascicles of the *Editio Critica Maior*).⁶ In the general consensus, there exists little room for scholarly doubt regarding this matter,⁷ and thus the deeper issues of theology and exegesis can proceed apace, with little regard given to any variation from the base NA²⁷/UBS⁴ or ECM text, except here and there as minor exercises in eclectic ingenuity considered worthy of publication in various journals.⁸

To be sure, various issues can be and have been raised regarding inadequacies when using UBS⁴ and NA²⁷ as hand editions *(Handausgaben)*,

---

6. B. Aland et al., eds., *Novum Testamentum Graecum: Editio Critica Maior, IV, Die Katholischen Briefe*: 1, Der Jakobusbrief; 2, Die Petrusbriefe; 3, Der Erste Johannesbrief (Stuttgart: Deutsche Bibelgesellschaft, 1997-2004), hereafter cited as ECM. The ECM volumes so far published have suggested that the NA²⁷ base text be changed in Jas 1:22; 2:3, 4; 1 Pet 1:6, 16 (2x); 2:25; 4:16; 5:9; 5:10; 2 Pet 2:6, 11, 15; 3:6, 10, 16 (2x), 18; 1 Jn 1:7; 5:10, 18. Otherwise, NA²⁷ = ECM = the *Ausgangstext*. Thus NA²⁷ in general is considered to represent the source text from which all other readings in each variant unit have derived ("a reconstruction which we believe to be the best hypothetical initial text that has been reached up to now without the knowledge of the extensive material being offered in the ECM," 1 John ECM, 28*).

7. C. C. Caragounis, *The Development of Greek and the New Testament: Morphology, Syntax, Phonology, and Textual Transmission* (WUNT 167; Tübingen: Mohr Siebeck, 2004), states, "Commentators as a rule follow the text of the *GNT* [= UBS⁴] or *NA*⁽²⁷⁾ without further ado. Where they do take up a variation unit for discussion, they normally accept the verdict of the editors and the explanation supplied by Metzger's commentary, which they express in their own words" (518).

8. F. Wisse, "The Nature and Purpose of Redactional Changes in Early Christian Texts: The Canonical Gospels," in *Gospel Traditions in the Second Century: Origins, Recensions, Text, and Transmission* (ed. W. L. Petersen; Christianity and Judaism in Antiquity 3; Notre Dame: University of Notre Dame Press, 1989), 39-53, suggests that, in many cases, "we are dealing with nothing more than educated guesses which lead nowhere and needlessly clutter the scholarly literature" (40). See also M. Goodacre, *The Case Against Q: Studies in Markan Priority and the Synoptic Problem* (Harrisburg, PA: Trinity Press International, 2002), 8-9, where he draws a close parallel between the Q hypothesis and New Testament textual criticism: "[Most scholars] will accept its broad finding and debate just a point here or a point there. The impression given is that the argument concerns merely the finer details of a text, the existence and overall character of which is unshakeable. In this important aspect, Q scholarship is aligning itself with the discipline of textual criticism; the broad consensus is established in the near unanimous use by scholars of the latest version of Nestle-Aland's critical text, but individual scholars will debate about one reading or another."

particularly in regard to the limited number of variant units cited (the same editorial team's UBS⁴ cites far fewer than NA²⁷; NA²⁷ cites fewer than the *Synopsis Quattuor Evangeliorum*;[9] and these cite far fewer than the comprehensive apparatuses of Tischendorf, Tregelles, or von Soden). The NA²⁷ preface specifically states (following the previously quoted portion) that

> It intends to provide the user with a well-founded working text together with the means of verifying it or alternatively of correcting it. Correspondingly the edition contains all the variants necessary for this purpose in as complete a form as possible within its limitations. The variants included are important either for their content or for their historical significance. The user can also gain an accurate impression of the amount of variation in the New Testament textual tradition, as well as of the general character of these variants, and of the motives and origins they reflect.[10]

Yet the claims so made raise valid questions, since the NA²⁷ edition is highly limited in its selection of variant units. When contrasted with the various editions of the Byzantine Textform,[11] for example, one finds that a large number of variant units — many of them significant for text-critical purposes — are *not* cited in the NA²⁷ apparatus. To illustrate, in Mark 11, NA²⁷ in 31 instances fails to cite differences between its text and the Byzantine Textform;[12] in Luke 7, NA²⁷ fails in 23 such instances;[13] in John

---

9. K. Aland, ed., *Synopsis Quattuor Evangeliorum* (15th rev. and exp. ed.; Stuttgart: Deutsche Bibelgesellschaft, 2001), hereafter cited as SQE. Allowing that the SQE contains a larger number of variant units than does NA²⁷, had the SQE been used for the Gospels section of the present paper, additional whole verses with zero support likely may have appeared.

10. NA²⁷, 45*-46*.

11. M. A. Robinson and W. G. Pierpont, eds., *The New Testament in the Original Greek: Byzantine Textform 2005* (Southborough, MA: Chilton Book Publishing, 2005); Z. C. Hodges and A. L. Farstad, eds., *The Greek New Testament according to the Majority Text* (2nd ed.; Nashville: Thomas Nelson, 1985).

12. Seven of these differences are merely orthographic; the remaining 24 cases reflect more significant changes involving word order, substitution, and matters of inclusion or omission.

13. Six of these differences are orthographic; the remaining 18 cases are more substantial.

Rule 9, Isolated Variants, and the "Test-Tube" Nature of the NA²⁷/UBS⁴ Text

7, NA²⁷ fails in 18 such instances.¹⁴ The same situation prevails in almost every chapter throughout the New Testament.¹⁵

A more basic question exists, however: just how *reliable* and *secure* for text-critical, exegetical, and hermeneutical purposes — even as a "working text" — is the main text of NA²⁷/UBS⁴/ECM as currently printed? Statistical comparison against a contrasting text such as the Byzantine Textform demonstrates that *all* texts share an approximate 90 percent (or greater) identity of wording.¹⁶ However, such a large amount of common agreement does *not* reflect the central area of concern for those involved in New Testament textual criticism. The primary issue involves the resultant base text and the *means* by which that text — whether NA²⁷, the Byzantine Textform, or any other — has been established, including the underlying theory, methodology, and applied praxis, since all these have coalesced to produce a text that is regarded either as "original," "closest to the original," a "base" or *Ausgangstext*, or simply a reasonably reliable "working text." The present essay addresses one aspect of the NA²⁷ text, since its text as published apparently stands in opposition to the text-critical rules established by Kurt and Barbara Aland in their *The Text of the New Testament*.¹⁷

---

14. Seven of these differences are orthographic; the remaining 11 cases are more substantial.

15. D. Trobisch, "From New Testament Manuscripts to a Central Electronic Database," in *Bible and Computer: The Stellenbosch AIBI-6 Conference, Proceedings of the Association Internationale Bible et Informatique "From Alpha to Byte," University of Stellenbosch 17-21 July, 2000* (ed. J. Cook; Leiden: Brill, 2002), 427-33, notes: "The Nestle-Aland edition collates a selected number of witnesses at a selected number of places. If the editors decided not to document variants for a specific text, there is no way for the users to know whether this text is transmitted without variants or not" (429). Even while acknowledging that "editors have to choose where they want to note variants and where not" (429), when speaking of the much more extensive but chronologically restricted ECM apparatus, Trobisch declares, "Ideally scholars should be presented with the complete data. To a Byzantine scholar, for example, the restriction [in ECM] to the first nine hundred years of transmission may limit the usefulness of this edition considerably" (430).

16. For example, when compared against the Byzantine Textform, Matt 13 in NA²⁷ has 94.8 percent of its wording (including word order) in common; in Acts 13, the same comparison finds 92.1 percent of the wording in common; Rom 13 finds 94.1 percent in common; Heb 13 finds 96.8 percent in common; and Rev 13 finds 91.6 percent in common.

17. K. Aland and B. Aland, *The Text of the New Testament* (2nd rev. ed.; Grand Rapids: Eerdmans, 1989).

MAURICE A. ROBINSON

Rule 9 versus the NA[27] Edition

The Alands list "twelve basic rules for textual criticism"[18] — many of which even Byzantine-priority advocates would accept.[19] Yet, whether consciously or not, one rule in particular continually is violated within NA[27]: Aland/Aland rule number nine:

> Variants must never be treated in isolation, but always considered in the context of the tradition. Otherwise there is too great a danger of reconstructing a "test-tube text" which never existed at any time or place.[20]

By neglecting this rule when constructing the NA[27] text as an *Ausgangstext*, the NA[27] text itself becomes the very "test-tube text" that two of its editors warned against. Why is this so?

Basically, the NA[27] main text, taken sequentially, represents a connected series of variant units, in which the main text in each individual variant unit bears the reading that has been determined as that from which all remaining variants in that particular unit are derived.[21] Little or no thought appears to have been given to the witnesses supporting one variant unit in conjunction with the witnesses supporting the surrounding

---

18. Aland and Aland, *The Text of the New Testament*, 280-81.

19. A similar tabulation of text-critical principles appears in M. A. Robinson, "New Testament Textual Criticism: The Case for Byzantine Priority," *TC: A Journal of Biblical Textual Criticism* 6 (2001) http://purl.org/TC/vol6/Robinson2001.html. The same list appears in the summary abridgement, M. A. Robinson, "The Case for Byzantine Priority," in *Rethinking New Testament Textual Criticism* (ed. D. A. Black; Grand Rapids: Baker, 2002), 125-39.

20. Aland and Aland, *The Text of the New Testament*, 281. See also the same rule in the German original, K. Aland and B. Aland, *Der Text des Neuen Testaments: Einführung in die wissenschaftlichen Ausgaben sowie in Theorie und Praxis der modernen Textkritik* (2nd rev. and enl. ed.; Stuttgart: Deutsche Bibelgesellschaft, 1989), 285: "Varianten dürfen nicht isoliert behandelt, sondern es muß stets der Kontext der Überlieferung beachtet werden, sonst ist die Gefahr der Konstituierung eines 'Textes aus der Retorte,' den es nirgendwann und nirgendwo real gegeben hat, zu groß."

21. Cf. *Dictionary of Biblical Interpretation* (2 vols.; ed. J. H. Hayes; Nashville: Abingdon, 1999), s.v. "Textual Criticism, New Testament," by K. Aland (rev. Beate Köster), 2:546-51: "A reading is most probably original if it easily explains the emergence of the other readings (the genealogical principle).... Textual criticism must always begin with the findings in regard to manuscript transmission. Only then can internal criteria... be considered, for they alone cannot substantiate a text-critical decision" (551).

variant units in the sequential connection of the overall text. This practice leads to contradictory levels of external support, whereby one variant unit's external support effectively cancels that of another neighboring variant unit. This situation progressively worsens as additional variant units are added to the overall sequence. The resultant text — even within relatively short segments — becomes an entity that apparently never existed at any time or place.[22]

The evidence by which to establish this repeated violation of Aland/Aland Rule 9 is the NA^{27} apparatus, in particular its attestation of "consistently cited witnesses."[23] Using the evidence presented in both the positive and negative apparatuses of the NA^{27} edition,[24] it can be demonstrated with success that more than 100 whole verses as printed in NA^{27} have *no apparent support* within the Greek manuscript tradition; in most (if not all) cases, no support exists for such whole verses even within the versional or patristic traditions.

Such a statement might seem puzzling and peculiar, since suppos-

---

22. Goodacre, *Case Against Q*, 8, correctly states: "The system inevitably tends to obscure the hypothetical nature of the document to which it refers. It has the clear potential to mislead students by giving them the impression of an established document, . . . the existence of which it would be foolish to question." So also 161-62: "Nestle-Aland^{27} offers at best only an approximation to the original texts of the Gospels. The sophistication of the critical text can all too easily seduce scholars into imagining that they are dealing with something far more concrete and stable than is in fact possible."

23. See NA^{27}, 50*: "The witness of these [consistently cited] manuscripts is always cited in the passages selected for the apparatus." The two "orders" of consistently cited witnesses include (1) "the papyri and the uncials which are independent of the Byzantine Koine text type, and a small number of minuscules which preserve an early [by this is meant non-Byzantine] form of the text"; and (2) "the more important uncials of the Koine text type, and a group of minuscules . . . related to the Byzantine Koine text type" (NA^{27}, 51*). Normally the MSS under group (2) are subsumed under the Gothic 𝔐 symbol (which includes the Byzantine Textform) where they do not otherwise explicitly deviate (see NA^{27}, 51*).

24. The positive and negative apparatuses are described in NA^{27}, 51*. The *positive* apparatus gives specific support for the NA^{27} main text reading *(txt)*; the *negative* apparatus gives specific support *only* for variants from the NA^{27} main text. The consistently cited witnesses for the NA^{27} main text generally can be calculated from the evidence of the positive and negative apparatuses, coupled with the list of manuscript lacunae appearing in NA^{27}, 684-713. A caution in this regard concerns the Gothic 𝔐 symbol and the negative apparatuses: due to various "flaws affecting the text of a manuscript, . . . the possibility should not be ruled out that on occasion a consistently cited witness is neither subsumed in the symbol 𝔐 nor in agreement with the text of this edition" (51*); this suggests that additional instances of zero support for whole verses may exist beyond those demonstrated in the present essay.

edly the only "conjectural"[25] reading in NA[27]/UBS[4] appears in Acts 16:12.[26] Yet the actual situation is not difficult to comprehend, since it reflects an inherent problem within the various forms of eclectic methodology:[27] because the system works primarily with individual variant units, the left hand has little or no regard for what the right hand may have done in a neighboring variant unit. The pattern is consistent: a decision regarding the "best" reading in one unit of variation normally is made on the basis of internal and external principles that pertain to that *specific* variant unit. These principles assign localized authority and "weight" *only* to the manuscripts whose general character and value happen to support the internal criteria favored within that particular variant unit.[28] Once this has been accomplished, the procedure commences anew for the next sequential variant unit, with little or no regard for what just had been determined, on what principles, or what witnesses may have supported the previous decision. Thus, it often happens that all or nearly all supporting witnesses for the "best" reading in one variant unit vanish from the list of witnesses supporting the eclectically determined "best" reading of the next sequential

---

25. In 2 Pet 3:10, ECM substitutes a conjecture for the NA[27] main text, choosing to follow certain Philoxenian Syriac MSS and the Sahidic/Dialect-V Coptic reading ουχ ευρεθησεται instead of the NA[27] ευρεθησεται (supported by ℵ B K P 0156^{vid} 323 1241 1739^{txt} *pc* sy$^{ph, hmg}$), or the Byzantine κατακαησεται.

26. The reading πρωτη[ς] μεριδος της is a conjecture made by Le Clerc (= Clericus) and later by others; at best this conjecture finds strained support in three late Vulgate manuscripts. UBS[4] provides a more comprehensive statement of the evidence regarding the various readings in this unit; text-critical issues and historical matters are discussed in B. M. Metzger, *A Textual Commentary on the Greek New Testament* (2nd ed.; Stuttgart: Deutsche Bibelgesellschaft, 1994), 393-95. A signed and strongly worded dissent in that volume by K. Aland and B. Metzger opposes such "ill-advised" conjecture; such becomes peculiar and ironic when the end product of the NA[27]/UBS[4] editorial procedure creates what amounts to conjecture in the aggregate in more than 100 whole verses of their shared New Testament text.

27. These include "rigorous" or "thoroughgoing" eclecticism; "reasoned" eclecticism; and the "local-genealogical" or "coherence-based genealogical" methods. Each of these leads to equally problematic results when the overall sequential context is considered.

28. Beyond the internal criterion of favoring the reading supposedly most likely to have given rise to all other readings within a particular variant unit, other internal criteria strongly influence such decisions. These include principles relating to the "more difficult," the "harmonizing," or the "shorter" reading, as well as other minor principles that in their subjective application remain subservient but highly necessary to the establishment of this initial overriding eclectic principle.

variant unit. As a result, while the witnesses cited in support of isolated variant units might appear significant, the level of overall support rapidly diminishes or vanishes once neighboring variant units are added to the totals. To illustrate this point, consider John 9:4f:[29]

John 9:4f
(a) <u>ημας δει</u> εργαζεσθαι τα εργα του πεμψαντος (b) <u>με</u> (c) <u>εως ημερα εστιν ερχεται νυξ οτε ουδεις δυναται εργαζεσθαι</u> (d) <u>οταν εν τω κοσμω ω φως ειμι του κοσμου</u>

(a) txt: P^{66} P^{75} ℵ* B (~D) L W 070 *pc* sa pbo bo   UBS^4 = {C}
(b) var: P^{66} P^{75} ℵ* L W *pc* pbo bo   UBS^4 = {C}
(c) var: C* L W 070 33 *pc* b d sy^{hmg} pbo bo
(d) var: sy^s

In John 9:4, the NA^{27} "best" sequence of variants (the *Ausgangstext*) reads (a) <u>ημας</u> δει followed by (b) πεμψαντος <u>με</u> (the intervening common text, εργαζεσθαι τα εργα του, has no variant units cited).[30] In variant unit (a), the NA^{27} apparatus shows the main text reading ημας to be supported by P^{66} P^{75} ℵ* B (~D) L W 070 *pc* sa pbo bo (D in fact reads δει ημας instead of ημας δει and thus differs from the NA^{27} text as printed).[31]

In the second variant unit (b), the NA^{27} apparatus shows the NA^{27}

---

29. The NA^{27} apparatus treats John 9:4 and John 9:5 as a single entity. This study considers such cases extended forms of single-verse support, following the decision of the NA^{27} editors. In the present instance, the only variant unit occurring within John 9:5 is (d), and that unit does not affect the discussion regarding diminishing support in John 9:4.

30. The Byzantine Textform at the same location reads the sequence (a) <u>εμε</u> δει and (b) πεμψαντος <u>με</u>. The Byzantine reading εμε in variant unit (a) is supported by 𝔐 ℵ^1 A C Θ Ψ f^1 f^{13} 33 lat sy ac^2 bo^{mss}. Variant unit (b) is read in common by both the Byzantine Textform and NA^{27} and shares the same supporting witnesses in that unit.

31. NA^{27} Appendix 2, *Variae Lectiones Minores*, 733, provides a full delineation of the readings of Greek manuscript witnesses enclosed in parentheses. As for the *"pc"* (= *pauci*) that indicates additional minor or insignificant minuscule support for this variant reading, the *Text und Textwert* volume for John shows the NA^{27} text reading in John 9:4, variant (a), to be supported additionally by only MS 849. Thanks are extended to Klaus Wachtel and the Institut für Neutestamentliche Textforschung for graciously providing this information prior to publication. See K. Aland, B. Aland, and K. Wachtel, eds., *Text und Textwert der griechischen Handschriften des Neuen Testaments, V: Das Johannesevangelium. I. Textstellenkollation der Kapitel 1–10, Band 1, 2: Resultate der Kollation und Hauptliste* (ANTF 36; Berlin: Walter de Gruyter, 2005).

main text reading με to have the support of the majority text (𝔐, including the Byzantine Textform). Yet the alternate (b) reading, ημας, is supported by P⁶⁶ P⁷⁵ ℵ* L W *pc* pbo bo. That group is almost the same as that which supported variant unit (a); the only defection is by B (D) 070 and the Sahidic version.³² When the NA²⁷ external support for *both* variant units is combined, the apparent greater degree of support for each unit taken separately is reduced in the aggregate *only* to that of B (D) and 070. The larger combination of witnesses P⁶⁶ P⁷⁵ ℵ* L W *pc* pbo bo actually reads the pattern (a) ημας and (b) ημας. Yet one cannot readily observe from the NA²⁷ apparatus the actual degree of support for the NA²⁷ main text combined reading, nor the combined support for the significant Alexandrian alternate, due to the manner in which the apparatus presents the data on a per-variant-unit basis.³³

Further, the support of B (D) 070 *pc* for the NA²⁷ main text reading of the combined variant units is reduced by the word order disagreement of D to only B 070. Then, if the third sequential variant unit (c) of John 9:4 is included (involving the NA²⁷ main text εως versus the alternate ως), even the support of 070 is lost, since 070 in variant unit (c) joins C* L W 33 *pc* b d sy^hmg pbo bo in reading ως.

Thus, in the space of three sequential variant units within the single verse John 9:4, the NA²⁷ text as printed is apparently supported by *only* Codex Vaticanus.³⁴ Thus it is not surprising to find hundreds of similar cases of single-manuscript support for whole verses of NA²⁷ throughout the New Testament.³⁵

---

32. The *Text und Textwert* volume for John shows the *pc* in the alternate reading of NA²⁷ John 9:4, variant unit (b), to be supported once more only by the additional MS 849 (which again represents the whole of the "*pc*" for this unit).

33. The UBS⁴ apparatus is more precise in addressing this sequence of variants, since it treats as one variant unit what NA²⁷ (and *Text und Textwert* for John) cites as two. UBS⁴ clearly shows that the main text reading (a) ημας δει followed by (b) πεμψαντος με is supported by "B (D δει ημας) 070 (it^d) syr^pal geo¹" and no other witnesses. However, due to its limited citation of variant units, the UBS⁴ apparatus does *not* include the variant unit immediately following (εως versus ως), and thus cannot show that the verse as printed is supported only by Codex Vaticanus.

34. This result is determined solely from the NA²⁷ apparatus concerning the three variant units involved; comparison against the actual text of Vaticanus might show additional deviation from the NA²⁷ main text as printed. Such, however, transcends the purpose of the present essay.

35. The present writer's tabulations show more than 180 (current count 190) whole

Rule 9, Isolated Variants, and the "Test-Tube" Nature of the NA²⁷/UBS⁴ Text

An even greater problem occurs when the tabulation of all variant units in sequence results in whole single verses that lack support from *any* existing Greek manuscript. In such cases, *no* commonalty of support exists for that verse. Yet such a puzzling scenario is clearly demonstrated in the NA²⁷ main text in more than 100 whole verses, deriving the results directly from the positive and negative apparatuses of NA²⁷. Further, in most of these cases no support is forthcoming even from the various versional or patristic traditions.

The methodological requirements for establishing this evaluation are simple:

(1) A given New Testament verse must have at least *two* variant units cited within the NA²⁷ apparatus.³⁶

(2) At least *one* of the variant units within the verse *must* be supplied in the apparatus with a statement of support for the NA²⁷ main text reading (i.e., the last entry of at least one variant unit *must* be *"txt,"* followed by the witnesses supporting the NA²⁷ main text reading for that variant unit).³⁷

(3) The remaining variant unit(s) within the verse must contain either

---

verses in NA²⁷ that have their aggregate support apparently in only one Greek manuscript. These single-support witnesses range from the papyri and old uncials (e.g., P⁶⁶, P⁷⁵, ℵ, B, C, D) to later uncials and minuscules such as L, W, Θ, Ψ, 0161, 0274, 0281, 33, 892, [2427], the archetype of f¹ or f¹³, and other witnesses. Such instances of single-manuscript support for an entire verse occur primarily in the longer NT books: Matt has 35 such verses; Mark has 13; Luke has 27; John has 24; Acts has 15; and Revelation has 38. In many of these cases, as soon as one or more variant units from the verses immediately preceding or following are included in the sequential tabulation, the amount of support drops from that single Greek MS to *zero* Greek MSS. In such cases, the result for the sequential variant units involved once more becomes a *de facto* conjectural text set forth as the supposed source *(Ausgangstext)* from which all other readings have derived. Such a scenario does *not* appear to reflect a proper view of historical textual transmission.

36. Except for the acknowledged conjecture at Acts 16:12, the NA²⁷ main text does not present (a) an entire NT verse containing (b) but a *single* variant unit in which (c) the reading of the NA²⁷ main text lacks the support of *all* known Greek manuscripts. All remaining instances necessarily occur in verses containing more than one variant unit.

37. A verse without an explicit *"txt"* statement in at least one variant unit *may* have zero support, but such would have to be determined by careful calculation. Wherever the *txt* reading — with or without other witnesses — is supported by *"rell"* (= *reliqui*, the remainder of the manuscript tradition), the support of the consistently cited witnesses must be determined by calculation.

(a) a *positive* apparatus (showing NA²⁷ *txt* support) for direct comparison with the other variant unit(s) containing *txt* support; or,

(b) a sufficient number of consistently cited witnesses in a *negative* apparatus (one without the citation of *txt* support) so as to permit the elimination of witnesses otherwise cited as *txt* in the other variant units within the same verse.[38]

Once all these conditions are present, it becomes a matter of comparison and reduction by elimination to determine the resultant support within any verse. The case of John 9:4 cited above showed how the process of elimination functions, even though its end result was single-manuscript support for a whole verse (Codex Vaticanus).[39]

The simplest demonstration of zero support for the NA²⁷ main text wording of an entire verse occurs when a verse contains two variant units, where the witnesses supporting one unit mutually exclude the witnesses supporting the other unit.[40] As an example, the NA²⁷ main text of Mark 11:3 contains only two variant units (indicated here by English letters),[41] and the external support for each is mutually exclusive of the

---

38. Any main text support by the collective symbol 𝔐 somehow must be eliminated (either in the positive or negative apparatus) in a competing variant unit within the same verse in order to establish zero support. One also must calculate whether any consistently cited witnesses of the second order are subsumed in 𝔐 (not always an easy task). If so, such might preclude zero support.

39. This method assumes only the accuracy of results determined on the basis of the NA²⁷ apparatus. Many other whole verses may have single- or zero-manuscript support that cannot be determined solely from that apparatus. Further examination of other text-critical resources would be necessary in order to determine additional cases.

40. The NA²⁷ apparatus presents 9 cases in which (a) the NA²⁷ main text displays only two variant units in a single verse, and (b) *none* of the witnesses supporting the first unit are identical to those supporting the second unit (i.e., they mutually negate each other). These 9 verses of "mutual exclusion" are the following: Mark 11:3; Luke 17:23; 24:50; John 5:2; 16:23; 18:1; Acts 27:8; 2 Cor 5:3; Rev 20:11. Some of the variant readings in these units indeed are minor, reflecting orthographic issues (such as αν versus εαν) or the presence or absence of an article before proper names (this type of variant seems overly emphasized in the NA²⁷ apparatus). The essential point remains: the NA²⁷ main text of these whole verses *as printed* finds *zero* Greek manuscript support for its purported archetypal or *Ausgangstext* reading. This not only demonstrates wide-ranging (even if unconscious) conjecture, but also calls into question the historical and transmissional likelihood of the NA²⁷ main text as published.

41. By text-critical convention, the Greek New Testament text is presented without

Rule 9, Isolated Variants, and the "Test-Tube" Nature of the NA²⁷/UBS⁴ Text

other. The portion of text involved in each variant unit is underlined for ease of reference:⁴²

Mark 11:3
και εαν τις υμιν ειπη τι ποιειτε τουτο (a) <u>ειπατε</u> ο κυριος αυτου χρειαν εχει και ευθυς (b) <u>αυτον αποστελλει παλιν</u> ωδε

(a) *txt: B Δ 2427 *pc* it
(b) *txt: ℵ D L 579 892 1241 *pc*   UBS⁴ = {B}

The support for the NA²⁷ text reading *(txt)* in the first (a) variant unit is B Δ [2427] *pc* it. The NA²⁷ text reading in the second (b) variant unit (rated {B} in UBS⁴)⁴³ is specifically stated to be ℵ D L 579 892 1241 *pc* (the support for alternate readings is not relevant to the discussion and is not presented). Obviously, the NA²⁷ text support for each variant unit is mutually exclusive, and thus — unless by sheer chance the relatively few and insignificant *"pc" (pauci)* minuscules that support variant unit (a) coincide with the limited *"pc"* minuscules that support variant unit (b) — a very unlikely scenario — the verse as printed in NA²⁷ has apparently *zero* support from *any* known Greek manuscript, version, or father.⁴⁴ On a *de facto* basis, the NA²⁷ main text *as printed* for this verse becomes a matter of *conjecture*, differing in its own manner very little from the acknowledged conjecture

---

capitalization, punctuation, or diacritical marks, following the pattern demonstrated in the early papyrus and uncial manuscripts.

42. The second NA²⁷ variant unit in Mark 11:3 also appears in the more limited apparatus of UBS⁴, and the main text reading is given a {B} rating as an indication of the editors' relative certainty regarding such. Further, any NA²⁷ variant unit paralleled by a UBS⁴ reading is discussed in Metzger's *Textual Commentary* in loc. The present essay cites the UBS⁴ evaluations where they occur, although their significance is debatable. See K. D. Clarke, *Textual Optimism: A Critique of the United Bible Societies' Greek New Testament* (JSNTSup 138; Sheffield: Sheffield Academic Press, 1997).

43. Many NA²⁷ variant units with UBS⁴ parallels in the present study are rated highly by those editors: 12 units have ratings of {A}; 32 units have ratings of {B}. The lower rated UBS⁴ variant units with {C} are strongly represented (35 units), but only 1 unit of the present study (Jude 5) has a rating of {D}. Most NA²⁷ variant units cited in this study have no UBS⁴ parallel. Given Clarke's questioning of the entire UBS⁴ rating system, such ratings likely remain irrelevant.

44. In the same verse, the Byzantine reading (a) <u>ειπατε οτι ο</u> plus (b) <u>αυτον αποστελλει</u> (without παλιν) is solidly supported within that Textform.

39

at Acts 16:12. The only real difference here is that the conjecture is spread among more than one variant unit.[45]

One should not presume that the NA[27]/UBS[4] editors are unconcerned about extended portions of text that lack Greek manuscript support. The NA[27] apparatus and the "Editionum Differentiae" appendix to that edition note two specific locations where the earlier NA[25] had zero support *(sine test.)* for its printed text — two oversights corrected in NA[27]:

(1) At John 7:46, the NA[25] main text reads ελαλησεν ουτως ανθρωπος ως ουτος λαλει ο ανθρωπος.[46] Both the NA[27] apparatus and the Editionum Differentiae appendix suggest that this wording had zero support.[47]

(2) Likewise, in the NA[27] Editionum Differentiae appendix (but surprisingly *not* in the NA[27] main apparatus), the NA[25] reading of 1 Pet 3:18 (περι αμαρτιων απεθανεν) also is cited as apparently having zero support.[48] Yet the NA[27] main apparatus presents the NA[25] reading with support *only* from vg$^{st,\ ww}$ Cyp and *no* Greek manuscripts. It thus appears that this NA[25] reading likewise should have had *"sine test."* appended.

Since NA[27] expresses such concern regarding zero-support readings found in NA[25] and other editions[49] — as well as noting in its apparatus the

---

45. In the same verse SQE presents four variant units rather than the two of NA[27]; this includes the remaining difference in the Byzantine text of this verse (ευθεως instead of ευθυς). The mutual exclusion of support in the two major variants remains unaffected by the additional material in SQE. It remains possible that many additional verses might be shown to have zero support if tabulation were made in the Gospels using the SQE apparatus instead of that of NA[27].

46. When the text of NA[25] differs from that of NA[27], the NA[27] apparatus indicates such by a dagger symbol (†) preceding the NA[25] reading (which always appears first within a given variant unit). See NA[27], 57*, for further explanation.

47. The NA[27] apparatus has *"sine test.?"* with the question mark suggesting some uncertainty. However, "Editionum Differentiae," in loc. (p. 758), has *"T M N (sine test.),"* *without* the question mark. The other letters indicate the various editions in which this identical zero-support reading (wrongly) appeared as the main text: Tischendorf^8 (T) and Merk (M), as well as NA[25] (N).

48. "T (H) M B N *(sine test.?),*" NA[27], Editionum Differentiae, 767. Once more other editions shared the same erroneous reading in their main text: NA[25] (N) here is joined by Tischendorf^8 (T), Westcott and Hort (H), Merk (M), and Bover (B).

49. Additional *"sine test."* notes appear in the Editionum Differentiae appendix, but these relate to editions other than NA[25] and do not pertain to the current study.

Rule 9, Isolated Variants, and the "Test-Tube" Nature of the NA²⁷/UBS⁴ Text

approximately 200 conjectural readings made by various commentators — it seems peculiar that the NA²⁷ editors end up printing a sequential text of single NT verses that have zero support when considered in their overall sequence — yet their own series of eclectic decisions claims to have determined the archetypal form or *Ausgangstext* for each variant unit within such a verse! That such a text when considered sequentially lacks a demonstrable existence among the Greek manuscript base throughout transmissional history seems not to have been a concern.[50]

Luke 17:23 demonstrates the same point. Once more, only two NA²⁷ variant units exist in this verse, and each mutually excludes the other. Thus the overall NA²⁷ main text as published for this verse presents what amounts to another conjectural reading:[51]

Luke 17:23
και ερουσιν υμιν ιδου (a) εκει [η] ιδου ωδε (b) μη απελθητε μηδε διωξητε

(a) txt: P⁷⁵ B 579 UBS⁴ = {C}
(b) var: P⁷⁵ B 579 f¹ f¹³ sy^hmg / L Δ *al*

Here the situation differs slightly from the first example, since only the first variant unit has *txt* support for the NA²⁷ main text reading (the "positive apparatus"); the second variant unit shows only the support for two separate variant readings that differ from the NA²⁷ main text (the "negative apparatus") but does not give the supporting evidence for the NA²⁷ main text reading.[52] However, it is clear that the three MSS supporting the

---

50. This assessment does *not* affect the approximately 90 percent of the NT text that remains basically free of significant variants. Nor does it affect the words in any zero-support verse that sequentially remain well supported apart from the anomalous situation created when the cited sequential variant units clash due to contradictory editorial decisions. Thus, in Mark 11:3, the remainder of the NA²⁷ main text is unaffected. This assessment does *not* involve the Byzantine Textform in comparison with NA²⁷: SQE correctly (and fully) shows that the Byzantine Textform differs from NA²⁷ in reading ευθεως for ευθυς and — in variant unit (b) — in excluding παλιν. But Byzantine support or lack of such remains irrelevant to the internal consistency issues affecting the NA²⁷ main text.

51. The Byzantine Textform in variant unit (a) reads ιδου ωδε η ιδου εκει and in variant unit (b) is identical with the NA²⁷ main text (μη απελθητε μηδε διωξητε).

52. The NA²⁷ Introduction, 50*-51*, explains its use of positive and negative apparatuses. The positive apparatus explicitly states the main text support by consistently cited wit-

41

(b) variant reading are the same ones that supported the NA²⁷ main text in variant unit (a). This therefore leaves the NA²⁷ main text as printed for this verse once more with zero support.⁵³

As one more example of a verse affected by only two variant units, John 5:2 as printed in NA²⁷ reads as follows:

John 5:2
εστιν δε εν τοις ιεροσολυμοις (a) <u>επι τη προβατικη κολυμβηθρα η επιλεγομενη</u> εβραιστι (b) <u>βηθζαθα</u> πεντε στοας εχουσα

(a) txt: P⁶⁶ᶜ P⁷⁵ B C T Ψ 078 f¹³ 𝔐 syʰ
(b) txt: ℵ (L) 33 it   UBS⁴ = {C}

Again, it is obvious that the NA²⁷ editors' choice of readings for this verse results in mutual exclusion among the two variant units. As a result, the text of the verse as printed in NA²⁷ does not appear in *any* known manuscript, nor in any apparent ancient version or patristic writer.⁵⁴

As additional variant units are included in a given verse, the level of mutual exclusion tends to increase, and calculation of overall support becomes more complex. Although one might presume the likelihood of zero manuscript support within a given verse continually to increase as the number of variant units multiply, such tends not to be the case (at least as

---

nesses of the first and second order. The negative apparatus requires calculation, leaving one to deduce main text support by subtracting the variant support of the consistently cited witnesses of both the first and second order, while taking account of any lacunae or illegibility in the text of those witnesses (lacunae are listed in NA²⁷ Appendix 1, "Codices Graeci et Latini," 684-720).

53. The bracketed [η] in the main NA²⁷ text of variant unit (a) does *not* affect the mutual exclusion issue, if the NA²⁷ main text is accepted *as printed*. With the bracketed word removed, the reading reverts to that of ℵ L *pc* as originally printed in NA²⁵. This then would leave ℵ alone in support of the entire verse (MS L in the second variant unit spells διωξητε differently than the NA²⁷ main text). SQE cites the same evidence for the NA²⁷ reading in (a), and adds to (b) only the minor witness of 205 and 1506.

54. So also SQE, which similarly cites no version or patristic writer in support of the combined NA²⁷ reading for this verse. SQE does add to variant unit (a) the support of f¹³ 892 1006 and 1342 (in NA²⁷ the constant witness 892 is subsumed in 𝔐), and to variant unit (b) the support of MS 1; these do not, however, alter the overall mutual exclusion. The Byzantine Textform in the same verse reads with NA²⁷ in variant unit (a), but reads βηθεσδα in variant unit (b).

Rule 9, Isolated Variants, and the "Test-Tube" Nature of the NA²⁷/UBS⁴ Text

evidenced by the NA²⁷ apparatus). Most frequently, zero-support verses contain 3, 4, or 5 variant units. After that, one finds diminishing results as the number of variant units within a verse increases.⁵⁵ A sample of each of the more typical situations is instructive and illustrates the various types of variant unit support that may be encountered:

Three variant units within a single verse:⁵⁶

Matthew 19:29
και πας οστις αφηκεν (a) <u>οικιας η αδελφους η αδελφας η πατερα η μητερα η τεκνα η αγρους</u> ενεκεν του (b) <u>ονοματος μου</u> (c) <u>εκατονταπλασιονα</u> λημψεται και ζωην αιωνιον κληρονομησει

(a) *txt: B (D) *pc* a n (sy^s)   UBS⁴ = {C}
(b) *txt: C D L W f¹ f¹³ 33 𝔐
(c) txt: ℵ C D^(*) W Θ f¹ f¹³ 33 𝔐 latt sy bo   UBS⁴ = {B}

Even though this verse contains three variant units, it requires only units (a)+(b) to establish zero support for the precise wording of the NA²⁷ main text.⁵⁷ The support for the various combinations of two variant units within this verse fluctuates: (a)+(b) clearly has zero support; (a)+(c) has zero support among Greek manuscript witnesses (the primary thrust of the current study; at most the combination *may* be supported by it^a, it^n, and sy^s); and (b)+(c) has the support of C W f¹ 33 𝔐 (D^[*] reads εκατονταπλασιον).⁵⁸ In any case, the overall NA²⁷ main text once more

---

55. The totals for NA²⁷ are as follows: the number of "zero-support" verses containing two variant units = 8; three variant units = 27; four variant units = 25; five variant units = 26; six variant units = 11; seven variant units = 6; eight variant units = 1; and nine variant units = 2. These represent all the cases that can be clearly and easily derived from the NA²⁷ apparatus.

56. Of the 26 zero-support verses containing three variant units, Matthew has 5, Mark has 3, Luke has 7, John has 2, Acts has 3, Paul has 3, the General Epistles have 2, and Revelation has 2.

57. The appended tables mark the key variant units that establish zero support with an asterisk. In many verses, the evidence of only two variant units suffices to render the NA²⁷ main text zero support, even if many more variant units exist within that verse. For example, a verse with six variant units may be established as zero support by only two out of the six (Jas 4:14 is one such case).

58. Had the spelling variation in D* not been included, the combination (b)+(c) would have added support from D, but that manuscript still would have been eliminated

clearly is shown to have zero support among the extant Greek manuscript base.[59]

Four variant units within a single verse:[60]

Acts 2:7
εξισταντο (a) <u>δε και</u> εθαυμαζον (b) <u>λεγοντες</u> (c) <u>ουχ</u> ιδου (d) <u>απαντες</u> ουτοι εισιν οι λαλουντες γαλιλαιοι

(a) *txt: B D 096 614 1241 *pm* gig r mae Eus
(b) *txt: P[74] ℵ A B C* 81 1175 *pc* r w vg Eus
(c) *txt: ℵ D E 81 1175 1891 *al*
(d) txt: P[74] ℵ A B[2] C D 096 323 945 1739 *al*

In each case, the NA[27] main text support is precisely stated, and one can readily calculate the degree of support for any combination of witnesses.[61] The appended asterisks show that only the *three* variant units (a)+(b)+(c) are necessary to establish the zero-support nature of the NA[27] main text in this verse.[62]

---

from whole-verse support by its irregular reading in variant unit (a) (omission of η πατερα; see NA[27] Variae Lectiones Minores, 720).

59. Versional support when all three variants are combined appears to be nil, since variant unit (b) shows no such support. Likewise, patristic evidence appears to be wholly lacking. The evidence in SQE does not alter the overall situation but at best adds only minor Greek manuscript support.

60. Throughout the NT, 25 such cases appear: Matt has 1, Mark has 2, Luke has 5, John has 4, Acts has 3, Paul has 4, the General Epistles have 4, and Rev has 2.

61. Variant units (a)+(b) are supported by B r Eus; (a)+(c) by D; (a)+(d) by D 096; (b)+(c) by ℵ 81 1175; (b)+(d) by P[74] ℵ A C*; and (c)+(d) by ℵ D. Note that correctors of a given MS are treated as distinct witnesses. For example, the combination of B and B[2] in readings (b) and (d) does *not* demonstrate common support of B for those two variant units. On the other hand, a manuscript cited as * (first hand) *is* considered identical with the same MS otherwise unmarked. Thus, in the present example, C and C* are identical witnesses, while B and B[2] are not.

62. The combination (a)+(b)+(d) also demonstrates zero support for this verse, but additional combinatory possibilities need not be marked or noted once zero support has been established.

Rule 9, Isolated Variants, and the "Test-Tube" Nature of the NA²⁷/UBS⁴ Text

Five variant units within a single verse:⁶³

Romans 2:16
(a) εν (b) ημερα οτε (c) κρινει ο θεος τα κρυπτα των ανθρωπων κατα το ευαγγελιον (d) μου δια (e) χριστου ιησου

(a) var: *conjecture* (Pohlenz)
(b) *txt: ℵ D G Ψ 33 1739 1881 𝔐 lat sy^h Spec
(c) *txt: B² Ψ 6 1241 *pc* (ℵ A B* D* G *sine acc.*)
(d) var: 69 d* sa^mss
(e) *txt: (ℵ*^vid) B [but ℵ* omits δια]⁶⁴   UBS⁴ = {C}

This verse in fact has only four actual variant units, since (a) is an acknowledged conjecture, unsupported by any MS, version, or father. Such acknowledged non-main-text conjectures are *not* counted in the tabulation of zero support within the present study.⁶⁵ This verse remains instructive for two reasons:

(1) The usual practice and preference of the NA²⁷/UBS⁴ editors is to *reject* conjectures throughout the NT (except in the case of Acts 16:12), even though numerous conjectures are mentioned in the apparatus.
(2) A variant unit may concern *only* the accentuation of a word (here κρίνει versus κρινεῖ). In this situation, the earlier uncials are ambiguous, since they lack accentuation. Thus, those uncials should be considered as supporting either reading, so long as they retain the same orthography of the word(s) in question. Even so, the verse as a whole

---

63. Throughout the NT, 26 such cases appear: Matthew has 2, Mark has 2, Luke has 4, John has 5, Acts has 1, Paul has 2, the General Epistles have 3, and Revelation has 7.

64. Witnesses surrounded by parentheses in the NA²⁷ apparatus differ in some manner from the wording of the reading for which they are cited. These therefore are *not* considered to support the NA²⁷ main text or variant reading in an identical manner with that of the other supporting witnesses cited for such. See NA²⁷, Introduction, 54*. The *precise* nature of the difference in a parenthetically enclosed MS is displayed in loc. in NA²⁷ Appendix 2, "Variae Lectiones Minores," 721-49.

65. Approximately 200 such conjectures are cited in the NA²⁷ apparatus; these "are identified either by their author . . . or by a more general reference" (NA²⁷ Introduction, 54*). Since none of these conjectures appear in the NA²⁷ main text, they are excluded from all tabulation of zero support.

still lacks support from any Greek MS, as determined by calculation of the various combinations of witnesses.[66]

Many more NA[27] zero-support examples could be given in detail, but space does not permit such. Instead, the complete list of whole-verse references and the variant units supporting such appears as an appendix. One last "worst-case" illustration still should be cited: 8 variant units in a lengthy 45-word verse[67] that includes bracketed text:[68]

Revelation 6:8
(a) και ειδον και ιδου ιππος κλωρος και (b) ο καθημενος (c) επανω αυτου ονομα αυτω (d) [ο] (e) θανατος και ο αδης (f) ηκολουθει (g) μετ αυτου και εδοθη (h) αυτοις εξουσια επι το τεταρτον της γης αποκτειναι εν ρομφαια και εν λιμω και εν θανατω και υπο των θηριων της γης

(a) var: 1854 2329 2351 𝔐^K gig vg^{cl} Bea   UBS^4 = {B}
(b) var: C
(c) *var: C 1611 2053 𝔐^A vgst / 1854 pc

66. Variant unit (a) is automatically excluded from calculation due to its conjectural nature. Variant unit (d) shows minor and insignificant support for the reading in question. Variant unit (c) is supported by B² Ψ 6 1241 pc and is accepted as supported by the old uncials ℵ A B* D* G. Only the combinations involving (b), (c), and (e) are relevant, with the following combinatory results: (b)+(c) has support from ℵ D* G Ψ; (c)+(e) from B*, assuming that B* in variant unit (c) supports the NA[27] accent; and (b)+(e) supported by *no* MSS, since ℵ*^{vid} is shown by the Variae Lectiones Minores (740) to differ from the NA[27] main text by omission of δια. Even though the omission of δια appears to be due to error on the part of the scribe ℵ* (ευαγγελιον μου χριστου ιησου is near nonsense), the *precise* combination (b)+(c)+(e) leaves the verse *as printed* in NA[27] with *zero* support. Had ℵ* not committed this error, ℵ conceivably could have supported the entire verse (assuming its unaccented κρινει supported the NA[27] main text).

67. As noted earlier, within the New Testament 11 zero-support variant units contain 6 readings; 5 zero-support units contain 7 readings; 1 such unit contains 8 readings; and 2 units contain 9 readings.

68. The NA[27] main text has 37 zero-support verses containing bracketed text (these are marked in the appended tables). Although the overall level of support for some of the zero-support verses would be affected were the bracketed words excluded, in the present instance (cf. Luke 17:23 above) the whole-verse zero support is *not* affected by the presence or absence of the bracketed [ο] in variant unit (d). In the remaining zero-support cases, 68 verses have *no* brackets present; these instances unambiguously demonstrate zero support.

(d) txt: A 𝔐
(e) *var: A
(f) var: 𝔐^A sy cop Vic
(g) *txt: A C 1611 𝔐^A
(h) var: 1611 1854 2329 2351 𝔐^K lat sy cop

The appended asterisks show that the positive apparatus witnesses in variant unit (g) — that is, those supporting the NA^{27} main text, A C 1611 𝔐^A — are negated within that verse when these same witnesses *depart* from the NA^{27} main text in variant units (c) and (e). MS A departs in variant unit (e), and C 1611 and 𝔐^A depart in variant unit (c). The remainder of 𝔐 (i.e., 𝔐^K) that appears in variant unit (d) becomes a non-issue in view of the departure of 𝔐^A in variant unit (c).[69]

Although Revelation might be considered a special case since its manuscript support is limited (slightly more than 300 Greek MSS and no lectionaries) and since the Byzantine Textform often is divided in that book, the principle remains stable. As the above example demonstrates, even if a zero-support verse contains eight (or even nine) variant units, usually only two or three units suffice to demonstrate the lack of external support. In fact, far more zero-support verses occur in the remainder of the New Testament (88 instances) than appear in Revelation (22 instances). Even in Jude, two whole verses (5, 15) have zero support in the NA^{27} text as printed.[70]

---

69. In Revelation *three* distinct forms of the "𝔐" symbol exist: 𝔐^A (the "Andreas" text), 𝔐^K (the "Koine" text), and m (the Byzantine/*Mehrheitstext*, where 𝔐^A and 𝔐^K coincide). Zero-support calculation in Revelation *must* ensure that the various 𝔐-groups are wholly negated within a verse, in addition to tabulation of the constant witnesses. Since 𝔐^A and 𝔐^K are *collective* entities, each comprising some 80 or so MSS, it cannot be assumed that *every* MS assigned to 𝔐^A or 𝔐^K necessarily differs from the reading for which the collective symbol is cited. For that, one would have to consult the detailed collations of H. C. Hoskier, *Concerning the Text of the Apocalypse* (2 vols.; London: Bernard Quaritch, 1929), and manually make the appropriate calculations (a time-consuming task). For the limited purpose of the present study, 𝔐^A and 𝔐^K are treated as unified witnesses.

70. Even though the textual situation in Jude is complex (see the relevant literature), it is somewhat surprising to find that the eclectic (or "local-genealogical") method creates a zero-support *Ausgangstext* for each of these two verses. Even in the textually complicated verses Jude 22-23 (with 4 variant units) the NA^{27} main text appears to be supported by Ψ (and, except for the spelling error αρπαζοτες for αρπαζοντες, by ℵ). Thus, even in a difficult passage, an eclectic method *could* base its text on at least one extant manuscript throughout

The *Editio Critica Maior* volumes on James, 1 Peter, 2 Peter, and 1 John do not address the zero-support issue,[71] even though ECM provides an extremely comprehensive apparatus regarding the six NA^{27} zero-support verses within these epistles (Jas 2:3; 4:14; 1 Pet 2:5; 5:9; and 1 John 3:1; 3:19).[72] Since the *Ausgangstext* was determined in an eclectic manner on a per-variant-unit basis (the "local-genealogical" method),[73] once the "best" reading has been established within any variant unit (on the primary ground of variant-based "genealogy"),[74] the methodological task proceeds

---

an entire verse, with no need to create a *de facto* conjectural text for that whole verse. Each problematic verse in Jude has at least one variant unit fully collated in K. Aland, ed., *Text und Textwert der griechischen Handschriften des Neuen Testaments. I. Die Katholischen Briefe. Band 1: Das Material* (ANTF 9; Berlin: Walter de Gruyter, 1987): Jude 5 (205-9, involving 2 of the 5 variant units in that verse); Jude 15 (210-12, involving 1 of the 4 variant units in that verse). Cf. in the same volume Jude 23 (215-20, involving 2 of the 4 variant units in that verse). *Text und Textwert* does *not* present the data regarding the remaining variant units in the given verses that would confirm (except for Jude 22-23) zero support. Note that in *Text und Textwert* the NA^{27} main text reading is always cited as group 2 (the Byzantine Textform as group 1). Jude 18 also would be zero support except for inclusion of the second-order constant witnesses 630 and 1505 within 𝔐 in one variant unit within that verse. However, the films of those two MSS reveal that even they differ from the NA^{27} main text in a non-cited variant unit (reading επιθυμιας αυτων instead of the NA^{27} εαυτων επιθυμιας); thus Jude 18 is likewise without support, although not considered so within the present study.

71. Although ECM offers a far more extensive apparatus than that of NA^{27}, the determination of zero support would be more time-consuming due to the ECM inclusion of many more variant units and manuscript witnesses.

72. In regard to zero-support readings, the ECM base text differs from that of NA^{27} in Jas 2:3 and 1 Pet 5:9. While the zero-support nature of the NA^{27} main text remains unaffected by these changes, the ECM main text in each instance regains minimal support from Greek manuscript witnesses (Jas 2:3 = B; 1 Pet 5:9 = P Ψ 1739).

73. The "local-genealogical" method is now termed the "Coherence-Based Genealogical Method" (ECM 1 John, "Preface," 22* and also 29*); in general, the same methodology and application is retained. "Coherence" earlier was discussed in ECM 1–2 Pet (23*-24*), but the terms "local-genealogical" and "Coherence-Based Genealogical Method" did not appear in that volume. The 1997 ECM James volume does not mention either term, nor does the word "coherence" appear therein.

74. ECM 1 John, "Preface," 22*: "The reconstruction of the text rests on an analysis of the primary transmission using the Coherence-Based Genealogical Method to explore the relationship among the witnesses." The essence of this "local-genealogical" method remains the establishment of the text by determining within each variant unit the presumed archetypal reading which *for that unit* serves as the source of all other manuscript readings that appear therein. This basically retains the older eclectic canon of favoring the reading presumed to have been the source of all others within a variant unit.

Rule 9, Isolated Variants, and the "Test-Tube" Nature of the NA²⁷/UBS⁴ Text

to the next sequential variant unit without regard for decisions made in the previous unit. Yet the resultant sequential *Ausgangstext*, once established as an entity, then is considered to be the overall hypothetical source text from which the *entire* transmissional tradition is derived.[75] At this point, the situation reverses itself: those witnesses that support any given variant unit are considered to represent only *derivative* and thus less accurate representations of the hypothetically determined *Ausgangstext*. No longer are these extant manuscript witnesses regarded (as they should be) as the basis by which the *Ausgangstext* is established — the manuscripts themselves now are transformed into imperfect reflections of the "more correct" but essentially conjectural *Ausgangstext*.[76] The circularity of this methodology is no coincidence, and yet this flaw propels the system.

Even while Kurt Aland and Beate Köster affirm that "Internal criteria . . . alone cannot substantiate a text-critical decision,"[77] Barbara Aland declares, "Considerations of the textual value of manuscripts are always dependent on internal criteria. . . . So a high degree of circular reasoning is involved."[78] Gerd Mink discusses the matter more explicitly, addressing the matter of "circular reasoning which cannot be entirely avoided in textual criticism":[79]

> There is a circular argument typical of textual criticism: witnesses are important for reconstructing the initial text, and they are important

---

75. G. Mink, "Problems of a Highly Contaminated Tradition: The New Testament. Stemmata of Variants as a Source of a Genealogy for Witnesses," in *Studies in Stemmatology II* (ed. P. van Reenen, A. den Hollander, and M. van Mulken; Amsterdam: Benjamins, 2004), 13-85, states, "Those witnesses with good genealogical coherencies with *A* [= the reconstructed *Ausgangstext* underlying ECM and NA²⁷] are of course of prime importance, since the variants in those witnesses could be expected to be part of the initial text" (82 n. 71).

76. ECM 1 John, 29*, states, "A high agreement with *A* [= the hypothetical *Ausgangstext*] reflects the quality of a witness." But the *Ausgangstext* as constructed is admittedly "an artificial witness" that serves as "the hypothetical initial text," transcending not only the manuscript witnesses that gave it existence, but even the NA²⁷ or ECM main text. Yet the *Ausgangstext* had to be constructed from the data present among the very MSS determined to be of high quality when compared with the *Ausgangstext*! Such sophisticated circularity not only parallels that of Westcott-Hort, but leaves the method with a questionable foundation and certainly begging the question.

77. K. Aland (rev. B. Köster), "Textual Criticism," 2:551.

78. B. Aland, "New Testament Textual Research," 69.

79. Mink, "Problems," 46.

because of the high number of agreements with the reconstructed initial text. In other words, witnesses are good because of their good variants, variants are good because of their good witnesses. This circle cannot be avoided [?], but it has to be controlled. We need a method, therefore, which can provide an overall view of the consequences of all the decisions we take, so that also the overall plausibility of what we are doing can be examined.[80]

In practice, this so-called "local-genealogical" or "coherence-based genealogical" method fails — not only because it presents the Westcott-Hort circular methodology cloaked in statistical garb, but also because as another form of eclecticism it continues to consider variant units in isolation, ignoring their sequential connection. The method thus abandons any semblance of *real* "coherence" in relation to sequential *external* support when producing its resultant critical text, choosing to place all its trust in statistical alignments. Although Mink repeatedly emphasizes "coherence,"[81] his use of the term relates primarily to a high percentage of agreement among manuscripts, by which the "local genealogies" presumably established for individual variant units are *statistically* but not *essentially* linked with those MSS that support sequential variant units. Yet Mink acknowledges,

> A global stemma can only be *true* if the relationships it shows between the witnesses are compatible with the relationships the witnesses have in every single place of variation *according to the relationships between their variants, as represented in the local stemmata.*[82]

Such at best remains a statistical and not an essential relationship in terms of intra-manuscript agreement. This then calls Mink's further claim into question, namely, that "The general textual flow *corresponds to the development of the text* (i.e. the variants) *throughout its history.* This development can be demonstrated *at every passage of the text* in local stemmata of variants."[83]

---

80. Mink, "Problems," 25.
81. Mink, "Problems," 29, 32, 46, 70.
82. Mink, "Problems," 29-30; emphasis added.
83. Mink, "Problems," 37; emphasis added. For further discussion of Mink's "local-genealogical" theory of "coherence," see G. Mink, "Eine umfassende Genealogie der

Rule 9, Isolated Variants, and the "Test-Tube" Nature of the NA²⁷/UBS⁴ Text

Yet when the internally determined *Ausgangstext* or initial reading of an individual variant unit is established as "best" *apart from* the external testimony that sequentially links one variant unit with another, the result becomes that which is stated by Jacquier in the opening epigram of this essay: "c'est faire oeuvre d'imagination et non de critique."[84]

The ECM editors (including Mink) specifically declare that "Internal criteria were often evaluated in a way similar to that used in NA/GNT," but "External criteria, however, have changed, drawing on much more information and also the perspective of genealogical coherence."[85] A most puzzling comment then follows: "One central external criterion is now whether a plausible textual flow can be assumed in a passage, i.e., transmission of the text by witnesses of high genealogical coherence."[86]

Given the thrust of the present essay and the multiplicity of zero-support verses in both NA²⁷ and ECM, a pertinent question arises: can "a plausible textual flow . . . be assumed" when the (re)constructed text of a verse in terms of its sequential variants does *not* appear in any known manuscript, version, or father, and apparently has *never* existed within the entirety of transmissional history? A negative answer obviously should be expected — but such is not the case with NA²⁷/UBS⁴/ECM. Rather, one finds not only a purported *Ausgangstext* that contains conjectures in specific single variant units (NA²⁷ Acts 16:12; ECM 2 Pet 3:10), but a text that in sequence has created numerous *de facto* whole-verse conjectures in its connected pattern of variant readings. Yet such a pattern of readings cannot be demonstrated ever to have had any real existence within the transmissional history of the New Testament text, nor can the hypothetical existence of such an *Ausgangstext* seriously be asserted when compared with the hard data of actual transmission.[87] A text that purports to be the

---

neutestamentlichen Überlieferung," *NTS* 39 (1993): 481-99; idem, "Editing and Genealogical Studies," 53; idem, "Was verändert sich in der Textkritik durch die Beachtung genealogischer Kohärenz?" in Weren and Koch, eds., *Recent Developments in Textual Criticism*, 39-68; idem, "Kohärenzbasierte Genealogische Methode — Worum geht es?" (2002) http://www.uni-muenster.de/NTTextforschung/Genealogische_Methode.html.

84. Jacquier, *Text*, 314: "It is to make a work of inspiration and not of criticism."
85. ECM, 1 John, 30.
86. ECM, 1 John, 30.
87. D. C. Parker, "Through a Screen Darkly: Digital Texts and the New Testament," *JSNT* 25 (2003): 395-411, states the fact quite bluntly: "[Modern eclectic] Textual critics, under the guise of reconstructing original texts, are really creating new ones . . . readjusting the

genealogical source of all other variant readings theoretically *should* reflect in its archetype a sequence generally maintained among the extant witnesses; otherwise, Calvin L. Porter's description of the eclectic method in general remains apt: "It seems to assume that very early the original text was rent piecemeal and so carried to the ends of the earth where the textual critic, like lamenting Isis, must seek it by his skill."[88]

At the very least, this suggests something of a wrong methodological approach and forces the reconsideration of Aland/Aland Rule Nine (here with added emphasis):

> *Variants must never be treated in isolation,* but *always* considered in the context of the [transmissional] tradition. Otherwise there is too great a danger of reconstructing a "test tube text" which *never* existed at *any* time or place.[89]

Yet such remains the situation within modern eclecticism, regardless of methodological approach (reasoned, thoroughgoing, "local-genealogical," or "coherence-based genealogical"). The resultant text — pieced together from disparate variant units — ultimately reflects a series of readings that lacks genuine historical existence, as well as even a plausible transmissional existence. This remains the case whether that text is considered to be the purported autograph, the transmissional archetype, a "working text," or the variant-based *Ausgangstext*. The results obtained within $NA^{27}/UBS^4/ECM$ continue to display what E. J. Epp termed a "symptom" and *not* a "solution."[90]

---

textual gene pool. . . . I do not mean that the texts we are creating are necessarily superior to earlier creations. It is more significant that they are the texts that we need to create" (401-402). One seriously might ask *why* such a "need" exists, and what is its nature; one then should inquire as to *how* a reconstruction that is *not* a solution can be acceptable (a satisfactory reply perhaps should not be expected).

88. C. L. Porter, "A Textual Analysis of the Earliest Manuscripts of the Gospel of John" (Ph.D. Diss., Duke University, 1961), 12.

89. Aland and Aland, *The Text of the New Testament*, 281; emphasis added.

90. E. J. Epp, "The Eclectic Method in New Testament Textual Criticism: Solution or Symptom?" *HTR* 69 (1976): 211-57 (reprinted in E. J. Epp and G. D. Fee, eds., *Studies in the Theory and Method of New Testament Textual Criticism* [SD 45; Grand Rapids: Eerdmans, 1993], 141-73).

Rule 9, Isolated Variants, and the "Test-Tube" Nature of the NA²⁷/UBS⁴ Text

An Alternative Hypothesis

In commenting upon the continuing research regarding "singular readings," Barbara Aland has suggested that the paucity of New Testament transmissional information prior to the fourth century permits a wide range of possible scenarios. As she critiques the various studies that have evaluated scribal habits on the basis of a manuscript's singular readings (i.e., the studies of Colwell, Royse, and Head),[91] she states the following:

> The method is still useful, although it should be underscored that there are no singular readings in the strictest sense. There is no way of knowing that what we regard as singular readings were not also to be found in the great mass of manuscripts that have been lost.[92]

By saying "no way of knowing," Aland's argument transcends the typical inferences made *ex silentio* and appeals *ad ignorantiam* to multivalent transmissional possibilities, particularly during the pre–fourth-century era. But such an appeal makes it impossible to rule out *any*

---

[91]. E. C. Colwell, "Method in Evaluating Scribal Habits: A Study of P⁴⁵, P⁶⁶, P⁷⁵," in his *Studies in Methodology in Textual Criticism of the New Testament* (NTTS 9; Grand Rapids: Eerdmans, 1968), 106-24; J. R. Royse, "Scribal Habits in the Transmission of New Testament Texts," in *The Critical Study of Sacred Texts* (ed. W. D. O'Flaherty; Berkeley: Graduate Theological Union, 1979), 139-61; idem, "Scribal Habits in Early Greek New Testament Papyri" (Th.D. Diss., Graduate Theological Union, Berkeley, 1981); idem, "Scribal Tendencies in the Transmission of the Text of the New Testament," in *The Text of the New Testament in Contemporary Research: Essays on the Status Quaestionis* (ed. B. D. Ehrman and M. W. Holmes; SD 46; Grand Rapids: Eerdmans, 1995), 239-52; P. W. Head, "Some Observations on Early Papyri of the Synoptic Gospels, Especially Concerning the 'Scribal Habits,'" *Bib* 71 (1990): 240-47; idem, "The Habits of New Testament Copyists: Singular Readings in the Early Fragmentary Papyri of John," *Bib* 85 (2004): 399-408.

[92]. B. Aland, "The Significance of the Chester Beatty Papyri in Early Church History," in *The Earliest Gospels* (ed. C. Horton; JSNTSup 258; London: T&T Clark, 2004), 108-21; the quotation is from 110 n. 12. A similar statement appears in Barbara Aland, "Neutestamentliche Handschriften als Interpreten des Textes? P⁷⁵ und seine Vorlagen in Joh 10," in *Jesus Rede von Gott und ihre Nachgeschichte im frühen Christentum: Beiträge zur Verkündigung Jesu und zum Kerygma der Kirche. Festschrift für Willi Marxsen zum 70. Geburtstag* (ed. D.-A. Koch et al.; Gütersloh: Gerd Mohn, 1989), 379-97: "Ich mit 'Kopierverhalten' nicht nur die 'scribal habits' des individuellen Schreibers einer vorliegenden Handschrift meine.... Die 'scribal habits' im engeren Sinne ... von den Singulärlesarten der Papyri ausging ... aber der Ausgangspunkt war eng gewählt, und wichtige Lesarten mußten von vornherein wegfallen" (380 n. 3).

transmissional hypothesis, and alternate possibilities equally can be postulated.[93] In particular, Aland suggests a bizarre sort of "majority text" hypothesis: a "great mass of manuscripts . . . have been lost," and that "great mass" *may (per ignorantiam!)* have contained any or all of what are known today only as "singular readings." By extension of the same argument, any or all of today's "singular readings" once *may* have existed in the numerical majority of MSS. If such an appeal to current ignorance were valid, text-critical decisions could no longer be made, since even internal criteria would offer little confidence regarding the plausibility of results.[94] Yet a "best guess" scenario need not be postulated.

   93. Such a line of argument allows anything and everything to be possible; thus, *any* proffered text could be accorded autograph status. In contrast, Wisse, "Nature and Purpose," 43, correctly suggests that one *cannot* "set this *undocumented* period apart from the *documented* history of the transmission of early Christian texts. There would have to be compelling reasons to make such an assumption." Wisse likewise strongly rejects the further Aland/Münster contention that the post–fourth-century "emerging orthodoxy" somehow ended "redactional freedom by deciding on a 'standard' text and by suppressing all manuscripts which deviated" (cf. K. Aland [rev. B. Köster], "Textual Criticism," 2:546: "From the time of Constantine on, . . . the bishops were able to guide the text . . . in a certain direction. They could choose a model text for the official scriptoria . . . and this text served as the basis for the [Byzantine] copies of the NT. . . . The medieval Byzantine church's attempt . . . to create a uniform NT text resulted in the oppressive [?] plurality of preserved NT manuscripts . . . containing the standard Byzantine text"). As Wisse correctly notes (45), "The church was in no position to establish and control the biblical text, let alone eliminate rival forms of the text. . . . Only beginning with the twelfth century, do we have evidence for a large scale effort. This is von Soden's group K^r which shows evidence of careful control. . . . There is no evidence for the Byzantine period or for an earlier date of efforts to eliminate divergent copies of New Testament manuscripts." Cf. also Wisse's further remarks (52-53): "This lack of evidence cannot be explained away by speculations about an extensively interpolated 'standard' text which was imposed by the orthodox leadership. . . . The Church certainly lacked the means and apparently also the will to do this. . . . The transmission process could not be effectively controlled even during the Byzantine period. . . . [Were the case otherwise,] the unanimous attestation of a relatively stable and uniform text during the following centuries in both Greek and the versions would have to be considered nothing short of a miracle."

   94. The same line of argument provides the theoretical basis for conjectural readings: any or all conjectural readings once *may* have existed and even at some point have held "majority" status during the obscure transmissional era prior to the fourth century. By such logic, the number of existing conjectures should be increased, lest a potential "original" reading otherwise be missed! Although this sounds absurd, a similar form of "conjectural originality" not only is permitted by Aland's line of argument, but for all practical purposes already exists in the current NA^{27}/UBS^4/ECM text.

Rule 9, Isolated Variants, and the "Test-Tube" Nature of the NA²⁷/UBS⁴ Text

Allowing that Aland makes a valid point (even if imperfectly stated),[95] an opposing hypothesis can be presented on a more secure basis. The lack of any thoroughly Byzantine MSS prior to the fourth century often has been urged against the Byzantine-priority hypothesis.[96] But, by applying Barbara Aland's argument regarding singular readings, the Byzantine Textform itself well may have existed in the pre–fourth-century era;[97] it may even have been widespread among a now-lost majority of MSS. Such theoretical speculation differs from that of Aland, however, in the sense that the Byzantine-priority hypothesis represents a *reasonable inference* based upon the *actual state* of the *existing* post–fourth-century textual evidence, and not upon a hypothetical assertion regarding what one cannot know due to historical ignorance. It is certain, for example, that

---

95. Certainly, various fathers make comments regarding readings known to them that today are found in few, one, or no extant manuscripts. Some of these readings are claimed by individual fathers to have been in "many" or even "most" copies known to them in their day. Yet one must allow that such statements *may* reflect only that which prevailed within a father's localized region, and not necessarily the true proportion of evidence that existed at that time on an Empire-wide basis. Nor do such statements establish that the majority or even a large minority of what are today known as singular readings have not in fact been singular since the time they appeared in the manuscript that presently contains them.

96. Just as some previously assumed "singular" readings now are known from recent discovery not to be singular, so also many Byzantine readings thought (particularly by Westcott and Hort) *not* to exist prior to the fourth century have been found in the early papyri; cf. H. A. Sturz, *The Byzantine Text-Type and New Testament Textual Criticism* (Nashville: Thomas Nelson, 1984); G. Zuntz, *The Text of the Epistles: A Disquisition upon the Corpus Paulinum* (The Schweich Lectures of the British Academy, 1946; London: The British Academy, 1953). Yet, while the specific Byzantine *pattern* of readings is not found in any extant MS, version, or father prior to the barrier of the fourth century, it becomes a more serious matter that the NA²⁷/UBS⁴/ECM pattern of readings cannot be shown to exist — nor plausibly *ever* to have existed — at *any* point in transmissional history, whether before or after the fourth century.

97. J.-F. Racine, *The Text of Matthew in the Writings of Basil of Caesarea* (NTGF 5; Leiden: Brill, 2004), has demonstrated that the earliest thoroughly Byzantine father is Basil of Caesarea (ca. 330-379). It is also plain that Greek fathers after this period (e.g., Gregory of Nyssa, Chrysostom, etc.) generally utilize a form of text that is more Byzantine than anything else. Since no evidence exists to support the notion that any of these fourth-century fathers *created* the Byzantine Textform, it must rather be presumed that they simply used an earlier form of text *already* current and readily obtainable in that specific region in which Greek was the primary language (from which region versional evidence necessarily did not exist and from which region *all* definitive pre–fourth-century patristic textual evidence is lacking).

now-lost Byzantine parent uncials had to have existed for the "orphaned" Byzantine minuscules of (at least) the ninth to eleventh centuries.[98] Equally, the parent uncials (or papyri) that once existed for the otherwise unrelated Byzantine uncials of the fourth through the ninth centuries are now lost.[99] An inference thus based upon a sufficient quantity of *existing* evidence provides a historically more reasonable scenario than an assertion *ad ignorantiam* suggesting what the "great mass" of MSS no longer extant *might* have read in quantity in relation to the "singular readings" of today's documents.[100]

Since more than 100 whole verses as printed in NA^{27}/UBS^4 *lack* extant manuscript support in the aggregate, to at least that extent the NA^{27}/UBS^4 text is based on conjecture and speculation, and not upon a logical inference from the actual data.[101] In contrast, within the Byzantine

---

98. K. Lake, "The Ecclesiastical Text," Excursus 1 in K. Lake, R. P. Blake, and S. New, "The Caesarean Text of the Gospel of Mark," *HTR* 21 (1928): 338-57, speaks with regard to the minuscules examined at Sinai, Patmos, and Jerusalem: "The amount of direct genealogy which has been detected . . . is almost negligible. . . . The manuscripts . . . are almost all orphan children without brothers or sisters" (348-49).

99. D^{abs1} and D^{abs2} of the ninth and tenth centuries respectively, as direct copies of the sixth century D/06 (Claromontanus) of Paul, appear to represent the only uncial exceptions to the "orphan" situation described by Lake, Blake, and New.

100. Royse, "Scribal Habits in Early Greek New Testament Papyri," 34-36, anticipated Barbara Aland on this point: "The alternative possibility . . . is that a singular reading was really part of a tradition, a tradition including at least the manuscript's *Vorlage*, but a tradition which left traces in one manuscript only. Is this alternative likely? . . . The fact that the New Testament has been transmitted by a tradition which is highly 'contaminated' and which has left such vast quantities of manuscript evidence, indicates that there were very few, if any, real 'dead ends' within this tradition. . . . Whatever the precise extent of . . . scribal correcting may have been, it would have worked to limit the continuation of one scribe's errors into subsequent manuscripts. And thus it would tend to ensure that some, at least, of the singulars . . . of one manuscript were not in fact part of a wider tradition, but were actually created by that manuscript's scribe." Cf. Royse's entire discussion, 33-41, regarding the likelihood that singular readings never were very widespread; also his concluding comment, 40: "Textual criticism is an empirical, historical discipline, whose results must rest ultimately on the data of the manuscripts. . . . Given the mass of data already available, carefully conducted studies of individual manuscripts are not likely to be made completely worthless by future finds."

101. This situation is exacerbated if one or more additional variant units from neighboring verses are added to the sequential tabulation. In such a case, many more short stretches of text demonstrate zero support, further calling into question the conjectural nature of the NA^{27} (re)constructed text. For example, the NA^{27} whole verse Matt 6:21 is sup-

Rule 9, Isolated Variants, and the "Test-Tube" Nature of the NA²⁷/UBS⁴ Text

Textform, nearly every verse of the NT steadfastly retains well over 90 percent general agreement among its component MSS regarding its text.[102] When this is contrasted with the situation in regard to the NA²⁷ text, one has to wonder *how*, under any putative theory of historical transmission, the presumed *Ausgangstext* (NA²⁷/UBS⁴/ECM) ever could have existed in actuality, let alone have given rise to all other forms of text while totally losing its own original identity among the extant manuscript base. Lack of perpetuation in this regard strongly suggests a lack of prior existence. It is certain that the NA²⁷ pattern of readings *cannot* be demonstrated ever to have existed within the whole of transmissional history, even within some shorter portions of text comprising but a single verse.[103]

In contrast to the *de facto* conjectural nature of the (re)constructed NA²⁷/UBS⁴/ECM text, the Byzantine Textform has a demonstrable historical existence: its line of transmission extends from (at least) the post–fourth-century era to the invention of printing.[104] Thus, in theory, the

---

ported by ℵ *pc*, while Matt 6:22 is supported by B W *pc*; thus there is zero support for the combined two verses. At least six clear instances of this phenomenon appear just within Matthew in NA²⁷: Matt 14:3 (MS 33) + 4 (B Z); 15:30 (ℵ *pc*) + 31 (C); 18:7 (L f¹ 892) + 8 (ℵ B); 19:16 (B) + 17 (ℵ L Θ); 24:30 (B L) + 31 (f¹ 892); 28:2 (ℵ B L-2211) + 3 (D 892). The remainder of the NT contains dozens of similar examples.

102. The general pattern of Byzantine coherence can be seen in the full collation data found in the *Text und Textwert* series. See K. Aland et al., eds., *Text und Textwert der griechischen Handschriften des Neuen Testaments*; I, Die Katholischen Briefe; II, Die Paulinischen Briefe; III, Die Apostelgeschichte; IV, Die Synoptischen Evangelien: 1, Das Markusevangelium; 2, Das Matthäusevangelium; 3, Das Lukasevangelium (ANTF 8-11, 13, 16-21, 26-31; Berlin: Walter de Gruyter, 1987-99). Note that the pattern of Byzantine coherence (as reflected in its overall consensus text) remains relatively stable, even when all Byzantine MSS copied after the eleventh century (80 percent of the total) are excluded from statistical tabulation.

103. Pertinent is the anecdote related by M. M. Parvis, "The Goals of New Testament Textual Studies," in *Studia Evangelica, Vol. VI: Papers Presented to the Fourth International Congress on New Testament Studies Held at Oxford, 1969* (ed. E. A. Livingstone; Berlin: Akademie-Verlag, 1973), 393-407: "Silva Lake told me that she often regretted the fact that she and Kirsopp Lake had 'reconstructed' the Caesarean text of the Gospel of Mark. She said that she realized that they had not reconstructed but had constructed a text of Mark that had never been seen in the ancient church" (397). It would appear that very much the same could be said in regard to the NA²⁷/UBS⁴/ECM text as published.

104. Parker, "Through a Screen Darkly," 403, seems to concede this point: "Texts are not inherently good or bad. The Byzantine text is [in Parker's view] certainly late, and certainly contains features lacking in the oldest copies, but it also happens to have been extremely successful, and to have existed as the honoured text of the orthodox for well over a

Byzantine Textform should retain a greater potential for preserving a preexisting archetype — a *non*-conjectural *Ausgangstext* that is historically and transmissionally superior to that presented in modern critical editions.[105] Such at least remains more plausible than a hypothetical archetype ultimately derived from sequential conjecture that has *no* demonstrable existence within the whole of transmissional history.

Those who maintain the status quo might reject such a claim as exceptional; yet it is the modern critical text that reflects *de facto* conjecture, transmissional abnormality, and historical implausibility. Ultimately, the question becomes whether confidence should be placed in a text that in the aggregate reflects conjectural speculation and lacks transmissional viability, or in a text with clear historical roots and a potential transmissional plausibility in its favor.[106] If one is willing to reexamine long-standing

---

thousand years." Cf. G. Zuntz, "The Byzantine Text in New Testament Criticism," *JTS* 43 (1942): 25-30: "The Byzantine Text must be reconstructed. . . . [It is] the only universal Greek text of the New Testament that ever existed. This, after all, was the book of books to medieval Eastern Christianity" (26-27).

105. Even B. Aland, "New Testament Textual Research," 69-72, testifies from her own perspective to this point: (1) *The Byzantine Textform is not recensional:* "If the Koine [= Byzantine] text were actually a recension, then one would expect it to have been edited systematically. But that is by no means the case" (71). (2) *Various "atypical" and "difficult" readings persisted without correction within the Byzantine Textform:* "[This] atypical Byzantine reading [εκ in Jas 2:18] . . . was copied throughout centuries by scribes with meticulous care" (71). (3) *The text of the Byzantine tradition remained highly stable:* "No scribe, no corrector dared to alter the sacred text" (71). (4) *Internal criteria utilized to establish the modern critical* Ausgangstext *are subjective and involve a methodological circularity:* "Considerations of the textual value of manuscripts are always dependent on internal criteria. . . . A high degree of circular reasoning is involved. . . . Considerations based on internal criteria are often ambiguous" (69-70). (5) *Most of the Byzantine Textform represents a good and valid form of the NT text:* "The Byzantine is not always a poor text. Only a relatively small number of variants, where the Byzantine tradition testifies to a reading as a consistent group against all other manuscripts, are secondary. . . . Apart from these passages the Koine text offers a good early textform" (71-72). The Byzantine Textform thus should not be seen as a recensional attempt (systematic or sporadic) to remove perceived difficulties, but instead as a good and stable text that persisted doggedly through the centuries with numerous difficulties left intact. While Byzantine-priority advocates obviously differ regarding Aland's claim as to its "secondary" status, they would welcome a reconsideration of the Byzantine Textform from such a basic perspective.

106. As H. C. Youtie, *The Textual Criticism of Documentary Papyri* (ed. E. G. Turner; Special University Lectures in Palaeography, University of London Institute of Classical Studies, Bulletin Supplement, 6; London: Institute of Classical Studies, 1958), 37, states, "Any-

scholarly opinion, the Byzantine-priority hypothesis becomes at least reasonably plausible, particularly in view of its actual historical existence when contrasted with the conjectural claims underlying the NA^{27}/UBS^4 text. Zero-support conjecture and a pattern of readings found in *no* extant manuscript, version, or patristic writer indeed creates the very "test-tube text" warned against by two of its own editors. If such an *Ausgangstext* lacks historical plausibility and results in conjecture-based whole verses, a problem exists; and the resultant text raises serious questions regarding whatever underlying transmissional history might be presupposed under the various eclectic theories.[107] In contrast, the overall pattern of readings that underlie the Byzantine Textform is *not* merely "a 'test tube text' which never existed at any time or place," but a text with a demonstrable historical existence and a potential transmissional originality.[108] The Byzantine-priority hypothesis thus is historically and transmissionally more probable than the conjectural vagaries derived from presumed genealogical "coherence" or varying forms of modern eclectic speculation.[109]

thing that goes beyond the minimum hypothesis is in danger of distorting the evidence." Youtie further suggests that "A hypothesis should embrace the data which it is meant to explain as closely as a well-fitting glove embraces the hand" (37); and (in a different context, but applicable *mutatis mutandis*), "If readings are to be correct, they must proceed from a correct intelligence of the text as a whole" (54).

107. The questionable historical and transmissional nature of the modern critical *Ausgangstext* finds a parallel in Streeter's comments regarding Fourth Gospel source criticism: "If the sources have undergone anything like the amount of amplification, excision, rearrangement and adaptation which the theory postulates, then the critic's pretence that he can unravel the process is grotesque. As well hope to start with a string of sausages and reconstruct the pig. . . . Even the more sober seeming of these . . . theories appear to me to be based on a method essentially unscientific"; B. H. Streeter, *The Four Gospels: A Study of Origins Treating of the Manuscript Tradition, Sources, Authorship, and Dates* (rev. ed.; London: Macmillan, 1930; rep. ed., 1956), 377.

108. Parvis, "The Goals," 405, states: "The *textus receptus* [TR, meaning the Byzantine Textform in general] may have a longer and more complicated line of descent than we have been accustomed to think. Beyond this, however, the *textus receptus* is an historical text. It is a text which was used by the Church." Ironically, as the printed TR editions displayed a less accurate form of their base Byzantine text, so also the NA^{27}/UBS^4/ECM "New Standard Text" editions display a less accurate form of their predominant base Alexandrian text — and the chance that "autograph" status is present in either set of editions remains minimal.

109. B. Aland, "Die Münsteraner Arbeit am Text des Neuen Testaments und ihr Beitrag für die frühe Überlieferung des 2. Jahrhunderts: Eine methodologische Betrachtung," in *Gospel Traditions in the Second Century: Origins, Recensions, Text, and Transmission* (ed. W. L. Petersen; Christianity and Judaism in Antiquity 3; Notre Dame: Uni-

MAURICE A. ROBINSON

Appendix: Zero-Support Verses by Number of Variant Units per Verse

2 VUs	3 VUs	4 VUs	5 VUs	6 VUs	7 VUs	8 VUs	9 VUs
Mk 11.3	Mt 19.29	Mt 16.21	Mt 8.13	Mk 14.72	Mt 20.23	Re 6.8	Lk 22.17fff
Lk 17.23	Mt 20.31	Mk 6.23	Mt 21.28	Jn 7.39	Mk 3.7f		Re 5.13
Lk 24.50	Mt 24.38	Mk 12.36	Mk 6.41	[Jn 17.11]	1Co 14.34f		
Jn 5.2	Mt 27.24	Lk 6.4	Mk 10.35ff	Ac 20.24	Re 6.11		
Jn 16.23	Mt 27.46	Lk 11.11	Lk 6.26	1Co 12.10	Re 18.19		
Jn 18.1	Mk 3.31	Lk 16.6	Lk 10:39	Jas 4.14	Re 9.20		
Ac 27.8	Mk 6.22	Lk 24.39	Lk 10.41f	Re 3.7			
2Co 5.3	Mk 6.33	Jn 6.23	Lk 13.35	Re 5.6			
	Lk 3.32	[Jn 8.7]	[Jn 8.9]	Re 13.15			
	Lk 3.37	Jn 13.2	Jn 10.7	Re 21.4			
	Lk 8.35	Jn 21.16	Jn 13.26	Re 21.16			
	Lk 12.54	Jn 21.17	[Jn 16.18]				
	Lk 13.27	Ac 2.7	Jn 18.31				
	Lk 21.11	Ac 15.4	Jn 20.17				
	Lk 22.30	Ac 18.7	Jn 21.4				
	Jn 14.10	Ro 8.11	Ac 1.14				
	Jn 21.24	1Tm 2.9	Ro 2.16				
	Ac 10.19	Phm 6	1Co 15.54f				
	Ac 13.14	He 13.21	Jas 2.3				
	Ac 23.30	1Pe 2.5	1Pe 5.9				
	1Co 10.9	1Jn 3.19	Jude 5				
	2Co 1.12	2Jn 1.12	Re 4.4				

---

versity of Notre Dame Press, 1989), 55-70, correctly asks: "zur letzen Frage: Welcher neutestamentliche Text kann überhaupt rekonstruiert werden?" ("Regarding the last question: what type of New Testament text can be reconstituted at all?"; 68). Yet she notes that "Wir in so sehr vielen Fällen ... so nahe an den ursprünglichen Text herenkommen!" ("We in so very many cases ... approach very near to the original text!"; 69). In response, one perhaps should consider the century-old remark of J. R. Harris, *Codex Bezae: A Study of the So-Called Western Text of the New Testament* (TS 2; Cambridge: University Press, 1891), 235: "In the field of New Testament Criticism, the unexpected is always happening: hypotheses which have been reckoned outworn reappear, and popular and attractive modern theories have frequently to be discarded." Perhaps the time for such reconsideration once more has come around, with Byzantine-priority at the vanguard.

Rule 9, Isolated Variants, and the "Test-Tube" Nature of the NA²⁷/UBS⁴ Text

2 VUs	3 VUs	4 VUs	5 VUs	6 VUs	7 VUs	8 VUs	9 VUs
	Heb 3.6	Jude 15	Re 7.1				
	1Jn 3.1	Re 1.20	Re 7.9				
	2Jn 1.8	Re 9.12f	Re 11.18				
	Re 13.8	Re 14.18	Re 14.8				
	Re 18.21		Re 19.17				
			Re 19.20				
Totals: 8	27	25 [26]	26 [28]	10 [11]	6	1	2

VUs = Variant units.
f, ff, fff = The verse cited plus the verse(s) following are treated as a single VU in NA²⁷.

61

The Significance of the Papyri in Revising the New Testament Greek Text and English Translations

Philip Comfort

In the past twenty years I have had the privilege of working in two fields of New Testament studies. I have had one hand in textual criticism and another hand in translation. My labor in textual studies has been with the early New Testament papyri, concerning which I have made several written contributions; the two most thorough books are *The Text of the Earliest New Testament Greek Manuscripts* and *Encountering the Manuscripts: An Introduction to New Testament Paleography and Textual Criticism* (both of which are often cited in this article). My work in translation has been serving as the coordinating editor for two editions of the New Living Translation, each term of service lasting seven years (1990-96, 1997-2003). One of my tasks in the translation was to be the textual critic; this gave me the opportunity to examine significant variant readings (especially the papyri) as they apply to English translation.

The New Testament papyri are generally recognized as being the most significant manuscripts because they provide the earliest extant evidence for the original wording of the New Testament text.[1] In addition to

---

1. There are 13 papyri I would date to the second century: $P^{4+64+67}$, P^{32}, P^{46}, P^{52}, P^{66}, P^{75}, P^{77} (and P^{103}), P^{87}, P^{98}, P^{104}, P^{109}, and P^{118}. There are another 14 manuscripts that could be dated to ca. 200 or early third century: P^{1}, P^{5}, P^{13}, P^{20}, P^{23}, P^{27}, P^{29}, P^{30}, P^{38}, P^{45}, P^{48}, P^{107}, P^{108}, and P^{121}. The papyri I would date to the second half of the third century and/or late third century are as follows: P^{9}, P^{12}, P^{15+16}, P^{17}, P^{18}, P^{24}, P^{28}, P^{35}, P^{37}, P^{40}, P^{50}, P^{53}, P^{70}, P^{72}, P^{78}, P^{80}, P^{86}, P^{91}, P^{92}, P^{101}, P^{102}, P^{113}, P^{114}, P^{115}, P^{119}, P^{120}. See P. Comfort and D. Barrett, *The Text of the Earliest New Testament Greek Manuscripts* (Wheaton: Tyndale, 2001), for an up-

The Significance of the Papyri in Revising the New Testament Greek Text

their early date, several of the early papyri bear telltale signs of having been produced by professional scribes capable of producing what is called the bookhand or literary hand. These professional scribes could produce a page with well-stroked letters (slowly formed), bilinearity (i.e., all letters except phi and psi are kept within imaginary upper and lower lines), with even spacing between letters in *scriptio continua* (continuous letters with no spaces between words), no ligatures, and no (or few) abbreviations of numerals. Literary hands also display punctuation and spacing at the end of sections.

Some of the early New Testament manuscripts, displaying what is called a bookhand or literary hand, were clearly produced by professionals who were able to produce literary texts. On the top of this list is the Gospel codex known as $P^{4+64+67}$ (displaying well-crafted calligraphy, paragraph markings, double columns, and punctuation). Other professionally produced manuscripts displaying a bookhand are P^{30} (with clear biblical uncial), P^{39} (a beautiful specimen of early biblical uncial), P^{46} (exhibiting stichoi notations, which are typical of scribes working for pay), P^{66} (most likely the product of a scriptorium or writing center), P^{75} (the work of an extremely well-trained scribe), $P^{77} + P^{103}$ (displaying well-crafted calligraphy, standard paragraph markings, and punctuation), P^{95} (showing a small portion of John), and P^{104} (a gem among the early papyri). The evidence of the extant papyri dated pre-A.D. 300 indicates that there are at least nine extant professionally made manuscripts whose calligraphy is well deserving of the description "bookhand": $P^{4+64+67}$, P^{39}, P^{46}, P^{66}, P^{75}, P^{77}, P^{95}, P^{103}, P^{104}. There are a number of other early papyri whose scribes were probably also professionals, but who did not have the capability (or perhaps the time) to produce a literary text. Rather, their texts display the workmanship of one trained in the craft of producing documents. In its better form (sometimes called the reformed documentary hand) this can be seen in the following papyri: P^1, P^{30}, P^{32}, P^{35}, P^{38}, P^{45}, P^{52}, P^{69}, P^{87}, P^{90}, P^{100}, P^{102}, P^{108}, P^{109}, P^{110}.[2]

---

to-date transcription of each of these papyri. The date of each manuscript is discussed prior to its transcription. See also P. Comfort, *Encountering the Manuscripts: Introduction to New Testament Paleography and Textual Criticism* (Nashville: Broadman & Holman, 2005), chap. 3, for a fuller discussion concerning the dates of each papyri.

2. For further discussion concerning professional manuscripts, both of the literary type and the reformed documentary type, see Comfort, *Encountering the Manuscripts*, 9-21. This volume also provides descriptions of each of the papyri discussed in this article, as well as arguments for joining P^4, P^{64}, and P^{67} as one codex (see pp. 56-77).

Several of the papyri displaying a literary hand are among the most trusted for providing an accurate text. For example, it is a well-known fact that the text produced by the meticulous scribe of P^{75} is a very accurate manuscript. It is also well known that P^{75} was the kind of manuscript used in formulating Codex Vaticanus; the texts of P^{75} and B are remarkably similar, demonstrating 83 percent agreement.[3] Prior to the discovery of P^{75} (which was published in 1961), many textual scholars were convinced that the second- and third-century papyri displayed a text in flux, a text characterized only by individual independence. Scholars thought that scribes at Alexandria must have used several such manuscripts to produce a good recension — as is exhibited in Codex Vaticanus. This was the opinion of such scholars as Kenyon[4] and Zuntz, who imagined that the Alexandrian scribes selected the best manuscripts and then gradually produced a text that reflected what they considered to be the original wording. In other words, they functioned as the most ancient of the New Testament textual critics. Zuntz believed that, from at least the middle of the second century to the fourth century, the Alexandrian scribes worked to purify the text from textual corruption.[5]

---

3. C. Porter, "Papyrus Bodmer XV (P75) and the Text of Codex Vaticanus," *JBL* 81 (1962): 363-76.

4. In "Hesychius and the Text of the New Testament" (in *Memorial Lagrange* [ed. V. Hugues; Paris: J. Gabalda, 1940], 251-58), F. Kenyon wrote, "During the second and third centuries, a great variety of readings came into existence throughout the Christian world. In some quarters, considerable license was shown in dealing with the sacred text; in others, more respect was shown to the tradition. In Egypt this variety of texts existed, as elsewhere; but Egypt (and especially Alexandria) was a country of strong scholarship and with a knowledge of textual criticism. Here, therefore, a relatively faithful tradition was preserved. About the beginning of the fourth century, a scholar may well have set himself to compare the best accessible representatives of this tradition, and so have produced a text of which B is an early descendant" (245). Much of what Kenyon said is accurate, especially about Alexandria preserving a relatively pure tradition. But Kenyon was wrong in thinking that Codex Vaticanus was the result of a scholarly recension, resulting from editorial selection across the various textual histories.

5. In *The Text of the Epistles* (London: Oxford University Press, 1953), G. Zuntz wrote: "the Alexandrian correctors strove, in ever repeated efforts, to keep the text current in their sphere free from the many faults that had infected it in the previous period and which tended to crop up again even after they had been obelized [i.e., marked as spurious]. These labours must time and again have been checked by persecutions and the confiscation of Christian books, and counteracted by the continuing currency of manuscripts of the older type. Nonetheless they resulted in the emergence of a type of text (as distinct from a definite edition) which served as a norm for the correctors in provincial Egyptian scriptoria. The fi-

The Significance of the Papyri in Revising the New Testament Greek Text

Both Kenyon and Zuntz were wrong. They cannot be faulted for this because P^{75} had not yet been discovered and shown to have such a close textual affinity with B. The "Alexandrian" text, as they called it, already existed in the late second century; it was not the culmination of a recension. Haenchen wrote:

> In P75, which may have been written around 200 A.D., the "neutral" readings are already practically all present, without any need for a long process of purification to bring them together *miro quodam modo* out of a multitude of manuscripts. . . . P75 allows us rather to see the neutral text as already as good as finished, before that slow development could have started at all; it allows us the conclusion that such manuscripts as lay behind Vaticanus — even if not all New Testament books — already existed for centuries.[6]

Kurt Aland's thinking was also changed by P^{75}. He used to speak of the second- and third-century manuscripts as exhibiting a text in flux or even a "mixed" text, but not after the discovery of P^{75}. He wrote, "P75 shows such a close affinity with the Codex Vaticanus that the supposition of a recension of the text at Alexandria, in the fourth century, can no longer be held."[7] Gordon Fee took this one step further — in an article appropriately titled "P75, P66, and Origen: The Myth of Early Textual Recension in Alexandria," Fee posited that there was no Alexandrian recension before the time of P^{75} (late second century) and Codex Vaticanus (early fourth) and that both these manuscripts "seem to represent a 'relatively pure' form of preservation of a 'relatively pure' line of descent from the original text."[8] Other early papyri also exhibit a very pure text. Of note is P^4, which exhibits 93 percent agreement with P^{75}.[9] Aside from its obvious errors, P^{46} is a

---

nal result was the survival of a text far superior to that of the second century, even though the revisers, being fallible human beings, rejected some of its own correct readings and introduced some faults of their own" (271-72).

6. E. Haenchen, *The Acts of the Apostles* (Philadelphia: Westminster, 1971), 59.

7. K. Aland, "The Significance of the Papyri for New Testament Research" in *The Bible in Modern Scholarship* (ed. J. P. Hyatt; Nashville: Abingdon, 1965), 336.

8. G. Fee, "P75, P66, and Origen: The Myth of Early Textual Recension in Alexandria," in *New Dimensions in New Testament Study* (ed. R. N. Longenecker and M. C. Tenney; Grand Rapids: Zondervan, 1974), 43.

9. According to a paper given by William Warren in November of 1998 at the Society of Biblical Literature convention.

representative of "a text of the superior, early-Alexandrian type."[10] The same holds true for P[66], especially in its corrected form.[11]

These papyri and several others have had an impact on some significant passages in the New Testament — or, at least, *should* have had an impact — as to both Greek text and English translations. To illustrate this, I have selected fourteen examples of significant passages involving readings of twelve different papyri — specifically P[4], P[5], P[39], P[46], P[47], P[65], P[66], P[69], P[75], P[104], P[106], and P[115]. This sampling includes some of the best-known papyrus manuscripts.

In this essay I will explore four different aspects of textual criticism involving these papyri: (1) how the papyri have influenced significant changes in the standard Greek text from Westcott and Hort (specifically in Luke 24); (2) how the papyri have affirmed significant changes decided upon by Westcott and Hort and continued in Nestle-Aland (specifically John 1:18; 1 Cor 2:1; 1 Thess 2:7); (3) how the papyri should influence further changes in Nestle-Aland (specifically in Matt 21:44; Luke 8:43; 22:43-44; 23:34; John 7:53–8:11; 9:38-39; Eph 1:1); and (4) how the papyri are divided in their testimony (specifically in John 1:34; Rev 13:18). In all of this, we will examine how English versions have or have not reflected these critical texts. For each of these, I will make a recommendation.

Matthew 21:44

text/WH NU

[καὶ ὁ πεσὼν ἐπὶ τὸν λίθον τοῦτον συνθλασθήσεται· ἐφ' ὃν δ' ἂν πέσῃ λικμήσει αὐτόν.]

And the one falling on this stone will be broken to pieces; and it will crush anyone on whom it falls.

א B C L W Z 0102 f[1,13] Maj cop
KJV NKJV RSVmg NRSV NASB NIV TNIV NEBmg REBmg NJBmg NAB NLT ESV HSB — bracketed

---

10. Zuntz, *Text of the Epistles*, 247.
11. For a full discussion of this, see Comfort, *Encountering the Manuscripts*, 313-15.

The Significance of the Papyri in Revising the New Testament Greek Text

Variant

omit verse

P^{104vid} D 33 it Origen Eusebius

RSV NRSVmg NIVmg TNIVmg NEB REB NJB NABmg NLTmg ESVmg HSBmg

Though this verse is included in the NU text, it is bracketed to signal the editors' doubts about it being a part of Matthew's original composition. The text has good documentary support, the kind that would usually affirm legitimacy for most textual variants. However, the reading of the text is challenged by the earliest manuscript, P^{104} (early second century), Origen, D, and other witnesses. The testimony of P^{104} (not cited in NA^{27})[12] heightens the suspicion that this verse may be an interpolation taken from Luke 20:18. One caution against this view is that one would have expected the interpolation to have been inserted (quite naturally) after Matt 21:42 (in order to get the two OT citations together, as in Luke 20:17-18), not after 21:43. Nonetheless, its position after 21:43 is not awkward and could have been intentional.

Most modern versions include the verse with a note about its omission. Those who exclude it are RSV NEB REB NJB. The evidence of P^{104} bolsters their case and may prompt changes in versions in the future.

Luke 3:22

text/WH NU

σὺ εἶ ὁ υἱός μου ὁ ἀγαπητός, ἐν σοὶ εὐδόκησα.

You are my Son, the beloved, in whom I am well pleased.

P^4 ℵ B L W 070 33 $MSS^{acc.\ to\ Augustine}$

KJV NKJV RSV NRSV ESV NASB NIV TNIV NEB REB NJBmg NAB NLT HCSB NET

---

12. P^{104vid} is not cited in the critical apparatus of NA^{27}. Though the manuscript is difficult to read, there is no way to account for a reconstruction of the text without the omission of Matt 21:44 (see my *Text of the Earliest New Testament Greek Manuscripts*, 644).

Variant

υιος μου ει συ, εγω σημερον γεγεννηκα σε

You are my Son; this day I have begotten you.

D it Justin (Clement) Hilary MSS[acc. to Augustine]
RSVmg NRSVmg ESVmg NEBmg REBmg NJB NABmg NLTmg NETmg

The reading of the text has the earliest and most diverse documentary support. The variant reading is later and more localized (in the West) — a true "Western" reading. Augustine knew of both readings, although he made it clear that the variant reading was "not found in the more ancient manuscripts" (*De Cons. Evang.* 2.14).

In spite of the documentary evidence, many scholars have defended the variant reading as being the more difficult reading and therefore more likely original. They argue that the reading was originally a full quotation of Ps 2:7, which (in the words of the NJB translators) shows Jesus to be "the King-Messiah of the Ps. [2:7] enthroned at the Baptism to establish the rule of God in the world." This reading was then harmonized to the baptism accounts in Matt 3:17 and Mark 1:11 by orthodox scribes trying to avoid having the text say that Jesus was "begotten" on the day of his baptism — an erroneous view held by the Adoptionists. However, it can be argued that the scribe of D (known for his creative editorialization) changed the text to replicate Ps 2:7 or was himself influenced by Adoptionistic views. Indeed, the variant reading was included in the second-century Gospel of the Ebionites, who were chief among the Adoptionists. They regarded Jesus as the son of Joseph and Mary, but elected Son of God at his baptism when he was united with the eternal Christ.

In any case, Ps 2:7 appears to have been used exclusively by NT writers with reference to Jesus' resurrection from the dead (Acts 13:33; Heb 1:5; 5:5). Since in Luke's book of Acts it is explicitly used to affirm the prophetic word about Jesus' resurrection, it would seem odd that he would use it to affirm Jesus' baptism. Given the reading of the text, it seems more likely that Luke was thinking of Ps 2:7 for the first part of the statement ("this is my beloved Son") and Isa 42:1 for the second part ("in whom I am well pleased"). The Isaiah passage is especially fitting given its connection with the Messiah's reception of the Spirit.

Luke 8:43

text/NU

ἥτις [ἰατροῖς προσαναλώσασα ὅλον τὸν βίον] οὐκ ἴσχυσεν ἀπ' οὐδενὸς θεραπευθῆναι

who spent all her living on physicians and was not able to be healed by anyone

ℵ A C L W Θ Ξ Ψ f[1, 13] 33 Maj
KJV NKJV RSVmg NRSV ESV NASBmg NIVmg TNIVmg NEBmg REBmg NJBmg NAB NLTmg HCSB NETmg

variant/WH

who was not able to be healed by anyone

P[75] B (D) 0279 syr[s] cop[sa] Origen
RSV NRSVmg ESVmg NASB NIV TNIV NEB REB NJB NLT HCSBmg NET

Though the above-noted clause ("spent all her living on physicians") is included in NU, it has been bracketed in the text to show the editors' doubts about its inclusion. On one hand, it looks as though it could be a true Lukan condensation of Mark 5:26; on the other hand, it is just as likely that the clause was borrowed by scribes from Mark 5:26 and 12:44. If it had been original, it is difficult to explain why the clause would have been dropped by the scribes of P[75] B D. Most modern translators thought the clause did not belong as part of Luke, and the testimony of P[75] especially strengthens their position, as does 0279, a manuscript discovered at St. Catherine's Monastery in the 1970s. Here is one case where a strong majority of modern translators have made a better decision than the editors of NU; the extra clause does not belong in the text at all.

PHILIP COMFORT

Luke 22:43-44

text/WH NU

include verses

43 [[ὤφθη δὲ αὐτῷ ἄγγελος ἀπ' οὐρανοῦ ἐνισχύων αὐτόν· 44 καὶ γενόμενος ἐν ἀγωνίᾳ ἐκτενέστερον προσηύχετο· καὶ ἐγένετο ὁ ἱδρὼς αὐτοῦ ὡσεὶ θρόμβοι αἵματος καταβαίνοντες ἐπὶ τὴν γῆν.]]

And an angel from heaven appeared to him, strengthening him. And being in agony, he prayed more earnestly, and his sweat became like great drops of blood falling down on the ground.

ℵ*, 2 D L 0171^vid 0233 f¹ Maj (with asterisks or obeli: D syr^s 1079 1195 1216 cop^bo) most Greek MSS^acc. to Anastasius MSS^acc. to Jerome MSS^acc. to Epiphanius Hilary Justin Irenaeus Hippolytus Eusebius
KJV NKJV RSVmg NRSV NASB NIV TNIV NEB REB NJB NAB NLT ESV HSB

variant 1

transpose verses to follow Matt 26:39

f¹³ (13*) and some lectionaries with additions

none

variant 2

omit verses

𝔓^69vid 𝔓^75 ℵ¹ A B T N W it^f syr^s cop^sa some Greek MSS^acc. to Anastasi MSS^acc. to Jerome some Greek and Old Latin MSS^acc. to Hilary

(NKJVmg) RSV NRSVmg NIVmg TNIVmg NEBmg REBmg NJBmg NABmg NLTmg ESVmg HSBmg

𝔓^69vid was not cited in UBS³ in support of the omission of Luke 22:43-44, but it is now noted in UBS⁴ in parentheses. NA²⁷ does not cite it at all. The editors of 𝔓^69 (see P. Oxy. 2383) were fairly confident that the only way to account for the size of the lacuna in 𝔓^69 (from Luke 22:41 to Luke 22:45) is that the copyist's exemplar did not contain Luke 22:43-44 and that the scribe's eye skipped from προσηύχετο in 22:41 to προσευχῆς in 22:45.

The manuscript evidence for this textual variant is decidedly in favor of the exclusion of 22:43-44. The Greek manuscripts (dating from the second to fifth century) favoring the exclusion of these verses form an impressive list: P⁶⁹ᵛⁱᵈ P⁷⁵ ℵ¹ B T W. (The first corrector of ℵ was a contemporary of the scribe who produced the manuscript of Luke; indeed, he was the diorthotes who worked on this manuscript before it left the scriptorium.) Other signs of its doubtfulness appear in manuscripts marking the passage with obeli or crossing out the passage (as was done by the first corrector of ℵ). Its transposition to Matt 26 in some manuscripts and lectionaries indicates that it was a free-floating passage that could be interjected into any of the passion narratives (see note on Matt 26:39).

The manuscript support for including the verses involves several witnesses, the earliest of which is 0171ᵛⁱᵈ (ca. 300). None of the other manuscripts is earlier than the fifth century. However, several early fathers (Justin, Irenaeus, Hippolytus, Dionysius, Eusebius) acknowledged this portion as part of Luke's Gospel.

When we turn to the writings of other early church fathers, we discover that many noted both the presence and absence of the "bloody sweat" passage in the manuscripts known to them. We have notes on this from Jerome, Hilary, Anastasius, and Epiphanius. For example, Epiphanius (*Ancoratus* 31.4-5) indicated that the verses were found in some "uncorrected copies" of Luke. This tells us that in the early course of textual transmission, the Gospel of Luke (in this chapter) was being copied in two forms — one that lacked the "bloody sweat" passage (as in P⁶⁹ᵛⁱᵈ P⁷⁵ T W) and one that included it (as in 0171). The question, then, is: Did Luke write these verses, which were later deleted, or did someone else add them later?

I affirm Metzger's view of this: "On grounds of transcriptional probability it is less likely that the verses were deleted in several different areas of the church by those who felt that the account of Jesus overwhelmed with human weakness was incompatible with his sharing the divine omnipotence of the Father, than that they were added from an early source."[13] Westcott and Hort also considered the "bloody sweat" passage to be an early (second-century) interpolation, added from an oral tradition concerning the life of Jesus.[14]

---

13. B. Metzger, *A Textual Commentary on the Greek New Testament* (rev. ed.; New York: United Bible Societies, 1994), 151.

14. B. F. Westcott and F. J. A. Hort, *Introduction to the New Testament in the Original Greek* (New York: Harper and Brothers, 1882), 64-67 (abbreviated in the text as WH).

One would think, then, that WH and NU would not have included the verses in a Greek text intending to represent the original writings. But both WH and NU include the bloody sweat passage (albeit in double brackets). Even though both groups of editors considered this passage to be a later addition to the text, it was retained because of its importance in the textual tradition. The RSV translators have been the only ones to exclude this passage. All other versions have kept Luke 22:43-44 in the text, many providing notes about its absence in ancient witnesses. I would urge the editors of the Nestle-Aland text to omit this passage. If they did so, more English translators would have the confidence to do the same.

Luke 23:34

text/WH NU

[[ὁ δὲ Ἰησοῦς ἔλεγεν· πάτερ, ἄφες αὐτοῖς, οὐ γὰρ οἴδασιν τί ποιοῦσιν.]]

And Jesus said, "Father, forgive them, for they do not know what they are doing."

א[*, 2] (A) C D² (E with obeli) L 0250 f[1, (13)] Maj syr[c, h, p] Diatessaron Hegesippus

all versions

variant

omit

P[75] א[1] B D* W Θ 070 it[a] syr[s] cop[sa]

NKJVmg RSVmg NRSVmg NIVmg TNIVmg NEBmg REBmg NJBmg NABmg NLTmg ESVmg HSBmg

The omission of these words in early and diverse manuscripts (the earliest being P[75]) cannot be explained as a scribal blunder. But were the words purposely excised? Westcott and Hort considered willful excision to be absolutely unthinkable.[15] But Marshall can think of several reasons why scribes might have deleted the words — the most convincing of which is that scribes might have been influenced by an anti-Judaic polemic and

---

15. Westcott and Hort, *Introduction*, 68.

therefore did not want the text saying that Jesus forgave the Jews who killed him.¹⁶ This would be especially true for Codex Beza, whose scribe has been charged with having anti-Judaic tendencies.¹⁷ However, there are four manuscripts — of diverse traditions — earlier than D (namely, P⁷⁵ B W ita), which do not include these words. Thus, D could not have been responsible for being the first to eliminate the words. The primary argument against excision (on the basis of an anti-Judaic polemic) is that Jesus was forgiving his Roman executioners, not the Jewish leaders. The grammar affirms this; in 23:33 it says εσταυρωσαν αυτον (they [the Roman execution squad] crucified him), then in 23:34 Jesus says, αφες αυτοις (forgive them) — i.e., the Roman execution squad.

Thus, it is more likely that the words were not written by Luke but were added later (as early as the second century — for they are attested to by Hegesippus and the Diatessaron). However, the words appear in the NU text and in all English translations because they have become so much a part of the traditional Gospel text that editors of Greek texts and Bible translators alike are not willing to excise this classic statement from their text. WH and NU double-bracketed this text to show their strong doubts about its inclusion. All English versions include it, and all (with the exception of KJV which does not have marginal notes) have marginal notes about its omission in various manuscripts. I would urge the editors of the Nestle-Aland text to omit this passage. If they did so, more English translators would have the confidence to do the same. But this will not come readily or easily. The first translators to omit this verse will suffer persecution, not to mention a decrease in Bible sales!

Luke 24:3, 6, 12, 36, 40, 51, 52

Westcott and Hort thought Codex Bezae (D) contained the original wording of Luke's Gospel in 24:3, 6, 12, 36, 40, 51, and 52. (All these portions are double-bracketed in WH to show the editors' strong doubts about their inclusion in the text.)¹⁸ Calling the omissions in D "Western non-

---

16. I. H. Marshall, *The Gospel of Luke* (Grand Rapids: Eerdmans, 1978), 867-68.
17. E. J. Epp, "The Ignorance Motif in Acts and the Antijudaic Tendencies in Codex Bezae," *HTR* 55 (1962): 51-62.
18. Westcott and Hort, *Introduction*, 71.

interpolations," they posited the theory that all the other manuscripts contain interpolations in these verses. This theory affected the Nestle text until its twenty-sixth edition, at which point this theory was abandoned — note the changes in Luke 24:3, 6, 12, 36, 40, 51, 52, where none of the portions are double-bracketed. This theory also affected several modern English versions — especially the RSV and NEB, which in nearly every one of these Luke 24 passages followed the testimony of D against all other early MSS. The NASB was also affected by this theory, but not as much as the RSV and NEB. After all three of these translations were published, P^{75} was discovered. And in every instance, P^{75} attests to the longer reading. P^{75} impacted the Nestle text, which now in every verse noted above follows the testimony of P^{75} et al. And P^{75} influenced the most recent versions (NIV NJB NAB NLT), which in every case follow its testimony to include those portions previously excluded by previous translations.

John 1:18

text/WH NU

μονογενὴς θεὸς

an only One, God (or, only-begotten God)

P^{66} ℵ* B C* L syr^p

NKJVmg RSVmg NRSV NASB NIV TNIV NEBmg NJBmg NAB NLT ESV HSBmg

variant 1

ο μονογενης θεος

the only-begotten God

P^{75} ℵ^1 33 cop^{bo}

NRSVmg NASBmg NIVmg

variant 2

ο μονογενης υιος

the only-begotten Son

A C^3 (W^s) Θ Ψ f$^{1, 13}$ Maj syr^c

The Significance of the Papyri in Revising the New Testament Greek Text

KJV NKJV RSV NASBmg NIVmg TNIVmg (NEB REB) NJB NLTmg ESVmg HSB

The two early papyri (P⁶⁶ and P⁷⁵), the earliest uncials (ℵ B C*) and some early versions (Coptic and Syriac) support the word θεος, and many church fathers (Irenaeus, Clement, Origen, Eusebius, Serapion, Basil, Didymus, Gregory of Nyssa, Epiphanius, Valentinians [according to Irenaeus], Clement) knew of this reading. The second variant with υιος was known by many early church fathers (Irenaeus, Clement, Hippolytus, Alexander, Eusebius, Eustathius, Serapion, Julian, Basil, and Gregory of Nazianzus) and translated in some early versions (Old Latin and Syriac). However, the discovery of two second-century papyri, P⁶⁶ and P⁷⁵, both of which read θεος (God), tipped the balance. It is now clear that μονογενης θεος is the earlier reading — and the preferred reading. This was changed, as early as the beginning of the third century — if not earlier — to the more ordinary reading, μονογενης υιος (the only-begotten Son).

After the discovery of the papyri, English translators started to adopt the reading "God." However, the entire phrase, μονογενης θεος, is very difficult to render, so translators have not known whether to treat μονογενης as an adjective alone or as an adjective functioning as a substantive. Should this be rendered "an only-begotten God" or "an only One, God" or "unique God"? Since the term μονογενης more likely speaks of "uniqueness" than of "only one born," it probably functions as a substantive indicating Jesus' unique identity as being both God and near to God, as a Son in the bosom of his Father. This is made somewhat clear in NET's translation: "the only One, who is himself God" or NIVmg — "God the only begotten." But note, even these translations add an article, and thereby follow the first variant. A literal translation as found in the NASB (and above — "the only begotten God") could lead readers to think mistakenly that the Son is a begotten God. Other translations offer conflated readings, which include both the readings "God" and "Son" — as in the NIV, TNIV, and NRSV, "God the only Son," and the NLT, "only Son is God himself." Of course, these translations are attempting to render μονογενης as "only Son," but this rendering ends up becoming a translation of the inferior textual variant. Several modern translations still follow the third reading: "the only Son" (NJB, HCSB) and "God's only Son" (REB). To accurately reflect what John wrote, an English translation could read, "No one has seen God at any time; a very unique One, who is God and who is in the bosom of the Father, has explained him."

John 1:34

text/WH NU

ὁ υἱὸς τοῦ θεοῦ

the Son of God

P^{66} P^{75} $\aleph^2$ A B C W Δ Θ Ψ 083
KJV NKJV RSV NRSV ESV NASB NIV TNIVmg NEBmg REBmg NJBmg NAB NLTmg HCSB NETmg

variant 1

ο εκλεκτος του θεου

the chosen One of God

P^{5vid} P^{106vid} $\aleph^*$ it^e syr$^{c,\ s}$
NRSVmg TNIV NEB REB NJB NLT HCSBmg NET

variant 2

chosen son of God

it^a syr^{pal} cop^{sa}
NETmg

Though both P^5 and P^{106} are listed as "vid" in UBS^4 (not cited in NA^{27}), it is fairly certain that both manuscripts read εκλεκτος, not υιος. The transcription of P^5 in *The New Testament in Greek, IV: The Gospel according to St. John* (Volume One, The Papyri), showing [υιο]ς, is incorrect. The spacing on the line calls for εκλεκτος, as judged by the original editors, Grenfell and Hunt.[19]

The text has excellent external support among the papyri and early uncials, but so does the first variant. Indeed, it is supported by two early papyri (P^5 and P^{106}), an early uncial ($\aleph^*$), and two of the most reliable early Western witnesses (it^e syr^s). The presence of the conflated reading, "chosen Son of God" (variant two), shows that both readings were present at an early stage of textual transmission. The second corrector of codex

---

19. See the Oxyrhynchus volumes on P^5 and P^{106}, and see Comfort, *Text of the Earliest Manuscripts*, 75, 646.

Sinaiticus (sixth or seventh century) deleted εκλεκτος and wrote the nomen sacrum for υιος in the margin.

Several scholars have argued that it is more likely that the reading εκλεκτος (chosen One) was changed to υιος (Son) than vice versa. For example, Gordon Fee thinks an orthodox scribe of the second century might have sensed "the possibility that the designation 'Chosen One' might be used to support adoptionism and so altered the text for orthodox reasons."[20] Or the change could have happened because scribes thought "Son" conformed with the Synoptic accounts of Jesus' baptism (where God calls Jesus "my Son") and/or suited John's Gospel better than "chosen One." Indeed, "Son of God" frequently occurs in John's Gospel, but not all who recognized Jesus' deity called him "the Son of God." For example, Peter called him "the holy one of God" (6:69). All these reasons strengthen the case for "chosen One" being the original reading.[21]

A growing number of translators have decided to follow the reading "chosen One." The recent publication of P[106] (early third century) has strengthened the case for the translators of the NEB, REB, NJB, NLT, TNIV, and NET to choose this text, while noting the other in the margin.

John 7:53–8:11

text/(WH — set as an appendix)

omit John 7:53–8:11

P[66] P[75] ℵ A[vid] B C[vid] L N T W Δ Θ Ψ 0141 33 it[a, f] syr[c, s, p] cop[sa, bo, ach2] geo Diatessaron Origen Chrysostom Cyril Tertullian Cyprian MSS[acc. to Augustine]

NKJVmg (RSV 1st printing) RSVmg NRSVmg NASBmg NIVmg TNIVmg NEBmg REB NJBmg NABmg NLTmg ESVmg HSBmg

---

20. G. D. Fee, "The Textual Criticism of the New Testament," in *The Expositor's Bible Commentary, I: Introductory Articles* (Grand Rapids: Zondervan, 1979), 431-32.

21. See Comfort, *Encountering the Manuscripts*, 336-37.

variant/NU

include John 7:53–8:11

D (F) G H K M U it[aur, c, d, e] syr[h, pal] cop[boMSS] Maj MSS[acc. to Didymus] E 8:2-11 with asterisks; L 8:3-11 with asterisks; f[1] after John 21:25; f[13] after Luke 21:38; 1333[c] 8:3-11 after Luke 24:53; 225 after John 7:36

English translations including the pericope after 7:52

KJV NKJV RSV NRSV NASB NIV TNIV NEB REBmg NJB NAB NLT ESV HSB

The pericope about the adulteress (John 7:53–8:11) is not included in any of the earliest manuscripts (second-fourth centuries), including the two earliest, P^{66} and P^{75}. The other witnesses to the exclusion of this passage are equally impressive, including all the fourth-century codices (ℵ A B C T), the Diatessaron, the early versions, and most of the early church fathers. Its first appearance in a Greek manuscript is in D (ca. 400), but it is not contained in other Greek manuscripts until the ninth century. (Didymus [died 398] indicates he knew of manuscripts containing the story.) When this story is inserted in later manuscripts, it appears in different places (after Luke 21:38; Luke 24:53; John 7:36; John 7:52; and at the end of John); and when it does appear it is often marked off by obeli or asterisks to signal its probable spuriousness. In most of the manuscripts that include this story, it appears at the beginning of John 8, probably because it provides an illustration of Jesus' resistance to passing judgment, which is spoken of in the following discourse (see 8:15-30). A marginal note in the NAB indicates that it is better suited after Luke 21:38 than after John 7:52 (see note in this commentary).

The inclusion of this story in the NT text is a prime example of how the oral tradition, originally not included in the text, eventually found its way into the written text. In its oral form the story may have been in circulation beginning in the early second century. Papias may have been speaking of this incident when he "expounded another story about a woman who was accused before the Lord of many sins, which the Gospel according to the Hebrews contains" (Eusebius, *Ecclesiastical History* 3.39.17). However, in the pericope of the adulteress there is no mention of many "sins," only one — that of adultery.[22]

22. F. F. Bruce, *The Gospel of John* (Grand Rapids: Eerdmans, 1983), 417-18.

The Significance of the Papyri in Revising the New Testament Greek Text

According to Ehrman, a story about a condemned woman being rescued by Jesus was extant in written form as early as the fourth century in three different versions: (1) as a story in which the religious leaders were trying to trap Jesus as to whether he would uphold the Mosaic law and in which he freely pardons a sinful woman — basically the story known to Papias and the author of the *Didascalia Apostolorum*; (2) the story of Jesus' intervention in an execution — an episode preserved in the Gospel according to the Hebrews and retold by Didymus in his commentary on Ecclesiastes; (3) the popular version found in most of the later manuscripts of John, "a version which represents a conflation of the two earlier stories."[23]

Not only is the external evidence against the Johannine authorship of the pericope about the adulteress potent (see above); so is the internal evidence. First of all, many scholars have pointed out that the vocabulary used in this pericope does not accord with the rest of John. For example, Wallace shows that the pericope does not match John's linguistic style or literary pattern.[24] Second, the insertion of the adulteress pericope at this point in John (after John 7:52 and before John 8:12) greatly disrupts the narrative flow and interrupts the connection between John 7:40-52 and 8:12-20.[25] John 8:12-20 is Jesus' response to John 7:52. In short, John 8:12-30 contains Jesus' rebuttal to these Pharisees who had boldly told Nicodemus that the Scriptures make no mention of even a prophet (much less the Christ) being raised up in Galilee. With respect to this assertion, Jesus made a declaration in which he implied that the Scriptures did speak of the Christ coming from Galilee. He said, "I am the light of the world; he who follows me will not walk in darkness, but will have the light of life." This statement was probably drawn from Isa 9:1-2: "But there will be no more gloom for her who was in anguish; in earlier times he treated the land of Zebulun and the land of Naphtali with contempt, but later on he will make it glorious, by the way of the sea, on the other side of the Jordan, Galilee of the Gentiles. The people who walk in darkness will see a great light, and the light will shine on those who live in the shadow of death." Both passages contain parallel images. Both Isa 9:2 and John 8:12 speak about the Messiah coming as the light among those who are walking in darkness and

---

23. B. Ehrman, "Jesus and the Adulteress," *NTS* 34 (1998): 24-44.
24. D. Wallace, "Reconsidering 'The Story of Jesus and the Adulteress Reconsidered,'" *NTS* 39 (1993): 290-96.
25. P. Comfort, "The Pericope of the Adulteress (John 7:53–8:11)," *BT* 40 (1989): 145-47.

sitting under the shadow of death to give them the light of life. Thus, John 8:12 parallels Isa 9:1-2 and thereby provides a reproof to the Pharisees' declaration in John 7:52 that the Scriptures nowhere speak of a prophet (not to mention the Messiah) having come from Galilee.

But most English readers of the New Testament will not see any of the connections mentioned above because the pericope of the adulteress is still printed in the text between John 7:52 and 8:12. True, the passage has been bracketed, or marked off with single lines (similar to the practice of marking obeli employed by several ancient scribes to the same passage), or set in italics. But there it stands — an obstacle to reading the true narrative of John's Gospel.

Thus it is very disappointing to realize that the pericope of the adulteress woman is included in the NU text, even though it is set in double brackets to signify the editors' serious doubts about its place in the text. I have no doubt that John never wrote it and that it has no place whatsoever being in the text. Of course, I am aware of how difficult it is to rid the Bible of spurious texts once they have gained a place in what people consider to be "Holy Scripture." When the RSV was first published, this pericope was taken out of the text and placed in a footnote, but the outcry against this was so vehement that it was placed back in the text in the next printing. The REB translators have moved the pericope to an appendix following the Gospel of John, just as was done by Westcott and Hort in their Greek text. This is the best approach.

John 9:38-39a

text/WH NU

ὁ δὲ ἔφη· Πιστεύω, κύριε. καὶ προσεκύνησεν αὐτῷ. καὶ εἶπεν ὁ Ἰησοῦς·

And he said, "I believe, Lord." And he worshiped him. 39 And Jesus said.

P^{66} ℵ^2 A B D L Q U Maj

all versions

The Significance of the Papyri in Revising the New Testament Greek Text

variant

omit

P^{75} ℵ* W it^b cop$^{ach2,\ saMS}$

NLTmg TNIVmg

The evidence for the omission of John 9:38-39a is impressive, inasmuch as the manuscripts that do not include it are early and geographically dispersed. The three early Greek manuscripts (P^{75} ℵ* W) are impressive enough, let alone the testimony of three early translations. It is usually argued that the omission was the result of a transcriptional error, but there is nothing in the text to suggest the usual kinds of error, such as homoeoteleuton or homoearchton. And even if it was an error, how could this have occurred in so many diverse manuscripts? Furthermore, εφη (I said) is rarely used in John (only in 1:23), the exact verbal form πιστευω (I believe) occurs nowhere else in John (except in the singular reading of P^{66} in 11:27) and is not used in John with "Jesus" as the direct object. These factors point to a non-Johannine origin.

If John did not write these words, why were they added? Brown suggests that "the words were an addition stemming from the association of John 9 with the baptismal liturgy and catechesis." He then elaborates:

> When the catechumens passed their examinations and were judged worthy of Baptism, lessons from the OT concerning cleansing water were read to them. Then came the solemn opening of the Gospel book and the reading of John 9, with the confession of the blind man, "I do believe, Lord" (38), serving as the climax. . . . After this the catechumens recited the creed.[26]

Porter argues that a similar interpolation found its way into Acts 8:37,[27] which is clearly a baptismal confession inserted into the text. Prior to his baptism, the Ethiopian eunuch says: "I believe that Jesus Christ is the Son of God." But these words are not found in any of the early manuscripts.

---

26. R. Brown, *The Gospel according to John I-XII* (Garden City, NY: Doubleday, 1966), 380-81.

27. C. Porter, "John IX. 38, 39a: A Liturgical Addition to the Text," *NTS* 13 (1967): 387-94.

The same kind of interpolation found its way into John 9, but at an early date, for it is present in P⁶⁶, a second-century manuscript. Therefore, it is not unlikely that certain manuscripts of the Gospel of John were affected by this addition by the middle of the second century, if not earlier. Thus, this passage is a prime example of how the New Testament text may have been affected by ecclesiastical practices such as baptismal confession.

It is disappointing to observe that not one English version has adopted the shorter reading, and only two note it (NLT TNIV). In the future, we may see some English versions reflecting the terser text, but that will be a long way off.

1 Corinthians 2:1

text/WH NU

τὸ μυστήριον τοῦ θεοῦ

the mystery of God

P⁴⁶vid ℵ* A C it^{a,r} syr^p cop^{bo}
NKJVmg RSVmg NRSV NIVmg TNIVmg NASBmg NEBmg REBmg NJB NAB NLT ESVmg HSBmg

variant

το μαρτυριον του θεου

the testimony of God

ℵ² B D F G Ψ 33 1739 Maj it^b syr^h cop^{sa}
KJV NKJV RSV NRSVmg NASB NIV TNIV NEB REB NJBmg ESV HSB

UBS³ cites P⁴⁶vid? in support of the text. The question mark follows "vid" because the editors were not sure that P⁴⁶ contains the word μυστηριον (mystery). Having examined the actual papyrus, I can affirm that the reading is μυστηριον (mystery), not μαρτυριον (testimony), because the Greek letter eta, though partially broken, is visible before the final four letters — also visible (ριον). The one letter makes all the difference in determining the reading. UBS⁴ (as well as the Nestle text) now lists it as P⁴⁶vid.

The text has uncontestable support from the earliest extant document, P⁴⁶. Several other witnesses, both early and diverse, also support the text. But the same can be said for the variant reading. So how then do we solve the problem? Competent textual critics such as Zuntz[28] and Fee[29] have argued that μυστηριον is a scribal emendation influenced by 2:7. Other scholars, such as Brown[30] and Metzger,[31] have argued that μαρτυριον is a scribal emendation influenced by 1:6. Actually, one can draw upon the context of 1 Corinthians 1–2 to support either word, because Paul's message in these chapters is that his mission was to testify only of Christ, who is the mystery of God. The immediate context seems to support "mystery," because chapter 2 focuses on the need for believers to receive revelation from the Spirit of God to truly understand all the hidden, secret riches of God that are in Christ Jesus (see 2:7-8). In summary, the internal and external evidence for this reading is divided, so it is not easy to make a decision regarding which variant is original. This indecision is displayed in the array of modern English versions. Though most versions use the word "testimony," these same versions print "mystery" in the margin.

Ephesians 1:1

Text/WH NU

τοῖς ἁγίοις τοῖς οὖσιν [ἐν Ἐφέσῳ] καὶ πιστοῖς ἐν Χριστῷ Ἰησοῦ,

to the saints being in Ephesus and faithful in Christ Jesus

B² D F G Ψ 33 Maj syr cop^sa
KJV NKJV RSVmg NRSV ESV NASB NIV TNIV NEB REB NJBmg NAB NLT NET

---

28. Zuntz, *Text of the Epistles*, 101.
29. G. Fee, "Textual-Exegetical Observations on 1 Corinthians 1:2; 2:1, and 2:10," in *Scribes and Scripture: New Testament Essays in Honor of J. Harold Greenlee* (ed. D. A. Black; Winona Lake: Eisenbrauns, 1992), 1-13.
30. R. Brown, *The Semitic Background of the Term "Mystery" in the New Testament* (Philadelphia: Facet Books, Biblical Series, 1968), 48-49.
31. Metzger, *A Textual Commentary*, 480.

variant 1

τοις αγιοις πασιν τοις ουσιν εν Εφεσω και πιστοις εν Χριστω Ιησου

to all the saints being in Ephesus and faithful in Christ Jesus

ℵ² A P it^b cop^bo

none

variant 2

τοις αγιοις τοις ουσιν και πιστοις εν Χριστω Ιησου

to the saints being _____ and faithful in Christ Jesus

𝔓⁴⁶ ℵ* B* 1739 Marcion
RSV NRSVmg ESVmg NASBmg NIVmg TNIVmg NEBmg REBmg NJB NABmg NLTmg NETmg

The insertion of πασιν (all) in the first variant is clearly a scribal attempt to harmonize this opening verse with several other opening verses in Paul's epistles, where Paul addresses "all" the saints in a particular locality (see Rom 1:7; 1 Cor 1:2; 2 Cor 1:1). The second variant represents the original text as it left the hand of Paul. There are three good reasons why we can be confident about this. (1) This reading has the support of the three earliest manuscripts: 𝔓⁴⁶ ℵ B, as well as 1739, a manuscript known for its textual integrity in the Pauline epistles. None of these manuscripts include the words εν Εφεσω (in Ephesus). (2) If the text had originally included "in Ephesus," there is no reason to explain why the words would have been deleted. In fact, the absence of "in Ephesus" makes for a very difficult sentence, grammatically speaking, because something has to follow the participle phrase τοις ουσιν. (3) The scribes of 𝔓⁴⁶ ℵ B 1739 could have done something to fix this grammatical problem, but they stayed true to their exemplars that retained the original form as it left the hand of Paul's amanuensis. (4) Thus, in the original document a blank space was left between τοις ουσιν (the ones being) and και πιστοις εν Χριστω Ιησου (and faithful ones in Christ Jesus). The blank would be filled in with the name of each local church ("in Ephesus," "in Laodicea," "in Colossae," etc.) as the epistle circulated from city to city. (5) Later manuscripts reflect the insertion of "in Ephesus" because Ephesus was the leading city in that region.

Paul probably intended this epistle to be a general encyclical sent to the churches in Asia, of which Ephesus was one of the leading churches.

No doubt, the epistle would have gone to Ephesus (perhaps first) and then on to other churches. Each time the epistle went to another church, the name of the locality would be supplied after the expression "to the saints [in _____]." Zuntz indicated that this procedure also occurred with some multiple copies of royal letters during the Hellenistic period; the master copy would have a blank for the addressee and would be filled in for each copy.[32] Zuntz considered the blank space in the address to the Ephesians as going back to the original. In the later textual tradition, certain scribes identified this epistle with Ephesus and thereby inserted "in Ephesus."

Regardless of the textual superiority of P^{46} B etc., English translators will not follow this reading because of the anacoluthon it creates in English. In short, some kind of prepositional phrase with the name of a city needs to be inserted — unless one allows for the translation, "Paul an apostle to the saints who are faithful in Christ Jesus."

1 Thessalonians 2:7

text/WH NU

ἐγενήθημεν νήπιοι ἐν μέσῳ ὑμῶν

we were infants in your midst

P^{65} ℵ* B C* D* F G I Ψ* it cop^{bo}
RSVmg NRSVmg ESVmg NASBmg TNIV NJBmg NABmg NLT HCSBmg NET

variant/TR

εγενηθημεν ηπιοι εν μεσω υμων

we were gentle in your midst

ℵ^c A C^2 D^2 Ψ^c 0278 33 1739 Maj
KJV NKJV RSV NRSV ESV NASB NIV NEB REB NJB NAB NLTmg HCSB

There is a one-letter difference (nu) between the variants: νηπιοι (infants); ηπιοι (gentle). Concerning transcriptional errors, it is difficult to know which reading produced the other. The first word (νηπιοι) could have

---

32. Zuntz, *Text of the Epistles*, 228.

been created by dittography — the preceding word (εγενηθημεν) ends in nu; or the second word (ηπιοι) could have been created by haplography — also influenced by the preceding word. The variant reading seems to be the most natural in context — especially in connection with the following metaphor: "we were gentle in your midst, like a nursing mother caring for her children."

However, there are several arguments against this. First, several manuscripts (ℵ C D Ψ) originally had the first reading but were later corrected. This strongly suggests that scribes and correctors had a problem with the meaning of the wording νηπιοι and then made an emendation. Second, the reading of the text has early and diverse attestation, including P[65] (third century). Third, Westcott and Hort argue that the adjective ηπιοι (gentle) is not compatible with the expression εν μεσω υμων (in your midst).[33] The appropriate word should be a noun, not an adjective.

But none of these arguments overcome the obstacle that the reading of the text seems to create a very contorted metaphor: "we were infants in your midst, like a nursing mother caring for her children." Yet it can be explained. Morris notes that in this very same chapter Paul likens himself to a father (2:11) and then an orphan (2:17).[34] This suggests that Paul was thinking of himself (metaphorically) as being a child who had been separated from his loved ones. His brief time with the Thessalonians, cut short by persecution and subsequent forced departure, caused him (and his coworkers) to acutely sense their separation. Thus, he used an emotive image in which he pictured himself as a child who had been orphaned from his parents. In like manner, in 2:7-8 he pictured himself as a babe in their midst to show that he was guileless, innocent, and unpretentious (see 2:3-6). In other words, he had no intention to take advantage of them. As such, the image of a child works.[35]

The majority of editors of UBS[3] and NA[26] decided to adopt the word νηπιοι because it has the earliest support (P[65] providing the earliest witness) and because it is the more difficult reading. Consequently, the Nestle text was changed to read νηπιοι. But two of the editors, Metzger and Wikgren, did not agree with the choice. However, they suggested that if this reading must be in the text, the punctuation must be changed (see

---

33. Westcott and Hort, *Introduction*, 128.
34. L. Morris, *1 and 2 Thessalonians* (Grand Rapids: Eerdmans, 1984), 56-57.
35. J. Weima, "But We Became Infants Among You: The Case for NHPIOI in 1 Thess. 2:7," *NTS* 46 (2000): 547-64.

TCGNT). Perhaps a change in punctuation could justify the following kind of translation of 2:7-8:

> 7 As apostles of Christ, we could have made demands on you, but we were infants in your midst. We were as a nursing mother who cares for her children — 8 being so affectionately desirous of you, we were willing to impart to you not the gospel of God only, but also our own souls, because you became dear to us.

In this way, the two metaphors of 2:7 are separated. The statement in 2:7a summarizes the message of apostolic purity in 2:3-6, and the statement in 2:7b is appropriately connected with 2:8.

Three recently published English translations, NLT TNIV NET, have followed the reading of the best text. Taking the lead were the translators of the NLT, which nicely separates the metaphors: "we were like children among you. We were like a mother feeding and caring for her own children." The NRSV deviates from the standard text at this point, under the influence of Metzger (head of the committee for the NRSV), who disagreed with the majority vote for the NU text (see above). Several translations provide a marginal note citing the reading "infants" out of deference to its presence in all the earliest MSS.

Revelation 13:18

text/WH NU

ἐξακόσιοι ἑξήκοντα ἕξ [= χξς]

666

P47 (ℵ) A P Maj Irenaeus Hippolytus

All

variant 1

εξακοσιοι δεκα εξ [= χις]

616

P115 C (5 11 — no longer extant) MSS[acc. to Irenaeus]
RSVmg NRSVmg ESVmg NASBmg NJBmg NABmg NLTmg HCSBmg

variant 2

εξακοσια εξηκοντα πεντε [= χξε]

665

2344

none

Writing in the late second century, Irenaeus (*Against Heresies* 5.30) was aware of the reading "616" but denounced it as "heretical and deceptive." He claimed that "666" was found in "all the good and ancient copies" and was "attested to by those who had seen John face to face." Three significant witnesses (P⁴⁷ ℵ A) must have their roots in those "good and ancient copies" because they read "666." However, the recently published P115 reads "616," as does Codex C. These are also among the "good and ancient copies," and the number they contain, "616," is not heretical. Either "666" or "616" could be original inasmuch as both symbolize "Caesar Nero." The number "666," abbreviated in ancient manuscripts as χξς, came from a Hebrew transliteration of "Nero Caesar" from Greek into Hebrew. The number "616," abbreviated in ancient manuscripts as χις, is a Latin equivalent of the name "Nero Caesar" by way of gematria (NETmg).[36] Both convey the same signification of the same person. As of yet, not one English translation prints "616" in the text, even though several note it. The note in HCSB says that one Greek manuscript plus other ancient evidence read "616." There are actually two ancient manuscripts, P¹¹⁵ and C.

Conclusion

As for the Greek text, the textual evidence, especially from the papyri, should prompt the Nestle-Aland/UBS committee to omit three passages from their text: Luke 22:43-44; 23:34; John 7:53–8:11, in addition to Luke 8:43a (which has been omitted by most versions anyway). I think Matt 21:44 should be double bracketed, as well as John 9:38-39a. All these changes would embolden translators to follow suit.

I would make one other recommendation: the Greek editors should have a way of noting variant readings that are just as likely to be original as

[36]. D. Aune, *Revelation 6–16* (WBC 52B; Dallas: Word, 1998), 770-71.

those printed in the text. I am especially thinking of John 1:34, but Rev 13:18 would be in the same category. English translators could do this with this wording in the marginal note: "Or, as in other manuscripts." The simple "or" lets the reader know that the translators think the variant reading could be just as original as that printed in the text. Though this is a simple suggestion, it could go a long way in helping English readers understand that not all variants should be treated equally but that some can be. As it now stands in nearly every English version, marginal notes tell readers only that there is a different reading in other manuscripts, without any kind of evaluation.

The Text and Luke 16:19-31

The Text of Luke 16

Barbara Aland

First of all, I agree with Dr. Robinson that the Byzantine text is by far not as bad as former generations thought. It's a good old text, but it has a number of bad readings and we have to eliminate them and then the text is a good old text. That means that if the Byzantine text agrees with P^{75} and Vaticanus, then it's a very trustworthy witness. That's my position.

Second, I think it's by no means sure that we are now able to establish the best text of the Gospels. For what we have done for the Catholic Epistles — that is, to strengthen the external criteria and gain trustworthy knowledge of all the extra manuscripts — we have not yet done for the Gospels. We have not constructed relational diagrams (see my major paper in this volume), and therefore we have not yet studied the contamination process of the Gospel tradition. The task is too big and therefore we could not do it so quickly. So we don't have precise knowledge of the value of all the extra manuscripts. We know, for example, about Vaticanus and P^{75}, that they are good and trustworthy manuscripts. But we don't know about their trustworthy descendants in the field of minuscules and that is our task. We should know trustworthy minuscules.

What is left to do now? I will mention two test passages for the section we are discussing in this book, Luke 16:19-31, in order to introduce their value for gaining insights into the textual transmission. The first test passage is Luke 16:20. We have the Byzantine reading: πτωχὸς δέ τις ἦν ὀνόματι Λάζαρος ὃς ἐβέβλητο, from which there are a number of descendants. We also have the so-called established text that is followed in our editions, the Nestle-Aland, GNT, and so on. The short text of 16:20, ὀνόματι Λάζαρος, names Lazarus, and the Byzantine texts add quite comprehensibly ἦν and ὅς, giving thereby a smooth sentence. That is, "the poor man *was* there named Lazarus *who* was laid at his gate full of sores." The short text edition of Nestle, considered to be the best possible text, is attested by only 16 witnesses. That is not much considering the fact that the Gospel of Luke is transmitted in about 2,000 manuscripts, only 16 out of 2,000. I nevertheless think that it is a good choice to have the short text as the primary text, for it is hardly conceivable that scribes would have altered the smooth sentence of the Byzantine text. But according to our current theory of textual criticism at the Institute of New Testament Textual Research, we should learn more about the value of all witnesses that attest the short reading. Therefore, we should know more about all the witnesses that attest the second reading. Right now we have that reading as the primary one in our editions. But we don't yet know what is the value of reading 1029 or 033. We have to know more about these manuscripts and then we could be more confident that we have chosen the right primary line.

The second test passage in Luke 16 is Luke 16:21: ἀπὸ τῶν πιπτόντων, or, as nearly all the manuscripts have it, ἀπὸ τῶν ψιχίων τῶν πιπτόντων; "Who desired to be fed with what fell from the rich man's table" or "Who desired to be fed with the crumbs (τῶν ψιχίων) that fell from the rich man's table." That's a Byzantine text, and Dr. Robinson has given very good reasons for this reading as a primary text reading. Only five manuscripts attest the reading without ψιχίων. Is that enough? It may not be. Only five manuscripts — P[75] 01 03 019 and 79. All the other manuscripts have a variant with ψιχίων. Why? We have to take into account that there may exist a parallel influence, although our text has no direct parallels in the Synoptic Gospels. But in Matt 15:27, the account of the Canaanite woman, it is written, "Yes, Lord, yet even the dogs eat the crumbs that fall from their master's table." It may be that very early in the history of copying there was a parallel influence from this Matthean passage that spread all over the witnesses of the Lukan text. But to be honest, I'm not sure about that. The manuscripts attesting our established texts are closely related to each other. Those attesting the reading of our primary text are closely related to each other. They are coherent, as we say in the Institute, so the shorter reading may have been introduced into this branch of the tradition in very early times. This reading may not be the primary text but a secondary mistake in this group. The only way to resolve the difficulties would be to know more about the witnesses that attest other readings than that of the so-called established text. That must be our goal — to know more about very good and trustworthy manuscripts in the field of minuscules. It is not enough to know that B is a good manuscript, as are P^{75} and perhaps Sinaiticus. We are not sure how good it is. But it is interesting that seven manuscripts that have the established text in 16:20, ὀνόματι Λάζαρος, do not attest the so-called established text in 16:21, "desire to be fed with what fell from the rich man's table" — that is, without mentioning crumbs. Why? Why don't all sixteen manuscripts that have the established text in 16:20 — that is, these sixteen minuscules — not read the text established in 16:21? What's the value of these seven manuscripts? All of them are in the group of Byzantine texts I have here in my manuscripts. I'm not sure if it is right what I am saying now. Nevertheless, I don't think that the longer texts with ψιχίων are the better text, since it doesn't seem likely that scribes would shorten the well-known wording of the Canaanite woman's story in editing. But this is not certain. And it may be instructive to learn how much there is still to know in textual criticism.

In conclusion, we may say that we have to learn more about the mass of extra minuscules and their value. There are minuscules that are as trustworthy as Vaticanus is. We can learn that with the help of the information that I explain in my major essay in this volume. On the other hand, there is another thing that I must say. I think the text of the Novum Testamentum Graece, the Nestle-Aland, and the GNT to be a very good and trustworthy text. That is no contradiction to working at the Editio Critica Maior. We have always found that the editors of the Nestle and the GNT have done very good and sensitive work. The question still open before us is how to provide conclusive evidence for the established text. And that's a very urgent task.

The Rich Man and Lazarus — Luke 16:19-31: Text-Critical Notes

Maurice A. Robinson

Since the narrative regarding the rich man and Lazarus is unique among the Gospels, it is less likely to be affected by scribal harmonizing tendencies as opposed to the more usual transcriptional forms of error or intentional alteration. The present comments involve only those readings in which the Byzantine Textform differs from the NA^{27}/UBS^4 critical text, since the two opposing textual theories concur regarding the bulk of the text of this pericope, even though such is determined by widely varying methodologies.[1]

The Byzantine form of this pericope[2] contains 251 words. The NA^{27}/UBS^4 text contains 244 words and is approximately 3 percent shorter. The differences between the Byzantine Textform and the NA^{27}/UBS^4 text involve 17 words in 15 variant units. Stated in relation to the Byzantine Textform, these differences are the following, arranged according to their increasing level of significance:

1. Within this pericope the predominant Byzantine Textform is stable, with no significant division among its supporting witnesses. The various Byzantine subgroup readings are excluded from the present discussion, since all such are minor, generally involving orthography and non-translatable variants.

2. M. A. Robinson and W. G. Pierpont, eds., *The New Testament in the Original Greek: Byzantine Textform 2005* (Southborough, MA: Chilton Book Publishing, 2005). See also Z. C. Hodges and A. L. Farstad, *The Greek New Testament according to the Majority Text* (2nd ed.; Nashville: Thomas Nelson, 1985), whose text agrees in this pericope with that of Robinson-Pierpont except in regard to minor orthographic matters, punctuation, and capitalization.

The Rich Man and Lazarus — Luke 16:19-31

4 words involve orthographic differences;
2 words are transposed (one variant unit);
2 words involve substitution;
1 word is added in NA²⁷/UBS⁴;
8 words (in 7 variant units) are lacking in NA²⁷/UBS⁴.

Thus, the NA²⁷/UBS⁴ text differs approximately 7 percent from that of the Byzantine Textform in this pericope, leaving 93 percent of its text fully established, regardless of theory or resultant text. Such demonstrates the relative stability of the New Testament text, even when considered from the perspective of differing text-types, text-critical theories, and resultant methodologies.

The variants between the Byzantine Textform and NA²⁷ are discussed by category, beginning with the least significant.

Orthographic Differences

Variant unit	Verse	Byzantine Textform	NA²⁷/UBS⁴
(1)	16:20	ηλκωμενος	ειλκωμενος
(2)	16:29	Μωσεα	Μωυσεα
(3)	16:31	Μωσεως	Μωυσεως
(4)	16:31	ουδε	ουδ

Very little comment is required in the case of alternate spellings. The Byzantine Textform basically follows a standardized orthography that reflects usage among the earlier Byzantine manuscripts.

(1) 16:20 ηλκωμενος → ειλκωμενος. The spelling variation between ηλκ- and ειλκ- represents a phonetic interchange with no difference in meaning.

(2) 16:29 Μωσεα → Μωυσεα, and (3) 16:31 Μωσεως → Μωυσεως. The alternate spellings of "Moses" as either Μω- or Μωυ- appear to reflect competing orthographic forms during the earliest Christian centuries. The Byzantine Textform tends to reflect the spelling Μωσ- in the Gospels[3]

---

3. H. F. von Soden, *Die Schriften des Neuen Testaments in ihrer ältesten erreichbaren Textgestalt* (2 vols. in 4 parts; Göttingen: Vandenhoeck und Ruprecht, 1911), shows the spelling Μωσ- here as dominantly supported within the Byzantine Textform by both K^x and the later (recensional) K^r.

and the first half of Acts,[4] while the same Textform prefers the spelling Μωυσ- in the remainder of the NT.[5] This orthographic shift among the Byzantine MSS appears to reflect some original intent, which later became blurred by scribes (and editors!).[6]

(4) 16:31 ουδε → ουδ. The elision of the final ε could be due to the normal practice of dropping a final vowel when the next word commences with a vowel. Equally, it could be the case that a small number of MSS omitted the final epsilon by haplography since the word following begins with epsilon. Accidental haplography becomes more likely when a manuscript is written in capital letters without word separation (ΟΥΔΕΕΑΝ → ΟΥΔΕΑΝ).

Transpositional Difference

Variant unit	Verse	Byzantine Textform	NA[27]/UBS[4]
(5)	16:27	ουν σε	σε ουν

(5) 16:27 ουν σε → σε ουν. This two-word transposition does not affect translation, exegesis, or interpretation. Since the postpositive conjunction ουν can readily stand in either location, the question concerns which order is more likely in view of Lukan usage and external evidence.

(a) In Luke-Acts, ουν with σε occurs nowhere else, although συ ουν occurs three times, and always in that order. The phrase ουν υμεις occurs in Luke 11:13 and Acts 23:15; Luke 12:40 has και υμεις ουν.

(b) Ουν occurs in Luke 44 times and in Acts 67 times, almost always in the normal postpositive second position. The exceptions occur when ουν is preceded by μεν (1 time in Luke; 27 times in Acts), and when following or imbedded within a prepositional phrase (Luke 13:14, εν ταυταις ουν;

---

4. Through Acts 7, the form Μωσ- reflects the dominant Byzantine usage; after Acts 13 the form Μωυσ- prevails (the name does not occur in Acts 8–12). Could such a spelling involve a shift from the Jewish-based church to the gentile mission, and thus affect the latter portion of Acts as well as the later books of the NT? This point requires further investigation.

5. This peculiarity is not mentioned in D. Trobisch, *The First Edition of the New Testament* (Oxford: Oxford University Press, 2000), even though such might strengthen his case for an early "canonical edition." This perhaps is due to Trobisch's general acceptance of NA[27]/UBS[4] as a base, in which editions the form Μωυσ- is universal throughout the NT.

6. The various *Textus Receptus* editions serve as an example, since their orthography varies widely between Μωσ- and Μωυσ-, even within a single NT book.

Luke 20:33, εν τη ουν αναστασει). The Byzantine reading ερωτω ουν σε thus tends to reflect Lukan style.

(c) Externally, the Byzantine ουν σε is supported by P⁷⁵ ℵ L Θ Ψ f¹ 𝔐 lat⁷ (a mixture of Alexandrian, Caesarean, and Western Old Latin witnesses); σε ουν of the NA²⁷ main text is supported by A B D f¹³ pc — individual MSS reflecting the Byzantine, Alexandrian, and Western types of text, but without serious support from their own relatives. This suggests unrelated independent transposition as underlying the NA²⁷ reading in this variant unit (σε *without* ουν appears in W 579 pc e f r¹ bo).

Substitutions

Variant unit	Verse	Byzantine Textform	NA²⁷/UBS⁴
(6)	16:21	απελειχον	επελειχον
(7)	16:26	επι	εν

(6) απελειχον → επελειχον. The word involved in this variant unit is *hapax* in the NT (including not only the Byzantine and NA²⁷ readings, but also the minor variants περιλειχον and ελειχον). Although the source verb differs, the general meaning is not affected. Between the Byzantine and NA²⁷ readings, the *only* difference involves the initial letter. This may have been altered unconsciously, perhaps (for ε-) by attraction to επιθυμων at the beginning of the verse; perhaps (for α-) by attraction to the earlier occurrence of απο; perhaps (for ε-) by the pronunciation of the immediately preceding -οι as *eh* or *ih*. Since the root verb is affected, it is classed as a substitution rather than an orthographic change, although either could apply; certainly substitution better fits the remaining minor readings.

The external evidence is decidedly one-sided. Απελειχον of the Byzantine Textform is joined by the purportedly "Caesarean" W and f¹³. Επελειχον of NA²⁷/UBS⁴ has mixed support from ℵ A B L Θ Ψ 33 1241 2542 pc. Since there is no compelling reason for scribal alteration of synonymous forms, unintentional transcriptional error must have occurred. In

---

7. 𝔐 in NA²⁷ includes not only the MSS comprising the Byzantine Textform, but also (where otherwise unspecified) the "constant witnesses of the second order": K N P Q Γ Δ 565 579 700 892 1241 1424 2542 L-844 L-2211. Of these, MS 579 here departs from 𝔐, and MSS P/024 and Q/026 have a lacuna.

such a case, it becomes transmissionally more likely that the vast majority of witnesses would preserve the original as opposed to a relatively small minority of witnesses, whose text may have resulted from unconscious accident.

(7) 16:26 επι → εν. The interchange between επι and εν is not unusual, since scribal substitution of one preposition for another commonly occurs within manuscripts. There is no compelling reason for intentional alteration in the present context, since meaning is unaffected;[8] thus, accidental error probably should be presumed.

In Luke and the NT, και εν clearly dominates (20 times in Luke; 154 times in the NT); και επι is less frequent (8 times in Luke; 51 times in the NT). However, Luke's use of επι or εν with πας differs significantly from usage elsewhere in the NT: the phrase επι πασιν occurs 7 times in Luke (only 3 times elsewhere in the NT!); εν πασιν occurs in Luke *only* at 9:48 (but 26 times in the remainder of the NT).[9]

Such does suggest a Lukan tendency to read επι in this location as opposed to εν.[10] Given that elsewhere in the NT the more common usage is to read εν with various forms of πας, and specifically to read εν πασιν as opposed to επι πασιν, the greater likelihood is that a minority of scribes would adjust their text to the more common NT style as opposed to the vast majority of scribes deliberately imitating Lukan style.[11]

It thus is not surprising that the actual state of the manuscript evidence strongly supports the Byzantine reading.[12] It is more likely that a few

---

8. In English translation some sort of paraphrase would be required to render either Greek idiom. Και εν/επι πασιν τουτοις is literally "and in/upon all these things" but in translation requires something such as "And in addition to," "Beyond," or "Besides" (all these things).

9. Similarly, in Luke, επι followed by any form of πας occurs 14 times (41 times in the NT), while εν followed by any form of πας occurs 6 times (92 times in the NT). This also reflects a Lukan preference for επι in such constructions as opposed to that of the NT as a whole.

10. Within this pericope, the preposition εν occurs 5x in the three verses immediately preceding (3 times in verse 23; 1 time in verse 24, 1 time in verse 25), whereas επι otherwise does not occur within this pericope, its last Lukan appearance being in Luke 15:20, and its next appearance in Luke 17:16. Harmonization to the immediate context by a minority of MSS thus becomes a reasonable surmise.

11. In the single Lukan occurrence of the phrase εν πασιν (Luke 9:48), von Soden shows only *one* MS (his I^a168 = Gregory-Aland 28) that changes εν to επι, clearly demonstrating that any scribal trend toward such correction would have to be in the opposite direction.

12. Επι is read by 𝔐 A D W Θ Ψ f^1 f^{13} a e, while εν is found only in P^{75} ℵ B L 579 *pc* lat.

The Rich Man and Lazarus — Luke 16:19-31

scribes would have altered a less familiar Lukan form of expression into that which was more common throughout the NT, particularly when such alteration could have been influenced by attraction to the numerous occurrences of εν in the immediate context. That the vast majority of scribes would alter a more common form of expression into one far less common and almost peculiarly Lukan appears minimal.[13]

Addition[14]

Variant unit	Verse	Byzantine Textform	NA[27]/UBS[4]
(8)	16:29	λεγει	λεγει δε

(8) 16:29 λεγει → λεγει δε. This is the only instance within this pericope in which the modern critical edition displays the longer reading in contrast to the Byzantine Textform. Even here, an Alexandrian shorter text (the lack of αυτω) immediately follows (this is discussed under variant unit 15 below). Neither NA[27]/UBS[4] nor SQE mentions the variant concerning δε. IGNTP Luke shows the NA[27] reading (+ δε; 76 MSS; -αυτω, 8 MSS) to be supported by P[75] ℵ B L 579 892 1241.[15]

One must consider not merely the external evidence but also transcriptional, stylistic, and transmissional factors. The following points appear significant:

(a) Transcriptional probability. No reason exists for the addition of δε by scribal error. On the other hand, δε could easily have been omitted by scribal error, since omission of short words is a common scribal failing. While accidental omission tends to be a widespread phenomenon, individual scribes do not tend to omit a word in the same location on the

---

13. External evidence coupled with transmissional probabilities normally should prevail over internal stylistic criteria. When transmissional probabilities and external evidence in fact *join* with internal stylistic criteria, the resultant case is strengthened significantly.

14. Two variant units occur simultaneously in this location. The first involves the NA[27] longer reading δε (*not* cited in the NA[27] apparatus); the second involves the Byzantine longer reading αυτω (which *is* cited in the NA[27] apparatus). These two variant units remain distinct: δε is *not* simply a substitute for αυτω.

15. The NA[27] apparatus cites MS 2542 in support of the omission of αυτω, but the same MS *also* omits δε — apparently the *only* MS that omits *both* δε and αυτω! MS 2542 thus should have been enclosed in parentheses within the NA[27] apparatus, and its precise reading stated in the section "Variae Lectiones Minores."

grand scale. The multiplicity of documents *not* containing δε in this location would seem to obviate accidental omission as a proximate cause of this variation. Intentional addition of the conjunction appears more likely, particularly in view of stylistic considerations.

(b) Style. Either Λεγει δε Αβρααμ (7 MSS) or Λεγει δε αυτω Αβρααμ (76 MSS) is less harsh than the abrupt Λεγει Αβρααμ or Λεγει αυτω Αβρααμ. Scribes would be tempted to correct such abruptness, even though asyndeton is not typical of Lukan style.[16] (Λεγει δε occurs elsewhere in Luke only at 19:22, and there only in the Byzantine Textform.[17] It would seem that the same Textform would not likely neglect such an expression at another point within the same book.) Also, Luke generally tends to avoid the historical present: ειπεν δε (53 times in Luke) and και ειπεν (also 53 times in Luke) clearly predominate. Where λεγει does occur in Luke (14 times), it rarely appears with a conjunction.[18] On balance, the reading without δε appears preferable from a stylistic viewpoint.

(c) Transmissional probability. Since it seems that only 84 MSS include the stylistically smoother δε at this point, leaving the vast majority of MSS not including such, it seems likely that the exclusion of δε must have been original to Luke. The exclusion coincides not only with Lukan style but also with transcriptional probabilities that would exclude accidental omission on the grand scale but would favor scribal addition of a perceived necessary conjunction in order to smooth the flow of the text. On strong transmissional grounds, therefore, the absence of δε is seen to be the "more difficult" reading; yet such conforms to Lukan style, and also reflects transcriptional probabilities.[19]

---

16. N. Turner, *Style*, vol. 4 of J. H. Moulton, *A Grammar of New Testament Greek* (Edinburgh: T. & T. Clark, 1976), does not mention asyndeton in his discussion of Lukan style, even while clearly mentioning such for the other Gospel writers (Mark, 12; Matt, 31; John, 70).

17. While NA[27] does not cite the Luke 19:22 variant unit, SQE offers the following evidence: λεγει alone is read by the main text and its cadre of consistently cited witnesses (calculation of such not made); λεγει δε is read by A W 33 892 1006 1342 1506 [E F H Δ 565 700 1424] 𝔐 bo[pt]; και λεγει is read by Θ 2542 bo[ms]; and ο δε ειπεν is read by D.

18. One does find και λεγει (16:7; 24:36); λεγει γαρ (5:39); αποκριθεις δε λεγει (3:11); and ο δε αποκριθεις λεγει (13:8).

19. Had the external evidence been reversed, one could justifiably argue for the inclusion of δε on the basis of Luke 19:22 as having at least minimal stylistic support within Luke. As it stands, however, transmissional probability stands against such.

The Rich Man and Lazarus — Luke 16:19-31

Omissions

Variant unit	Verse	Byzantine Textform	NA²⁷/UBS⁴
(9)	16:20	τις **ην** ονοματι	τις ονοματι
(10)	16:20	Λαζαρος **ος** εβεβλητο	Λαζαρος εβεβλητο
(11)	16:21	των **ψιχιων** των πιπτοντων	των πιπτοντων
(12)	16:23	ορα **τον** Αβρααμ	ορα Αβρααμ
(13)	16:25	απελαβες **συ** τα	απελαβες τα
(14)	16:26	μηδε **οι** εκειθεν	μηδε εκειθεν
(15)	16:29	λεγει **αυτω** Αβρααμ	λεγει δε Αβρααμ

The 7 "shorter reading" units found in NA²⁷/UBS⁴ tend to be typical of the Alexandrian "shorter text" and in general reflect the eclectic editorial preference for such, despite the mounting evidence that such may more likely reflect early scribal omission as opposed to a longer source text.[20] While the shorter text remains intelligible even in translation, the question as to which reading is more likely original remains the essence of New Testament textual criticism.[21]

(9) 16:20 τις ην ονοματι → τις ονοματι, and (10) 16:20 Λαζαρος ος εβεβλητο → Λαζαρος εβεβλητο. These two variant units are grouped together in the NA²⁷ apparatus (also in *Text und Textwert: Luke*).[22] The

---

20. E. C. Colwell, "Method in Evaluating Scribal Habits: A Study of P⁴⁵, P⁶⁶, P⁷⁵," in his *Studies in Methodology in Textual Criticism of the New Testament* (NTTS 9; Grand Rapids: Eerdmans, 1968), 106-24; J. R. Royse, "Scribal Habits in the Transmission of New Testament Texts," in *The Critical Study of Sacred Texts* (ed. W. D. O'Flaherty; Berkeley: Graduate Theological Union, 1979), 139-61; idem, "Scribal Habits in Early Greek New Testament Papyri" (Th.D. diss., Graduate Theological Union, 1981); idem, "Scribal Tendencies in the Transmission of the Text of the New Testament," in *The Text of the New Testament in Contemporary Research: Essays on the Status Quaestionis* (ed. B. D. Ehrman and M. W. Holmes; SD 46; Grand Rapids: Eerdmans, 1995), 239-52; M. A. Robinson, "Scribal Habits among Manuscripts of the Apocalypse" (Ph.D. diss., Southwestern Baptist Theological Seminary, 1982); P. W. Head, "Some Observations on Early Papyri of the Synoptic Gospels, Especially Concerning the 'Scribal Habits,'" *Bib* 71 (1990): 240-47; idem, "The Habits of New Testament Copyists: Singular Readings in the Early Fragmentary Papyri of John," *Bib* 85 (2004): 399-408.

21. In addition to the studies of scribal habits by Colwell, Royse, Robinson, and Head, see also in this regard M. A. Robinson, "In Search of the Alexandrian Archetype: Observations from a Byzantine-Priority Perspective," in *The New Testament Text in Early Christianity: Proceedings of the Lille Colloquium, July 2000* (ed. C.-B. Amphoux and J. K. Elliott; HTB 6; Lausanne: Éditions du Zèbre, 2003), 45-67.

22. K. Aland et al., eds., *Text und Textwert der griechischen Handschriften des Neuen*

Byzantine Textform here reads τις ην ονοματι Λαζαρος ος εβεβλητο, with the underlined words omitted in the NA²⁷ main text. The difference is stylistic and can be reflected in translation: "Now **there was** a certain poor man named Lazarus, **who** had been cast at his gates" (Byzantine) or "Now a certain poor man named Lazarus had been cast at his gates" (NA²⁷/ UBS⁴). Since both variants appear in tandem, the alteration (in whichever direction) was recensional, rather than a matter of scribal oversight.²³ Thus, in this case, either the witnesses for the longer reading (A W Θ f¹ f¹³ 𝔐 lat sy sa)²⁴ or those for the shorter reading (P⁷⁵ ℵ B D L Ψ 33ᵛⁱᵈ 579 1241 L-844 L-2211 *al* a e Mcion^A Cl) are recensional.²⁵

One must consider what Luke does in similar instances. Luke *alone* in the NT uses the phrase τις ην (4 times elsewhere in Luke; 4 times in Acts), and two occurrences of such appear in close context (16:1, 19; the other occurrences are in 14:2 and 18:2). Luke also follows a noun or descriptive adjective with a relative pronoun 17 times (Acts 7 times), while the same is found 10 times in Matt, 6 times in Mark, and 6 times in John. Such seems also to be characteristic of Lukan style. Both forms come together in 16:1 (ανθρωπος τις ην πλουσιος ος ειχεν), and that passage may set the pattern for this chapter.

The use of ονοματι regarding a particular named individual is almost wholly Lukan. Only 2 cases out of 30 appear in the other Gospels: Simon of Cyrene in Matt 27:32 and Jairus in Mark 5:22. The remaining Lukan instances thus become a point of focus. However, such results are inconclusive: Luke *could* have used any of a number of forms in this re-

---

Testaments, IV: Die Synoptischen Evangelien, 3, Das Lukasevangelium (ANTF 31; Berlin: Walter DeGruyter, 1999). The data presented in *Text und Textwert* contains full collation data regarding continuous-text Greek manuscript support not only for variant units (9)-(10), but also for variant unit (11), and its evidence will be cited accordingly in summary fashion.

23. Had the presence or absence of ην not been an issue, either Λαζαρος ος could have resulted from dittography or Λαζαρος alone could have resulted from haplography (skipping from ος to ος).

24. MS P* and 59 other MSS omit ην and retain ος (see *Text und Textwert: Luke* in loc., variant 3, 3b, 3c) — the only non-Byzantine variant in this unit with more than the 16 MSS of NA²⁷ in support. This reading certainly derives from the Byzantine reading by simple omission, since a scribe would have been unlikely to have added only ος in an awkward position.

25. *Text und Textwert: Luke* shows a total of 1,569 continuous-text MSS supporting the Byzantine longer reading, and 16 MSS (P⁷⁵ ℵ B D L X Ψ 4 157 579 1029 1241 1604 1612 2290 2546) supporting the NA²⁷ main text reading.

The Rich Man and Lazarus — Luke 16:19-31

gard.²⁶ Luke's general practice (19x in Luke-Acts) is *not* to associate ονόματι with either ην or a relative pronoun;²⁷ this *may* have been a factor leading to stylistic revision away from the longer reading — such certainly would appear more likely than the deliberate inclusion of ην and ος when such is not Luke's usual practice. While 16:1 (in particular) and 16:19 *could* have prompted scribal alteration, transmissionally such would be more likely to have appeared in a *small* number of MSS as opposed to the larger mass (it is easier to explain scribal failure or intentional alteration when the manuscript support for such is limited; once the external support exceeds that which could be explained by coincidence, the issue becomes recensional).

There would be no need to assume attraction from 16:1, since 16:19 (which also deals with a πλούσιος) was *not* altered to harmonize with that contextual parallel, nor with the Byzantine form of 16:20. Influence from 16:1 to 16:19, 20 appears nonexistent; likewise influence from 16:20 (either form) back to 16:1 or 16:19. It thus appears that 16:20 was shortened recensionally in order to produce a smoother reading.

The Byzantine reading reflects a more verbose structure: "There was a certain poor one named Lazarus, who had been cast." The shorter reading is smoother: "A certain poor one named Lazarus had been cast." This suggests recensional activity in the interest of smoothness and readability. That the shorter and smoother reading also appears among a small minority of (generally) localized Greek MSS reflecting elements of the Egyptian text-type (the Sahidic, Syriac, and Latin all side with the Byzantine Textform) further reflects the limited locus of such recensional activity.²⁸

(11) 16:21 των ψιχιων των πιπτοντων → των πιπτοντων. In theory,

---

26. One need only compare the following: τις ην ονόματι . . . ος (Acts 9:36; 10:1); τις ην ονόματι (Acts 10:1; 16:1; cf. Acts 9:10 ην δε τις . . . ονόματι); τις ονόματι . . . ος (Acts 9:33; 16:14; 18:7).

27. Luke's 19 dominant forms are either τις ονόματι standing alone (Luke 1:5; 10:38; Acts 5:1; 8:9; 18:2, 24; 19:24; 20:9; 21:12; 27:1) or a noun followed by ονόματι standing alone (Luke 5:27; 19:2; 23:50; Acts 5:34; 9:11, 12; 11:28; 12:13; 17:34).

28. Such is the thrust of J. C. O'Neill, "The Rules Followed by the Editors of the Text Found in the Codex Vaticanus," *NTS* 35 (1989): 218-28, who suggests that specific editorial activity, accidental error, and attempted reconstruction characterized the recension that produced the original Alexandrian archetype (reflected in its later P⁷⁵/B descendants): "Their first rule was, 'Prefer the shorter reading'; and their second rule was, 'Make pertinent (if difficult) sense always' . . . . They aimed for small-scale lucidity" (222). Both these factors characterize the Alexandrian reading in the present variant unit.

the NA²⁷/UBS⁴ editors agree with Metzger regarding the supposed originality of the shorter reading and his explanation of the rise of the longer Byzantine reading:²⁹ "The more picturesque expression τῶν ψιχίων ('the crumbs') was introduced by copyists from Matt 15.27."³⁰ However — *contra* Metzger — it seems unlikely that harmonization to a remote phrase in a non-parallel location would occur, simply since such is not a widespread phenomenon among MSS of the Gospels.³¹ The most obvious cause of variation that the average text-critical reader would suspect in the present instance would be accidental omission due to homoioteleuton. A skip from τῶν to τῶν found in but five Greek manuscripts (P⁷⁵ ℵ* B L 79*)³² is far more likely than a suggestion that the vast majority of scribes harmonized to a remote, isolated phrase in a non-parallel pericope that specifically mentioned crumbs falling from a table. If such were not present in the Lukan passage, and if that passage were already sensible, scribes *en masse* would not be likely to add a phrase that did not appear in their exemplar. Assuming that the shorter text is original, it already reads sensibly (cf. the RSV: "to be fed with what fell from the rich man's table"). No addition is required to complete the sense, so this therefore would not create a reason for scribal search and assimilation to a remote parallel.³³ The various studies of scribal habits have shown clearly that scribal leaps from the

---

29. B. M. Metzger, *A Textual Commentary on the Greek New Testament* (2nd rev. ed.; Stuttgart: Deutsche Bibelgesellschaft, 1994), 141. Since the *Textual Commentary* provides a rationale for the decisions made by the NA²⁷/UBS⁴ Committee, unless a signed dissenting note appears (which here it does not), a general concurrence of the Committee with Metzger's explanation should be presumed.

30. The UBS⁴ text assigns a {B} rating to its preferred reading in this unit, which (to those editors) now "indicates that the text is almost certain" (UBS⁴, "Introduction," 3*; earlier UBS editions said that the {B} rating "indicates some degree of doubt").

31. Harmonization to words and phrases in *parallel* pericopes does occur fairly frequently — mostly in a small minority of witnesses at any given point. Harmonization merely on the *phrase* level *outside* of parallel pericopes is virtually nonexistent.

32. The complete evidence regarding all continuous-text Greek MSS for this variant unit appears in *Text und Textwert: Luke*. Various elements within the Western and patristic tradition also omit these words and are cited in NA²⁷/UBS⁴. Such may have come about by scribal error (particularly sa^mss or bo^pt), or by error in a common exemplar (it^(b, c, e, ff2, i, l, q, r1); sy^(s, c, pal)). The patristic quotations derive specifically from the Western tradition (Marcion^(acc. to Adamantius) Clement Ambrose Gaudentius).

33. The various studies of scribal habits have clearly shown that harmonization to remote non-parallel pericopes is nearly nonexistent, and that harmonization to parallel passages is far less frequent than harmonization to the immediate context.

The Rich Man and Lazarus — Luke 16:19-31

same to the same represent the most common form of error in the early manuscripts.³⁴ Accidental omission in at least a common archetype therefore should be taken as primary, given that only four textually interrelated Greek MSS (P⁷⁵ ℵ B L) contain the shorter reading (most certainly, the unrelated MS 79* omitted των ψιχιων by independent error).

While the remote passage Matt 15:27 does mention crumbs falling from a table, using the identical wording of the Byzantine Textform in Luke 16:20 (απο των ψιχιων των πιπτοντων απο της τραπεζης), the context differs radically.³⁵ The passage is not parallel, and — assuming a "sensible" reading already to be in place in Luke — there would have been no reason for assimilation to have occurred in order to establish verbal identity among non-parallel situations. Scribes would not be likely to seek out remote non-harmonizing parallels merely to improve their present narrative. At best, unconscious expansion due to familiarity with a common form of expression could be postulated, but if so, various other words (e.g., βρωματων or ψωμιων) could have been inserted — but no other words appear in this location,³⁶ apart from various cases of error-based omission.³⁷

---

34. In addition to the studies of scribal habits mentioned previously, cf. the assessment made by J. R. Royse, "The Treatment of Scribal Leaps in Metzger's *Textual Commentary*," NTS 29 (1983): 539-51. Royse demonstrates that a "simpler" transcriptional explanation — not only when merely possible but even when highly likely — is often passed by in silence as the *Commentary* attempts to justify the editorial preference for the NA²⁷/UBS⁴ shorter reading.

35. Matt 15:27 concerns the Canaanite woman, who states, και γαρ τα κυναρια εσθιει απο των ψιχιων των πιπτοντων απο της τραπεζης των κυριων αυτων. The *true* parallel account to that pericope appears in Mark 7:28, with a *non*-harmonized wording: και γαρ τα κυναρια υποκατω της τραπεζης εσθιει απο των ψιχιων των παιδιων. Since harmonization did not occur in the *immediate* parallel account, it is far *less* likely that harmonization occurred in a remote location in Luke, specifically in regard to only two words that could appear in a similar phrase.

36. MS 192 reads the contextually meaningless orthographic variant ψυχων (certainly *not* "souls"), while MSS D and 355 read the nonsensical ψιχων.

37. *Text und Textwert: Luke* provides some insight into the scribal process within this variant unit: απο is omitted carelessly in MS 1602; των *ante* ψιχιων is omitted in MS 1353; πιπτοντων is omitted by skipping from των to των in MS 1205. In MS 1335* πιπτοντων is written as πτοντων, skipping from π to π. In MSS 2457 and 2680, των πιπτοντων is omitted by haplography, skipping from των to -των. Lastly, the phrase απο των . . . πιπτοντων is omitted in *seven* MSS (759* 1139 1166 1314 1403 1542 2533) due to a scribal leap from απο to απο — yet even this results in a "sensible" reading: "and he desired to be fed from the table"! These examples clearly demonstrate that similar letters, words, and endings make haplog-

(12) 16:23 ορα τον Αβρααμ → ορα Αβρααμ. This variant is untranslatable, but it involves a matter of Greek and Lukan style. In this pericope, Abraham is mentioned six times: twice in direct address (which does not take the article),[38] three times *without* the article, and here alone possibly with the article. In general, the first occurrence of a name within a given pericope might lack the article, with subsequent references possibly having the article when indicating a person or object previously mentioned.

In 16:23, the Byzantine Textform appears to follow this practice: the rich man sees that particular Abraham whose bosom was previously mentioned in 16:22. The omission of the article in a small number of witnesses (P^{75} ℵ B D L X Θ Marcion) could be due to accident, perhaps in a common early archetype; or perhaps by intent, in order to harmonize with the immediate context, in which all remaining occurrences of Abraham lack the article.

Luke mentions Abraham more than any other Gospel writer (Matt 7 times, Mark 1 time, Luke 15 times, John 10 times; cf. Acts 7 times). In addition, Luke retains the article before Abraham 4x while omitting the article 10x. Acts has Abraham with the article only in 7:17 and without the article 6x. Given Luke's infrequent use of the article with Abraham, coupled with its nonappearance in the other 5 occurrences within this pericope, it becomes likely that a small number of scribes might have presumed the article to be erroneous or superfluous and deliberately omitted it. Such a supposition commends itself far more than any presumption that nearly all scribes would add just one article to a name that otherwise wholly lacked such within the close context.[39] Similarly, the vast majority of scribes did *not* attempt to add the article before Abraham in the remaining 10 anarthrous occurrences within Luke. This apparent anomaly in Luke 16:23 suggests that the article stood in the autograph and was preserved in transmission, save for a small number of MSS or their common archetype,

---

raphy a likely cause for any omissions within this variant unit. The few Egyptian MSS P^{75} ℵ B L or their archetype simply represent one aspect of this total situation, and thus are very unlikely to reflect the "original" or *Ausgangstext* in this variant unit.

38. Codex Bezae (D) adds another vocative occurrence in 16:27; but this does not affect the main discussion.

39. Cf. the minority K^r group and a few other witnesses (W f^{13} 71 280 659 1071 1279) that add the article before Abraham in 16:22. This action was *not* followed by the remainder of the manuscript tradition. (These data are taken from von Soden and converted into Gregory-Aland format. Neither NA^{27} nor SQE mentions this variant.)

which either omitted the article by accident or by intent chose to conform the name Abraham to its dominant anarthrous form in this pericope.[40]

(13) 16:25 απελαβες συ τα → απελαβες τα. This variant unit is not cited in NA[27] but does appear in SQE. The longer Byzantine reading is supported by (~A) W Ψ f[1] 892 1006 1342 1506 [E F Δ 205 565 700] 𝔐 b (support for the NA[27]/SQE main text reading must be inferred). IGNTP Luke shows 35 MSS and 4 lectionaries that omit συ; among these are P[75] ℵ B D G H L N Θ Π* f[13], Old Latin MSS e a aur c d f ff[2] g[1] gat i l q r[1], and a number of fathers (Athanasius, Basil the Great, Catena on Luke [Cramer], Chrysostom, Cyril of Alexandria, Gregory of Nyssa, Isidore of Pelusium, Nectarius, Nilus, Origen, Marcion). No transcriptional reason exists for omission or addition. Given the small number of MSS that omit the pronoun, it would appear that the omission of συ may have been intentional, perhaps to reduce the level of emphasis. Grammatically, either expression would be suitable; however, the two cases of possessive σου that follow appear to require the triple emphasis: "Child, remember that *you* received *your* good things in *your* life"). Omission of the initial συ could have been an attempt to reduce and stylistically smooth an already emphatic statement. Certainly, perhaps *some* scribes could have added an initial συ in order to enhance the overall emphasis, but it would be unlikely that nearly all remaining scribes would follow suit — particularly when a double emphasis already exists within the sentence.

Triple emphasis in Luke is rare but not unknown:[41] the Byzantine text of Luke 19:42 reads και <u>συ</u> και γε εν τη ημερα <u>σου</u> ταυτη τα προς ειρηνην <u>σου</u>.[42] Further, Luke does use the emphatic συ frequently (24 times), and συ follows the finite verb (as here) at least 4 times.

Transcriptionally and transmissionally it is more likely that a short word would be omitted than that an unnecessary emphatic pronoun would be added, particularly when additional emphasis is not required.

(14) 16:26 μηδε οι εκειθεν → μηδε εκειθεν. In Luke, μηδε followed by

---

40. Luke's *last* use of the article with Abraham occurred in 3:34(!). No other occurrences of the article with Abraham appear after Luke 16:22.

41. The only other occurrences of triple emphasis in the Gospels appear in Matt 6:6, 17. The double emphasis (συ ... σου) is far more frequent (21 NT occurrences, including 6x in Luke and 2x in Acts).

42. NA[27] in Luke 19:42 has a distinctly different reading, which appears to be recensional, attempting to reduce to one an original Lukan triple emphasis: ει εγνως εν τη ημερα ταυτη και συ τα προς ειρηνην (supported as a whole by only ℵ B L 579 pc). *Text und Textwert*: Luke does not cover the inclusion/omission of the final σου in the Byzantine Textform.

an article occurs 4 times while μηδε not followed by an article occurs 7 times. Also, εκειθεν elsewhere in Luke-Acts (6x) is anarthrous. Since Lukan style favors the *lack* of an article in such cases, it would not be likely that a large number of scribes ever would add such, since they certainly did not do so in those other locations in which such alteration equally could have occurred. Transcriptionally, a small number of scribes (P[75] ℵ* B D f[13]) or their archetypes could easily have omitted the article accidentally. There is no good reason for intentional insertion, since μηδε εκειθεν already is sensible.

While one might assume that οι was added to create balance, had such been the case the addition likely would not have been merely that of οι, but rather οι θελοντες, to parallel the first portion of the contrast. Since such did not occur, it remains transmissionally more likely that the article accidentally was omitted in a few witnesses, either independently (D, f[13]) or in relation to a common archetype (P[75] ℵ* B).

(15) 16:29 λεγει αυτω Αβρααμ → λεγει δε Αβρααμ. The NA[27] addition of δε was discussed above, variant unit 8. Here the question is whether the omission or inclusion of αυτω is more likely original. The NA[27] main text is supported by 7 MSS and one father: P[75] ℵ B L 579 892 1241 Ephr (δε αυτω is read by ca. 76 MSS).

Luke rarely follows λεγει with αυτω (Matt 20 times; Mark 13 times; Luke 4 times; John 44 times; Acts 1 time), nor does the conflate phrase λεγει δε αυτω found in 76 MSS occur in the NT. Luke normally writes ειπεν αυτω (59 times). Certainly some scribes could have been tempted to add αυτω in the present context based on familiar NT usage elsewhere. However, transmissional expectation would presume that only a small number of scribes would make such an addition (cf. the 76 that added δε in this variant unit); thus, such an addition would tend to have only a limited amount of perpetuation within the manuscript tradition. Yet here the vast majority of scribes retain αυτω, with only a small handful of interrelated MSS (P[75] ℵ B L 579 892 1241) omitting it (while adding δε at the same time). The omission of αυτω apparently was present in the Alexandrian archetype, either as a result of accident or due to intentional stylistic improvement, related to the use of the historic present in a dramatic narrative ("But Abraham said" is more dramatic than the plodding and verbose "But Abraham said to him"). Were αυτω not original, no good reason would exist for its addition, whereas were αυτω originally present, the text would read more acceptably but less smoothly and dramatically. Thus, the presence of αυτω appears to represent the more difficult reading and should be preferred.

Two Illustrations of Scribal Gap Filling in Luke 16:19

Philip Comfort

In studying textual variants in the Greek New Testament, textual critics realize that many of the differences in the manuscripts came about as the result of transcriptional errors, but they also realize that other variants were created during the process of reading. Whether consciously or unconsciously, the scribe would alter the text as he or she made a new copy and thereby left a written legacy of his or her individual readings. The good scribe is expected not to have really processed the text but to have mechanically copied it word by word. But no matter how meticulous or professional, a scribe would still become subjectively involved with the text and — whether consciously or unconsciously — would produce a transcription that differed from his exemplar. Scribes internalized the text in the process of reading it and transcribing it.

According to reader-reception theory, the meaning of any text is not inherent in the text but must be actualized by the reader. A reader must act as co-creator of the text by supplying that portion of it which is not written but only implied. Each reader uses his or her imagination to fill in the unwritten portions of the text, its "gaps" or areas of "indeterminacy." In other words, as the reader adopts the perspectives thrust on him or her by the text, experiences it sequentially, has expectations frustrated or modified, relates one part of the text to the other, imagines and fills in all that the text leaves blank, its meaning is gradually actualized.

Whereas readers do this gap-filling in their imaginations only, scribes sometimes took the liberty of filling the unwritten gaps with written words.

In other words, some scribes went beyond just imagining how the gaps should be filled and actually filled them. The historical evidence shows that each scribe who made a text created a newly written text. Although there are many factors that could have contributed to the making of this new text, one major factor is that the text constantly demands the reader to fill in the gaps.

Scribes frequently encountered perceived gaps in narrative portions of the New Testament (Gospels-Acts), gaps that often prompted some kind of filling, so as to make the text more lucid for their readers. Such insertions, whether one word or one sentence, account for the ever-expanding text of the New Testament throughout the course of its transmission.[1] By way of example, gap-filling is nowhere more evident than in the interpolations that were created by the scribe of codex Bezae (D) in Luke and Acts. Other scribes did the same, even those who are known for their meticulousness — as we will soon see with respect to the scribe of P^{75}.

The first verse of this pericope (Luke 16:19) provides two examples of narrative gap-filling: one from the scribe of D and another from the scribe of P^{75}. The scribe of codex D introduced the pericope of the rich man and Lazarus with the words "and he spoke another parable." This act of scribal gap filling shows that the scribe of D wanted his readers to understand that this pericope was a parable and not a historical account. In like manner, modern interpreters tend to call it an illustration or an example story (see current standard commentaries on Luke).

This is the only parable told by Jesus in which one of the characters is given a name; the blind beggar is called Lazarus (Luke 16:20). Later in the narrative we are introduced to another named person, Abraham (16:22-25). But the rich man is nameless, thereby leaving a perceived gap in the narrative. The scribe of P^{75}, who is known for his professionalism in producing a faithful text, stepped out of character here. He gave the rich man a name: Neuh, which may be a synonym for Nineveh, the wealthy city that came under God's judgment. One Coptic Sahidic manuscript reads Nineue. Grobell has argued that the Coptic scribe adopted the name Nineue, meaning "Nobody," from an Egyptian folktale, written in Demotic, about Samte's descent into Amnte. He then conjectured that the scribe of P^{75} took his name from a Coptic Sahidic version.[2] However, it is

---

1. For further discussion on this, see P. Comfort, "Scribes as Readers: Looking at New Testament Textual Variants according to Reader Reception Analysis," *Neot* 38 (2004): 28-53.
2. K. Grobel, "Whose Name Was Neves?" *NTS* 10 (1964): 373-82.

just as likely that the scribe of P⁷⁵ also knew the story — or another similar story — and inserted a name of his own choosing.

Other scribes and translators have given the rich man various names. Metzger said that, according to a pseudo-Cyprianic text (third century), the rich man is called Finaeus. Priscillian also gave him the name Finees, which is probably an alternate to Phinehas, Eleazar's father (Exod 6:25; Num 25:7, 11). Peter of Riga called him Amonofis, which is a form of Amenophis, a name held by many Pharaohs.[3]

So the scribe of P⁷⁵ was not alone in supplying the rich man with a name; his is simply the earliest extant record of having done so. (P⁷⁵ dates back to the end of the second century.)[4] Even after the early centuries, readers of this pericope also sensed the lack and provided the rich man a name. In fact, the lack of a name for the rich man was so pronounced that the Latin adjective "dives" (meaning "rich") was assumed to be the man's name. Since the time of Chaucer, the rich man has been known as "Dives" in Latin and English literature.[5]

---

[3]. B. Metzger, *A Textual Commentary on the Greek New Testament* (New York: United Bible Societies, 1994), 140-41.

[4]. For a thorough discussion of the dating of P⁷⁵ to the late second century, see P. Comfort, *Opening the Manuscripts: Introduction to New Testament Paleography and Textual Criticism* (Nashville: Broadman & Holman, 2005), 152.

[5]. The Merriam-Webster's *Collegiate Dictionary* (11th edition) defines "Dives" as "Latin for rich, rich man; misunderstood as a proper name in Lk 16:19."

PART 2
TRANSLATION

Assessing Translation Theory:
Beyond Literal and Dynamic Equivalence

Stanley E. Porter

No doubt the best-known name in Bible translation today is still that of Eugene Nida. Clearly no one has had as much positive and constructive — and even controversial — influence upon the field of Bible translation over the last half century or more than has Nida.[1] In fact, his influence reaches

---

1. The history of translation, especially Bible translation, is discussed and traced in many works, including the following: R. Brower, ed., *On Translation* (Cambridge, MA: Harvard University Press, 1959); H. J. Störig, ed., *Das Problem des Übersetzens* (Darmstadt: Wissenschaftliche Buchgesellschaft, 1963); B. F. Westcott, *A General View of the History of the English Bible* (2nd ed.; London: Macmillan, 1872); E. A. Nida, *Toward a Science of Translating* (Leiden: Brill, 1964), esp. 11-29; F. F. Bruce, *History of the Bible in English* (3rd ed.; Guildford: Lutterworth, 1978); S. Kubo and W. Specht, *So Many Versions? Twentieth Century English Versions of the Bible* (Grand Rapids: Zondervan, 1975); D. Ewert, *From Ancient Tablets to Modern Translations: A General Introduction to the Bible* (Grand Rapids: Zondervan, 1983); H. M. Orlinsky and R. G. Bratcher, *A History of Bible Translation and the North American Contribution* (Atlanta: Scholars Press, 1991); B. M. Metzger, *The Bible in Translation: Ancient and English Versions* (Grand Rapids: Baker, 2001). My own views of the history and development of Bible translation are found in a number of writings: S. E. Porter, "Some Issues in Modern Translation Theory and Study of the Greek New Testament," *Currents in Research: Biblical Studies* 9 (2001): 350-82; "Modern Translations," in *The Oxford Illustrated History of the Bible* (ed. J. Rogerson; Oxford: Oxford University Press, 2001), 134-61; "Language and Translation of the New Testament," in *The Oxford Handbook of Biblical Studies* (ed. J. W. Rogerson and J. M. Lieu; Oxford: Oxford University Press, 2006), 184-210; "Translations of

---

I wish to acknowledge the help and support in development of this essay of my friend and colleague, Dr. Matthew Brook O'Donnell.

far beyond that of Bible translation. If one consults many of the standard works in translation theory and practice (not specifically addressing issues of Bible translation), one is almost bound to find reference to at least the theory if not also the practice of Nida.[2]

Nida's success can be judged in at least three ways — by the number of translation projects that he has birthed, so that today the Good News Translation (GNT; formerly Today's English Version and Good News Bible) is a recognized and standard translation (still underestimated for its innovation, literary quality, and readability);[3] by the number of supportive projects that he has sponsored, such as the United Bible Societies' Greek New Testament *(UBSGNT),* the journal *The Bible Translator,* and numerous interpreters' and translators' guides; and, especially, by the development and utilization of his model of dynamic and functional equivalence translation — along with the controversy that has attended his work, in terms of reaction both by those who do not share his premises and by those who wish to go further and in other directions.

In some ways, Nida's personality and energy have been so overpowering that most discussion of translation theory today still focuses upon differences between literalist/formalist and dynamic equivalence translation.[4] In some circles, in fact in most biblical circles, it is almost as if these are the only two choices of how to conceive of translation. Although other approaches to translation are sometimes mentioned — including those such as relevance theory — they are rarely included in the larger discussion, and there is little to relate these models to each other.[5] The impres-

---

the Bible (Since the KJV)," in *Dictionary of Biblical Criticism and Interpretation* (ed. S. E. Porter; London and New York: Routledge, 2007), 362-69.

2. Nida also has a particular place in the life of McMaster Divinity College, since we recognized him in 2003 with an honorary Doctor of Letters degree to commemorate and recognize the significant work that he has done to promote biblical translation.

3. I could and probably should also mention the Contemporary English Version (CEV). See S. E. Porter, "The Contemporary English Version and the Ideology of Translation," in *Translating the Bible: Problems and Prospects* (ed. S. E. Porter and R. S. Hess; Sheffield: Sheffield Academic Press, 1999), 18-45.

4. For a recent sympathetic assessment of Nida and his work, see the following essays in *BT* 56, no. 1 (2005): W. J. Porter, "Life and Works of Eugene Albert Nida," 1-7, and S. E. Porter, "Eugene Nida and Translation," 8-18. See the recent biography by P. C. Stine, *Let the Words Be Written: The Lasting Influence of Eugene A. Nida* (Leiden: Brill, 2004).

5. See, e.g., D. A. Carson, *The Inclusive Language Debate: A Plea for Realism* (Grand Rapids: Baker, 1998), 71. Cf. D. A. Carson, "The Limits of Dynamic Equivalence in Bible

Assessing Translation Theory

sion that one often gets is that these methods are all addressing the same set of translational issues, even if in slightly different ways.

I do not believe that such is the case. Utilizing the levels of analysis pioneered in the OpenText.org project, this essay attempts to show that various translation models tend to focus upon particular ranks of linguistic analysis, even if they touch on other levels, and that the level at which a translation functions helps to determine the particular features of the approach and the kinds of issues it addresses. Once this analysis is complete, I think that we will be able to see that translation theory has been well served in some areas, but not as well served in others, and I have some suggestions to make in this regard.

Models of Translation Theory

Before I explicate the different models of translation theory that I want to explore, I wish to outline briefly the model of textual analysis pioneered by the OpenText.org project. This project can be found on the web at www.opentext.org.[6] The goal of this project is to provide a richly annotated structured corpus of Greek texts from the Hellenistic world.[7]

Let me say something briefly about each of the items noted. The corpus is of Greek texts, so that we can make comparisons across the range of Hellenistic Greek literature. The corpus is structured to provide representative genres or literary types, weighted to reflect not just what remains by accident but proposed registers of usage in the ancient world. The rich annotation goes well beyond what other annotated texts provide. These other texts are confined to the level of morphology (with some serious depar-

---

Translation," *Evangelical Review of Theology* 9 (1985): 200-213; revisited in "The Limits of Functional Equivalence in Bible Translation — And Other Limits, Too," in *The Challenge of Bible Translation: Communicating God's Word to the World* (ed. G. G. Scorgie et al.; Grand Rapids: Zondervan, 2003), 65-113; and many of the essays in A. Brenner and J. W. van Henten, eds., *Bible Translation on the Threshold of the Twenty-First Century: Authority, Reception, Culture and Religion* (Sheffield: Sheffield Academic Press, 2002).

6. The OpenText.org site has a number of postings that give insight into the project. See the articles under the resources section.

7. For a description of this idealized corpus, see M. B. O'Donnell, "Designing and Compiling a Register-Balanced Corpus of Hellenistic Greek for the Purpose of Linguistic Description and Investigation," in *Diglossia and Other Topics in New Testament Linguistics* (ed. S. E. Porter; Sheffield: Sheffield Academic Press, 2000), 255-97.

119

tures from this that simply serve to confuse the annotation), whereas the OpenText.org database annotates from the word up to the level of the discourse. Morphologically based annotation is important, but it is clearly limited in what it can provide.

The smallest unit of meaningful or disambiguating structure in the OpenText.org model is the word group. Word groups consist of such things as nominal groups, with a substantive as the head-term and dependent modifiers; or verbal groups, with the verbal element as the head-term and dependent modifiers.

The next level is the clause. The tendency in much Greek grammatical discussion is to move directly to the sentence, not realizing that the sentence is itself an ambiguous notion. The clause level is confined to a unit of independent meaning that can stand alone, often with a predicator as its minimal unit. The major elements of clausal structure are the subject, predicator, complement, and adjunct, with adjuncts often consisting of participle or infinitive phrases.

The next largest unit is the clause complex, in which various clauses are connected together, through the use of asyndeton and various types of conjunction.

The level of the paragraph is a group of clauses/clause-complexes that form a structural unit of meaning,[8] and it is concerned with the structure of groups of primary, secondary, and embedded clauses. Primary clauses (to use geometric metaphors) function at the horizontal level to propel the line of discourse forward. Secondary clauses function at the vertical level to provide either background or development off the line of the main discourse. Embedded clauses function similarly to secondary clauses, but within the structure of the clause itself.

The discourse sub-unit is concerned with units that join together a number of paragraphs, to mark off sub-sections within a discourse. Narratives often consist of formal introductions, various discurses, and digressions, as well as the main narrative, which may have a number of sub-units. The letter-form consists of various letter sub-units, such as the salu-

---

8. The paragraph is a notoriously difficult unit of structure to define. See S. E. Porter, "Pericope Markers and the Paragraph: Textual and Linguistic Considerations," *The Import of Unit Delimitation on Exegesis* (Pericope 7; ed. R. de Hoop, M. C. A. Korpel, and S. E. Porter; Assen: Van Gorcum, 2008), 175-95; cf. S. Crisp, "Scribal Marks and Logical Paragraphs: Discourse Segmentation Criteria in Manuscripts of the Pauline Corpus," *UBS Bulletin* 198/199 (2005): 77-87.

tation, thanksgiving, body, paranesis, and closing — each one of these is a discourse sub-unit that consists of one or more paragraphs. The discourse itself consists of the entirety of the grammatico-lexical and communicative unit and conforms to a discourse type. The basic discourse types are narrative and exposition, although some might also wish to include such types as poetry, hortatory texts, procedural texts, and the like.[9]

Analysis of these levels in terms of the components of register — field, tenor, and mode — provides a means of describing the context of situation of the given document, that is, the situation that would have generated such a document, within its wider context of culture, with culture including the range of cultural norms and assumptions, including the literary types available.

The OpenText.org project has completed rich annotation of the Greek New Testament from the level of the word/word group to the level of the paragraph, and is currently developing the theoretical basis for further annotation. The project has also already extended its scope to extrabiblical documents, such as papyri, the *Didache,* and the *Gospel of Peter,* among others. Not only word order and syntactical information are annotated, however, but also semantic domain information. The goal is to be able to provide a means of analysis of a wide and expanding body of Greek texts from the individual words to their context of culture, as the basis of intensive comparative linguistic analysis.

A graphic diagram of the various levels of annotation as described above that I am using in this paper is as follows:

Context of Culture
Context of Situation
Discourse
Sub-Discourse Unit
Paragraph
Clause Complex
Clause
___Word Group___   (minimal rank of meaningful structure)
Word
Morphology

---

9. One of the best discussions of these types is R. E. Longacre, *The Grammar of Discourse* (2nd ed.; New York: Plenum, 1983), 20.

I now wish to introduce briefly the major translation models that are currently being employed in various ways[10] and to attempt to correlate them with this scheme above of levels of language.[11] I will use the first few verses of the passage in Luke 16:19-31 regarding Lazarus as a test-case to illustrate some of the issues raised by these models of translation. I will not engage in extended critique of the individual models, except to note how some of the translation models have developed in response to others.

Literalist/Formal Equivalence Translation

The relevance of literalist or formal equivalence translation is not so fully appreciated today as it once was — although there have been recent efforts to defend it.[12] In the English-speaking world, as long as the King James or Authorized Version (KJV/AV) of the Bible held preeminence, literalistic translation theory was the major explicit theory of Bible translation. It is not as if this theory developed without thought and consideration, however. To a large extent it was predicated upon a desire to be faithful to the original text, and it mirrored the kind of translation that was often done in classical studies when renderings were made out of the original into a

---

10. A somewhat comparable study is provided by Mojola and Wendland, but several of what they identify as "contemporary translation approaches" are less approaches than responses to and critiques of other methods. See A. O. Mojola and E. Wendland, "Scripture Translation in the Era of Translation Studies," in *Bible Translation: Frames of Reference* (ed. T. Wilt; Manchester: St. Jerome, 2003), 1-25, esp. 13-24. After I had delivered this paper, I came across J. Munday, *Introducing Translation Studies: Theories and Applications* (London: Routledge, 2001), who treats some of the same methods of translation as I do, although in some differing ways. The methods he treats are the following: "equivalence and equivalent effect" (Jakobson, Nida, Newmark), "translation shift approach" (Catford), "functional theories of translation," "discourse and register analysis approaches" (Halliday, Baker, Hatim, and Mason), "systems theories," "cultural studies," the work of Venuti in terms of "translating the foreign," and "philosophical theories of translation" (e.g., Steiner).

11. See J. C. Catford, *A Linguistic Theory of Translation* (London: Oxford University Press, 1965), 25-26.

12. See, e.g., L. Ryken, *The Word of God in English: Criteria for Excellence in Bible Translation* (Wheaton, IL: Crossway, 2002), 9-10, who prefers the term "essentially literal translation" (which acknowledges problems with strict formalism); and W. Grudem et al., *Translating Truth: The Case for Essentially Literal Bible Translation* (Wheaton, IL: Crossway, 2005), where the term is taken up by not only Ryken but Grudem in their essays.

modern language — the translation itself was seen as a guide to how well the translator understood the original document. A literalistic approach is still found in a number of translations, such as the Revised and New Revised Standard Version (RSV/NRSV), the New American Standard Bible (NASB), the English Standard Version (ESV), and the Holman Christian Standard Bible (HCSB).[13]

Some of the principles that govern literalistic or formalist translation theory are worth noting.[14] Such translations are generally concerned with being as close to a one-to-one correspondence as possible — although one notices a shift in what this means in more recent literalistic translations, such as the NKJV. Thus there is emphasis upon the iconicity of form and meaning, the need for faithfulness to the wording of the original in terms of both lexis and syntax, an emphasis upon translating the words themselves consistently, and attention to the literary types of the original. In other words, the emphasis is upon the original meaning of the text and preserving it in a form as close as possible to that of the original, including stylistic variations. These kinds of translations are characterized by a purported fidelity to the original text, often a consistency in rendering vocabulary, a word-order that attempts to maintain closeness to the original, and often a use of archaic or at least stilted modern language, either because of a felt need to maintain a tradition of biblical translation or because of a hesitance to become overly colloquial and perhaps jeopardize the proper sound of the venerated text. This type of translation has often characterized translation of ancient languages, where staying close to the original was seen as a sign of understanding it. This tradition, dating from the Renaissance, was firmly established in classical studies in the nineteenth century and has been maintained by

---

13. There have been various attempts to categorize translations. See Porter, "Modern Translations," 134-47. Cf. C. J. Collins, "What the Reader Wants and the Translator Can Give: First John as a Test Case," in Grudem et al., *Translating Truth*, 77-112, esp. 84.

14. The means of defining literalistic or formalistic translation is complicated by the fact that there are few places that actually do so. Even those that purport to be doing so present their definition more by way of negation of other forms of translation. In some ways, Nida's definition of formal equivalence (*Science*, 159) is a more concise and better definition than that found elsewhere (and the basis for mine above). See also A. L. Farstad, *The New King James Version: In the Great Tradition* (Nashville: Nelson, 1989), 120-21, but he wishes to call the technique of the New King James Version (NKJV) "complete equivalence," which is literal translation that benefits from linguistic analysis (124-25).

some to this day (as is evidenced by some translations, such as the NASB).

There is a tradition, no doubt established by the KJV, to begin the parable in Luke 16:19 with the phrase "there was a certain rich man." The same phrasing is used at Luke 16:1 to start the parable of the unjust steward. This is apparently the way that one begins a parable in the literalistic tradition, since similar phrasing is used in such translations as the NKJV, RSV/NRSV, NASB, ESV, and HCSB. The phrasing could have been rendered even more literalistically (and arguably more accurately and at least as idiomatically) with "and a certain man was rich," but this would not have indicated the parabolic convention. Luke 16:20 is rendered similarly in the KJV with "and there was a certain beggar named Lazarus," which is followed by some, but not all, literalistic translations. The NKJV and NASB follow this, while the RSV/NRSV and ESV render it "and at his gate lay a poor man named Lazarus." The KJV probably renders v. 20 this way to continue the indication of a parable. Having begun this way, the KJV reflects a reading in Alexandrinus and the majority text with a relative clause: "which was laid at his gate," while the NASB retains the Greek clausal syntax in the Alexandrian tradition with "was laid at his gate." The RSV/NRSV retains the Greek clausal syntax but shifts individual clausal components. The HCSB is similar to the RSV/NRSV in v. 19, but the NASB in v. 20 reads: "there was a rich man who would dress in purple. . . . But a poor man named Lazarus, covered with sores, was left at his gate." What is pertinent to note is that there is a high consistency in the vocabulary used, in the style of rendering to indicate a parable, and in the retention of similar word groups even if the clausal syntax is changed.

These examples, in conjunction with the principles laid out in discussion of formalist translation, indicate that literalistic or formal equivalence translation retains its orientation to the individual word or the word group, even if it is not as formal as it might be. The major differences are, for the most part, confined to variations in how individual words are rendered, and occasionally the moving of a clausal component.

Context of Culture
Context of Situation
Discourse
Sub-Discourse Unit
Paragraph
Clause Complex
Clause
___Word Group___   Literal/Formal Equivalence Translation
Word
Morphology

Dynamic/Functional Equivalence

"Dynamic or functional translation equivalence" is usually the alternative to literalistic translation when translational models are discussed. Some would argue that such an alternative to a literalistic or formalistic translation model has always been with us. In a sense they are correct, if for no other reason than that an entirely consistent literalistic model that makes sense in the receptor language is not possible — there is always the need for accommodation to the fact that the source and receptor languages are not equivalent and that adjustments in syntax are required (as already noted above). Nevertheless, the development of the explicit theory of dynamic or functional equivalence is the responsibility of Eugene Nida.[15] As Nida told me when he gave lectures to my graduate students at my previous institution, he wrote his first book on translation because he could not find a book that laid out the principles of translation in a systematic way.[16] He took that occasion to begin to systematize the principles that he increasingly developed and refined in the course of his work. The first fully informed translation that utilized the principles of dynamic equivalence was the GNT. Since then, there have been a number of other dynamic equivalence translations. These include some directly inspired by Nida, such as the CEV, in some ways an attempt to bring the GNT up to date for

---

15. Some want to argue that functional has replaced dynamic equivalence (e.g., Carson, *Inclusive Language Debate*, 71), but others question the shift. See N. Statham, "Nida and 'Functional Equivalence,'" *BT* 56, no. 1 (2005): 29-45.

16. This book was E. A. Nida, *Bible Translating* (New York: American Bible Society, 1947).

a new generation. There are also other dynamic equivalence translations, however, such as the (Today's) New International Version (NIV/TNIV) and New Living Translation (NLT).

Nida defines his dynamic equivalence translation in terms of a number of categories regarding the source language[17] and the receptor language:[18] As a result, (1) a translation must aim primarily at reproducing the message of the source language, (2) a translation is to seek equivalence of the message rather than conserving the form of the utterance, (3) the closest natural equivalent is to be used, (4) meaning is given priority over structure, and (5) style, though secondary to content, must still be preserved.[19]

The way these principles work is illustrated by Nida's use of his theory of kernel sentences.[20] Nida distinguishes between surface structure and underlying kernel sentences. Even though surface structures may be the same, the underlying kernels may be different. An example at the level of the word group is "the will of God," which has a kernel of "God wills," which is different from the surface structure "Jesus of Nazareth," which has a kernel of "Jesus comes from Nazareth." The process that Nida specifies is that one analyses a construction in the source language into its kernel and then transfers this into the receptor language, rendering its equivalent kernel into the surface structure of the receptor. An example that Nida has used on several occasions[21] is Mark 1:4, which says that John preached "a baptism of repentance for the forgiveness of sins." Nida posits that the "ba-

---

17. E. A. Nida and C. R. Taber, *The Theory and Practice of Translation* (Leiden: Brill, 1969), 6-8: (1) the biblical languages are languages like any other languages, with the same limitations; (2) the biblical writers expected to be understood; and (3) a translation should reproduce the meaning of a given passage according to the understanding of the writer.

18. Nida and Taber, *Theory*, 3-6: (1) each language has its own distinctive characteristics; (2) these characteristics must be respected, rather than altered; (3) what can be said in one language can be said in any other; and (4) the content of the message must be preserved even if the form must be changed.

19. Nida and Taber, *Theory*, 12-14.

20. Nida and Taber, *Theory*, 33-55; cf. Nida, *Science*, 9. Correlations have been drawn with N. Chomsky's phrase-structure grammar in *Syntactic Structures* (The Hague: Mouton, 1957).

21. E. A. Nida, *God's Word in Man's Language* (New York: Harper & Row, 1952), 33-34; Nida and Taber, *Theory*, 44, 51-53; E. A. Nida, *Good News for Everyone* (Waco, TX: Word, 1977), 99-101. I have examined this example in S. E. Porter, "Mark 1.4, Baptism and Translation," in *Baptism, the New Testament and the Church* (ed. S. E. Porter and A. R. Cross; Sheffield: Sheffield Academic Press, 1999), 81-98.

sic kernels" that make up the phrase in Mark 1:4 are five: (1) "John preached X" (in which X stands for the entire indirect discourse), (2) "John baptizes the people," (3) "The people repent," (4) "God forgives X," (5) "the people sin."[22] Nida then determines a number of relationships between the five kernel sentences,[23] and then proposes two means of rendering the phrase, as a result of his kernel analysis. For languages that do not have passive formations, a rendering might be "I will baptize you" or "You will receive baptism." For languages that have passive formations, of which English is one, a rendering might be "John preached, 'Repent and be baptized, so that God will forgive the evil you have done.'"[24]

In examining some dynamic equivalence translations, we encounter some surprises. The NIV/TNIV begins our example passage with "There was a rich man" and continues: "At his gate was laid a beggar named Lazarus," language similar to many of the formal equivalence translations.[25] The GNT renders Luke 16:19-20 thus: "There was once a rich man who dressed in the most expensive clothes and lived in great luxury every day. There was also a poor man named Lazarus, covered with sores, who used to be brought to the rich man's door." The GNT retains many of the conventions established by the KJV tradition in rendering the Greek with the impersonal construction for the introduction of both the rich man and Lazarus, although the reference to lying at the rich man's door appears at the end of the verse in the GNT. The NLT prefaces the unit by stating that "Jesus said," but then renders the two verses in language very much like the

---

22. Nida and Taber, *Theory*, 51.

23. He finds the following relationships. First, the goal of kernel 1 is kernels 2-5, with the result that, in many languages, he believes, it is appropriate to render indirect discourse into direct discourse. Secondly, "Kernel 3 precedes kernel 2 in time, as two related events combined by *and*. This set of kernels is equivalent to the expression 'repent and be baptized'" (Nida and Taber, *Theory*, 51-52). Thirdly, for Nida "Kernel 5 is the goal of the verb of kernel 4," and fourthly, apparently on the basis of the preposition *eis*, "Kernel 4 (with its goal, kernel 5) is the purpose of kernels 3 and 2. That is to say, the forgiveness of sins is not related merely to repentance but to the combined expression 'repent and be baptized'" (Nida and Taber, *Theory*, 52).

24. Nida and Taber, *Theory*, 52. The above is taken from Porter, "Some Issues in Modern Translation Theory," 354-56.

25. This is consistent with where some scholars place the NIV/TNIV and NLT, as between formal and dynamic equivalence. See W. Grudem, "Are Only Some Words of Scripture Breathed Out by God? Why Plenary Inspiration Favors 'Essentially Literal' Bible Translation," in Grudem et al., *Translating Truth*, 19-56, here 22.

RSV: "there was a certain rich man who . . . at his door lay a diseased beggar named Lazarus." The speech margin is somewhat similar to the added words in manuscript D: "and he spoke another parable."

The nature of these changes should not be as surprising as one might expect in the light of the apparent radical disjunction posited between formal and dynamic equivalence translation. Dynamic equivalence translation has a number of features in common with literalistic translation, so much so that some of these dynamic translations retain the similar distinguishing characteristics of the literalistic renderings in terms of parabolic markers, impersonal constructions, the sound of a traditional translation, and even some word order. However, there are also a number of slight changes at the clausal level. It is worth noting that the formalist and dynamic equivalence methods have much in common theoretically (e.g., Nida's kernel model) and practically. Theoretically they both put an emphasis upon the language and meaning of the original or source language over the receptor language. This is no doubt partly why they are both tied to more fundamental or lower levels of language usage, the word group and the clause.

Context of Culture
Context of Situation
Discourse
Sub-Discourse Unit
Paragraph
Clause Complex
Clause   Dynamic/Functional Equivalence Translation
___Word Group___   Literal/Formal Equivalence Translation
Word
Morphology

Functionalist Translation

The functionalist approach to translation is not to be confused with the functional equivalence advocated by Nida and his followers. The functionalist approach, which draws heavily upon the early Hallidayan linguistic work of scale and category grammar, began to be developed in the 1960s, especially in the work of J. C. Catford, and was further developed by Peter

Newmark, among others.[26] The key to the functional analysis that Catford lays out is the notion of levels of language usage and the difference between form and substance. Thus, when language is used, three levels of abstraction can be exemplified: grammatical/lexical form, consisting of grammar and lexis; medium form, consisting of phonology and graphology; and medium substance, consisting of phonic substance and graphic substance. These exemplifications exist within a situation (or situation substance) and context, which Catford defines as an interlevel between the levels noted above. Whereas most theories of translation are concerned with the contextual meaning, that is, what is associated with grammatical/lexical forms, Catford argues that meaning is larger than this restricted notion. He posits five units of hierarchy, a rank scale, of grammar for English, from the largest to the smallest unit. These are: sentence, clause, group, word, and morpheme, in which elements of the lower ranks function as exponents of the elements of the higher rank (when the movement is in the other direction, one has rank shifting). Munday emphasizes the notion of "shifts" between various forms of exponence as a major emphasis of Catford's translational theory.[27]

With this framework in mind, Catford defines translation as follows: "the replacement of textual material in one language (SL [= source language]) by equivalent textual material in another language (TL [= target language])."[28] After noting distinctions between full and partial translation and total and restricted translation, as well as making the kinds of distinctions being made in this essay regarding a rank level analysis of translation, Catford posits various levels of translational equivalence, including phonological and graphological.

Rather than being concerned with formal equivalence, Catford believes that textual equivalence is necessary. This means that emphasis is not upon the source language but upon the target language, such that the target language form is deemed to be the equivalent of the source language. How-

---

26. Catford, *Linguistic Theory*; idem, "Translation and Language Teaching," in *Linguistic Theories and Their Application* (n.p.: Aidela, 1967), 125-46; P. Newmark, *A Textbook of Translation* (New York: Prentice Hall, 1988); M. Baker, *In Other Words* (London: Routledge, 1992). Note that Munday *(Translation Studies)* puts Halliday and Baker, Catford, and Newmark in three separate categories. See *Halliday: System and Function in Language* (ed. G. Kress; Oxford: Oxford University Press, 1976).

27. Munday, *Translation Studies*, 60-62.

28. Catford, *Linguistic Theory*, 20.

ever, it is not satisfactory in Firthian linguistic terms to simply state that the two texts have the "same" meaning. Meaning is determined in terms of the situation and context in which the translation is used, so that a given target language text has its meaning within the context of its being a target language, and similarly for the source language. As a translation, therefore, the target language translation must use the elements of the language with consistent internal values.[29] The target language may have values, however, that have been established by the source language through a process of transference, but these are the values in the target language, not those of the source language, and this is not what is normally thought of as translation. One of the places where this has become most obvious of late is in terms of translation of the singular masculine pronoun of Greek. It is now thought that English does not use the masculine singular pronoun as inclusive, as it was clearly used in Greek, thus justifying various forms of expression in English that are not the "same" as they were in the original Greek. Not as readily apparent, but perhaps even more important, are issues related to translation of verbal aspect (tense forms) and causality (voice forms) in Greek, where English does not have iconicity. The various synthetic aspects in Greek are captured with differing English analytic realizations (the present-tense form rendered by the English progressive), or the Greek middle is captured by an entire clausal predicator unit.

Catford posits a number of restrictions upon a functionalist approach as well. One is that he believes there are limits to translation where there is a crossing of significant boundaries, such as a difference in medium. Another is that having linguistic relevance is not the same as having functional relevance, with translation concerned with the latter. A final restriction to mention here is linguistic untranslatability. Catford rejects the hard form of this notion (that items cannot be translated from one language to another) but does note that there are circumstances that limit translatability, such as shared exponence (same realization for differing features) or polysemy.

I do not know of a readily accessible biblical translation that exemplifies the functionalist approach to Luke 16.[30] However, there are some

---

29. Catford, *Linguistic Theory*, 43.

30. In fact, as one respondent says of Catford's theory, "what is proposed here has no connection with applied linguistics, either in theory or in practice" (Culioli, response to Catford's article, *Linguistic Theories*, 146). Much the same could be said about a number of these models.

applications that might be relevant. A contextual determination of the use of a parable might dictate an indication in the receptor language that this is a parable, but that would not necessarily indicate use of the phrase "there was a . . ." As with the NLT, there might be a speech margin, such as "Jesus continued with this parable. . . ." This would eliminate the need to use the common introductory formulas in vv. 19 and 20 and could allow the clause-level rendering to be more expressive in the receptor language. This could be something as simple as "a rich man was always dressing in expensive clothing . . . But a poor man named Lazarus was sprawled at his door . . ."

On the basis of the position of Catford, one could argue that the functionalist approach addresses the context of situation. Although Catford does mention this element of translation, when it comes to actually analyzing examples of how translation is done he confines himself to the clause complex as the largest category that he discusses. He limits the theory in practice to dealing with the linkage of individual clauses into larger units. The orientation is more focused upon the function of the target language, and hence tends to move up the scale, more so than functional equivalence.

Context of Culture
Context of Situation
Discourse
Sub-Discourse Unit
Paragraph
Clause Complex   Functionalist Translation
Clause   Dynamic/Functional Equivalence Translation
___Word Group___   Literal/Formal Equivalence Translation
Word
Morphology

Discourse Analysis (Text-Linguistics)

The importance of discourse analysis, or text-linguistics, for translation of the New Testament has only recently been realized. Discourse analysis is a composite method of textual treatment that encompasses various forms of linguistic analysis. This is especially true of discourse analysis that is bottom up in nature, since it bases its discourse structures upon the concatenation of smaller linguistic units. In that sense, all of the elements that have already been discussed, including word groups, clauses, etc., are a part of discourse analysis. However, the role of discourse analysis in translation also provides something unique that goes beyond other forms of analysis so far discussed. Two major books have been written on the role of discourse in translation, both by Basil Hatim and Ian Mason.[31] Neither book is written as a "how to" book on translation, in the sense that other books are written as guides to translational technique. Instead, these books bring together various elements of linguistic analysis and place them in the overall context of how discourse considerations affect translational practices. This has two major results. The first is that analysis is primarily concerned with elements that are beyond the sentence, and the second is that Hallidayan linguistics has had a large influence upon such model-building, especially the Hallidayan notion of register.[32] In that sense, the discourse analytic treatment of translation is a further development and extension of the model proposed above by Catford.

The result is a discussion that takes up issues not typically found in traditional treatments of translation, most if not virtually all of which are beyond the sentence in scope. Sometimes this extension beyond the sentence goes quite a bit beyond the sentence, and even beyond an individual discourse itself. Thus, Hatim and Mason recognize the general issues of translation — such as issues of objectivity and subjectivity, liberal and free translation, form and content, and author- and reader-centered translation — before undertaking to provide their analysis of how to handle the major issues. They believe that the kind of dynamic equivalence model proposed by Nida, and reflective of Chomskyan notions of deep structure, has moved translation away from its primary concern, communication.[33]

Instead, they wish to focus on the communicative dimensions of translation. These include a number of major factors. One is register anal-

---

31. B. Hatim and I. Mason, *Discourse and the Translator* (London: Longman, 1990) and *The Translator as Communicator* (London: Routledge, 1997).

32. For discussion of register in terms of New Testament study, see S. E. Porter, "Dialect and Register in the Greek of the New Testament: Theory," and "Register in the Greek of the New Testament: Application with Reference to Mark's Gospel," in *Rethinking Contexts, Rereading Texts: Contributions from the Social Sciences to Biblical Interpretation* (ed. M. D. Carroll R.; JSOTSup 299; Sheffield: Sheffield Academic Press, 2000), 190-208 and 209-29.

33. Hatim and Mason, *Discourse*, 32.

ysis, a distinctly Hallidayan notion as it is utilized here. Within the context of situation and culture, register captures the elements of what is often called "dialect" or individual difference, but in terms of the field, mode, and tenor of discourse. Hatim and Mason place these within the linguistic context of pragmatics. In their discussion of pragmatics, they recognize that there is a complex interplay among communication, pragmatics, and semiotics. The field of discourse is concerned with the genre of discourse, the tenor with the discourse itself, and the mode with the text. Hatim and Mason wish to move beyond the de Saussurian and related notions of *langue* and *parole,* since these notions have restricted development of analysis of the communicative possibilities of language by not treating *parole* but concentrating on *langue.* Analysis of language use has shown that *parole* is in fact structured and not the chaotic exemplification that Saussurian models have posited.[34] These larger patterns of usage that create structure in texts and give texture to discourses are important parts of the meaning in context. In fact, Hatim and Mason wish to go beyond the text to include intertextuality within the scope of issues that a full discourse analytic translational model discusses, since these intertextual references are part of the communicative intent of the discourse.

As with the functionalist approach, there is, to my knowledge, no conscious rendering of this Lukan passage that reflects the principles articulated in terms of discourse analysis. One of the first questions for the discourse analyst to ask is whether the passage is a parable or some other literary type. There are a number of features to consider in this determination. One is the fact that one of the central human participant characters is mentioned by name, something that rarely if ever happens in the parables of Jesus (and in P[75] the rich man is named as well, but this naming is only found in that one manuscript). If the passage is determined to be a parallel, and if indicating such is important, then the discourse-based translator would need to render this appropriately. If the passage is determined to be something else — some have taken it to be a historically/theologically based account — then appropriate adjustments would need to be made. The discourse is structured in several distinct parts, around the individual participants. This may reflect an original oral mode, now transformed into a tripartite participant-based written text: rich man and Lazarus; rich man and Abraham; and then rich man, Abraham, and Lazarus. For the sake of

---

34. Hatim and Mason, *Discourse,* 107-108.

textual cohesion, a means of rendering the parallel references to the characters would need to be found, taking into account the full forms used for Lazarus and Abraham. The discourse sets up an opposition between named and unnamed characters, with the named ones siding against the unnamed. One such rendering might start thus: "There were two men, one very rich who dressed in the best clothes and enjoyed life immensely, and the other a poor diseased man named Lazarus who begged outside his door."

The level of analysis with which discourse analysis is concerned jumps a number of steps up on the rank scale that I have posited above. Discourse analysis, as noted above, treats all of the elements below, but it puts them within the larger context of the discourse itself, with all of its communicative references and intents, as well as means of expression.

Context of Culture	
Context of Situation	
Discourse	Discourse Analysis
Sub-Discourse Unit	
Paragraph	
Clause Complex	Functionalist Translation
Clause	Dynamic/Functional Equivalence Translation
___Word Group___	Literal/Formal Equivalence Translation
Word	
Morphology	

Relevance Theory Translation

Relevance theory grows out of a critique of two major notions. The first is the code theory of language. Sperber and Wilson[35] contend that the code theory of language does not satisfactorily answer the question of how communication takes place, since there remains an unbridgeable gap between linguistic expression and meaning. This is especially seen when individual sentences are examined outside of a particular context. For example, in the sentence "I will see her next Thursday," Sperber and Wilson would say that

---

35. D. Sperber and D. Wilson, *Relevance: Communication and Cognition* (2nd ed.; Oxford: Blackwell, 1995).

Assessing Translation Theory

the general semantic sense of "I" as including a singular speaker does not provide adequate information that can be gained only by knowing the "I" in a specific context. The same can be said of "her." The reference to "next Thursday" only communicates if one knows what day it is today, rather than simply knowing that Thursday is the day after Wednesday. Even when the notion of inference is included, they believe that communication cannot be adequately accounted for. It is fair to say that a code theory of language has clearly dominated both major forms of translational theory, the formalist and the dynamic equivalence models. Instead, Sperber and Wilson believe that language always invokes much beyond the words themselves, and as a result they look to a cognitive model of communication to develop the notion of inference further. This results in their second critique, that of Paul Grice's implicatures of conversation.[36]

A number of trenchant criticisms have been brought to bear on Grice's maxims. The first is that it has been shown that Grice's implicatures are probably particularly well suited to English, because they emphasize brevity, sincerity, and relevance.[37] These are not necessarily the same values that are emphasized in conversation in all cultures, whether ancient or modern. The second is that some implicatures have been shown to be of less pertinence or content when they are examined more closely. Included in these would be the criterion of the "maxim of relation," which was subject to subjective analysis based on intuition, rather than objective analysis.[38] As a result, Sperber and Wilson developed their reassessment of Grice in terms of the notion of ostensive-inferential communication, working within the overarching notion of relevance. Ostention and inference make clear that certain information is being put forward as constituting the assumptions for communication. This is then evaluated in terms of relevance.

Relevance theory would be concerned with the amount of information that is put forward and its degree of relevance to the parable account. The use of the word rendered "certain one" in some of the translations would possibly suggest the abstract and hence potentially fictitious account, in which the specific character is not named. However, Lazarus is

---

36. P. Grice, "Logic and Conversation," repr. in *Studies in the Way of Words* (Cambridge, MA: Harvard University Press, 1989), 22-40.
37. Baker, *In Other Words*, 237.
38. Baker, *In Other Words*, 236, citing Sperber and Wilson, *Relevance*, 36.

named, which raises questions about the relevance of this naming and speculation regarding the factuality of the account. If this is a parable, this might well be an instance in which the ancient storyteller went beyond what might be considered relevant by today's interpretive standards. The details that are given regarding the two men are seen to be relevant through their creation of a stark contrast between them. The one man is dressed in the best clothing and enjoys life to the fullest every day. The phrase "every day" is particularly relevant. This is in contrast to the other man, named (perhaps it is significant that he has a name even though he is in dire straits), who is poor and begging at the other's door, full of sores.

Relevance theory itself, however, is not a theory of translation, but a theory of cognition, especially regarding language. It is in the work of Ernst-August Gutt that the theories of Sperber and Wilson have been applied directly to the area of translation. As Gutt states, "The central claim of relevance theory is that human communication crucially creates an expectation of optimal relevance, that is, an expectation on the part of the hearer that his attempt at interpretation will yield *adequate contextual effects at minimal processing cost*."[39] The basic principles here are that there should be maximal understanding with minimal effort on the part of the hearer. Further, when a reader engages in more effort, the expectation is that there will be a commensurably larger amount of understanding to warrant the effort. Otherwise, material that is not relevant is being processed. Mojola and Wendland use the CEV as an example[40] — not because it was written with relevance translation theory in mind, but because it was done in an effort to minimize processing and maximize understanding. The CEV goes further than even the GNT in its rendering of the opening of the parable: "There was once a rich man who wore expensive clothes and every day ate the best food. But a poor beggar named Lazarus was brought to the gate of the rich man's house." The use of "once" probably replaces "certain" in the other translations. It is more than a word-for-word substitution, but it is at the level of the clause, changing an element of a nominative phrase into an adjunct. The reference to lying at the rich man's door appears at the end of the verse in the CEV, as in the GNT. In the CEV,

---

39. E. A. Gutt, *Translation and Relevance: Cognition and Context* (Oxford: Blackwell, 1991), 20, cited in Mojola and Wendland, "Scripture Translation," 20-21. See also E. A. Gutt, *Relevance Theory: A Guide to Successful Communication in Translation* (Dallas: Summer Institute of Linguistics, 1992).

40. Mojola and Wendland, "Scripture Translation," 21.

one notices that there is no reference to the man having sores in v. 20. This phrasing is moved to v. 21, which reads: "He was happy just to eat the scraps that fell from the rich man's table. His body was covered with sores, and dogs kept coming up to lick them." A number of features of the CEV clearly are made in terms of optimizing relevance in terms of a given context of situation of the parable.

Context of Culture	
Context of Situation	Relevance Theory
Discourse	Discourse Analysis
Sub-Discourse Unit	
Paragraph	
Clause Complex	Functionalist Translation
Clause	Dynamic/Functional Equivalence Translation
___Word Group___	Literal/Formal Equivalence Translation
Word	
Morphology	

Descriptivist Approach

The descriptivist approach to Bible translation is concerned with describing the specific cultural context of a translation, rather than prescribing what such a translation should be like.[41] Their approach to some extent grows out of the debate over the nature of literary translation in terms of its source and receiver cultures. Descriptivists view the predominant models of translation — formalist and dynamic equivalence — as prescriptive, in that they are concerned to formulate rules and guidelines to guide translation, as well as developing practical means by which translators can learn to perform their task. Instead, a descriptivist approach, again in some ways dependent upon a systemic-functional model of linguistics, as are several of the methods noted above, is concerned with the general principles that govern translation and how these general principles are manifested. In that sense, they have been described as being more concerned with the "product" than with the "process" of translation. In the

---

41. I am dependent here upon Mojola and Wendland, "Scripture Translation," 17-19. See also Munday, *Translation Studies*, 119-21, cf. 108-19.

words of Hermans, one of the advocates of the approach, descriptivists are much more concerned with theory than with activity and have a

> view of literature as a complex and dynamic system; a conviction that there should be a continual interplay between theoretical models and practical case studies; an approach to literary translation which is descriptive, target-oriented, functional and systemic; and an interest in the norms and constraints that govern the production and reception of translations, in the relation between translation and other types of text processing, and in the place and role of translations both within a given literature and in the interaction between literatures.[42]

The major issue with literary translations is not the question of what constitutes literature per se, but how the text is perceived within different cultures. That something is seen as literature is based upon the culture in which it is found, not on any inherent features. Whereas there may or may not be a text in the source language that is a literary language, by virtue of translation virtually any text is going to be seen as a literary text in a receptor culture and thus be expected to follow the patterns of similar literary texts within that culture. It is this reception that establishes the guidelines for a given translation.

A descriptivist approach would want to begin by asking questions about the literary quality of the translation, especially in terms of the available literary types. The KJV and translations that follow its practice of indicating genre with standardized introductory renderings would probably be labeled as sacrificing the literary quality of the receptor text for an admittedly rigid integrity of the source text. The descriptivist would want to evaluate a translation on the basis of its literary function in the receptor culture. Such an evaluation would include assessment of the choice of words to describe the two characters of the parable. Language regarding being dressed in purple and fine linen would need to be scrutinized.

Like several of the methods noted above, but perhaps more than most, the descriptivist approach is less an approach to translation than it is

---

42. T. Hermans, *Translation in Systems — Descriptive and System-oriented Approaches Explained* (Manchester: St. Jerome, 1999), 32, cited in Mojola and Wendland, "Scripture Translation," 17-18.

an attempt to describe the context in which translation occurs.[43] It certainly draws heavily upon the context of culture, but it functions within the context of situation in which the source text is rendered into the receptor language. Its descriptive characteristics are less a method of translation than a model for evaluating translations within their specific contexts of situation.

Context of Culture
Context of Situation   Relevance Theory; Descriptivist Approach
Discourse   Discourse Analysis
Sub-Discourse Unit
Paragraph
Clause Complex   Functionalist Translation
Clause   Dynamic/Functional Equivalence Translation
___Word Group___   Literal/Formal Equivalence Translation
Word
Morphology

Cultural/Postcolonial Theory

Cultural ideology can and does play a role in most kinds of translation.[44] However, this factor has not often been noticed. A number of models of translation — including the literalist and dynamic equivalence models — purport to be objectivist translational methods, but there are subjective factors involved. In recent years, there has been a backlash against both particular kinds of translations and the translation process itself.

Lawrence Venuti has specifically criticized the dynamic equivalence model of Nida from an ideological point of view.[45] It strikes some as odd in

---

43. See the essay by Alain Gignac in this volume, on the *Bible, nouvelle traduction*, 146-66.

44. See Hatim and Mason, *Discourse*, 143. I put here what Mojola and Wendland, "Scripture Translation," 24-25, label as foreignization versus domestication. See also Munday, *Translation Studies*, 126-61.

45. L. Venuti, *The Translator's Invisibility: A History of Translation* (London: Routledge, 1995); cf. also his *The Scandals of Translation: Towards an Ethics of Difference* (London: Routledge, 1998). See also S. Bassnett, *Translation Studies* (rev. ed.; London: Routledge, 1991); and S. Bassnett and H. Trivedi, eds., *Post-Colonial Translation: Theory and Practice* (London: Routledge, 1999).

the light of Nida's own cross-cultural experience and anthropological background that his program of translation is seen by some[46] to impose a cultural hegemony of the receptor language, since the translation is meant to be a fluent and fully comprehensible rendering in the receptor language — while neglecting the character and context of the original.[47] In addressing the issue of culture in terms of the receptor language, Venuti argues for foreignizing translations that restrain what he calls "the ethnocentric violence of translation," which attempts to exert hegemonic control over the translated text.[48] He sees this in Anglo-American culture and translational practice, which he claims is dominated by "domesticating theories" of translation that strive to produce fluent translations, but in which an "illusion of transparency" hides the fact that the translation is a "partial interpretation."[49] He contends that Nida's emphasis upon "naturalness of expression"[50] involves domestication, such that unrecognizable source-language features are replaced by those in the target language.[51] When Nida argues for accuracy in translation, Venuti claims, he is arguing for creating the same effect in the target-language readers as was produced in the source-language readers. In other words, the differences in language and culture that separate the two are overcome by forcing the one to submit to the other. Venuti argues, however, that this creates a translation that enshrines "target-language cultural values while veiling this domestication in the transparency evoked by a fluent strategy."[52] He goes further and claims that Nida does not take into account "the ethnocentric violence that is inherent in every translation process."[53]

Venuti attributes Nida's position to several factors. One of these is what he claims is his "transcendental concept of humanity as an essence that remains unchanged over time and space."[54] He recognizes that this is related to what he labels Nida's Christian evangelism and cultural elitism.

---

46. E.g., Venuti, *Invisibility*, 21-23.
47. See J. M. Watt, "Eugene A. Nida's Contributions to Sociolinguistics," *BT* 56, no. 1 (2005): 19-29.
48. Venuti, *Invisibility*, 20.
49. Venuti, *Invisibility*, 21.
50. Nida, *Science*, 159.
51. Venuti, *Invisibility*, 21.
52. Venuti, *Invisibility*, 22.
53. Venuti, *Invisibility*, 22.
54. Venuti, *Invisibility*, 22; cf. Nida, *Science*, 2.

Assessing Translation Theory

Venuti sees these as going together, in that Nida wants to promote a translated text that is "centred in Christian dogma" and that "seeks to impose" a "specific dialect of English as well as a distinctly Christian understanding of the Bible."[55]

Venuti's solution is a foreignizing translation that, while not free from its own cultural political agendas, "resists dominant target-language cultural values so as to signify the linguistic and cultural difference of the foreign text."[56] Even if one were to change the rendering of a particular problematic word in a translation by Nida, according to Venuti, one has not addressed the issues that have been raised. According to Venuti, Nida creates a partial translation — but that could be argued for any translation, admittedly including the kind of foreignizing translation for which Venuti argues. Venuti recognizes that there are ideological and cultural (read also political) issues at stake in such a debate.[57] Venuti is not suggesting a corrective that argues for a theory-neutral or value-free translational model. There is not only a recognition that Nida's model is not neutral, but an outright acknowledgment and endorsement of a competing ideology.

The translation process itself has also been the target of much postcolonialist theory, and translation is often held up for criticism.[58] The basis for such criticism is that translation never occurs without a particular context but, to the contrary, is linked to the notions of empire, power, wealth, cultural domination, colonialization, indoctrination, and dilution of native cultures. Translations are made by those in the ascendancy at the expense of others. Thus, translation becomes an insidious tool of those who wish to extend their power and influence and dominate those who are unable to resist. The result is that translations do much more than simply render a text into the language of an indigenous people; translations become the tools of domination by others, since the translations themselves end up reflecting the assumptions and biases of the dominant culture. Rather than simply communicating with those with whom they have contact, those who sponsor the translation end up helping to perpetuate their domination through the translation itself. This is supposedly seen to be at its worst in terms of

---

55. Venuti, *Invisibility*, 23.

56. Venuti, *Invisibility*, 23; cf. L. Venuti, ed., *Rethinking Translation: Discourse, Subjectivity, Ideology* (London: Routledge, 1992).

57. See also, e.g., P. Zlateva, ed., *Translation as Social Action: Russian and Bulgarian Perspectives* (London: Routledge, 1993).

58. Mojola and Wendland, "Scripture Translation," 22-23.

Christianity using translation as a means of evangelizing, for the purpose of conversion, those for whom the translation is accomplished. The problem is not so much that there may be individual translational choices that are questionable when specifics are examined; from a postcolonial theoretical standpoint the problem is the much larger one that translation is taking place from a particular standpoint or viewpoint.

A postcolonial or ideological translation would need to address several issues. One is the set of cultural values reflected in the parable. The contrast of rich and poor might be suspect, as is the kind of work ethic displayed, and the types of people who populate the establishment, even if no one else cares. The standard scenario of the rich having power over the poor has been with us for some time, but it is thwarted in this story by the rich man being condemned, while the poor man is triumphant. J. B. Phillips's translation was made before the rise of postcolonial theory, but its origins in providing a translation for the disenfranchised youth of a depressed Britain reveal a similar orientation. This is perhaps why Phillips labels the parable of Luke 16:19-31 as "Jesus shows the fearful consequence of social injustice." His translation, though earlier, has similarities with the GNT and CEV.

Context of Culture	Cultural/Postcolonial Theory
Context of Situation	Relevance Theory; Descriptivist Approach
Discourse	Discourse Analysis
Sub-Discourse Unit	
Paragraph	
Clause Complex	Functionalist Translation
Clause	Dynamic/Functional Equivalence Translation
___Word Group___	Literal/Formal Equivalence Translation
Word	
Morphology	

Areas of Need for Translation Theory

A number of observations may be made regarding areas of need in translation theory. The first concerns criticism of the particular methods of translation noted above. Once such limitations are recognized, there are, secondly, areas in which further research in translation theory is needed.

Each of the perspectives above may legitimately be criticized. I have space here only to name a few general points.

Literalistic translation tends to lose sight of meaning in maintenance of form and preserves religious-sounding language long after it has lost its immediacy. There is often an unjust level of standardization that loses sight of contextual meaning, since the focus is upon the word group as the primary translational unit.

The dynamic or functional equivalence approach moves the level of discussion to the level of the clause complex, but fails to move explicitly to larger units beyond the clause. The emphasis upon the translation of meaning as found in the source language, when the translational unit is the clause, still tends to be limited and to lose sight of larger meaning units. The tendency is to neglect and overlook difficulties in the source text in an effort to create a readily understood receptor text. There is also a tendency to over-objectivize the translational process, when the unit of translational equivalence is limited to the clause.

The functionalist approach provides a more comprehensive model, but to date it, too, has found it difficult to move beyond the clause complex or sentence. There are some trans-sentential elements noted in some later developments, but the clause or clause complex still seems to be the largest unit of translational equivalence. The functionalist approach shifts emphasis from the source to the receptor language, but a fragmentation in method occurs, since translational equivalence is seen in terms of various levels of translation.

The discourse analytic method continues the move in the right direction so far as units of analysis are concerned, with attention rightly paid to the entire discourse. Like most discourse methods, however, this one suffers from a surfeit of data without a comprehensive means of coordinating the results. The discourse method is dependent upon other forms of linguistic analysis, and hence it is subject to some of the same limitations as the methods noted above.

The limitations of relevance theory itself are also those of relevance-theory-based translation. The theory is better at explaining after the fact how a given element is relevant, and explaining the relationship between processing effort and meaning, than it is in developing a method by which translations should be created. Again, this approach is dependent upon the results of other methods of translation when it comes to performing the translational task itself.

The descriptivist approach helps to take context, whether of situation or culture, into account, but its descriptive nature limits its procedural benefit. The recognition of the role of context, especially in terms of the literary characteristics of a translation, verges on being a truism at this stage in translational analysis, especially since the method is not designed to create translations but to examine the factors that go into recognition of a literary translation in the receptor language.

Lastly, cultural or postcolonial theorizing regarding translation, while certainly bringing the context of culture to the forefront and the recognition that sensitivity to the original text and twenty-first-century worldview are different things, does little to aid in analysis and the creation of translations. Those like Venuti acknowledge that they have no particular translational choice that they wish to criticize; rather, they are simply not happy with the attempt to make the translation not sound like a translation, that is, to lose its foreign element in the process of domestication. Those who criticize translations for their ideological framework often fall into the trap of criticizing Christianity itself for its use of translations as a form of evangelism. The criticism of translation is blurred by the rejection of the claims of Christianity as an evangelistic and missionary religion and in their minds renders much of the linguistic effort as without foundation once these elements are removed. Thus, some of these methods hold out more promise than others in terms of utilization in translation itself.

The areas in which there is still need of further analysis are several. One is the recognition that we must move beyond the simple disjunction between literalistic and dynamic equivalence translation. For so long, the standard discussion has weighed and debated only these two options for describing and characterizing translational practice. These two code-based models are perhaps worth comparing, but even they do not speak to the same level of analysis. Literalistic translation addresses the word group, and hence it is bound to remain unidiomatic to the point of not being expressive of meaning, since the word group does not involve sentential syntax. However, dynamic equivalence only moves to the clause, still restricting meaning to a rather narrow set of configurations. The first stage is therefore to recognize the limitations of these two models, in terms of both their internal limitations and their limitations with regard to each other and the rank structure of language.

A second area for further analysis is the recognition and development of appropriate translational tools to move beyond the clause to the full discourse. As has been noted above, virtually all of the models that move to the discourse level or further also address the issue of context, whether of situation or of culture, or both. This move to the level of discourse and beyond opens up a whole new range of tools for exploration in translation. These especially include matters of pragmatic theory, which traditionally have not been considered in translational theory. However, this move also raises the question that has often been raised in linguistic circles regarding suitable criteria for analysis of super-sentential levels of usage. Whereas one can describe the syntax of the clause, even of the clause complex, there are no similar structural criteria for analysis of the sub-paragraph or paragraph. Some posit that there is no such thing as syntax for units larger than the clause or sentence, while others believe that such a syntax awaits development. In any case, no consistent and coordinated criteria for the practice of translation using discourse analysis have been developed. The amount of data available when treating discourses has resulted in a set of possible methods garnered from other forms of linguistic analysis but without the kind of overall pattern to make such tools useful for actually producing translations.

A third area to note is that those methods that address such things as context of situation and context of culture, while providing a useful and potentially enlightening reminder regarding worldview and assumptions, have, at least to date, provided less in terms of the actual practice of translation. This is even, so far, true of relevance theory, since it relies upon the methods of traditional translational approaches. This is even more the case with such methods as cultural or postcolonial theory, where the issue is not individual renderings but the larger enterprise of what cultural baggage the very act of translation itself brings to the task.

What is needed is a coordinated method of translation theory that divides the task up in the way that the functionalist method does, but that extends the scope of translation practice beyond the clause complex to encompass the paragraph, discourse, and even context of situation and context of culture.

A Translation That Induces a Reading Experience: Narrativity, Intratextuality, Rhetorical Performance, and Galatians 1–2

Alain Gignac

> *Je m'étonne que si vite vous vous détourniez de celui qui vous a convoqués par la grâce de Jésus Christ, pour accueillir une annonce différente: il n'y en a pas d'autre. Il y a seulement des gens qui vous bouleversent et veulent dénaturer l'Annonce du Christ.*
>
> *Mais si nous-mêmes, si un messager venu du ciel se faisait porteur d'une annonce différente de celle que nous vous avons portée, qu'il soit anathème!*
>
> *Comme nous l'avons prédit, et aujourd'hui encore je vous le dis, si quelqu'un se fait porteur d'une annonce autre que celle que vous avez reçue, qu'il soit anathème!*
>
> *Écoutez maintenant: est-ce que je cherche à convaincre les hommes ou Dieu? Est-ce que je cherche à plaire aux hommes? Si je voulais encore plaire aux hommes, je ne serais plus l'esclave du Christ.*
>
> > *Sachez-le, en effet, mes frères,*
> > *l'Annonce dont j'ai été porteur n'est pas à la mesure de*

This essay is part of my research on *Filiation, engendrement, problématique du sujet. La lettre aux Galates comme laboratoire de théologie narrative et discursive,* funded by the Social Science and Humanities Research Council (SSHRC) of the Government of Canada. I would like to thank my research assistants Danielle Jodoin, Alain Bihan, and Clervaux Dessalines for their help. I am also grateful to Sybil Murray-Denis for translating this essay from the original French.

A Translation That Induces a Reading Experience

> *l'homme;*
> *ce n'est pas non plus de l'homme que je l'ai reçue ou apprise,*
> *mais par ce que Jésus Christ m'a dévoilé.*
>
> (Gal 1:6-12, *Bible, nouvelle traduction*)

Let me hasten to say that I consider myself quite inadequate as a translator. The hermeneutical challenge of translation leaves me in a state close to paralysis, perhaps because I am so keenly aware of all the demands and even paradoxes the task involves. I struggle with the Greek, then with the French; the text is defiant in its opaqueness. How can I express in the target language what I *fail* to understand in the source language? As I discern one trail of meaning in the text and then another, I feel its meaning slip away from me. Must I, paraphrasing Paul, cry out: "Wretched man that I am! Who will rescue me from this textual body?" (cf. Rom 7:24). But in another passage from Romans, I do find some consolation, since the text hints that what today is so hard to read and translate was, yesterday, just as painful and soul-rending to put into writing: "I am speaking in human terms because of your natural limitations" (Rom 6:19, NRSV). Paul might have added: ". . . and because of my own limitations."

Translation is an impossible task: it requires rendering, with clarity, an original text written in another language, while still paying homage to its obscurities. An intelligent translation must already feed on textual interpretation and yet still avoid being a preemptive interpretation of the text: the translator must make every effort to step back and leave the interpretive task up to the reader. The question is how to translate so as to induce a renewed and spiritually replenishing reading experience.

I am here confiding my reflections on translation as they emerge from two specific experiences. On the one hand, my teaching experience in exegesis leads me toward a more and more literary and synchronic approach. When the accent is placed on know-how (that is, knowing how to read) rather than on knowledge, I see that a close reading of the text, with its rough spots and its difficulties, is of more service to students than piles of encyclopedic knowledge of the Bible — knowledge liable to change considerably from one decade to the next. In other words, the presentation of very ingenious but always hypothetical reconstructions of the world *behind* the text is always secondary to the imperative of learning to inhabit

and explore the world of the text itself.¹ On the other hand, at the outset of
my university career I had the opportunity to participate in a very innovative translation project, initially called "Bible 21" (for the twenty-first century) and now known under the name *Bible, nouvelle traduction*. This was
a destabilizing and thus stimulating experience, and it is the one with
which I shall begin my exposé. I shall then present the conception of text
and reading that underlies my interpretation and thus my translation,
pleading in favor of a synchronic approach to the text (though, let it be
said once and for all, not to the exclusion of other methods). Thirdly, on
the basis of the example of Galatians 1 and 2, I shall outline how paying attention to the narrativity, intratextuality, and rhetorical performance embedded in the text can help us renew our understanding of the text and
thus our translation. In sum, starting from concrete experience, I next take
a somewhat theoretical stance and then return to the concrete reality of the
text.

Experience of *Bible, nouvelle traduction* (Bayard-Médiaspaul)

The French world, like the English world, has its shelves of biblical translations, three of which are particularly outstanding: *Bible de Jérusalem*
(1973), *Traduction œcuménique de la Bible* (TOB, 1972 for the NT) and
Segond (1975).² Except for a few superficial revisions, these Bibles date
from the 1970s and follow in the effervescent wake of Vatican II. Then, in
1995, Frédéric Boyer, Jean-Pierre Prévost, and Marc Sevin sowed the seeds
of a new translation project at the publishing houses of Bayard (France)
and Médiaspaul (Québec). The initial idea consisted in pairing an exegete
with a writer for each book of the Bible, so as to reflect the scientific movements of the past thirty years and the style of literary French in the early
twenty-first century. This was the first time a substantial team of Quebec
theologians would be associated with such a project and with its roster of
prestigious avant-garde writers (for example, Florence Delay of the

---

1. Here I agree with the remarks formulated by D. J. A. Clines, "The Postmodern Ad-
venture in Biblical Studies," in *Interpretation of the Bible: International Symposium on the Interpretation of the Bible, Ljubljana, Slovenia, 1996* (ed. J. Krasovec; Ljubljana: Slovenska
akademija znanosti in umetnosti, 1998), 1603-16.

2. J.-M. Auwers, ed., *La Bible en français: Guide des traductions courantes* (Connaître
la Bible 11-12; Brussels: Lumen vitae, 1999).

A Translation That Induces a Reading Experience

Académie française and Jean Echenoz, recipient of the Prix Goncourt). For my part, I was paired with the writer Marie Depussé and entrusted with the translation of the letters to the Romans and to the Galatians.[3]

When published in the fall of 2001, the Bible was the talk of the new literary season in France and Quebec. In the Paris metro, statistics told the tale: "20 writers/27 exegetes/73 books/3,200 pages/in 1 volume." On 650 Montreal buses, the public was solicited by this ad: "Still the same old story. The Bible better written than ever." Hardly the kind of thing you would expect to see in a secularized Quebec. A little anecdote: The launch was scheduled for the 12th of September. We all know what happened on the eve of that date. The Quebec poet Jacques Brault, invited to read an excerpt of his translation of the Apocalypse, chose Apocalypse 18, giving a universal and contemporary import to this passage — and showing that the Bible can be confiscated by various points of view. For the first time, a translation of the Bible was making the headlines, drawing media attention, and stirring debate.[4] The Bible became a bestseller at Costco. The first run of 150,000 copies was quickly sold out. But, once the dust settles, what, if anything, will this all add up to?

The *Bible, nouvelle traduction (BNT)* presents the text in a seamless flow, without titles or paragraphs, shifting all notes to the end of the volume and even moving the location of verses into the margins. The tone has been set: the Bible is *to be read* as a continuous text and not parceled out in pericopes. The style is vivid, the punctuation sparse, the layout often audacious — reflecting the traits of contemporary French poetry and prose.

---

3. M. Depussé and A. Gignac, "Lettre aux Romains (traduction)," in *Bible, nouvelle traduction* (ed. F. Boyer, J.-P. Prévost, and M. Sévin; Paris: Bayard; Montréal: Médiaspaul, 2001), 2475-502; "Lettre aux Galates (traduction)," in *Bible, nouvelle traduction*, 2554-61.

4. Survey of media attention: See C. David, "Une nouvelle traduction, pour quoi faire?" *Nouvel Observateur* 1921 (2001); N. Gueunier, "À propos de 'La Bible Bayard' dite 'Nouvelle Traduction,'" *Études* (Décembre 2001): 694-700; "La Bible, monument littéraire iconoclaste?" *L'Humanité* (18 Octobre 2001): 22; V. M. La Meslée, "La Bible, roman," *Le Point* 1512 (7 Septembre 2001); P. Lançon, "Dieu reconnaîtra les siens," *Libération* (6 Septembre 2001); J.-Y. Thériault, "Une réussite à apprivoiser," *Le Devoir* (3-4 Novembre 2001): D12. For more in-depth and scientific analyses, see Jean-Marie Auwers, "La Bible revisitée. À propos d'une nouvelle traduction de la Bible," *RTL* 32 (2001): 529-36; Michel Gourgues, "Étude critique. Le Nouveau Testament dans la nouvelle traduction de la Bible en français," *ScEs* 54 (2002): 205-23; Pierre Grelot, "À propos de la Bible Bayard. Une pluralité de regard," *Esprit et vie* 47 (2001): 3-14; Olivier-Thomas Venard, "La culture de la 'Bible Bayard,'" *Kephas* 1 (2002): 129-40, also available on the Web: ttp://www.revue-kephas.org/02/1/Venard129-140.html.

What we have is a translation that shakes off the stylistic uniformity of the *Bible de Jérusalem* or the pedagogical gloss of the *TOB* and sets out to "revive reading." Far more, the *BNT* resolutely sheds the traditional theological/ecclesiastical vocabulary that, often inherited from Latin and now worn thin with use, has become mere cant. This new translation reflects the Bible's stylistic, theological, and literary diversity, in something like an exploded view. The translation of each of its books must be examined individually, since there is nothing unifying the project as a whole. In sum, this is the Bible as it has never been read before.

In a manner similar to the legendary translation of the Septuagint,[5] each team of translators worked almost in isolation, but the collective work partakes of the same spirit (here, we should say of the same breath).[6] In retrospect, I realize that the *BNT* has banked on a synchronic approach to the text, giving full attention to its aesthetic aspect. The work of translation is an opportunity to enjoy a spiritual experience that progresses not solely through cognitive but also through emotional and aesthetic channels. How do we translate in such a way that the text bearing signs of divine revelation will again become a Penuel-like encounter?[7]

The future will confirm or invalidate the impact made by the *BNT*'s public reception. Some Catholic circles have sharply denounced it; others

---

5. According to legend, 72 sages (6 for each tribe of Israel), each working separately, are supposed to have translated the Torah in 72 days, with virtually the same result. We have two accounts of the translation of the Septuagint from Hebrew to Greek: (1) Philo of Alexandria ("De Vita Mosis," in *Oeuvres de Philon d'Alexandrie* [ed. R. Arnaldez, C. Mondésert, J. Pouilloux, and P. Savinel; Paris: Cerf, 1967], II:25-44), and (2) Aristeas (*Lettre d'Aristé à Philocrate* [ed. A. Pelletier; Sources chrétiennes 89; Paris: Cerf, 1962]).

6. Without really consulting each other, since all were free in their choice of words, all of the translations render πνεῦμα as *souffle* (breath) and not as *Esprit* (Spirit) — but it sounds better in French than in English.

7. See Gen 32:22-32, the story of Jacob's struggle: "So Jacob called the place Peniel, saying, 'For I have seen God face to face, and yet my life is preserved.' The sun rose upon him as he passed Penuel, limping because of his hip" (vv. 30-31). I use the image of encounter according to the French title (*Le texte de la rencontre: L'interprétation du Nouveau Testament comme écriture sainte* [trans. J.-C. Breton and D. Barrios-Auscher; Montréal: Fides, 1995]) of the translation of S. M. Schneiders, *The Revelatory Text: Interpreting the New Testament as Sacred Scripture* (San Francisco: Harper San Francisco, 1991). In Schneiders' book there are clear signs of Gadamer's influence; see H. G. Gadamer, *Vérité et méthode: les grandes lignes d'une herméneutique philosophiques* (trans. P. Fruchon, J. Grondin, and G. Merlio; L'Ordre philosophique; Paris: Seuil, 1996; *Truth and Method* [trans. J. C. Weinsheimer and D. G. Marshall; 2nd ed.; London: Sheed and Ward, 1989]; German original 1964).

A Translation That Induces a Reading Experience

have labeled it elitist (the Saint-Germain-des-Prés Bible); and others have seen it as the Bible for non-Christians. But, with this translation, all have been given the chance to reappropriate the Bible as a classic of Western culture. Can this translation be called (post)modern — with all the semantic ambiguity that this catch-all term conveys? To do so would be toying with provocation. Whatever the case may be, this is the first post-Wittgenstein and post-Saussure Bible, assuming there is anything to what has been called the "language revolution." Reading is no longer just decoding a text to find its message, but also consenting to be swept along by a surprising metaphor, to be swayed by the rhythm of a poem, to be held rapt by the plot of a story — in a relentless pursuit of the text's significations. "On the contemporary market of biblical translation, the *BNT* inhabits the core of the tension between the 'pole of the signified' (the world of the text) and the 'pole of the signifier' (the work on language), to take up Nicole Gueunier's useful distinction once more."[8] The result might seem strange: it is neither a literal nor a dynamic translation, the two extremes that usually frame the spectrum of classification. But it is a literary translation, sometimes quite literal, sometimes adaptive — always creative and attentive to the sonority of the language.

My "binomial" experience with Marie Depussé was *revelatory*. Together we sought to understand the meanderings of Paul's argumentative Greek, looking for just the right formula to remove the dust from the text. This agnostic writer showed me another facet of the text, a text to which she, of all persons, devoted a sacred reverence that would have edified many a Christian. It was a constant struggle, made up of much compromise — especially since we were not exactly at home in the same language (being from different sides of the Atlantic) and did not always share the same understanding of the text. It was a friendly struggle between the two of us and with the text — as my colleague sums it up in the biographical note she prepared for the launching of the Bible:

---

8. P. Lassave, *La traduction des alliances. Sociologie d'un événement culturel* (Paris: Centre d'Études Interdisciplinaires des Faits Religieux, École des Hautes Études en Sciences Sociales, 2003), 65 — the author cites N. Gueunier, "Une traduction biblique peut-elle encore aujourd'hui être littéraire?" in *La Bible en littérature: actes de colloque international de Metz (septembre 1994)* (ed. P.-M. Beaude; Paris: Éditions du Cerf; Metz: Université de Metz, 1997), 259-69. Lassave, since then, has published a restyled edition of his study: *Bible: La traduction des alliances: Enquête sur un événement littéraire* (Logiques sociales; Paris: L'Hormattan, 2005).

Striving to read a text afresh, by renouncing the ideologies we all accumulate along the way. Submitting to this text without passion. Meeting the text armed only with the tools of translation. The exegete/writer couple has met these demands. In these strange couplings, one member must inevitably get the best of the other, an exhausting affair for both. Whether a believer or not, the writer does not believe in the prior meaning of a word. The writer also knows that the meanings of words wear thin with use. He will seek their meaning in that series of sentences of which the text is composed.

In preparing the introduction to Romans, I wrote down a paragraph summing up my approach, but, owing to space/time constraints as well as the financial pressures that shaped the final product, this summary could not be published:

Our translation has been guided by a few intuitions. First of all, we wanted a fresh version of the text that would wake readers up, whether readers who believe they know the text or those approaching it for the first time. Give the reader a taste of its violent tone! So, to rediscover the power of the images, we avoided words such as *faith, gospel, glory, spirit, baptism, apostle* which are impregnated with two thousand years of interpretive efforts, often replacing them with *adherence (or faithfulness), message, splendour, breath, immersion, envoy*. We had to respond to a twofold challenge. On the one hand: respect the Greek text — its rhythm, its forcefulness, its syntactic breaks — but do so without twisting its clarity. (We often chose to keep the ambiguity, perceiving it as a springboard for rhetorical argumentation.) On the other hand: succeed in rendering the Greek into an elegant French whose resonance would guard against any literalism and thus enable readers to appreciate the text's literary aspect while also compelling them to reflect *on it*. For the sake of readability, we have not always translated the same Greek word by its French equivalent. This plays up the immediate context and mutes established intratextual echoes. Several Greek passives have been turned into pronominal constructions. The rather repetitive conjunctions of Greek have been variously translated to coincide with what we (as interpreters!) believe to be the progress and pace of the argumentation. The result is an intersection of two sets of compromises: those associated with the two challenges identified

A Translation That Induces a Reading Experience

above and those associated with the collaboration between a theologian and a writer, each with a different approach to and understanding of the text. We therefore wanted to leave the reader free to accompany the text off the well-beaten paths, not to say the ruts, of interpretation. This being said, translating necessarily brings the translator's understanding [of the text] into play. It is an illusion to believe that any translation can be absolutely transparent. The preceding remarks apply particularly to *Romans*.

After much trial and error, we came to a rather audacious decision. In Greek, the word πίστις covers several semantic fields, including that of faith, trust, faithfulness, and steadfastness. We tried, almost experimentally and to the greatest extent possible, to avoid using the word *faith*, for several reasons: first, because it narrows the semantic field and carries with it an intellectual connotation (belief); next, because it is weighted with the whole history of Christianity; finally, because it induces a false sense of security in the reader, a sort of double ignorance — we think we know what it is all about, whereas this can only be known at the end of the letter (and perhaps not even then!). We also opted for a subjective reading of the expression πίστις χριστοῦ (the faith lived by Christ), as opposed to the traditional objective understanding (faith seeking Christ). By cultivating surprise and playing on several registers at once, we took the risk of opening up the meaning:

> *Faith* is a movement which originates in the life, death, and resurrection of Jesus, recognized as Christ by his *faithfulness*, a movement by which they who hear this account of *faithfulness* decide to write out their own life in the wake of Christ's (see Gal 2:16; 2:20; and 3:22) and, thus, "requite His faith."[9]

A person is saved not by accomplishing the Law but by *adhering* to the saving acts of Jesus, to his person and to his example. Anyone who *adheres* with *trust* to this extraordinary Message is made alive by the same Breath that enlivens the risen Christ, and that person can then fulfill the requirements of the Law, which was only a teacher. In a note, I do warn readers about this pluri-vocal style, so that they will not be trapped by this

---

9. A. Gignac, "Introduction et notes de la Lettre aux Galates," in *Bible, nouvelle traduction*, 3052-54 (here 3053).

experimental approach but will always remember that *trust* in each case implies *adherence* and *faithfulness* and vice versa.[10]

Pierre Lassave, in his study of the *BNT*, sums up a paragraph analyzing our translation of Romans with these words: "Paul and his translators engage in a linguistic wrestling match — with losses and gains."[11]

What Is a Text? What Is Reading?

"Tell me how you define or describe a text or the act of reading it and I will tell you how you conceive interpretation." One of the sessions of my course in biblical hermeneutics (which treats various theories of interpretation) begins with this pastiche of a famous Spanish proverb.[12] There are several ways of understanding the reality of the text and the act of reading. Mine has been deeply influenced by Paul Ricoeur, who focuses attention on the text and the reader.[13]

What is a text? It is a living organism to be contemplated in its complexity and not a cadaver to be dissected.[14] The text, like a snowbound brook, begins to flow under the reader's gaze. Whoever attempts to seize its flow will catch only a few drops that slip off his fingers. But anyone who so desires can keep going back to drink from the brook. Or, etymologically speaking, the text is a *tissue* woven of multifarious threads,[15] something like a tapestry.[16] To translate is to deliver the reader a living organism.

---

10. Gignac, "Introduction et notes de la Lettre aux Galates," 3053 (note for Gal 3:14).

11. P. Lassave, *La traduction des alliances*, 59.

12. Quoted by Lord Chesterfield in a letter to his son: "Tell me whom you live with, and I will tell you who you are."

13. See, in particular, P. Ricoeur, "Qu'est-ce qu'un texte?" in *Du texte à l'action: Essais d'herméneutique II* (Paris: Seuil, 1986; article originally published in 1970), 137-59; "La fonction herméneutique de la distanciation," in *Du texte à l'action* (article originally published in 1975), 101-17; *La métaphore vive* (L'ordre philosophique; Paris: Seuil, 1975); *Temps et récit* (Points, essais; Paris: Seuil, 1985). English translations are available.

14. Stephen D. Moore, "How Jesus' Risen Body Became a Cadaver," in *The New Literary Criticism and the New Testament* (ed. E. S. Malbon and E. V. Mcknight; Sheffield: JSOT Press, 1994), 269-81.

15. See the interesting developments in W. G. Jeanrond, *Introduction à l'herméneutique théologique: Développement et signification* (trans. P.-L. Lesaffre; Cogitatio Fidei; Paris: Cerf, 1995; English 1991), 121-22.

16. The metaphor is used by B. Witherington III, *Paul's Narrative Thought World* (Louisville: Westminster John Knox, 1994), 1.

A Translation That Induces a Reading Experience

What is the act of reading? For Ricoeur it is an act of self-understanding in front of the text. The text comprises a structure of signification that allows the reader to draw meaning from it:[17] "the subject interpreting a text ends up in self-interpretation, gaining greater self-knowledge, another form of self-knowledge or even the first glimmer of self-knowledge."[18] The shortest human path to self-knowledge is this long detour through the text. Though Ricoeur explicitly rejects the analogy between reading and dialogue,[19] this analogy, so it seems to me, is not without relevance and can be useful in our reflection on translation. The text resists and challenges us, whereas *we* approach the text with our personal baggage, our presuppositions, and our questions. Out of all the text's possibilities we construct a meaning. To put it in negative terms, reading is not primarily the search for a meaning hidden, like a treasure, in the text, nor for a message to be decoded. Of course, like the farmer's sons in the Jean de Lafontaine fable, we dig up the soil of the text to find the treasure, but the very *act* of reading is an end in itself.

Reading is rather like a hike in a forest with dense underbrush. There are several trails, and each, whenever taken, reveals a new landscape. The reader finds a path. Reading one of Paul's letters is like trying to form the most coherent picture possible from a scattering of puzzle pieces. As the reading progresses, meaning is constructed from images, metaphors, and concepts that are often dark at first but then gradually grow clearer as the reader weaves correspondences and discerns the harmonics among them. For example, several major themes run through Galatians: the Law, justification, filiation, the Gospel, and the relation between slavery and freedom. But none of them can claim to exhaust the letter's content. A good translation will allow readers to make their own way through the text, without imposing a particular path upon them.[20]

---

17. Ricoeur, "Qu'est-ce qu'un texte?" 153.
18. Ricoeur, "Qu'est-ce qu'un texte?" 152.
19. Ricoeur, "Qu'est-ce qu'un texte?" 138-39.
20. Judge from the following paraphrase of Rom 3:25 proposed by Alfred Kuen, which a student has shown me: "Dieu l'a destiné d'avance à prendre sur lui la punition que méritaient nos péchés. En mourant sur sa croix sanglante, Jésus était la victime offerte pour nous en sacrifice qui nous purifie et nous rend la faveur divine [God predestined him to take on himself the punishment merited by our sins. By dying on his bloody cross, Jesus was the victim offered for us as a sacrifice which purifies us and returns us to divine favour]" (*Parole vivante: Transcription dynamique du Nouveau Testament* [Braine-l'Alleud, Belgium: Editeurs de littérature biblique, 2001]).

Now, this exploration of the textual world is a struggle that will not leave us unscathed; it will not always be easy. Reading is a transformative experience that goes along paths of pleasure and of asceticism:

> Paul's text is difficult, from several points of view. First of all, because of its style. The syntax is often heavy, complex. There are several incomplete sentences. Images are linked with little regard for coherence, sometimes as if by free association — one must never push the metaphors "into a corner." The text plays on the recurrence of certain verbal roots, usually impossible to render in translation — intratextual echoes, often several chapters apart, abound; several paragraphs are structured around word play. There are numerous biblical references to key passages in the Jewish Scriptures which are not as familiar to us as they were to 1st century readers.[21]

There is an obvious correspondence between these brief theoretical remarks and the *BNT* experiment described above as designed to "revive reading." Now, this view of the text and the reader turns the current paradigm for exegetical interpretation upside down. If, for Ricoeur, the referent of the text — that of which it speaks — is the reader, this implies recognition of a radical division between the author and his work, though in Ricoeur the author and his world do still remain in the background of the main plot involving the text and reader.[22] There is no denying that current mainstream English exegesis is investing the major share of its energies in reconstructions of the world *behind the text*. For example, Louis Martyn speaking of Galatians used to say that he wanted to listen to the letter as Christians in Galatia might have done in the first century.[23] Nanos's

---

21. A. Gignac, "Introduction et notes de la Lettre aux Romains," in *Bible, nouvelle traduction*, 3035-42 (here 3036).

22. Ricoeur does not rule out historical research but rather minimizes it. Historical reconstruction is useful, for "explaining more means understanding better," but it is only an additive to the principal task of interpretation, which consists in self-understanding through the text. The book co-authored with the historical/critical exegete André Lacocque illustrates that: reconstructions are very interesting, but the reading Ricoeur then proposes does not seem rooted in them. See A. Lacocque and P. Ricoeur, *Thinking Biblically: Exegetical and Hermeneutical Studies* (trans. D. Pellauer; Chicago/London: University of Chicago Press, 1998).

23. J. L. Martyn, *Galatians: A New Translation with Introduction and Commentary* (AB 33A; New York/Toronto: Doubleday, 1997), 42.

Galatians Debate is also symptomatic:²⁴ to understand the letter's structure, its biographical elements, or the issues motivating it, most studies look to extra-textual data as the organizing principle of the text. Understanding the text means going outside of the text. The text is thus forced into one or more of the rhetorical molds typical of antiquity, as handed down to us in extant school manuals. Biographical data from Galatians 1 and 2 are compared to other autobiographies of the period or to the chronological framework of Acts, or else fitted into the Greco-Roman sociohistorical framework. Finally, the attempt is made to identify the circumstances that may have given rise to the letter: on Paul's side, on the side of the "foolish Galatians," or on the side of those bringing them another gospel. Then, this attempt leads back to the letter itself.

A few warnings have, however, been sounded. According to Mark Seifrid, much more attention should be paid to the internal analysis of Paul's letters, which would be of "considerable virtue in keeping one's feet on the ground."²⁵ John Barclay had already been recommending the greatest rigor and prudence in what concerns the reconstruction of an Identikit portrait of Paul's opponents.²⁶ Finally, Beverly R. Gaventa has this to say:

> This weighty consensus [Gal 1–2 as apologetic] has virtually precluded examination of the purpose of Galatians 1 and 2 or their function in the letter as a whole.... Whatever their value, these approaches perpetuate the tendency to view Paul's personal narrative as divorced from his theological argument.²⁷

Without denying the importance of a historical-critical approach to the text, what I try to do instead is immerse myself in the Greek text, to steep myself in the world it fashions, and then to render this world to the reader. As an exegete, my intention is to visit the text as one would visit a monument. A cathedral exists, above all else, as architecture, lines of force,

---

24. M. D. Nanos, *The Galatians Debate: Contemporary Issues in Rhetorical and Historical Interpretation* (Peabody, MA: Hendrickson Publishers, 2002).
25. M. A. Seifrid, "Review of 'Nanos, *Galatians Debate*,'" *Trinity Journal* 25 (2004): 267-70.
26. J. M. G. Barclay, "Mirror-Reading a Polemical Letter: Galatians as a Test Case," *JSNT* 31 (1987): 73-93.
27. B. R. Gaventa, "Galatians 1 and 2: Autobiography as Paradigm," *NovT* 28 (1986): 309-26 (here 310 and 312).

a particular aesthetic, a theology in stone. At dawn, at noon, at twilight, it gives rise to a different experience. Surely, I *could* ask myself about its architect or wonder about the socio-economic conditions of its construction or the motives of its builders. But I have decided to question the text in its own existence as a coherent whole. Some European philosophers have made this synchronic choice with surprising but nonetheless refreshing results.[28] Why couldn't a theologian take the same path?

Observations in Galatians 1–2

The *BNT* experience shows that a translation born of compromise is never perfect and can always be improved. Revisiting the beginning of the Epistle to the Galatians, I would like, in this last section, to give a concrete illustration of what a synchronic approach could contribute to the translation process, especially as regards its focus on traces of rhetorical *elocutio*, on intratextual play, and on the letter's numerous narrative elements.

In the wake of Hans Dieter Betz, Galatians has been the ideal terrain for rhetorical analysis. The ensuing debate has been practically monopolized by the identification of rhetorical genre (forensic, deliberative, epideictic) and of the *dispositio* they entail. But little attention has been given to discovering in the letter those traces of *elocutio* which remind us that its discourse also sets a scene and gives a performance.[29] Paul shouts at the Galatians (1:6; 3:1, 15; 4:11; 6:1); swears (1:20); pronounces anathemas (1:8-9); declares his involvement by use of the first-person singular ("I say" — 1:9; 3:15, 17; 4:1; 5:2, 16; "I want" — 3:2; 4:20; etc.); and asks questions

28. I am thinking of Alain Badiou, Giorgio Agamben, Jacob Taubes, and Slavoj Zizek. See my article, "Taubes, Badiou, Agamben: Reception of Paul by Non-Christian Philosophers Today," in *Society of Biblical Literature 2002 Seminar Papers* (Atlanta: SBL, 2002), 74-110; republished in *Reading Romans with Contemporary Philosophers and Theologians* (ed. D. Odell-Scott; Romans through History and Culture Series 7; New York: Clark, 2007), 155-211.

29. Exceptions to the rule: P. J. J. Botha, "Letter Writing and Oral Communication in Antiquity: Suggested Implications for the Interpretation of Paul's Letter to the Galatians," *Scripture* 42 (1992): 17-34; J. D. Hester, "The Use and Influence of Rhetoric in Galatians," *TZ* 42 (1986): 137-46; Martyn, *Galatians*, 21 and 23: "The oral communication for which the letter is a substitute would have been an argumentative sermon preached in the context of a service of worship — and this rhetoric proves to be more revelatory and performative than hortatory and persuasive."

(1:10; 2:14, 17; 3:1, 2, 3, 5, 19, 21; 4:9, 15, 16, 21, 30; 5:7, 11; 6:14), questions to which he sometimes responds with his μὴ γένοιτο (2:17; 3:21; 6:14); etc. Translations are too often pale, flat, and still presented in conventional formats, whereas what is needed is some rendition of the fiery vigor of the style.

When translating Paul, it is particularly difficult to follow along with the subtleties of semantic cross-references within a single paragraph or even between two chapters that are quite far apart. Let's give a few examples. The interplay of prepositions presents a headache from the opening of the letter (I shall come back to this). Prefixes present a similar case: What is the difference in shade of meaning between παραλαμβάνω (1:9, 12) and ἀπολαμβάνω (4:5)? or between μεταστρέφω (1:7), ὑποστρέφω (1:17) and ἐπιστρέφω (4:9)? Conversely, is it significant that the prefix "meta" is repeated twice in two verses: μετατίθημι (1:6) and μεταστρέφω (1:7)? Certain images echo each other: Paul's race (2:2) in contrast to that of the Galatians (5:7); the grace that the letter reactivates (1:3; 6:18), that the Galatians have received (1:6), that they may lose (5:4), and upon which Paul's ministry is also founded (1:15; 2:9-21). The relationship between words of the same family is often no longer visible in the target language, words such as "evangelize" (εὐαγγελίζω; 1:8, 9, 11, 16, 23; 4:13), "extraordinary message" (εὐαγγέλιον; 1:6, 7, 11; 2:2, 5, 7, 14), "promise" (ἐπαγγελία; 3:14, 16, 17, 18, 21, 22, 29; 4:23, 28) and "angel" (ἄγγελος; 1:8; 3:19; 4:14)! Or again, some puns are hard to translate, such as the quadruple occurrence of the verb δοκέω (2:2, 6, 9). Sometimes, the intratextual link is quite subtle: Paul speaks of himself as an apostle (ἀπόστολος; 1:1) and as set apart by God (ἀφορίζω 1:15); now, in 2:12, he speaks of Peter in similar words: ὑποστέλλω and ἀφορίζω; he thus poses Peter as his antithesis.[30] All these subtleties are stumbling blocks for translators.

Though Pauline texts do not, strictly speaking, present themselves as narratives, they abound in narrative elements, not only beneath the text, as one current research trend suggests,[31] but well and truly in the

---

30. In French this could be rendered: "moi Paul, je suis un *envoyé*, *isolé* par Dieu; lui Pierre, il s'est *fourvoyé* et *isolé* à Antioche (I, Paul, am called, set apart by God; Peter, withdrew and held himself aloof at Antioch)."

31. According to this trend in Pauline studies, which follows in the wake of R. B. Hays — whose 1983 thesis has been recently reedited: *The Faith of Jesus Christ: The Narrative Substructure of Galatians 3:1–4:11* (Biblical Resource Series; Grand Rapids: Eerdmans; Dearborn: Dove Booksellers, 2002) — the argumentation of the letters, it would seem, brings out the

text. The discourse puts characters on the stage, in a space and time setting. Furthermore, the narrative character of some sections of the letters (including Galatians 1 and 2) are even more obvious, as when the Pauline "I" gives an autobiographical account and enters the plot as a narrator involved in the story he is telling.[32] It is not a matter of asking whether or not the Pauline narrative is true to historical facts but rather of examining how the narrativization configures a new world where the notions of revelation, gospel, and apostle link up in a new way to become theology.[33] Thus:

- The text presents characters and makes them interact: Paul, the Galatians, those who preach another gospel (which is not really a gospel), the other apostles (including James and Peter), God, Jesus, the churches of Judea, etc. — these characters slowly take shape before our eyes, and we can classify them according to their importance and role in the story (protagonists, walk-ons, "ficelles").
- The text situates the characters in space: Paul in Judaism, in his mother's uterus, set apart, among the pagans, in Arabia, in Damascus, in Jerusalem, in Syria-Cilicia, in Antioch; the Galatians outside of this sinful world;[34] Christ in Paul (1:16; 2:20); Peter aloof; etc.
- The text first portrays the characters in a dualistic temporality, be-

---

meaning, the pattern, the theme *(dianoia)* of an earlier narrative *(mythos)* but one on which this argumentation is, at the same time, closely dependent. In other words, the text would presuppose a narrative infrastructure that perhaps occasionally rises to the surface of the argumentation. For an introduction to the debate, we would suggest: B. W. Longenecker, "Narrative Interest in the Study of Paul: Retrospective and Prospective," in *Narrative Dynamics in Paul: A Critical Assessment* (ed. B. W. Longenecker; Louisville: Westminster John Knox, 1994), 3-16.

32. In narratological analysis, we then speak of the homodiegetic narrator, according to the theoretical categories of G. Genette, *Figures III* (Paris: Éditions du Seuil, 1972); idem, *Nouveau discours du récit* (Poétique; Paris: Seuil, 1983).

33. For a more exhaustive presentation, see A. Gignac, "La gestion des personnages en Ga 1-2. Pour que les narrataires s'identifient au héros 'Paul,'" in *Et vous, qui dites-vous que je suis? La gestion des personnages dans les récits bibliques* (ed. P. Létourneau and M. Talbot; Sciences bibliques 16; Montréal, Médiaspaul, 2006), 203-28; "Intrigue, temporalité et spatialité en Ga 1-2. Comment la mise en récit fait-elle théologie?" in *Regards croisés sur la Bible: Études sur le point de vue* (Lectio Divina; Paris: Cerf, 2007), 419-38.

34. It would be more exact to speak of another character, "we," which is probably made up of Paul, the brothers with him, and the churches in Galatia.

fore and after the revelation of Jesus Christ (1:10, 13-15), then moves on with a succession of irenic encounters (after three years, after fourteen years) to end up with the *coup de théâtre* of an undated and conflictual encounter (with Peter in Antioch).
- The text brings into play several levels of narration: the first level of an "I" who speaks to the Galatians, a second level where the churches of Judea echo the narrative level 1 (1:23-24) and where Paul "tells" Peter about the transformation they have undergone, as Jews (2:14b-21).
- The text establishes a contrast between two transformations: the apocalyptic transformation experienced by "us" (1:4), by Paul and by Peter; the regressive transformation experienced by Peter and the people of James, which the Galatians are tempted to imitate.
- In fact, the story told is not that of the gospel (except in passing and in an oblique and laconic manner in 1:4), but that of preaching the gospel and of its effects.

This whole narrative mechanism (which functions differently in Galatians 3-6) operates a double-action identification process:[35] (1) Paul, though a Jew, joins in solidarity with the Galatians and champions their cause; (2) the Galatians must identify with the transformation experienced by Paul and not turn back. Thus the central affirmation of Gal 4:12: "Friends, I beg you, become as I am, for I also have become as you are" (NSRV).[36]

Rhetorical performance, intratextuality, and narrativity are not compartmentalized aspects of the discourse; instead, they intersect to form its structure and sometimes serve to highlight reading perspectives that would otherwise be left in the shadows. In closing I would like to describe two key theological motifs that appear little by little thanks to a synchronic approach: (1) a revelation without mediation and (2) extraction, condition of a new birth.

---

35. See the enlightening remarks of Paul E. Koptak, who, though he situates his work in Kenneth Burke's rhetorical line, has, to my mind, taken a narratological approach ("Rhetorical Identification in Paul's Autobiographical Narrative," *JSNT* 40 [1990]: 97-115).

36. This is the thesis of Gaventa, "Galatians 1 and 2."

ALAIN GIGNAC

Revelation without Mediation

Following the studies by James Louis Martyn, it is now acknowledged that the theological framework of Galatians is highly apocalyptic.[37] The apocalyptic setting generally presupposes a mediation between heaven and earth, between God and the seer (whether the latter remains on earth or is taken to heaven). It often involves an angel. Now, Galatians keeps vehemently affirming the absence of mediation, to the point of putting theology and the Law in peril: "Is the Law then opposed to the promises of God? Certainly not!" (Gal 3:21). If attention is paid to words with the root *αγγελ* and to the interplay of prepositions (δια, ἀπο, κατα, παρα), a correlation can be established between many "figures"[38] of transmission: the apostle's mission (1:1), the reception of the gospel by the Galatians (1:8; 4:14) and by Paul (1:11-12), and the gift of the Law to Israel (3:19-20):

Paul	1:1	ἀπόστολος οὐκ ἀπ' <u>ἀνθρώπων</u> οὐδὲ **δι'** <u>**ἀνθρώπου**</u> ἀλλὰ **διὰ 'Ιησοῦ Χριστοῦ** καὶ θεοῦ παρτὸς
	1:11-12	τὸ εὐαγγέλιον [. . .] οὐκ ἔστιν κατὰ <u>ἄνθρωπον</u>· οὐδὲ γὰρ ἐγὼ παρὰ <u>ἀνθρώπου</u> παρέλαβον αὐτὸ οὔτε ἐδιδάχθην ἀλλὰ **δι' ἀποκαλύψεως 'Ιησοῦ Χριστοῦ**.
Galatians	1:8	ἀλλὰ καὶ ἐὰν ἡμεῖς ἢ <u>ἄγγελος</u> ἐξ οὐρανοῦ εὐαγγελίζηται ὑμῖν
	4:14	ἀλλὰ ὡς <u>ἄγγελον</u> θεοῦ ἐδέξασθέ με, ὡς Χριστὸν 'Ιησοῦν
Israel	3:19-20	Τί οὖν ὁ νόμος; τῶν παραβάσεων χάριν προσετέθη, ἄχρις οὗ ἔλθῃ τὸ σπέρμα ᾧ ἐπήγγελται, διαταγεὶς **δι'**

---

37. Besides his commentary, see the essays collected in J. L. Martyn, *Theological Issues in the Letters of Paul* (Nashville: Abingdon, 1997). Martyn, in some ways, has filled in the piece missing in J. C. Beker, *Paul the Apostle: The Triumph of God in Life and Thought* (Philadelphia: Fortress, 1980).

38. I use "figure" in the sense of Greimassian semiotics: a signifier without direct or instantaneous signification. This signifier receives its signification from the association with other signifiers and is opened to a transformation in the process of the discourse. See D. Patte, *Structural Exegesis for New Testament Critics* (Guides to Biblical Scholarship, New Testament Series; Minneapolis: Fortress Press, 1990); A. J. Greimas and J. Courtés, *Sémiotique: dictionnaire raisonné de la théorie du langage* (Hachette université, Linguistique; Paris: Hachette, 1993).

A Translation That Induces a Reading Experience

ἀγγέλων ἐν χειρὶ μεσίτου. ὁ δὲ μεσίτης ἑνὸς οὐκ ἔστιν, ὁ δὲ θεὸς εἷς ἐστιν.

This correlation merits a few remarks.[39] First, any human or angelic mediation is excluded regarding the gospel's transmission, no matter which preposition is used: δια, ἀπο, κατα, or παρα (1:1, 11, 12; 3:19). Second, angelic mediation is devalued and brings about a devaluation of the Law in comparison to the Gospel (1:8; 3:19-20). Third, the question of number seems to be important: the oneness of God seems to exclude the plural as an agent of transmission — what comes from God can come neither from humans (1:1) nor from angels (3:19) — and even disqualifies the singular, when linked to the plural — no intervention from any human (1:1) nor from a mediator (3:20).[40] The text does, however, prompt us to temper the preceding remarks on the absence of mediation, giving rise to three other "counter-remarks." Fourth, according to whether one gives an objective or subjective meaning to the expression δι' ἀποκαλύψεως Ἰησοῦ Χριστοῦ (1:12) — linked also to the affirmation: ἀποκαλύψαι τὸν υἱὸν αὐτοῦ ἐν ἐμοί (1:16)[41] — it could be that in 1:1 and 1:12 Jesus Christ is being presented as mediator. Fifth, the narrative paradox created by the figure of the angel must be noted: the figure is negative in 1:8 and 3:19-20, but Paul applies it to himself in 4:14. Finally, sixth, some thought must also be given to the fact that the duality Jesus Christ/God the Father in verse 1:1 is not without causing some problems in the numerical logic stated in 3:19-20 (see above, remark 3).

In summary, the criteria for the evaluation of a good translation would be: Can the reader perceive the paradoxical statements concerning transmission in Galatians? Can she feel the impact of the mediation motif in the discourse?

---

39. Also see L. Panier, "Les marques d'énonciation dans l'épître aux Galates. Essai d'organisation et d'interprétation," in *Regards croisés sur l'Épître aux Galates* (ed. J.-P. Lémonon; Lyon: Profac, 2001), 123-36 (here 129). Strangely, Martyn does not pay much attention to the correlation or to the apocalyptic significance of "angel," even though the apocalyptic context is the key of his reading (see *Galatians*, 113 and 421).

40. Gal 3:20 is a stumbling block for any commentator.

41. Commentators diverge on this. For example, for Richard N. Longenecker, Jesus Christ reveals himself (*Galatians* [WBC 41; Dallas: Word Books, 1990], 24); whereas for Martyn (*Galatians*, 144), God reveals Jesus Christ.

ALAIN GIGNAC

Extraction, Condition of a New Birth

The themes of filiation and fathering are very noticeable in Galatians, and yet they are ignored by research. In Paul God reveals his *Son*, after having set Paul apart *from his mother's womb* (1:15), making him an apostle (1:1) so that Christ lives *in him* (2:20). God has sent his *Son, born of a woman* (4:4). Believers are *heirs* of Abraham from whom Christ is *descended*, by becoming *adoptive sons* of God (3:6-4:7). Paul describes himself as the mother of the Galatians, these *little children to whom he gives a second birth in suffering* until Christ is *formed in them* (4:19). To Paul's new apostolic identity corresponds that of those baptized in Christ: they are neither Jew nor Greek, slave nor free, man nor woman (cf. 3:28). This new identity corresponds to the division between two types of sons, the son of the free woman and the son of the slave woman (4:21-31), or to the division of a subject split between *the flesh and the spirit* (chs. 5-6). We have a *mother*, the Jerusalem from above (4:26). To be added to these few examples there is the question of *circumcision* and its relation to the Law (of the Father?), which runs through the whole argumentation.

In Galatians 1, we observe that the affirmation of the paternity of God with regard to Jesus (1:1), to "us" (1:4),[42] and to Paul (1:15) is always linked to the idea of separation, of leaving one space (the world of the dead, the actual sinful world, his mother's uterus) for an unnamed space beyond. This pattern is not devoid of a relation with the apocalyptic context previously evoked. Thus, we find another correlation:

Jesus   1:1   διὰ Ἰησοῦ Χριστοῦ καὶ θεοῦ <u>πατρὸς</u> τοῦ ἐγείραντος αὐτὸν **ἐκ** νεκρῶν

Us   1:4   ὅπως **ἐξέληται** ἡμᾶς **ἐκ** τοῦ αἰῶνος τοῦ ἐνεστῶτος πονηροῦ κατὰ τὸ θέλημα τοῦ θεοῦ καὶ <u>πατρὸς</u> ἡμῶν

Paul   1:15   Ὅτε δὲ εὐδόκησεν ὁ θεὸς ὁ ἀφορίσας με **ἐκ** κοιλίας <u>μητρός</u> μου

Paul's being set apart is not usually understood as being torn from his mother. The Greek ἐκ κοιλίας μητρός μου is generally translated as an idiomatic expression drawn from the Septuagint (through an intertextual

---

42. Here I develop an observation made by Panier, "Les marques d'énonciation," 131.

A Translation That Induces a Reading Experience

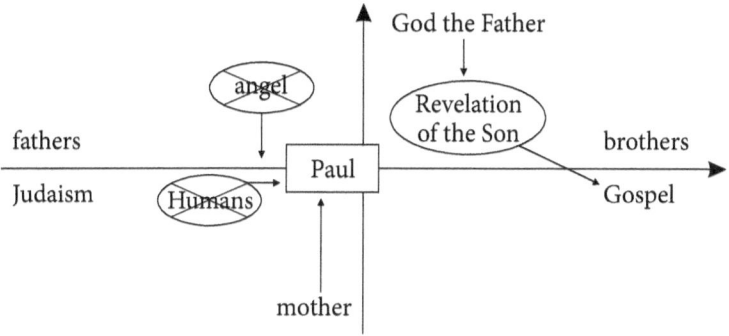

link with Jer 1:5 and Isa 49:1) that means "from my birth,"[43] or "from the time I was in my mother's womb." Now, the immediate context of the Pauline narrative uses words that also refer to birth: "immediately, without consulting flesh and blood" (1:16).[44] Risking for a moment a reading of the type "cesarean,"[45] the following working hypothesis could be formulated: the birth of "Paul" as a son of the Father coincides with a radical severance from his human moorings. He was extracted from his mother's womb; according to Gal 1:14, the revelation of the son in him also means a break with his fathers and the youth of his generation: "I advanced in Judaism beyond many among my people *of the same age*, for I was far more zealous for the traditions of my *ancestors* (τῶν πατρικῶν μου)" (NRSV). Again, a good translation should help the reader to see this correlation between the three "figures" of birth in Galatians 1, or at least should not hide it.

The figure at the top of this page sums up the observations concerning "mediation" and "extraction" in Galatians. Horizontally, Paul is moved on a trajectory from Judaism (of his fathers and of his peers) to the new fraternity of the gospel. Vertically, he is brought apart, severed from his mother, to receive directly from above the revelation of the Son that makes

---

43. Longenecker, *Galatians*, 30; NSRV: "But when God, who had set me apart *before I was born* . . ." (emphasis mine). It is impossible to follow the intratextual play of the preposition ἐκ.

44. The NRSV paraphrases: "I did not confer with any human being," obliterating the key image of flesh and blood and forgetting the chronological reference *at once* (εὐθέως).

45. Remember that in 1 Cor 15:8, when recounting the apparition from which he benefits, Paul also uses the semantic register of birth: "Last of all, as to one *untimely born*, he appeared also to me," literally: little runt, baby born dead.

165

him become a son. The gospel is not transmitted horizontally by human beings, nor vertically by angels, but only by God.

In sum, these few observations show that the translator must try not to betray the text and the reader, even to gain some apparent clarity. Here is the challenge: to render, in the target language, not so much the text's ideas as its images and semantic potentialities, so that readers can, in their own language, do the same work as they would on the Greek. What on one side remains an impossible objective must on the other side become a motivational ideal.

Conclusion

On the basis of my use of synchronic exegesis, my reflection on the theories of interpretation, and my participation in the *BNT* project — which I have in passing rather provocatively qualified as (post)modern — I have proposed that, in the translation process, emphasis should be placed on the text as fare for reading, with the intention of renewing the reading experience. How does one step back from ready-made, ready-to-think theologies and go about translating so that readers will encounter the text in all its newness and its transforming power? Galatians 1–2, with its narrative and rhetorical wealth, its network of intratextual cross-references, its metaphors and linguistic inventions, has allowed us to illustrate this perspective, which has its strengths and also its weaknesses.

En définitive, comme traducteur, j'espère seulement ne pas être trop réducteur.[46]

---

[46]. "When all is said and done, I only hope that, as a translator, I have not been too reductionist."

Hebrews 10:32-39 and the Agony of the Translator

Luke Timothy Johnson

When I was a very young man indeed, perhaps 15 years old, I was enchanted by Ronald Knox's translation of the Vulgate.[1] Knox may have been working in a version rather than in the original Hebrew and Greek, and he may not always have shown the greatest piety toward his source text, but he sure could write. I can still recall the majestic Anglo-Saxon alliteration in his rendering of 1 Sam 17:50: "Thus David slew the Philistine; with sling and stone he smote and slew him." Small wonder that I eventually found my way also to Knox's *Trials of a Translator,* in which he recounted some of the tribulations of his craft, one that at that time I had no thought of cultivating.[2]

I still can't claim to be a translator of Knox's formidable ability, even though I have managed to turn into some form of English a not insubstantial portion of the Greek New Testament: Luke and Acts, James, Paul's First and Second Letters to Timothy.[3] These translations were all done as the basis for commentaries. And as I struggled, *sans* committee and *sans* theory

---

1. *The Holy Bible: A Translation from the Latin Vulgate in the Light of the Hebrew and Greek Originals, Authorized by the Hierarchy of England and Wales and the Hierarchy of Scotland* (trans. R. A. Knox; New York: Sheed and Ward, 1950).

2. R. A. Knox, *Trials of a Translator* (New York: Sheed and Ward, 1949).

3. See L. T. Johnson, *The Gospel of Luke* (SP 3; Collegeville: Liturgical Press, 1991); idem, *The Acts of the Apostles* (SP 5; Collegeville: Liturgical Press, 1992); idem, *The Letter of James: A New Translation with Introduction and Commentary* (AB 37A; New York: Doubleday, 1995); idem, *The First and Second Letters to Timothy: A New Translation with Introduction and Commentary* (AB 35A; New York: Doubleday, 2001).

— with *nada* of Nida in my portfolio — I have grown more rather than less respectful of those whose entire endeavor is to translate the Sacred Word into words intelligible to the contemporary reader in every part of the globe, and keenly aware of how helpful a committee would be in discussing alternative renderings and bearing shared responsibility for the final and inevitably inadequate result.

The translator's trials have afflicted me most powerfully, however, over the past two years, as I have labored over a commentary on the Letter to the Hebrews for the Westminster/John Knox series, The New Testament Library.[4] Rarely in my scholarly life — one not lacking in humiliations — have I felt so consistently and depressingly incompetent as in my efforts to "English Hebrews" — to use another of Knox's phrases.[5] No need to elaborate on the reasons for regarding myself as incompetent; these are as obvious to me as they are to others. But Hebrews has a way of exposing the nerve-endings of even its best interpreters, much in the manner that it says God's living word lays bare human necks to the all-seeing God (4:12-13). No need either to expound at length all the challenges that Hebrews puts to the translator, but I can quickly state two interconnected factors that are obvious to us all and are assumed in this essay.

The first is the self-consciously rhetorical character of the composition: at the level of style, its diction, grammar, and syntax all reveal a more elevated form of *koine* than one meets elsewhere in the New Testament; at the level of invention, its choice of *pathos, ethos,* and *logos* arguments is impressive and sustained;[6] and at the level of arrangement, it impresses by its powerful alternation of exposition and exhortation, by its subtle manner of introducing and interweaving themes, and by its powerful movement toward resolution.[7]

---

4. This has now appeared as L. T. Johnson, *Hebrews: A Commentary* (NTL; Louisville: Westminster John Knox Press, 2006).

5. R. A. Knox, *On Englishing the Bible* (London: Burns and Oates, 1949).

6. The fullest display of these elements and the most consistent reading of the composition according to the standard rhetorical arrangement is found in C. R. Koester, *Hebrews: A New Translation with Introduction and Commentary* (AB 36; New York: Doubleday, 2001), especially pp. 87-92.

7. Although I think that Hebrews is better considered as deliberative rather than epideictic discourse, I agree with Harold Attridge that the most important rhetorical aspect of Hebrews is to be found in its invention rather than in its arrangement; see *The Epistle to the Hebrews: A Commentary on the Epistle to the Hebrews* (Hermeneia; Philadelphia: Fortress Press, 1989).

Hebrews 10:32-39 and the Agony of the Translator

The second is the strange way in which Hebrews is at once so isolated in terms of the conditions of its composition — we remain uncertain about its author, readers, date, and destination — and at the same time so intricately connected to the wider cultures of Hellenism and Judaism as well as the symbolic world of the nascent Christian movement.

To illustrate the ways in which Hebrews tests the translator, I have chosen in this presentation to consider a single passage, Heb 10:32-39. The passage serves within the overall argument as something of a transition, appearing immediately after the solemn warning against apostasy in 10:26-31 and immediately before the roll call of the heroes of faith in 11:1-40. The passage itself falls rather neatly into two parts as well, with the first lines recalling to the hearers their earlier days of endurance, and the last lines declaring the need for continuing in their endurance in order to obtain the promise.

In my comments, I will touch on specific points of grammar and syntax, but will focus particularly on the way in which intratextual and intertextual connections cause problems for the translator that defy easy solution.[8] As a warning against high expectations, I should note immediately that my own translation of Hebrews does not really solve any of these problems, either. But here it is:

> 10:32 But remember the earlier days when, after you were enlightened, you endured a great contest of sufferings. 33 You were both publicly shamed by revilings and afflictions, and you became partners of those who lived that way. 34 For you even shared the suffering of prisoners and you accepted the seizure of your property with joy, since you knew that you yourselves had a better and permanent possession. 35 So don't lose your confidence. It has a great reward. 36 For you need to have endurance, so that, by having done God's will, you might receive the promise. 37 Now, "yet a little while — he who comes will arrive and he will not delay, 38 and my righteous one will live from faith," and, "if he draws back, my soul will not be pleased with him." 39 But we do not draw back — to our destruction. Rather, we have faith — to the securing of our life.

---

8. I use these terms as described by V. K. Robbins, *The Tapestry of Early Christian Discourse: Rhetoric, Society and Ideology* (London: Routledge and Kegan Paul, 1996).

The Significance of a Participle

I begin with the problem created by the participle *phōtisthentes* in 10:32. As a predicative participle it functions adverbially to define the circumstances attendant on the main verb *hypemeinate* ("you endured"). The aorist indicates time prior to the main verb, the passive voice an action received by the hearers rather than done by them. The verb from which the participle is formed, *phōtizein* ("to illumine, enlighten"), appears earlier in the composition in the same participial form, among other expressions that clearly allude to the hearers' initial experience of entry into the community (6:4), so that we may legitimately take the circumstance to be their experience of conversion or baptism (see also Eph 5:8-14). So far, so good.

But now, two questions arise. Should the participle be translated more strictly as "having been illumined, enlightened," or more broadly as "having been converted/baptized" or even "having entered the community"? In favor of the narrower rendering is the fact that the author has, immediately before this, spoken of their earlier condition as "having received the recognition of the truth" (10:26). Thus, the translation "having been enlightened" makes good contextual sense. On the other side, the point here does not seem so much to be the hearers' state of cognition or awareness as to be their initiation into the community. This dilemma, in turn, points to a more serious issue concerning the translation of the participle, namely its relation to the main clause. Is the link only temporal — this happened and then that happened — or does the author want to indicate another sort of connection between circumstance and action? The circumstantial participle, we know, can express a number of such relations, ranging from concession to cause to purpose. Here, it could well express a causal relationship. It is precisely *because* they had been enlightened, that is, entered the community, that they were exposed to dangers. Their suffering is a consequence of their commitment rather than simply a circumstance that followed their commitment.

The Merging of Metaphors

The same sentence contains another challenge, this time connected to a second and more pervasive metaphor than enlightenment. The author states that they have endured a *pollēn athlēsin pathēmatōn*. The phrase poses two difficulties. The first is that no English term adequately captures the meaning of the Greek *athlēsis*. With other translators, I have rendered it as "contest," but in contemporary culture, that could refer to anything from a lottery or poker game to a quiz show. The noun "competition" would come closer to the Greek, but might mislead by suggesting rivalry among the readers or between readers and outsiders. The real difficulty is that this single word suggests one of the most important metaphors in the composition, namely THE LIFE OF FAITH = OLYMPIC GAMES.[9] The metaphor is itself complex in structure, because in Greek culture, athletic games — and the training for such games — had already served as metaphor for moral education. Actually, this is a metaphoric field in which tenor and vehicle merge, since the gymnasium was the locus for both bodily training (carried out through exercise) and mental and moral education (carried out through the reading of poets and philosophers). Hebrews reintroduces the metaphor in 12:1-4, at the climax of the roll call of faith, when the writer invites his readers to strip themselves of every encumbrance and "look to Jesus," the pioneer and perfecter of faith, as one who runs ahead of them in a great race that is viewed by a great cloud of witnesses. And he elaborates the metaphor in 12:5-13, when he reminds his hearers that they "are enduring for the sake of an education" when they receive instruction/discipline from God as Father. It is impossible for any English term — or any combination of terms — to capture either the metaphorical weight or the intratextual allusions of *athlēsis*.

Translation of the phrase is made even harder, however, by the genitive *pathēmatōn* (literally, "of sufferings"). The genitive serves to characterize the contest or struggle. It was not simply accompanied by sufferings *(meta pathēmatōn)* but actually consisted in sufferings. The contest had to do with how they could deal with the sufferings that came upon them as a result of their confession of Christ, and their "enduring" *(hypemeinate)* marks their success in the contest. They did not fall away or leave the game. They stayed the course. But there is a deeper resonance to this phrase that is impossible to capture by translation, namely the role the author has assigned to suffering in the process of education in genuine son-

9. For background to the metaphor, see V. C. Pfitzner, *Paul and the Agon Motif: Traditional Athletic Imagery in the Pauline Literature* (NovTSup 16; Leiden: Brill, 1967), especially 1-75; for the application specifically to Hebrews, see N. C. Croy, *Endurance in Suffering: Hebrews 12:1-13 in Its Rhetorical, Religious, and Philosophical Context* (SNTSMS 98; Cambridge: Cambridge University Press, 1998).

ship. This theme is struck first in 5:7-9, when the author declares that although Jesus was a son he learned obedience from the things he suffered. As all commentators recognize, the phrase *emathen aph' hōn epathen* echoes the proverbial Greek expression *mathein pathein*, "to learn is to suffer," which, once again, finds its home in the context of the educational world of the Hellenistic gymnasium. Jesus was to be perfected through the suffering that was obedient faith and endurance (2:10).[10]

Hebrews clearly does not mean only Jesus' passion and death, but the entire progression of his human existence, from the moment he came into the world crying "I have come to do your will, O God" (10:7), to the moment when, crying out with tears, he was heard because of his piety (5:7). The author understands Jesus' human obedience as an education in sonship, and he understands the discipleship of his hearers in exactly the same way. His exhortation to them to advance from childhood to maturity in 5:11-14 is therefore couched in terms of educational progress, as is his final exhortation in 12:5-13. The translator who is sensitive to these overlapping metaphorical fields and to their intratextual connections can only sigh in frustration at the phrase *pollēn athlēsin pathēmatōn* and at the difficulty of finding a rendition better than "great contest of sufferings."

The Sharing of Shame

The passage presents still another set of translation difficulties as it begins to spell out the nature of the sufferings the hearers of this discourse endured in their earlier days, first in more general (v. 33) and then in more specific terms (v. 34). The overall sense of 10:33 is clear enough: the hearers' great contest of sufferings has involved on one side *(touto men)* things that have been done to them, and on the other side *(touto de)* their association with others. What is difficult to communicate through translation are the cultural nuances of shame and fellowship, nuances that would have been obvious to the first hearers of this discourse, but which are not at all obvious to contemporary readers.

---

10. See C. H. Talbert, *Learning through Suffering: The Educational Value of Suffering in the New Testament and Its Milieu* (Zaccheus Studies; Collegeville: Liturgical Press, 1991), 1-23, 58-74; J. Coste, "Notion Grecque et Notion Biblique de la 'Souffrance Educatrice,'" *RSR* 43 (1955): 481-523.

One of the great advances in our knowledge of antiquity generally has been the recovery of the cultural importance of honor and shame in the ancient Mediterranean world,[11] and one of the great advances in the interpretation of Hebrews has been the recognition of how pervasively and powerfully it uses this register of language.[12]

Understanding the importance of the present passage for setting up the final hortatory section of the discourse, in turn, is enhanced by recognizing the presence of honor-shame language within it. In 12:1-2, the hearers are told to run the race that lies before them with endurance *(di' hypomonēs)*, as they "look to Jesus, the pioneer and perfecter of faith," who, for the sake of the joy that lay before him, endured a cross *(hypemeinen stauron)*, "despising [its] shame" *(aischynēs kataphronēsas)*. That exhortation gains specific meaning as the climax of the roll call of the heroes of faith in 11:1-40, and even more from the recognition that the hearers are themselves enduring shame because of their commitment to a messiah who died shamefully but is now "crowned with glory and honor" at the right hand of God (2:7-9; 12:2).

So, in describing the contest of sufferings they had earlier endured, the author chooses to use the participle *theatrizomenoi* in 10:33, a New Testament *hapax legomenon*. The *theatron* ("theater") of an ancient city was the place where dramas were performed (Herodotus, *Persian War* 6.67) and often where the populace of the city gathered as an *ekklēsia* (see Acts 19:29, 31). It is a most public place. The (also rare) verb *theatrizein*, logically enough, means to perform a play or put something on display in a public manner. The use of the passive voice here suggests that such display was not chosen: the hearers had been "made a spectacle" or had been "put on public display." Given the low repute of actors in the ancient honor-shame calculus, and given the involuntary character of this "being put on display," we are justified in regarding this public exposure as a form of shaming. The closest analogy in the New Testament is Paul's statement that he and his associates "have become a spectacle *(theatron)* to the world" (1 Cor 4:9). The author of Hebrews clearly intends to evoke the image of a theater, for he will speak in 12:1 of a "great cloud of witnesses" gathered to

---

11. For its pertinence to all New Testament literature, see D. A. deSilva, *The Hope of Glory: Honor Discourse and New Testament Interpretation* (Collegeville: Liturgical Press, 1999).

12. See D. A. deSilva, *Despising Shame: Honor Discourse and Community Maintenance in the Epistle to the Hebrews* (SBLDS 152; Atlanta: Scholars Press, 1995).

witness the "race" (literally, *agōna*, "contest") to be run by those who are enduring in faith. Here, however, the great contest of suffering is carried out before a public gaze that is hostile.

The two terms that describe the means of such public shaming are found frequently in the New Testament in similar settings. The verb *oneidizein* ("to revile or reproach") is used frequently for the rejection of Jesus (Matt 27:44; Mark 15:32; Rom 15:3) or for the rejection of those associated with Jesus (Matt 5:11; Luke 6:22; 1 Pet 4:14). The use of the noun form *oneidismos* — a reproach or censure, with the nuance of shame brought on the one reproached (see Plato, *Republic* 590C) — is especially significant here, for the author will shortly speak of how Moses preferred the reviling for Christ *(oneidismos Christou)* that he received to the wealth of Egypt (11:26), and, at the end of the discourse, will summon his hearers to go out of the city, bearing his (that is, Christ's) reproach *(oneidismos autou,* 13:13). The shame that they had borne with endurance in the former days, and which they are now being called to bear, is one already borne by the crucified Jesus. The term *thlipsis,* in turn, has a definite physical dimension. In the Septuagint, the noun is used for the hard things that come upon the people Israel (Gen 35:3; 42:21; Exod 4:31; Deut 4:29). In the New Testament, *thlipsis* tends to be used for the troubles experienced by those associated with the Christ (Matt 13:21; 24:9; Acts 11:19; Rom 5:3; 2 Cor 1:4). In combination, the terms "revilings" and "afflictions" suggest both verbal and physical abuse in public at the hands of others. These, the author says, they have endured.

In addition to the ridicule and pain they have themselves undergone, they made themselves partners *(koinōnoi)* of those likewise situated. Here we see the second set of cultural associations that the author assumes among his hearers — this time, those gathered around the Hellenistic topos on friendship *(peri philias).*[13] Ancient philosophical discussions on friendship, like that in books 8 and 9 of Aristotle's *Nicomachean Ethics,* emphasize the degree of intimacy and sharing among friends in all things reflected in such proverbs as "friends are one soul" or "friends hold all things in common" or "friendship is fellowship" *(philia koinōnia).* To make oneself a "partner/fellow" in the sufferings of another is to show oneself bound by the deepest and purest form of allegiance. This is clear enough.

---

13. For essays on friendship, see J. T. Fitzgerald, ed., *Friendship, Flattery, and Frankness of Speech* (NovTSup 82; Leiden: Brill, 1996).

More difficult is deciding how to render the phrase that describes those with whom the hearers have made themselves partners, *tōn houtōs anastrephomenōn*. The most obvious way to translate the middle voice of *anastrephein* would be "conducting oneself" as in 1 Tim 3:15 and also, later in this same discourse, Heb 13:18. The RSV and Attridge, however, take *anastrephesthai* as a passive form, "those who were so treated."[14] This translation refers the *houtōs* ("thus") to the indignities suffered. But *houtōs* can equally refer to the endurance that the hearers have shared with others. They have therefore made themselves partners to those who likewise endure various hard things. This translation has the support of an intratextual link: they have shown the same disposition to share in the endurance of sufferings as the Messiah Jesus, who joined the destiny of those who "share in flesh and blood" (2:14) and therefore also in suffering and mortality.

The resonance of the topos on friendship is pertinent in the next verse as well, when the author spells out the form of suffering in reverse sequence, touching first on the way the hearers partnered the suffering of others, then turning to their own experience of deprivation. Here the issue is how to translate the verb *sympathein*. The prefix *syn-* points to the common life and experience of friendship. The verb is commonly used for the moral disposition of "having sympathy toward" another (see 4 Macc 13:23). But the contemporary meaning of "sympathy" is so weak that I have translated (with Attridge), "shared the suffering" of prisoners, a rendering that continues the theme of friendship struck by the characterization of them as "partners" *(koinōnoi)* in the previous verse.[15] Once more, the word choice provokes another intratextual echo. The same disposition is ascribed to Christ: in 4:15, the high priest is himself tested in every way and is therefore able to sympathize with their weaknesses. In this case, the hearers have identified themselves with those being held as prisoners *(desmioi)*. We are even allowed to suspect that the author was striving to suggest a form of identification that goes beyond mere "sympathy." In 13:3, he tells his hearers to "keep in mind the prisoners as though you were fellow prisoners (literally, 'bound together with,' *syndedemenoi*), those who are being badly treated *(tōn kakouchoumenōn)* as though you were in the same body." This last phrase, *hōs kai autoi ontes en sōmati*, is notoriously

---

14. Attridge, *Hebrews*, 297-99.
15. Attridge, *Hebrews*, 297-99.

difficult, but at the very least it signifies a form of identification that is profoundly somatic in character.

Hebrews' language in this passage, we begin to see, not only draws from the rich cultural associations attaching to games, education, shame, and friendship, but does so in a manner that establishes strong intratextual links between the earlier experience of the hearers and their call to follow in the path of still earlier people of faith, above all Jesus, the pioneer and perfecter of faith. The same tendency appears in the continuation of 10:34, where the author makes explicit the form of *thlipsis* that his hearers earlier endured, namely the forcible seizure of their property. Since *hyparchonta* can refer to any sort of possession (see Luke 8:3; 11:21; 12:15; 16:1; Acts 4:32), it is not clear what property they have lost, but the noun *hapargē* indicates that they were the victims of a violent seizure of what they owned (see Xenophon, *Memorabilia* 2.3.14; Josephus, *Antiquities* 20.214; *Testament of Judah* 23.3). We cannot know how such expropriation occurred, although the case of Qumran reminds us that a sect can experience as traumatic the seizure of its property by a more powerful rival (1QpHab 8.13; 12.1-15). What we do know is that the author's language in 10:33 suggests that such a loss of property was an experience of public exposure and shame, toward which the natural response would be grief and anger.

The author's focus, however, is not on the loss itself but on the hearers' manner of experiencing this *thlipsis*. He says that they "accepted [it] with joy." The verb *prosdechomai* has the nuance not just of a passive "acceptance" (see Heb 11:35) but even of a "welcoming" (compare *Letter of Aristeas* 257; Luke 15:2; Rom 16:2; Phil 2:29), and that nuance is made explicit with the modifying phrase "with joy" *(meta charas)*. The term "joy" is a distinctive part of the early Christian lexicon of virtues (see, e.g., Matt 25:21; Luke 1:14; John 16:20; Rom 15:13; Gal 5:22; Col 1:11; 1 Thess 2:19). I use the term "virtue" advisedly, for something more than an emotion is meant by the term; it signifies a moral disposition. Unlike happiness, for example, which depends on positive circumstances, joy is a moral disposition of contentment/receptivity even in the context of suffering (see 2 Cor 7:4; 1 Thess 1:6; Jas 1:2). As with other terms in this passage, this diction serves the author's hortatory purposes. In 12:11, he will note that those experiencing discipline at the hands of their father do not "consider it joy" while it is occurring, but afterward it brings about the peaceful fruit of righteousness. Even more directly, he will speak of Jesus as enduring the cross and despising its shame because of "the joy that was set before him" (12:2).

They were able to accept their loss joyfully because of a certain perception of reality. In this case, the participle *ginōskontes* must surely be taken as explanatory: it is "because they knew" the nature and certainty of God's promise that they had earlier been able to endure their shameful losses joyfully rather than "abandon their assemblies" as some others had done (10:25). They know, the author says, that they themselves have a better *(kreittona)* and permanent *(menousan)* possession *(hyparxin)*. In so saying, he touches on a fundamental point of his extended argument: what they hope for is not something material and transitory, but the realization of God's presence through the exaltation of Christ. Once more, the language deliberately anticipates the encomium on faith that follows immediately after this passage in 11:1-40. There, the author portrays the patriarchs as "desiring a better *(kreittonos)* country, that is, a heavenly one" (11:16). At the same time, the author anticipates his climactic assurance to his hearers in 13:14: "we do not have a permanent city here. We are seeking a city to come."

God Speaks through Prophets

This passage shows how translation difficulties are posed not only by Hebrews' astonishing ability to weave metaphors drawn from Hellenistic culture into its rhetoric of alternating exposition and exhortation, but also by its distinctive use of intertexture drawn from Scripture. That this composition both dwells within and constructs a "scriptural world" is obvious to any reader;[16] the degree to which its argument relies upon a subtle and sophisticated rereading of Scripture has been one of Hebrews' abiding fascinations for scholars.[17]

The warning delivered to his hearers against apostasy in 10:26-31 concludes with an appropriately harsh citation from Deut 32:35, "Vengeance is mine, I will repay," and a mixed citation from Deut 32:36 and Ps 135:14, "The Lord will judge his people," with the author adding as a coda one of his most famous and frightening lines, "It is a fearful thing to fall into the hands of

---

16. See L. T. Johnson, "The Scriptural World of Hebrews," *Int* 57 (2003): 237-50.

17. See G. H. Guthrie, "Hebrews' Use of the Old Testament: Recent Trends in Research," *CBR* 1, no. 2 (2003): 271-94, and F. Schroeger, *Der Verfasser des Hebraeerbriefes als Schriftsausleger* (Biblische Untersuchungen 4; Regensberg: Friedrich Pustet, 1968).

the living God" (10:31). This complex citation is introduced in a manner typical of this composition, not as a written text, but as a spoken word from God, "we know the one who said" (10:30). For the author of Hebrews, God is constantly speaking to humans; in the past God spoke through the prophets, and in these last times, God has spoken through his Son (1:1). But if it is God who speaks through the words written in Scripture, then the words of Scripture are not dead texts significant only for the past, but living voices speaking powerfully to the present. Nowhere is this conviction more impressively displayed than in the author's insistence that the words of LXX Ps 94:7-11 continue to be addressed to his own generation: "Today if you hear his voice, do not harden your hearts" (4:7).

This more positive exhortation in Heb 10:32-39 also closes with a scriptural citation to which the author appends a concluding coda. The citation is prepared for by the author's plea to the hearers not to throw away the confidence *(parrhēsia)* with which they have been gifted (see 3:6; 4:16; 10:19), because this is a confidence or boldness — *parrhēsia* itself has a complex significance in this composition[18] — that has a "great reward" *(megalē misthapodosia)*. The language again has intratextual implications: in 11:6, the author will state that those who approach God must believe that he exists and that he is a "rewarder *(misthapodotēs)* of those who seek him," and in 11:26, Moses is said to endure suffering because he "looked to the reward *(misthapodosia).*" The phrase "great reward" corresponds to the "great contest" that they endured in their earlier days.

The next verse seems at first simply to repeat the same point, but there is a subtle difference. Their confidence has a great reward, but only if they hold on to it the way they did in the past. They need to continue to "endure" *(hypomenein)*. This will be the powerful lesson driven home time after time in the next chapter: all of the heroes of Israel's past held on to their faith, and the supreme exemplar of faith did as well: Jesus endured the cross (12:2-3). The verse also spells out more fully the significance of this endurance. It is an articulation of the faith that wins a reward. Once more, Jesus is the example. He entered the world proclaiming, in the words of LXX Ps 39, "I have come to do your will, O God" (10:7), and it is by that will that they have been sanctified (10:10). Now, the hearers are told that it

---

18. In general, see S. B. Marrow, "Parrhesia and the New Testament," *CBQ* 44 (1982): 431-46; and in particular, see A. C. Mitchell, "Holding on to Confidence: *PARRHESIA* in Hebrews," in *Friendship, Flattery, and Frankness of Speech*, 203-26.

is by "doing God's will" *(to thelēma tou theou poiēsantes)* that they will be able to receive the reward that is the promise *(epangelia)* made available to them through the death and exaltation of Jesus (for the promise, see 4:1; 6:12, 15, 17; 7:6; 8:6; 9:15). Again, the language anticipates the next section, for all the heroes of the past endured for the sake of the promise (11:9, 13, 17, 33), even though they did not receive it (11:39) because they were not to be perfected apart from those whom our author addresses (11:40).

The concluding (mixed) citation in 10:37-38 is meant to elaborate and secure the statements of vv. 35-36, as the inferential *gar* ("for") in v. 37 indicates.[19] Strikingly, the citation has no formal introduction at all. With the addition of *gar* in v. 37 and *kai* in v. 38, the author has seamlessly made the words of Scripture his own words. No better evidence could be found for his conviction that the prophets speak directly to his own time. The citation proper is introduced by an allusion to LXX Isa 26:20, "yet a little while." I have placed a dash between these words and the rest of the citation to preserve the anacoluthic character of the quotation. The words from Isaiah heighten the eschatological urgency that is characteristic of this composition (see 10:25, 30).[20]

The main body of the citation is from Hab 2:3-4, a passage favored by other Jewish writers of the first century. The sectarians at Qumran devoted a pesher-style commentary to the Hebrew text of the prophet that included an interpretation of this verse (1QpHab 7.14–8.1), and Paul twice quotes the same passage in a more abbreviated form in his arguments concerning the righteousness that comes to humans through the faith of Jesus (Rom 1:17; Gal 3:11). The citation in Hebrews depends entirely on the Septuagint rather than the Masoretic Text.[21] The original Hebrew contained a vision concerning God's judgment, delivered to the prophet who had taken his stand on the watchtower: "it will surely come, it will not delay" (RSV). Hebrews makes the present Greek participle *erchomenos* — already present in the LXX — both personal and specific, by adding the definite article, thus

---

19. Despite its absence from P[13, 104], and a Vulgate MS, the presence of *gar* is otherwise overwhelmingly supported.

20. The classic essay is the one by C. K. Barrett, "The Eschatology of the Epistle to the Hebrews," in *The Background of the New Testament and Its Eschatology* (ed. W. D. Davies and D. Daube; Cambridge: Cambridge University Press, 1956), 363-93.

21. For full discussion, see R. Gheorghita, *The Role of the Septuagint in Hebrews: An Investigation of Its Influence with Special Consideration to the Use of Hab 2:3-4 in Heb 10:37-38* (WUNT 2, Reihe 160; Tübingen: J. C. B. Mohr [Paul Siebeck], 2003), especially 148-224.

forming *ho erchomenos,* "the one who is coming." As a result, the passage appears to speak of a judgment to be carried out by the Messiah (for "the coming one" with reference to Jesus, compare Matt 3:2; Luke 7:19; John 1:9; 3:31; 6:14), a judgment that the author has already stated that Jesus would come to perform (see 9:28).

The remainder of the passage in Hebrew reads, "Behold, he whose soul is not upright in him shall fail, but the righteous one shall live by his faith" (Hab 2:4 RSV). The Septuagint, followed by our author, translates the first clause as "if he draws back, my soul will not be pleased with him." Our composition also reverses the sequence of the clauses, so that the statement concerning the righteous one and faith precedes rather than follows the statement concerning the one who draws back *(hyposteilētai).* As a result, the prophet's words do not stand for two classes of people on whom judgment will fall, but for two ways of responding to God's visitation, the way of the apostate and the way of the faithful.

Finally, both the LXX and our discourse employ the personal pronoun "my" rather than the personal pronoun "his" found in the Masoretic Text. In some manuscripts of the Septuagint, indeed, the personal pronoun "my" modifies the noun "faith," making this statement, "the righteous one will live out of my faith," with the "my" in this instance referring to God. Our author, however, agrees with those manuscripts of the LXX in which "my" refers to the righteous one, making this statement: "my righteous one *(dikaios)* will live out of faith *(ek pisteōs)*." The programmatic character of this citation is obvious. This is the first of three occurrences of "righteous" in the composition. In 11:4, we shall learn that it was because of his faith that Abel was testified to (by God) as righteous *(dikaios).* And in 12:23, the hearers are told that they are approaching close to the city of the living God — and to the spirits of righteous ones *(dikaioi)* who have been made perfect. As for faith *(pistis),* it will immediately be given a descriptive definition (11:1) and become the metronomic introduction to every hero of Israel's past whose praises the author proclaims: all of them lived "in faith."

The final sentence in this passage provides a final challenge to the translator — as though one more challenge were still needed — because, like all gnomic utterances, it is extremely compressed in its manner of expression. The sentence begins, "but we are not" *(ouk esmen),* followed by two genitives: "of drawing back" *(hypostolēs)* and "of faith" *(pisteōs).* Each of these is followed in turn by prepositional phrases that form final clauses: *eis apōleian* and *eis peripoiēsin psychēs.* The last of these phrases is especially ambiguous. Does *psychē* mean "soul" or "life" (see Heb 4:12; 6:19; 12:3; 13:17)? And should the noun *peripoiēsis* have its possible sense of "hold as a possession" (see Eph 1:14; 1 Pet 2:9; 1 Tim 3:13; Acts 20:28)? The most striking parallel is Luke 17:33, "Whoever seeks to possess/secure *(peripoiēsasthai)* his life/soul *(psychē)* will lose it *(apolesei autēn)*." Certainly, the nuance of "gain as a possession" would be appropriate in the context, for it opposes this acquisition of their (true) lives or souls to the expropriation of their material property.

Rendering the sentence as a whole clearly demands some decisions. Mine were to change the genitival phrases to verbal phrases: "we do not draw back" and "we have faith." Then I use dashes to help indicate the result clauses. Thus, "But we do not draw back — to our destruction. Rather, we have faith — to the securing of our life." That the consequence of "drawing back," that is apostasy, is destruction has been the burden of the author's exhortation in the preceding passage (10:26-30). That an enduring faith leads to the saving of life or the securing of the soul will be demonstrated by the roll call of the heroes of Israel's story that follows immediately.

The Impossible but Necessary Task

I do not draw any grand conclusion from these observations on a single passage in Hebrews, but I do draw some comfort. I have emphasized the frustration and struggle *(agōnia)* inherent in translating a composition as stylistically sophisticated and rhetorically complex as Hebrews. It is certainly true that adequacy in translation is, in such a case, an ever-receding goal. But I should close with the acknowledgment — understood if not always admitted by all who labor at this impossible task — that the search for a more adequate translation, one that comes to grips with the complex webs of intratexture and intertexture drawn from Mediterranean culture and the symbolic world of Scripture, is both necessary (for the life of the church requires a living word in every age) and joyful (for the richness of the scriptural word enlivens even as it challenges). The translation of Hebrews that I am now endeavoring to complete will, in all likelihood, be the last effort of this sort I will make. Even as I suffer the pains that it has inflicted, I am grateful for the chance to have received the education it enables.

Translation and Luke 16:19-31

Comparative Discourse Analysis as a Tool in Assessing Translations, Using Luke 16:19-31 as a Test Case

Stanley E. Porter and Matthew Brook O'Donnell

Introduction to Comparative Discourse Analysis

The use of the Internet by multinational bodies such as the European Union to publish and archive constitutions, legislation, and standards in multiple languages provides opportunities for the study of translation practice through empirical corpus-based analysis. Corpus linguistics is the computational and statistical analysis of representative samples of naturally occurring language to identify patterns of meaning.[1] The method has been utilized primarily in the study of individual languages using monolingual corpora.[2] However, the benefit of language corpora for translation

---

1. For introductions to corpus linguistics, see T. McEnery and A. Wilson, *Corpus Linguistics* (2nd ed.; Edinburgh: Edinburgh University Press, 2001); D. Biber, S. Conrad, and R. Reppen, *Corpus Linguistics: Investigating Language Structure and Use* (Cambridge Approaches to Linguistics; Cambridge: Cambridge University Press, 1998); G. Kennedy, *An Introduction to Corpus Linguistics* (London: Longman, 1998); C. F. Meyer, *English Corpus Linguistics: An Introduction* (Cambridge: Cambridge University Press, 2002); S. Hunston, *Corpora in Applied Linguistics* (Cambridge Applied Linguistics; Cambridge: Cambridge University Press, 2002). For an exploratory investigation of how corpus-based methods could be applied to the study of an epigraphic language like Hellenistic Greek, see M. B. O'Donnell, *Corpus Linguistics and the Greek of the New Testament* (New Testament Monographs 6; Sheffield: Sheffield Phoenix Press, 2005).

2. In the past, translated material has tended to be excluded from corpora on the grounds that the source language is likely to influence the grammar and structure of the translation. This, it is argued, makes translated material less representative of the target lan-

185

studies and particularly the availability of "parallel corpora" — a corpus that contains the same document in two or more languages — has gained wide acceptance.[3] Discussing the use of corpora in translation studies, Olohan makes use of the three models of translation studies put forward by Chesterman.[4] They are: (1) *the comparative model*, which explores the correlations between translations and their source texts, (2) *the process model*, where the focus is upon the history of and developments in the translation of particular documents, and (3) *the causal model*, which focuses upon the cultural, political, and cognitive factors that influence and are influenced by translations.[5]

The comparative model has been the predominant one in translation studies. Features are selected from the source language and compared to their target-language translation. The analysis has traditionally taken place at the sentence level through the construction of comparative syntaxes or grammars. Aligned parallel corpora have sentences in the source matched up with corresponding sentences in the target language. For the comparison of Bible translations, verse demarcations provide a ready-made alignment mechanism.[6] The Open Scripture Information Standard (OSIS) project[7] provides a standardized encoding method for Bible translations,

---

guage. See S. Johansson, "On the Role of Corpora in Cross-Linguistic Research," in *Corpora and Cross-Linguistic Research* (ed. S. Johansson and S. Oksefjell; Amsterdam: Rodopi, 1998), 3-24.

3. Olohan provides a comprehensive introduction, considering both the theoretical and practical aspects of utilizing corpora in translation studies. See M. Olohan, *Introducing Corpora in Translation Studies* (New York: Routledge, 2004), esp. 24-34 where definitions of the term "parallel corpus" are reviewed.

4. A. Chesterman, "A Causal Model for Translation Studies," in *Intercultural Faultlines: Research Models in Translation Studies I: Textual and Cognitive Aspects* (ed. M. Olohan; Manchester: St. Jerome, 2000), 15-27.

5. See Olohan, *Introducing Corpora*, 9-11.

6. The majority of translations maintain chapter and verse divisions. Translations adhering to a more literal translation method are more likely to treat these divisions as closely akin to linguistic, i.e., sentence, boundaries. Versions such as the CEV, which utilize the dynamic equivalence model, see these verse divisions as secondary to prose structure, i.e., sections, sub-sections and paragraphs. However, they are still bound to a certain degree by the accepted verse divisions to a particular ordering of material.

7. OSIS is "an XML schema for marking up scripture and related text, part of an 'open scripture' initiative composed of translators, publishers, scholars, software manufacturers, and technical experts who are coordinated by the 'Bible Technologies Group'" (from OSIS website http://www.bibletechnologies.net/OSISinformation/ [accessed May 2005]). For the

facilitating their alignment and comparison.[8] A range of features across source and target languages could be examined. One could search, for instance, to see if a particular phrase in the source texts is consistently translated. However, it is possible to expand the comparative approach above the sentence/verse and the syntactical level to align discourse units for comparison.

In the present context, we are able to do little more than sketch an idea of how the comparative model of translation might be applied at the discourse level.[9] A core tenet of discourse analysis is that meaning and communicative function and intent result not from the combined meaning of individual words, but from a complex of features that make up a single discourse. This means that a source document and its translation might appear to have strong equivalence at the word and sentence level, but might have quite different "meaning" at the level of discourse. Conversely, the measure of an effective translation is not then how well it matches at the word-to-word or sentence-to-sentence level, but whether a discourse analysis of the source and target language versions produces equivalent results.

Analysis of Luke 16:19-31 according to the OpenText.org Discourse Model

Discourse analysis is "data intensive" in the sense that it requires the analyst to keep track of the occurrence and patterns of a large number of linguistic features across a large stretch of text. The following sections present a discourse analysis of Luke 16:19-31 utilizing the model developed in the OpenText.org project.[10]

---

description of an earlier but similar initiative to create a parallel corpus of Bible translations, see P. Resnik, M. Broman Olsen, and M. Diab, "The Bible as a Parallel Corpus: Annotating the 'Book of 2000 Tongues,'" *Computers and the Humanities* 33, no. 1-2 (1999): 129-53.

8. See http://thebibletool.com for a tool that allows the parallel comparison of a wide range of translations.

9. This paper attempts to provide an example of translation at the discourse level, following the scheme in Porter's "Assessing Translation Theory," pp. 117-45 in this volume.

10. See www.opentext.org for both the method and the results. The entire marked New Testament is available on-line according to the ranks of word group and clause. We use the terminology and method of OpenText.org in this essay.

STANLEY E. PORTER AND MATTHEW BROOK O'DONNELL

Identifying and Justifying Paragraph Boundaries

The first topic we will treat is identifying and justifying paragraph boundaries. Defining the paragraph has proved highly problematic in linguistic circles.[11] Many discourse linguists believe that there is a unit of structure above the sentence, but so far no one has provided a convincing identification of that structure, especially in grammatical terms. Nevertheless, we must begin with the discourse and its constituent parts. The structure of Luke 16:19-31 can be laid out as follows.

Paragraph 1 (vv. 19-21): Introduction of Characters and Setting
19 C83 ||s ἄνθρωπος (cj δέ) τις |p ἦν |c πλούσιος[57] ||
   C84 ||cj καὶ |p ἐνεδιδύσκετο |A πορφύραν καὶ βύσσον
         |A [[P εὐφραινόμενος[25] |A καθ' ἡμέραν |A λαμπρῶς]]||
20 C86 ||s πτωχὸς[57] (cj δέ) τις ὀνόματι [33] Λάζαρος [93] |p ἐβέβλητο[15]
         |A πρὸς τὸν πυλῶνα αὐτοῦ
         |A [[P εἰλκωμένος[23]]]
21   [[cj καὶ |p ἐπιθυμῶν[25] |c [[P χορτασθῆναι[23]
         |A[[P ἀπὸ τῶν πιπτόντων[15] |A ἀπὸ τῆς τραπέζης τοῦ
         πλουσίου[57]]]]]||
   C91 ||cj ἀλλὰ |cj καὶ |s οἱ κύνες |A[[P ἐρχόμενοι[15]]]|p ἐπέλειχον[23]
         |c τὰ ἕλκη[23] αὐτοῦ ||

The first paragraph introduces the two main characters of the parable, with grammaticalized references. Each one is the first clausal element in a primary clause with subject-predicator . . . structure (SPC and SPAA).[12] The setting is established through the description of the poor man as thrown at the rich man's gate, and the use of embedded clauses focused upon the poor man — covered with sores and desiring to be fed. The major point of dramatic tension is also introduced in a primary clause in v. 21 — the dogs were coming to lick the sores of the poor man right under the (grammatical) nose of the rich man.

---

11. For a survey of opinion, see S. E. Porter, "Pericope Markers and the Paragraph: Textual Linguistic Considerations," in *The Impact of Unit Delimitation on Exegesis* (Pericope 7; ed. R. de Hoop, M. C. A. Korpel, and S. E. Porter; Assen: Van Gorcum, 2008), 175-95.

12. S = subject, P = predicator, C = complement, A = adjunct, cj = conjunction.

Paragraph 2 (vv. 22-24): First scene

22 c93   ‖p ἐγένετο |cj δὲ |s ‖p ἀποθανεῖν²³ |s τὸν πτωχὸν⁵⁷ ‖
           ‖cj καὶ |p ἀπενεχθῆναι¹⁵ |s αὐτὸν |a ὑπὸ τῶν ἀγγέλων
           |a εἰς τὸν κόλπον⁸ Ἀβραάμ⁹³ ‖‖
   c96   ‖p ἀπέθανεν²³ |cj δὲ |cj καὶ |s ὁ πλούσιος⁵⁷ ‖
   c97   ‖cj καὶ |p ἐτάφη ‖
23 c98   ‖cj καὶ |a ἐν τῷ ᾅδῃ a‖p ἐπάρας¹⁵ |c τοὺς ὀφθαλμοὺς⁸ αὐτοῦ ‖|a‖p
           ὑπάρχων |a ἐν βασάνοις²⁴ ‖|p ὁρᾷ |c Ἀβραὰμ⁹³ |a ἀπὸ μακρόθεν
           καὶ Λάζαρον⁹³ ἐν τοῖς κόλποις αὐτοῦ ‖
24 c101   ‖cj καὶ |s αὐτὸς |a‖p φωνήσας³³ ‖|p εἶπεν³³ ‖
   c103   ‖add Πάτερ¹⁰ Ἀβραάμ⁹³ |p ἐλέησόν |c με ‖
   c104   ‖cj καὶ |p πέμψον¹⁵ |c Λάζαρον⁹³ ‖
   c105   ‖cj ἵνα |p βάψῃ |c τὸ ἄκρον τοῦ δακτύλου⁸ αὐτοῦ |a ὕδατος ‖
   c106   ‖cj καὶ |p καταψύξῃ |c τὴν γλῶσσάν⁸ μου ‖
   c107   ‖cj ὅτι |p ὀδυνῶμαι²⁴ |a ἐν τῇ φλογὶ ταύτῃ ‖

The first scene is introduced with an ἐγένετο construction, often used to mark stages in New Testament narrative. What happened was that the poor man died, as did the rich man. We note that description of these two events is in predicator-subject constructions. This is clearly a scene about death. This is confirmed by the string of fronted elements about death, burial, and Hades. The dead rich man calls upon Abraham (direct address of Abraham, using the vocative) and pleads with him.

Paragraph 3 (vv. 25-26): Abraham speaks

25 c108   ‖p εἶπεν³³ |cj δὲ |s Ἀβραάμ⁹³ ‖
   c109   ‖add Τέκνον¹⁰ |p μνήσθητι ‖
   c110   ‖cj ὅτι |p ἀπέλαβες⁵⁷ |c τὰ ἀγαθά⁵⁷ σου |a ἐν τῇ ζωῇ²³ σου ‖
   c111   ‖cj καὶ |s Λάζαρος⁹³ |a ὁμοίως |c τὰ κακά ‖
   c112   ‖a νῦν |c δὲ |a ὧδε |p παρακαλεῖται²⁵ ‖
   c113   ‖s σὺ |cj δὲ |p ὀδυνᾶσαι²⁴ ‖
26 c114   ‖cj καὶ |a ἐν πᾶσι τούτοις |a μεταξὺ ἡμῶν καὶ ὑμῶν |s χάσμα μέγα
           |p ἐστήρικται ‖
   c115   ‖cj ὅπως |s‖p οἱ θέλοντες²⁵ |c‖p διαβῆναι¹⁵ |a ἔνθεν |a πρὸς ὑμᾶς
             ‖|a μὴ⁶⁹ |p δύνωνται ‖
   c118   ‖cj μηδὲ⁶⁹ |a ἐκεῖθεν |a πρὸς ἡμᾶς |p διαπερῶσιν¹⁵ ‖

In response to the pleading of the post-mortem rich man, Abraham speaks. Already introduced above, Abraham speaks in a predicator-subject construction and addresses the rich man ("child"). He recounts the rich man's position in a series of short clauses, concluding by noting that a great chasm separates him from others.

Paragraph 4 (vv. 27-28): Rich man speaks
27 c119 ||p εἶπεν³³ |cj δέ ||
   c120 ||p Ἐρωτῶ³³ |c σε |cj οὖν |add πάτερ¹⁰ ||
   c121 ||cj ἵνα |p πέμψῃς¹⁵ |c αὐτὸν |A εἰς τὸν <u>οἶκον</u>¹⁰ τοῦ <u>πατρός</u>¹⁰ μου ||
28 c122 ||p ἔχω⁵⁷ |cj γὰρ |c πέντε <u>ἀδελφούς</u>¹⁰ ||
   c123 ||cj ὅπως |p <u>διαμαρτύρηται</u>³³ |c αὐτοῖς ||
   c124 ||cj ἵνα |A μὴ⁶⁹ |A καὶ |s αὐτοὶ |p ἔλθωσιν¹⁵ |A εἰς τὸν τόπον τοῦτον τῆς <u>βασάνου</u>²⁴ ||

The rich man responds. Whereas Abraham's language is straightforward and contained for the most part in a series of primary clauses, until he reaches his explanation (secondary clauses), the request of the rich man is found in secondary clauses. These are used to state the purpose and result of his request: that his relatives would not have to come to this place.

Paragraph 5 (vv. 29-31): Conclusions
29 c125 ||p <u>λέγει</u>³³ |c δὲ |s Ἀβραάμ⁹³ ||
   c126 ||p ἔχουσι⁵⁷ |c Μωϋσέα⁹³ καὶ τοὺς προφήτας ||
   c127 ||p ἀκουσάτωσαν²⁴ |c αὐτῶν ||
30 c128 ||s ὁ |cj δὲ |p <u>εἶπεν</u>³³ ||
   c129 ||A Οὐχί |add πάτερ¹⁰ Ἀβραάμ⁹³ ||
   c130 ||cj ἀλλ' |c ἐάν |s τις |A ἀπὸ <u>νεκρῶν</u>²³ |p <u>πορευθῇ</u>¹⁵ |A πρὸς αὐτοὺς ||
   c131 ||p μετανοήσουσιν ||
31 c132 ||p εἶπεν³³ |cj δὲ |c αὐτῷ ||
   c133 ||cj Εἰ |c <u>Μωϋσέως</u>⁹³ καὶ τῶν προφητῶν |A οὐκ⁶⁹ |p ἀκούουσιν²⁴ ||
   c134 ||cj <u>οὐδ'</u>⁶⁹ |cj ἐάν |s τις |A ἐκ <u>νεκρῶν</u>²³ |p <u>ἀναστῇ</u>²³ ||
   c135 ||p <u>πεισθήσονται</u>³³ ||

An interchange between Abraham and the rich man closes the episode. Abraham says that the rich man's relatives have Moses. There are two concluding conditional statements. The rich man says that if someone were to come back from the dead they would repent, while Abraham counters that if they have Moses and the prophets and they do not hear them, they would not be persuaded by one coming back from the dead.

Thematization Patterns

Thematization patterns typically revolve around the element that is first in the ordering of units. In terms of Greek discourse, thematization occurs at every rank of exponence. For this study, we wish to analyze thematization in terms of the level of the clause complex. The thematized element is the grammaticalized participant as actor in a process chain, expressed by a nominal group in a primary clause.[13] At the level of the clause complex, the thematized element is the element that is expressed by a grammaticalized form (as opposed to a reduced or implied form) as the subject or actor of a clause.

In this discourse, the thematized elements are placed to the left margin, according to the paragraphs noted above, analyzing the primary clauses.

Paragraph 1
19 Ἄνθρωπος δέ τις ἦν πλούσιος, καὶ ἐνεδιδύσκετο πορφύραν καὶ βύσσον
  εὐφραινόμενος καθ' ἡμέραν λαμπρῶς (there was a rich man, and he
  was clothed in purple and linen, rejoicing each day splendidly),
20 πτωχὸς δέ τις ὀνόματι Λάζαρος ἐβέβλητο πρὸς τὸν πυλῶνα αὐτοῦ
  εἱλκωμένος 21 καὶ ἐπιθυμῶν χορτασθῆναι ἀπὸ τῶν πιπτόντων ἀπὸ
  τῆς τραπέζης τοῦ πλουσίου (a poor man named Lazarus was cast at
  his gate, having sores and desiring to be fed from the things falling
  from the table of the rich man)
ἀλλὰ καὶ οἱ κύνες ἐρχόμενοι ἐπέλειχον τὰ ἕλκη αὐτοῦ (but indeed dogs,
  coming, were licking his sores)

This paragraph has three thematized elements: the rich man, the poor man named Lazarus, and the dogs.

---

13. See S. E. Porter and M. B. O'Donnell, *Discourse Analysis and the Greek New Testament* (forthcoming), ch. 3, for this terminology.

Paragraph 2

22 ἐγένετο δὲ ἀποθανεῖν τὸν πτωχὸν καὶ ἀπενεχθῆναι αὐτὸν ὑπὸ τῶν ἀγγέλων εἰς τὸν κόλπον Ἀβραάμ· ἀπέθανεν δὲ καὶ ὁ πλούσιος καὶ ἐτάφη. 23 καὶ ἐν τῷ ᾅδῃ ἐπάρας τοὺς ὀφθαλμοὺς αὐτοῦ, ὑπάρχων ἐν βασάνοις, ὁρᾷ Ἀβραάμ ἀπὸ μακρόθεν καὶ Λάζαρος ἐν τοῖν κόλποις αὐτοῦ (it happened that the poor man died and he was taken up by the angels into the bosom of Abraham, and the rich man died and was buried. And in Hades, looking up his eyes, being in torment, he saw Abraham at a distance and Lazarus in his bosom)

24 καὶ αὐτὸς φωνήσας εἶπεν, Πάτερ Ἀβραάμ, ἐλέησόν με καὶ πέμψον Λάζαρον ἵνα βάψῃ τὸ ἄκρον τοῦ δακτύλου αὐτοῦ ὕδατος καὶ καταψύξῃ τὴν γλῶσσάν μου, ὅτι ὀδυνῶμαι ἐν τῇ φλογὶ ταύτῃ (and he, calling, said, Father Abraham, have mercy on me and send Lazarus to touch the tip of his finger in water and cool my tongue, because I am suffering in this flame)

All of the material is rhematic, that is, without thematized material until the introduction with the reduced (pronoun) form of the rich man. Here the subject is within a speech margin (speech margins are found in vv. 24, 25, 27, 29, 30, 31). The thematized character is the one who initiates conversation here.

Paragraph 3

25 εἶπεν δὲ Ἀβραάμ, Τέκνον, μνήσθητι ὅτι ἀπέλαβες τὰ ἀγαθά σου ἐν τῇ ζωῇ σου, καὶ Λάζαρος ὁμοίως τὰ κακά· νῦν δὲ ὧδε παρακαλεῖται σὺ δὲ ὀδυνᾶσαι. 26 καὶ ἐν πᾶσι τούτοις μεταξὺ ἡμῶν καὶ ὑμῶν χάσμα μέγα ἐστήρικται, ὅπως οἱ θέλοντες διαβῆναι ἔνθεν πρὸς ὑμᾶς μὴ δύνωνται, μηδὲ ἐκεῖθεν πρὸς ἡμᾶς διαπερῶσιν (but Abraham said, Child, remember that you received your good things in your life, and Lazarus likewise the bad things; but now here he is comforted but you are suffering. And in all these things between us and you a giant chasm is erected, so that those willing to pass through from here to you are not able, nor from there to us are they able to pass)

As in paragraph 2, though established at the outset, the theme is Abraham, who speaks throughout the paragraph (speech margin).

Comparative Discourse Analysis as a Tool in Assessing Translations

Paragraph 4

27 εἶπεν δέ, Ἐρωτῶ σε οὖν, πάτερ, ἵνα πέμψῃς αὐτὸν εἰς τὸν οἶκον τοῦ παρτός μου, 28 ἔχω γὰρ πέντε ἀδελφούς, ὅπως διαμαρτύρηται αὐτοῖς, ἵνα μὴ καὶ αὐτοὶ ἔλθωσιν εἰς τὸν τόπον τοῦτον τῆς βασάνου (but he said, I am asking you therefore, father, to send him to the house of my father, for I have five brothers, so that he might be a testimony to them, so that they might not also come into this place of torment)

There is only rhematic material in Paragraph 4, as the rich man has already been introduced.

Paragraph 5

29 λέγει δὲ Ἀβραάμ, ἔχουσι Μωϋσέα καὶ τοὺς προφήτας· ἀκουσάτωσαν αὐτῶν (but Abraham said, They have Moses and the prophets; let them hear them)

30 ὁ δὲ εἶπεν, Οὐχί, πάτερ Ἀβραάμ, ἀλλ' ἐάν τις ἀπὸ νεκρῶν πορευθῇ πρὸς αὐτοὺς μετανοήσουσιν. 31 εἶπεν δὲ αὐτῷ, Εἰ Μωϋσέως καὶ τῶν προφητῶν οὐκ ἀκούουσιν, οὐδ' ἐάν τις ἐκ νεκρῶν ἀναστῇ πεισθήσονται (but he said, No, father Abraham, but if someone might come from the dead to them they might repent. But he said to him, If they do not hear Moses and the prophets, not even if someone rises from the dead will they be persuaded).

The grammaticalized form is used for Abraham's final comment, and the reduced form (the pronominal use of the article) for the rich man's final comment. The theme is not returned to Abraham, even though he is given the final comment, as the statement is a further elaboration of the comment by the rich man.

Thus, there are the following thematized elements: the rich man, the poor man named Lazarus, the dogs, the rich man, Abraham, Abraham and the rich man. These thematized elements capture the dominant actors and actions in the discourse.

Participant Reference

Participant reference indicates those who participate in the discourse, whether they are thematized or not. A discourse often includes more participants than it does thematized actors.

There are three major participants in this discourse (rich man, poor man, and Abraham), one minor participant (dogs), and several non-participant references (father, brothers, Moses, and prophets). One of the features of this discourse is that when one of the major participants is introduced, the participant is usually introduced with the conjunction δέ. This occurs with the rich man in vv. 19 and 30, Abraham in vv. 25 and 29, and the poor man in v. 20 — the first reference to each one.

The rich man is the first major participant introduced. He is never named (in our established text), but is referred to with a grammaticalized form in v. 19 and v. 21 (table of the rich man), and in v. 25 with the appellative "child." He is introduced by reduced forms in vv. 19 ("one"), 20 ("his"), 23 ("his"), 24 (pronouns: "he," "me," "my"), 25 ("your" and "you"), 26 (pronouns for "you"), 27 ("my"), 30 ("he"), 31 ("him"), and implied forms in vv. 19 (verb form), 22 (verb forms), 23 (verb form), and 27 (verb forms).

The poor man is the second major participant introduced. He is referred to with a grammaticalized form, his name, in vv. 20, 23, 24, and 25, and as "the poor man" in vv. 20 and 22. He is referred to with reduced forms in vv. 21 ("his"), 22 ("he"), 24 ("his"), 26 (possibly "us"), 27 ("him"), 30 ("someone"), 31 ("someone"), and implied forms in vv. 24 (verb forms), 25 (verb form), and 28 (verb form).

The third major participant is Abraham. Abraham is referred to in grammaticalized form, by name, in vv. 22, 23, 24, 25, 29, and 30, and as "father" in vv. 27 and 30. He is referred to in reduced form in vv. 26 ("us") and 27 ("you"), and in implied form in vv. 24 (verb form), 25 (verb form), and 27 (verb form).

Transitivity Analysis and the Main Discourse Participants

The examination of transitivity in relation to the major participants indicates the types and kinds of processes involved in the discourse.

The actions of the rich man are as follows, in terms of the rich man as the subject and actor of a primary clause:

[he] was clothed (v. 19)
the rich man died (v. 22)
[he] was buried (v. 22)

Comparative Discourse Analysis as a Tool in Assessing Translations

[he] saw (v. 23)
he said (v. 24)
[you] remember (v. 25)
you received the good things (v. 25)
you are being tormented (v. 25)
[he] said (v. 27)
I ask you (v. 27)
[he] said (v. 30)

The actions of Abraham are as follows:

[you] have mercy (v. 24)
[you] send (v. 24)
Abraham said (v. 25)
Abraham said (v. 29)
[he] said (v. 31)

The actions of the poor man are as follows:

[he] was cast at the door (v. 20)
[he] is comforted (v. 25)

The transitivity system related to the major participants reveals an interesting configuration that helps to get to the heart of the discourse. The first thing to note is that, just as the condition might imply, the poor man is the passive agent who is the recipient of the action. The parable states that he was cast at the door (by others or his illness) and was comforted (by being in Abraham's bosom) — two uses of the passive verb. The second observation is that the rich man pleads with Abraham to have mercy and to send Lazarus. However, Abraham does not do any of these actions. Instead, Abraham simply speaks. Abraham speaks words of description and hence judgment and condemnation on the rich man. The rich man is clearly the most active, but his processes too are limited. There are two major kinds of processes that the rich man is involved in. One is speaking and the other is being the recipient of actions. He dies, is buried, and receives good things and torment. There is a clear indication that the rich man speaks, but out of a context that does not merit his speech, as he is not a contributor but a receiver.

Semantic Domains

As indicated above in the paragraph and clausal diagram, a number of different semantic domains are represented in this discourse.[14] The major ones are as follows:

93.	Names of Persons and Places	12
33.	Communication	11
15.	Linear Movement	11
23.	Physiological Processes and States	10
57.	Possess, Transfer, Exchange	9
10.	Kinship Terms	7
24.	Sensory Events and States	6
69.	Affirmation, Negation	6
8.	Body, Body Parts, and Body Products	4
25.	Attitudes and Emotions	4
79.	Features of Objects	3
88.	Moral and Ethical Qualities and Related Behavior	3

Several of these should be placed together. For example, numbers 93 and 10 go together, and include: Abraham, Lazarus, and Moses under domain 93, and father, child, house, and brothers under domain 10. We have already commented above that the participants are often referred to with a full grammatical form, and this accounts for the references in domain 93. Some of the minor participants are indicated in terms of their familial relation to the rich man, which accounts for those in domain 10.

Another set of domains that should be placed together are domains 23, 24, and 25. The sequence of the numbers indicates that they are contiguous in the domain lexicon, and they include the following:

23. Physiological Processes and States — εἰλκωμένος (covered in sores; v. 20), χορτασθῆναι (feed; v. 21), ἐπέλειχον τὰ ἕλκη αὐτοῦ (licking his sores; v. 21), ἀποθανεῖν and ἀπέθανεν (die; v. 22), ζωῇ (life; v. 25), νεκρῶν (dead; vv. 30, 31); ἀναστῇ (rise; v. 31)
24. Sensory Events and States — βασάνοις/ου (torment; vv. 23, 28), ὀδυνῶμαι/ᾶσαι (agonize; vv. 24, 25), ἀκούω (hear; vv. 29, 31)

---

14. We use the semantic domains as found in J. P. Louw and E. A. Nida, *Greek-English Lexicon of the New Testament Based on Semantic Domains* (2 vols.; New York: ABS, 1988).

25. Attitudes and Emotions — εὐφραινόμενος (rejoice; v. 19), ἐπιθυμῶν (desire; v. 21), παρακαλεῖται (comfort; v. 25); θέλοντες (will; v. 26).

The effect of the use of semantic domains is several. First, semantic domains help to establish and clarify the basic subject matter of the parable, its ideational semantics. It is common in biblical texts to have high incidence of domain 33, communication, as well as domain 15, linear movement, because people are often going from place to place and saying, teaching, or proclaiming things. The question is, What they are proclaiming? The indications from the domains are that this parable focuses upon people (domain 93) in relationship (domain 10) undergoing some kind of physiological or emotional transformation (domains 23, 24, and 25) that also involves, in a more limited way, the possession, transfer, or exchange of something (domain 57). That is what this discourse is about: the interaction of the rich man, poor man, and Abraham over the death and final disposition of one who is wealthy and one who is poor.

Semantic domains also establish textual cohesion.[15] Texts cohere around a variety of factors. Some of these have already been noted, such as the use of δέ to introduce participants and their speech, or the introduction and continued presence of the major participants (through grammaticalized, reduced, and implied forms of reference). Another form of cohesion is provided through semantic chains, that is, through the use of lexical items from the same or similar semantic domains. Domains 23, 24, and 25 have eleven different words used in twenty instances in this discourse. They are distributed throughout each paragraph: six instances in paragraph 1, six in paragraph 2, two in paragraph 3, one in paragraph 4, and five in paragraph 5. The result is that these domains serve a cohesive function by creating a semantic chain of words related to these physiological or emotional transformations.

Discourse Translation of Luke 16:19-31

The final step is to produce a discourse-based translation of this passage. Here is an attempt to capture some of the elements noted above (others

15. See Porter and O'Donnell, *Discourse Analysis*, ch. 5.

have not been explored and so are not emphasized below), in terms of both layout and rendering:

> There was a certain rich man — and he was dressed in purple and linen, and he was rejoicing each day splendidly.
> Then there was a certain poor man named Lazarus — cast down at his door, covered with sores and desiring to be fed from what dropped from the table of the rich man.
> And the dogs also, coming, were licking the sores of this one.

> The poor man, it so happened, died, and he was taken up by the angels into Abraham's bosom. And the rich man also died and was buried. And he, in Hades, lifted up his eyes, as he was in torment, and saw from a distance Abraham, and Lazarus in his bosom.
> And he, calling out, said: Father Abraham, be merciful to me and send Lazarus to touch the tip of his own finger in water and cool my own tongue, because I am in agony in this flame.

> Then Abraham said: Child, remember that you received your good in your life, and Lazarus likewise his bad, but now he is comforted here but you are in agony. And between us and you in all of these places there stands erected a giant chasm, so that those who wish to pass are not able to pass across from here to you, nor are they able to pass over from there to us.

> Then he said: I ask you therefore, father, to send him to my father's household, for I have five brothers, so that he may clearly testify to them, so that they themselves might not come into this place of torment.

> Then Abraham said: They have Moses and the prophets. Let them hear them.

> Then he said: No, father Abraham, but if someone from the dead might come to them they might repent.
> Then he said to him: If they do not listen to Moses and the prophets, neither will they be persuaded if someone from the dead rises up.

Conclusions

Discourse analysis has not been widely applied to biblical translation (or to biblical, especially New Testament, analysis for that matter). However, attention to a variety of discourse features has the potential to influence how we understand the source text, how we understand the receptor text, and how we understand the process that leads from one to the other. In this essay, we have taken the first steps in comparative discourse translation of a text of the New Testament, the story about Lazarus and the rich man and Abraham. We have noted the structure of the text, the thematized elements, the main participants, the transitivity patterns of the processes, and the semantic domains that establish the ideational and cohesional structure. Once these elements are understood in the source text, they can be applied to the creation of a translation of that passage. The next step is to compare the findings regarding the source text and the resultant translation with translations produced by other, more conventional methods of translation. We believe that the next major step in translational theory and practice is to extend analysis to elements at and above the clause level and to find ways of rendering these into our translations, as a reflection of our understanding of the source text.

Synchronic Observations on Luke 16:19-31 as Preparation for a Translation

Alain Gignac

When I translate a text such as Luke 16:19-31, I first translate it literally, paying attention to the interplay between verb tenses, prepositions, prefixes, same-family words, puns, etc. Then, before consulting any commentary, I take a careful look at the text: its characters, its spatialization, its temporalization, the semantic domains of its vocabulary, the transformations that take place in it, and the oppositions that gradually take shape in it. As I do this, I also look for incongruities, oddities, ambiguities, or even contradictions. If I find cracks in the wall that I want to climb — a wall apparently smooth and uniform — I will then be able to reach the top. In other words, I try to raise questions and brace myself against quick answers too easily pulled from my hat. These questions can open up new ways of looking at the text, and from them can also emerge seminal theological insights.

Here, I propose at random six observations on this text, which is so well known that it is almost no longer open at all to reading — a story of a rich man and his poor neighbor who ends up withdrawing from him: (1) difficulties of translation; (2) semantic domains; (3) narrative structure; (4) spatialization; (5) characterization; (6) implied reader.

First, it is always instructive to check how far the translations depart from the harshness of the original Greek, for various reasons. For this exercise, I consulted six translations, three in French, three in English.[1] Let

1. *Bible de Jérusalem* (1998) = BJ, *Traduction œcuménique de la Bible* (1974) = TOB, *Bi-*

Synchronic Observations on Luke 16:19-31 as Preparation for a Translation

me give a few examples. In v. 21, we have the participle form ἐπιθυμῶν, a very strong verb. Now, we see that the three French translations are much softer than the original Greek:

BJ:	Il aurait bien voulu se rassasier	ASV:	and desiring to be fed
TOB:	Il aurait bien voulu se rassasier	NRSV:	who longed to satisfy his hunger
BNT:	Il espérait calmer sa faim²	NIV:	and longing to eat

In the French translations, any reference to a strong desire is omitted, contrary to Liddell and Scott's definition of ἐπιθυμῶν: "to set one's heart upon a thing, lust after, long for, covet, desire." This story is a story of desire, from beginning to end: it appeals to the reader's own desire.

In v. 23, we have the sentence (A) καὶ ἐν τῷ ᾅδῃ (B) ἐπάρας τοὺς ὀφθαλμοὺς αὐτοῦ, (C) ὑπάρχων ἐν βασάνοις (D) ὁρᾷ Ἀβραάμ. Four Bibles have changed the word order thus: A + C + B + D (BJ, TOB, NIV, NRSV): "In Hades, where he was being tormented, he looked up and saw Abraham" (NRSV). This sentence may be more logical and elegant, but perhaps the Greek word order has its own agenda — the locus and state of torment is framed between two verbs of sight. Does that make a difference in the final interpretation? As Christians, since Origen, we are "textual maniacs," as every detail of the text is crucial and significant. Should we respect the word order?

In vv. 22-23, we encounter the idiom κόλπον Ἀβραάμ, κόλποι αὐτοῦ first in the singular, then in the plural. The Bibles we are comparing translate it as follows:

BJ:	dans le sein d'Abraham/en son sein	ASV:	into Abraham's bosom/
TOB:	au côté d'Abraham/à ses côtés		in his bosom
	(singular and plural are respected)	NIV:	to Abraham's side/by his side
BNT:	auprès d'Abraham/dans ses bras	NRSV:	to be with Abraham/by his side
	(singular and plural are respected)		

The variation from singular to plural in two adjacent verses is an enigma in itself — only TOB and BNT respect this slip. Furthermore, κόλπον is a

---

ble Nouvelle Traduction (2001) = BNT, *American Standard Version* (1901) = ASV, *New International Version* (1965) = NIV, *New Revised Standard Version* (1989) = NRSV.

2. "He would have liked to satiate himself," "He hoped to calm his hunger."

metaphor, but a strange one, alien to our culture. The BJ is very particular, making Abraham a female: "in his womb." And why not? The general meaning is clearly intimacy, proximity. The difficulty lies in respecting the metaphor. Should we find an equivalent metaphor for today? Here, BNT is more audacious ("in his arms"), but TOB, NIV, and NRSV might hit the target too.

Second, I discern in Luke three semantic domains that can guide the interpretation, and hence the translation, of this passage. Many words indicate the importance of family: father Abraham (vv. 24, 30), father (v. 27), my father (v. 27), child (v. 25 — not son!), brothers (v. 28). Green's commentary explains this with reference to the socio-historical background of the first-century Mediterranean world and its clan-like structure.[3] The rich man has the control of his clan; each of its members is defined by his family solidarity. This is very interesting, but can we draw any theological insight from the presence of this vocabulary? In the New Testament, filiation and sonship are not just socioeconomic realities or trivial questions, but central issues that intersect every NT book. Why does the rich man acknowledge Abraham as his father, and why does Abraham reply to him with a kind of ironic euphemism: "child"? How can the rich man have two fathers in verse 27? "Then, father, I beg you to send him to my father's house." Is it possible that the father's house could be Israel? I think that these kinds of questions, apparently foolish, could lead us to interesting discoveries and open up new reading possibilities. We must also try to explain the text's literary mechanics.

We observe another semantic domain around suffering: Lazarus is covered with sores (twice, vv. 20, 21), and in Hades the rich man is subject to torture (twice, vv. 23, 28) and torment (twice, vv. 24, 25). Thus, the storyteller strongly emphasizes suffering. Linked to this is a third semantic domain concerning the body. In v. 21, the dogs are licking Lazarus, but the reader should see that in v. 24 the rich man wants desperately to lick just the tip of Lazarus's finger.

Third, the narrative structure presents two plots successively, a plot of resolution (vv. 19-23) with a stereotyped and minimalist *mise en scène*, and a revelation plot (vv. 24-31), with a very long dialogue (for the Bible!) in which the proud rich man, even in Hades, dares to make three requests to use Lazarus as his servant, each of which Abraham refuses. The first

---

3. J. B. Green, *The Gospel of Luke* (NICNT; Grand Rapids: Eerdmans, 1997).

Synchronic Observations on Luke 16:19-31 as Preparation for a Translation

part (vv. 19-23) sets up a story of reversal — as we shall see in our analysis of the spatialization — in the same line as the *Magnificat* (Luke 1:51-53).[4] First the beggar wants to reach the rich man, but to no avail; this sets the scene for the reversal in the second part (vv. 24-31), a very polite conversation that mixes different motifs about eschatology, resurrection, and the testimonial function of Scriptures. The rich man begs Abraham to let the former beggar reach him — but in vain. In a sense, the tableau is almost surrealistic: in a very casual tone, Abraham and the rich man — two men far apart, one of them suffering *à l'extrême* — have a long theological exchange that seems to go nowhere.

It is interesting to compare these results with what one commentator has to say about this passage.[5] Marshall, too, sees the two parts of the story. But in a historico-critical perspective, he looks for the Egyptian or Jewish version that could be the ancestor of Luke's story; for Marshall, the presence of a short story of reversal — a very classic motif in the Ancient Near East — combined with a dialogue, presupposes a complex editorial process, probably very far from Jesus' teaching. These genealogical observations, even though hypothetical, are fascinating. But again, we also have to try to explain the text with its own literary mechanism.

Fourth, the spatialization of the text is particularly intriguing — it is condensed in the following chart:

	Verticality	**Horizontality**
Before death	rich/Lazarus	Lazarus toward the rich man's gate
After death	Lazarus/rich man rich man is buried ↓ Lazarus ↑ angels	Lazarus could go toward the rich man Lazarus could go toward the brothers
Resurrection	to rise *from* the dead (Abraham's point of view)	go to them commissioned *by* the dead (rich man's point of view)

The fundamental vertical and hierarchic positions before death are reversed after death: first, the rich man is above Lazarus, and then Lazarus is

---

4. "He has brought down the powerful from their thrones, and lifted up the lowly; he has filled the hungry with good things, and sent the rich away empty."

5. I. H. Marshall, *The Gospel of Luke: A Commentary on the Greek Text* (NIGTC; Grand Rapids: Eerdmans, 1978).

above the rich man. There are also horizontal and vertical movements. Horizontally, Lazarus "tries" to go toward the rich man or his brothers, before and after death, but is unable to do it. Vertically, the rich man goes down (in the tomb and then in Hades) and Lazarus goes up, with the angels' help. From a socio-historical perspective, to be buried is a sign of wealth, and it seems logical that Lazarus would have gone to the "common grave." But in the narrative, the vertical contrast is in favor of Lazarus. One last detail to note: from Abraham's point of view, the resurrection is vertical (τις ἐκ νεκρῶν), in contrast with the rich man's point of view, where it is described horizontally (τις ἀπὸ νεκρῶν).

Fifth, the characterization creates three main characters, two active (the rich man and Abraham) and one passive (Lazarus). Apart from the mention of angels, God is absent. The following chart shows the contrast between the rich man and Lazarus:

	Space 1	Character 1	Character 2	Space 2
vv. 19-21		man	—	
			[with the dogs]	
		rich person	poor	near the rich man's door
		• purple, linen ($)	• sores	under rich man's table
		• feasting each day ($)	• hunger	
		—	Lazarus	
vv. 22-23	[low]	buried ($)	carried away by the angels [heaven]	[high] κόλπος
	in Hades			with Abraham
	[low] (looking up)			far away [from the rich man point of view]
	in torments (plural)			ἐν τοῖς κόλποις (plural)
vv. 24-31	in this fire	five brothers		
	in this place of torture	tormented		
		ACTIVE	**PASSIVE**	

As I keep looking for the contradictions, oppositions, and oddities in the text, I retain the following observations:

- The rich man is anonymous (despite the effort of some manuscripts[6]) but still has a human rank.

6. See the remarks of the text-critical colleagues in this volume.

- Lazarus is always shown in reference to the rich man; he is ranked at the level of a dog; he says nothing. We could affirm that he is nothing, or the shadow of the other man. The word ἄνθρωπος is not applied directly to him (despite many translations), but he has a name.
- Before his death, Lazarus is hungry, while after his death, the rich man is thirsty.
- In v. 24, the rich man is willing to lick Lazarus, like a dog.
- The narrator speaks about "tortures" (plural, v. 23), the character "rich man" speaks of torture (singular, v. 28) about himself. Is the suffering less intense from the rich man's perspective?
- Abraham comments in v. 25 on the narration of vv. 19-23: the story itself gives its own interpretation.
- The rich man knows Lazarus's name, but the reader does not learn that fact until the middle of the narrative (v. 24) — this new clue provokes the reader to change her evaluation of the character: "the rich man was a bad guy, indeed, knowing his neighbor's situation from the beginning!"[7]
- Lazarus becomes the (virtual) mediator between Abraham and the rich man, the rich man and his brothers. For a nobody, a non-person, a silent figure of the text, a shadow, this central function is paradoxical. The poor marginal character is at the structural center of the text.
- There is a close intimacy between Abraham and Lazarus and a formal father-son relationship between Abraham and the rich man.

Sixth, one last word concerning the implied Christian reader. If we place ourselves in an intertextual perspective, and not in a historico-critical perspective of sources or tradition history, could we risk the hypothesis that the figure of Luke's Lazarus has a link with the story of Lazarus of Bethany returning from the dead, as found in John 11? The end of Luke's story could allude to John's story.

These few observations do not exhaust the exegetical work. In this limited space I wanted only to demonstrate the fruitfulness of a synchronic, narrative approach. We explored only the text itself, notwithstanding its narrative context:[8] this story is told by Jesus to the Pharisees,

---

7. R. Hurley, "Le lecteur et le riche," *ScEs* 51 (1999): 65-80.
8. See Luke Timothy Johnson, "Narrative Perspectives on Luke 16:19-31," pp. 207-11 in this volume.

in the overall complex plot of the Gospel, and it interacts with other stories, such as "One father had two sons" (Luke 15:11-32), and "A man was going down from Jerusalem to Jericho" (Luke 10:29-37), stories of sonship and of being a neighbor. We should consider the function of our story in the Lukan narrative project.

Returning to Luke 16:19-31, one thing struck me. If we define a parable as a story that ends in a disturbing and awkward fashion, the story of the rich man and Lazarus is a particularly efficient parable. This is not a moralizing story (be good to the poor), nor a positivistic description of the afterlife, nor an intriguing debate on the proof of the resurrection, nor even an appeal for ethical conversion. After a vivid exposition of contrasted characters, the reader is left in the middle of nowhere, with no other suspense than the repeated refusals of Abraham to the demands of the rich man. The story is open-ended and leaves the reader orphaned. One task remains: to complete the ending with the help of Moses and the prophets, a reservoir of stories. At last, our story leads the reader toward other stories.

Narrative Perspectives on Luke 16:19-31

Luke Timothy Johnson

I take this exercise as one of discovering what can be learned about a specific text when it is approached from a variety of self-consciously adopted perspectives. My perspective on Luke 16:19-31, as on any other Gospel passage, is that of narrative criticism. This is not, for me, so much a deliberately chosen approach as it is a perspective shaped by early practices of reading — specifically that of *lectio continua* in the Divine Office when I was a Benedictine monk — and by youthful exposure to the new criticism associated with Cleanth Brooks and company. Narrative criticism, as it developed within New Testament studies, seemed to me merely to provide discipline for a self-evidently reasonable way of reading stories.

For contemporary readers as for ancient — the main difference being whether the text is experienced through oral proclamation or not — stories unfold their meaning in sequence or not at all; readers work with the text to construct meaning bit by bit, with each new segment of the narrative confirming, amplifying, or altering the sense of the story as heard to that point. The critic simply occupies the position of a super-competent hearer, who has heard this story told before any number of times, and so is not utterly naïve, yet whose discipline enables him or her to remain open to new ways of hearing at each repetition.

Fundamental to my approach is the premise that narratives create meaning precisely as narratives: the story is itself the vehicle of meaning. In terms of Aristotle's *Poetics*, it is the *mythos* ("Plot") and *ethos* ("Character") as fully developed that reveal the *dianoia* ("Meaning" or "Argument"). Narrative is read, in short, as a form of rhetoric, in which both invention (the story elements chosen to relate) and arrangement (the sequence in which the story elements are told) work together to shape an argument. A second premise follows from the first, namely, that each part of the overall story serves a function for the shaping of the larger narrative argument. The narrative critic asks for any specific pericope of a Gospel, therefore, not simply "what is it saying?" but also "what is it doing?" Narrative interpretation requires the subtle evaluation of the reciprocal effect of the part on the whole and the whole on the part.

If we look at Jesus' parable of Lazarus and the rich man in isolation from its narrative context, we can make a number of interesting and even important observations. We can note its resemblance to other ancient Mediterranean stories of after-death reversal; we can see its narrative enactment of the Lukan beatitude ("Blessed are you poor") and woe ("Woe to you who are rich," Luke 6:20, 24); we can therefore correlate this story with other Lukan statements in order to construct the evangelist's teaching on material possessions; and we can draw some inferences concerning Luke's understanding of eschatology and of the moral teaching of the law and prophets. We can even note the way in which this parable resembles another of Luke's most memorable stories — the one about the lost son (15:11-32) — in appending a conversation between two characters at the end of the parable. These are all observations worth making.

But what reading the parable in isolation from its narrative context does not enable us to observe is precisely what narrative criticism allows us to see, namely what this parable is doing within the story and how it contributes to the construction of the larger story. Narrative criticism allows us to ask about the narrative function of the parable, to ask not only what it says, but also why it is being said here. This question is especially important for interpreting Luke-Acts, for in this composition the *sequence* of the narration is distinctively significant: Luke regards a story told *kathexēs* as having a particularly convincing character (see Luke 1:3; Acts 11:4). In Luke-Acts, *where* something is said is as important as *what* is said.

Starting with the widest circle — the narrative of Luke-Acts as a whole — it is possible to spiral in a rapid series of turns to the parable of Lazarus and the rich man in its immediate narrative context, in order to ask just that question: what is it doing here? Allow me to stipulate, then, a number of points that can be, and have been, supported by careful analysis, but that analysis will not be in this essay. Luke-Acts as a whole makes an argument in defense of God's fidelity by using a prophetic model: not only does the story of Jesus and the church fulfill God's prophecies of old, but Jesus and the apostles are themselves prophetic in speech and deed. Specifically, Luke constructs his story on the model of the prophet Moses, whose twofold sending to Israel and twofold rejection by the people is sketched in Stephen's speech in Acts 7:17-50: the Gospel shows the first sending of Jesus as God's prophet who brings God's visitation, his first rejection, and his vindication by God; the sequel shows the second visitation of the people through Jesus' prophetic representatives and shows how some of the people responded in faith, so that the mission to the Gentiles was an extension rather than a replacement of Israel as God's people.

The parable of Lazarus and the rich man appears in a part of Luke's Gospel narrative that is entirely his literary construction, namely the long account of Jesus' journey toward Jerusalem that extends from 9:51 to 19:44. Having established that Jesus is the prophet-messiah who embodies God's visitation of the people in 3:1–7:50, and having shown that prophet gathering a remnant people defined by faith around him in 8:1–9:50, Luke constructs this long journey that occupies a full ten chapters of his Gospel. As in Mark, this middle part of the narrative is marked by passion predictions: readers see Jesus as the prophet who is moving toward his destined death in Jerusalem. But while he is journeying, Jesus is also constantly teaching. Here is where Luke has placed the great bulk of the Q material he shares with Matthew and his own distinctive L material. In contrast to Matthew's habit of organizing Jesus' sayings into set discourses, however, Luke weaves his teaching with subtle verisimilitude into the situations Jesus faces while on this great journey: sayings on hospitality are spoken at meals, calls to follow him are issued while Jesus is on the road.

Two further compositional features distinguish Luke's arrangement of these saying materials. The first is that he carefully distinguishes what sort of thing Jesus says to each of the three groups that are around him as he moves on his journey. To the anonymous crowd, he issues warnings and calls to discipleship; to those who join him on the journey, he provides instruction on the use of possessions, prayer, and patience in persecution; to his opponents, the Pharisees and lawyers, he speaks words of rejection in response to their rejection of the vision of the world he offers through his deeds and speech. The second is that he arranges these in an alternating pattern, addressing first one audience, then another, thereby creating a sense both of movement and of growth, as Jesus gathers a remnant prophetic people around himself even as he spurs his enemies to their climatic rejection of him.

Now I must bring these sweeping claims to bear on the immediate context of our parable. I note in the first place that the three parables of the lost and found (sheep, coin, son) in 15:3-32 are told not to the disciples, but specifically in response to the Pharisees and scribes, who in 15:1-2 had grumbled because Jesus "welcomed sinners and ate together with them." The closing dialogue between the father and the elder son therefore unmistakably serves to interpret this narrative setting: the correspondence between the law-abiding elder son who rejects table-fellowship with the sinful younger son and the narrative setting established by Luke can scarcely be missed. The parable serves to interpret Luke's larger story of the prophet and the people. I note in the second place that Jesus next turns in 16:1-13 to a parable and maxims delivered *pros tous mathētas* ("to his disciples"), and however strange or difficult we find 16:1-13, it is clearly meant to be positive instruction concerning *phronēsis* ("cleverness/sagacity") in the use of material possessions.

I note in the third place that the entire sequence of 16:14-31 is once more spoken to Jesus' enemies, the Pharisees. In 16:14, Luke identifies them as *philargyroi* ("lovers of money") who reject Jesus precisely upon "hearing all these things" that Jesus said about sharing possessions through almsgiving. However difficult it is to find a connecting thread running through the obscure sayings in 16:14-18, it can be asserted with considerable probability that Luke intended them to serve the narrative function of distinguishing the teaching of the prophetic messiah from that of his opponents. And I note in the fourth and final place that, in this sequence, the parable of Lazarus and the rich man forms the same sort of climactic and interpretive role as did the parable of the lost son in the previous sequence — we see that in 17:1 Jesus once again addresses "his disciples."

From this narrative perspective, then, we can conclude that the dialogue between Abraham and the rich man is far from an afterthought; it is, indeed, the intended climax of the parable, which serves to morally indict the rich man (and the money-loving Pharisees) in a manner that the basic story does not: if the rich man and the Pharisees had truly been committed to Moses and the prophets, they would have recognized that the sharing of possessions with the poor among the people was at the heart of Torah and would never cease being normative for God's people (see 16:17), and the rich man would have fed and clothed the man he passed every day at his gate (16:19).

We can conclude further that Luke placed the parable in this place to serve his narrative purpose at this place, which was to show the division within the people caused by the prophetic Messiah Jesus: the self-justifying Pharisees (see 16:15) are designated as "lovers of money" (16:14) precisely because they do not share Jesus' prophetic vision of God's care for the poor and therefore the covenantal obligation to share possessions with the poor.

We can conclude, finally, that Abraham's closing declaration, "If they do not listen to Moses and the prophets, neither will they be convinced if someone rises from the dead" (16:31), serves as a narrative anticipation of Luke's second volume, when the proclamation and demonstration of Jesus as the prophet whom God has raised will again gather the outcast but leave the wealthy and powerful unconvinced (see Acts 2:41–5:42).

PART 3
THEOLOGY

Mistranslation and the Death of Christ: Isaiah 53 LXX and Its Pauline Reception

Francis Watson

As traditionally understood, textual criticism is the attempt to recover the text as it left the hand of its author or final redactor. Modern biblical translators and exegetes seek from textual critics a text approximating as closely as possible to that original state of the text. The assumption is that canonical scripture is a singular object with an essentially singular form, which every critical edition or translation seeks to represent as accurately as possible, stripping away the accumulated errors of generations of scribes. This model of the canonical text has great achievements to its credit and remains indispensable for many kinds of exegetical activity. Yet it has its limitations. Above all, it underplays the irreducibly plural forms of canonical scripture that are actually operative within communities of faith.

This essay is devoted to the Septuagintal translation of Isaiah 53, the "Fourth Servant Song," a text crucially important for early Christian reflection on the death of Jesus.[1] Its importance is evident already in Paul, not just in his explicit citations but also in his use of language drawn from this text. What is striking is that this Christian appropriation of Isaiah 53 is heavily dependent on statements that seem to deviate from and mistranslate the probable underlying Hebrew. The term "mistranslation" is used here in an extended sense, to cover not just the translator's errors but every feature of the Greek text that could not in principle have been predicted in

---

1. Throughout this essay I refer for convenience to "Isaiah 53," meaning "Isa 52:13–53:12."

advance on the basis of the Hebrew. "Mistranslation" thus covers a wide range of linguistic phenomena — omissions, insertions, or substitutions, grammatical or syntactical modifications, debatable semantic decisions, and so on. Some if not all of these phenomena may be covered by the term "paraphrase." They represent *mis*-translation in the sense that semantic possibilities present in the original Hebrew are obscured or lost in the Greek and are replaced by new semantic possibilities that cannot unambiguously be derived from the Hebrew.

A translation both *represents* an original, whose semantic content it strives to convey in a new linguistic medium, and *displaces* that original. Indeed, it is precisely because the translation represents the original that it also displaces it. Henceforth the text will be associated not with the barely accessible language of its original composition but with the vernacular. The original text is marginalized. For Greek-speaking communities, the Isaianic prophecy announces that "the virgin will conceive and will bear a son" (Isa 7:14): that is what the scriptural text says, for the scriptural text is now the text in Greek. Admittedly, the bilingual may propose that "young woman" would be more in keeping with the semantic range of the Hebrew. Yet the monolingual may prove surprisingly resistant to any suggestion that a translation be modified — and not only when doctrinal issues are at stake. In the case of the Septuagint, the legend of its miraculous origin functions precisely to inhibit the possibility of appealing to the Hebrew against the Greek.[2] The legend originally related only to the Pentateuch but was extended by Christians to "the prophets," i.e., to scripture as a whole.[3] Thus the translators who at Isa 7:14 rendered *'almah* as *parthenos*

---

2. In its earliest extant form, the legend serves the same function but without appeal to miracle. In the *Letter of Aristeas*, the translators produce an agreed version that is approved by the Jewish community of Alexandria, who pronounce a curse on any who modify it (*Letter of Aristeas* 302, 308-11; cf. Josephus, *Ant.* 12.103-109, where the curse is replaced by an exhortation to practice textual criticism). In Philo's *Life of Moses*, however, the translators become inspired prophets who each independently produce the same translation (*Life of Moses* 2.37-40). The Greek and the "Chaldean" versions are to be regarded "as sisters, or rather as one and the same," and the authors of the Greek "not as translators but as hierophants and prophets" (40). It was this "miraculous" version of the legend that was taken up and developed by Greek-speaking Christians.

3. See Justin, *1 Apol.* 31; Ps-Justin, *Coh. ad Graec.*, 13; Clement of Alexandria, *Strom.* 1.22; Irenaeus, *Adv. haer.* 3.21.1-3 (with particular reference to Isa 7:14). In Pseudo-Justin and Irenaeus, the translators are shut up in individual rooms, thereby ensuring the miraculous status of the common translation. This version of the story recurs in Cyril of Jerusalem,

did so under the inspiration of the Holy Spirit. Even where there is an awareness of a possible discrepancy between translation and original, the inspired translation retains its own autonomous authority; it is this that the appeal to inspiration is intended to safeguard.

If "scripture" is inseparable from the forms in which it functions in particular communities, it is appropriate to follow the early church in regarding Greek Isaiah as a canonical text in its own right. This means that the quest for a singular, "original" text loses its urgency: scripture incorporates various text-forms and is an inherently plural phenomenon. Instances of "mistranslation" will serve only to underline the distinctive, autonomous existence of the new text, which displaces the original and functions as normative scripture in its own right. If Paul and other early Christians appeal to texts where the Greek is an imperfect rendering of the Hebrew, this need not be seen as a problem, to be corrected perhaps by reconstructing a Hebrew original and interpreting Isaiah 53 solely on that basis. A text's original sense may prove to be less significant than what happens to it in the process of its transmission. Isaiah 53 seems to have occasioned little interpretative interest before early Christians found in its Greek form lexical and semantic resources that enabled them to understand Jesus' death in its positive soteriological significance.[4]

The Suffering Servant in Greek

If certain kinds of "mistranslation" occur in the passage from Hebrew to Greek, this presupposes that we have access to relatively stable Hebrew and Greek texts that can be compared with each other. If there are marked divergences between the Masoretic text and the Greek translation as attested in the early uncials, we cannot exclude the possibility that equally significant divergences may have occurred within the Hebrew and Greek textual

---

Epiphanius, and Augustine and is criticized by Jerome; on this, see M. Müller, *The First Bible of the Church: A Plea for the Septuagint* (Copenhagen International Seminar 1; Sheffield: Sheffield Academic Press, 1996), 68-97.

4. It was once widely believed that Isaiah 53 was significant for pre-Christian Jewish messianic beliefs and for Jesus' sense of his own vocation: see for example O. Cullmann, *The Christology of the New Testament* (trans. S. C. Guthrie and C. A. M. Hall; London: SCM Press, 1959), 51-82, and, for a recent restatement, N. T. Wright, *Jesus and the Victory of God* (London: SPCK, 1996), 588-91, 601-4.

traditions themselves. That would make it harder to identify mistranslations in the passage from the one to the other, for a discrepancy between the Greek and the Hebrew might represent a discrepancy within the Hebrew tradition itself. In fact, however, it does prove possible to identify relatively stable Hebrew and Greek texts of Isaiah 53, as is clear from a comparison between the Masoretic text and the Qumran Isaiah manuscripts, and between the Greek Isaiah and early Christian citations.

The Hebrew Text

The full text of Isa 52:13–53:12 is found in 1QIsaiah[a] (col. XLIV) and 1QIsaiah[b] (col. VIII). Fragments of this text are found in three manuscripts from Cave 4, 4QIsaiah[b] (fr. 39: Isa 53:11-12); 4QIsaiah[c] (fr. 37-39: Isa 52:13–53:3, 6-8); and 4QIsaiah[d] (fr. 11 ii: Isa 53:8-12).[5] These texts produce a total of 14 variant readings (9 of them from 1QIsaiah[a]), of which the most significant are the following:

- Isa 53:3 MT "a man of sufferings and known [וידוע] of sickness"; 1QIsa[a, b] "knowing [וי[ו]דע] sickness" (two letters have been transposed, perhaps by being mistaken for each other).
- Isa 53:8 MT "stricken for the transgression of my people [עמי]"; 1QIsa[a] "his people [עמו]."
- Isa 53:9 MT "he gave [ויתן] his grave with the wicked"; 1QIsa[a] "they gave [ויתנו]."
- Isa 53:10 MT "he has made [him] sick [החלי]" (?); 1QIsa[a] "he has pierced him [ויחללהו]."
- Isa 53:11 MT "from the distress of his soul he will see [יראה]"; 1QIsa[a, b], 4QIsa[d] "he will see light [יראה אור]."
- Isa 53:11 MT "the righteous one, my servant [עבדי] will justify many"; 1QIsa[a] "his servant [עבדו]."[6]

---

5. For the texts from Caves 1 and 4, see D. W. Parry and E. Qimron, *The Great Isaiah Scroll (1QIsa[a]): A New Edition* (STDJ 32; Leiden: Brill, 1999); D. Barthélemy and J. T. Milik, *Qumran Cave 1* (DJD 1; Oxford: Clarendon Press, 1955): 1QIsaiah[b]; E. Ulrich et al., *Qumran Cave 4: The Prophets* (DJD 15; Oxford: Clarendon Press, 1997): 4QIsaiah[b,c,d].

6. The other 8 variants are: 52:14 משחת (MT), משחתי (1QIsa[a]); 52:15 כי (MT), כיא (4QIsa[c]); 53:6 נבוה (MT), ינבוזהו (1QIsa[a]); 53:9 במתיו (MT), בומתו (1QIsa[a]); 53:9 פיו (MT), פיהו (4QIsa[d]); 53:10 יאריך (MT), האריך (4QIsa[d]); 53:12 נמנה (MT), נמנא (1QIsa[a]); 53:12 ולפשעם (MT), ולפשעים (1QIsa[a]).

Mistranslation and the Death of Christ

Only two of these variants provide any support for a Septuagintal reading: v. 3, where LXX reads, "and knowing [what it is] to bear weakness" (καὶ εἰδὼς φέρειν μαλακίαν); and v. 11, where LXX reads, "[And the Lord willed to remove] the distress of his soul, to show him light . . ." (δεῖξαι αὐτῷ φῶς). In vv. 8, 11, a third-person singular pronominal suffix takes the place of a first singular one, resulting in a change of speaker but not of referent. The most significant Qumran variant, "he will pierce him," is unsupported by the Greek. Conversely, the most significant Greek variant (εἰς θάνατον in v. 8, suggesting "stricken unto death" [למות for למו] in the Hebrew exemplar?) is unsupported by the Qumran textual evidence. Overall, the Greek does not significantly affect the textual criticism of the Hebrew in this passage. While the Qumran Isaiah manuscripts provide a series of interesting variants, their potential impact on the sense of the text is limited. We are dealing here with a relatively stable text: at the turn of the eras, Isaiah 53 was already being read in forms closely corresponding to the Masoretic one. There is no evidence in the Qumran material of a radically different text-form, which could be used to explain the divergences in the Greek.[7]

The Greek Text

The stability or otherwise of the Greek text of Isaiah 53 can best be assessed by way of the earliest Christian citations from this chapter.[8] A citation that deviates from the Greek text as attested in the major uncials could, of course, simply be a free citation rather than representing a deviant text-form. In fact, however, deviations from the received text are remarkably

---

7. A. van der Kooij seeks to align 1QIsaiah[a] with Isaiah LXX, on the grounds that both texts represent a free approach in relation to their *Vorlagen* ("The Old Greek of Isaiah in Relation to the Qumran Texts of Isaiah: Some General Comments," in *Septuagint, Scrolls and Cognate Writings: Papers Presented to the International Symposium on the Septuagint and Its Relations to the Dead Sea Scrolls and Other Writings* [ed. G. J. Brooke and B. Lindars; Atlanta: Scholars Press, 1992], 195-213, here 198-99). In the case of Isaiah 53, however, the differences between 1QIsaiah[a] and MT are of a quite different order of magnitude than the differences between Isaiah LXX and MT.

8. Among the older papyri, material from the Fourth Servant Song is attested only in the fourth century P.Ryl. Gr. 460 (= Rahlfs 958), which consists of fragments of a testimony-book that included Isa 42:3-4; 52:15; 53:1-3, 6-7, 11-12; 66:18-19 (J. Ziegler, *Isaias* [Septuaginta XIV; 2nd ed.; Göttingen: Vandenhoeck & Ruprecht, 1967], 11).

few. Early Christian citations are extant both of Isaiah 53 as a whole (1 Clem. 16; Justin, *Dial.* 13) and of individual passages:

- Isa 52:10–54:6 = Justin, *Dial.* 13.2-9. In Isa 52:14, there are a transposition[9] and an abbreviation (*Dial.* 13.3).[10] At 53:7, an explanatory pronoun is added (τὸ στόμα αὐτοῦ),[11] and a redundant pronoun is omitted (ἐναντίον τοῦ κείραντος [αὐτόν]) (*Dial.* 13.5). At 53:11, τὰς ἁμαρτίας αὐτῶν becomes τὰς ἁμαρτίας ἡμῶν (*Dial.* 13.7).
- Isa 52:15 = Rom 15:21. There are no significant variants either between or within the Pauline or the Septuagintal textual traditions.[12]
- Isa 53:1-12 = 1 Clem. 16.3-14. The citation of the entire chapter shows that early Christian readers could view it as a distinct literary unit.[13] At v. 3, Clement reads παρὰ τὸ εἶδος τῶν ἀνθρώπων for παρὰ πάντας ἀνθρώπους (Alexandrinus), or παρὰ τοὺς υἱοὺς τῶν ἀνθρώπων (Vaticanus; Justin, *Dial.* 13.4), or the harmonizing παρὰ πάντας τοὺς υἱοὺς τῶν ἀνθρώπων (Sinaiticus). Clement is probably paraphrasing here.[14] In v. 6, it is said that "the Lord gave him up to our sins [ταῖς ἁμαρτίαις ἡμῶν]"; Clement's substitution of ὑπὲρ τῶν ἁμαρτιῶν ἡμῶν (1 Clem. 16.7) is clearly shaped by traditional Christian terminology.[15]
- Isa 53:1 = Rom 10:16; John 12:38. No variants.

9. πολλοὶ ἐπὶ σέ for ἐπὶ σὲ πολλοί.
10. τὸ εἶδος καὶ ἡ δόξα σου for τὸ εἶδός σου καὶ ἡ δόξα σου ἀπὸ τῶν ἀνθρώπων.
11. Justin thereby harmonizes the first occurrence of this phrase with the second, later in the same verse. Note also the similar explanatory pronoun in v. 8, ἐν τῇ ταπεινώσει αὐτοῦ, where Justin's reading (*Dial.* 13.6) is supported by the majority reading of Acts 8:32 but not by P[74] ℵ A B.
12. The variation in word order in Ambrosiaster and Vaticanus is an attempt to improve the awkward syntax (so C. R. Stanley, *Paul and the Language of Scripture: Citation Technique in the Pauline Epistles and Contemporary Literature* [SNTSMS; Cambridge: Cambridge University Press, 1992], 184 n.). Surprisingly, some commentators take it to be original (e.g., C. E. B. Cranfield, *Romans* [vol. 2; ICC; Edinburgh: T. & T. Clark, 1979], 765; J. D. G. Dunn, *Romans 9–16* [WBC; Dallas: Word Books, 1988], 865).
13. It is an exaggeration to claim that "the modern isolation of the Servant Songs . . . was completely unknown in that day" (J. Jeremias, *TDNT*, 5:682). Note also the citation of the "First Servant Song" in Matt 12:18-21 (= Isa 42:1-4).
14. The additional reference to the servant's "form" is derived from the opening of v. 3 (ἀλλὰ τὸ εἶδος αὐτοῦ ἄτιμον ἐκλεῖπον).
15. Other variants in Clement's citation are: the paraphrastic insertion of καὶ πόνῳ after ἐν πληγῇ ὤν (v. 3; 1 Clem. 16.3); the substitution of ἥκει for ἤχθη (v. 8; 1 Clem. 16.9, so also Justin, *Dial.* 13.6); and the transposition of βούλεται κύριος (v. 10; 1 Clem. 16.12).

- Isa 53:4 = Matt 8:17. Here the evangelist reads αὐτὸς τὰς ἀσθενείας ἡμῶν ἔλαβεν καὶ τὰς νόσους ἐβάστασεν in place of the LXX's οὗτος τὰς ἁμαρτίας ἡμῶν φέρει καὶ περὶ ἡμῶν ὀδυνᾶται. Matthew's rendering appears to represent an independent retranslation from the Hebrew.[16]
- Isa 53:5 = Barn. 5.2. Barnabas attests the order διὰ τὰς ἀνομίας ἡμῶν/ διὰ τὰς ἁμαρτίας ἡμῶν, with Alexandrinus and Sinaiticus. The nouns are transposed in 1 Clem. 16.5, Justin, *Dial.* 13.5, and Vaticanus.
- Isa 53:7 = Barn. 5.2. Here ἄφωνος is transposed, so that the text reads ὡς ἀμνὸς ἄφωνος ἐναντίον τοῦ κείραντος αὐτόν rather than ὡς ἀμνὸς ἐναντίον τοῦ κείραντος αὐτὸν ἄφωνος (B A S). The transposition is not supported by the fuller citation in Acts 8:32-33.
- Isa 53:7-8 = Acts 8:32-33. In the only extended New Testament citation from Isaiah 53, there are no significant variants.
- Isa 53:9 = 1 Pet 2:22. In the first of several allusions to Isaiah 53, the author draws upon v. 9, ἀνομίαν οὐκ ἐποίησεν, οὐδὲ εὑρέθη δόλος ἐν τῷ στόματι αὐτοῦ, but replaces ἀνομίαν with ἁμαρτίαν. In 1 Pet 2:24, τὰς ἁμαρτίας ἡμῶν αὐτὸς ἀνήνεγκεν derives from Isa 53:4 (οὗτος <u>τὰς ἁμαρτίας ἡμῶν</u> φέρει) and 53:12 (<u>αὐτὸς</u> ἁμαρτίας πολλῶν <u>ἀνήνεγκεν</u>). Also derived from Isaiah 53 are οὗ τῷ μώλωπι ἰάθητε (1 Pet 2:24; Isa 53:5, τῷ μώλωπι αὐτοῦ ἡμεῖς ἰάθημεν), and ἦτε γὰρ ὡς πρόβατα πλανώμενοι (1 Pet 2:25; Isa 53:6, πάντες ὡς πρόβατα ἐπλανήθημεν). There is no evidence here of any variants within the text used by the author of 1 Peter.
- Isa 53:12 = Luke 22:37; Mark 15:28 (majority reading). In Luke 22:37, the command to buy a sword is explained by the need to fulfill what is written: καὶ μετὰ ἀνόμων ἐλογίσθη. In Mark 15:28 (not attested in ℵ A B C D etc.), the same citation is applied to Jesus' crucifixion between the two thieves. It is drawn from Isa 53:12: καὶ ἐν τοῖς ἀνόμοις ἐλογίσθη. The wording of Mark 15:28 is probably dependent on Luke 22:37, and the deviation from the Septuagint is explicable if Luke, like the later copyist of Mark, has in mind the "two other criminals" (Luke 23:32) with whom Jesus was crucified.[17] The Septuagint's "among the lawless" would imply more than two.

---

16. On Matthew's scriptural citations, see most recently M. J. J. Menken, *Matthew's Bible* (Leuven: Leuven University Press, 2004).

17. On this see J. Fitzmyer, *The Gospel according to Luke X–XXIV* (AB; New York: Doubleday, 1985), 1433.

The earliest Christian citations of Isaiah 53 produce few interesting textual variants. Matt 8:17 is an independent translation, intended to exploit the reference to sickness present in the Hebrew but not in the Greek; Luke 22:37 has adapted Isa 53:12 to the realities of the passion narrative. Otherwise, early Christian citations correspond remarkably closely to the text as rendered in the major Septuagintal manuscripts — in spite of the common tendency of short citations to deviate through imprecision or adaptation. Like its Hebrew counterpart, Isaiah 53 in Greek is a relatively stable text by the first century CE — and therefore no doubt earlier as well. Yet there are radical differences *between* the two textual traditions, most of which appear to have arisen in the process of translation rather than representing a deviant Hebrew exemplar.

Divergences

Having established the relative stability of both the Hebrew and the Greek texts of Isaiah 53, we must now identify the major points at which they diverge, verse by verse.[18] Since there is little evidence of fundamentally different Hebrew text-forms in this chapter, we may assume that many (not all) of these divergences will represent "mistranslations," in the sense that they could not have been predicted in advance on the basis of the Hebrew.[19]

- 52:13 Ἰδοὺ συνήσει ὁ παῖς μου καὶ ὑψωθήσεται καὶ δοξασθήσεται σφόδρα.

Here, "my servant" (עבדי) is introduced as ὁ παῖς μου.[20] The rendering of עבד as παῖς is common throughout the Septuagint, although other Greek terms may also be selected (δοῦλος and θεράπων are both used frequently; Aquila and Symmachus replace παῖς here with δοῦλος).[21] While παῖς nor-

---

18. The Greek text here is that of Ziegler, *Isaias*, apart from a conjectural emendation in 53:2, which I would reject, and a transposition in v. 5. With the exception of the emendation, Ziegler's text for Isa 52:13–53:12 is identical to that of A. Rahlfs, *Septuaginta*.

19. See also the discussion of Isa 52:13–53:12 LXX in K. H. Jobes and M. Silva, *Invitation to the Septuagint* (Grand Rapids: Baker, 2000), 215-27.

20. As in Isa 41:8, 9; 42:1; 43:10; 44:1, 2, 21, 26; 45:4; 49:6; 50:10.

21. Readings from later translators are derived from J. Ziegler, *Isaias*, ad loc.

mally represents עבד and is used only occasionally for the Hebrew terms for "child," "boy," or "son," use of this term may have facilitated the early Christian appropriation of this passage by suggesting a connection with sonship language (cf. Acts 3:13, 26; 4:25, 27, 30).[22] In the New Testament, παῖς means "boy" or "child" more often than "servant."[23] συνήσει ("will understand") is within the normal semantic range of שכל hiph. (cf. Gen 3:6; Isa 41:20; 44:18);[24] "will prosper" (cf. 1 Sam 18:14, 15) would have been an alternative. The two future passive verbs represent an abbreviation of the Hebrew (ירום ונשא וגבה מאד)[25] and seem to have influenced the Johannine view of the crucifixion (ὑψωθήσεται: cf. John 3:14; 12:32, 34; δοξασθήσεται: John 7:39; 12:16, 23; 13:31); note the proximity of the passage where the two terms coincide (12:23, 32, 34) to a citation from Isa 53:1 (John 12:38).

- 52:14 ὃν τρόπον ἐκστήσονται ἐπὶ σὲ πολλοί — οὕτως ἀδοξήσει ἀπὸ ἀνθρώπων τὸ εἶδός σου καὶ ἡ δόξα σου ἀπὸ τῶν ἀνθρώπων —

In MT this refers to a past event (שממו), in LXX to a future one (ἐκστήσονται, ἀδοξήσει).[26] The Greek here retains the second-person singular address in the parenthesis; MT reverts to the third person ("his appearance," "his form") and is followed in this by Aquila (ὅρασις αὐτοῦ καὶ μορφὴ αὐτοῦ). The almost identical ἀπό-clauses do not do justice to the Hebrew parallelism (מאם // מבני אדם), although the translator elsewhere renders the "son of man" idiom literally (Isa 51:12). Symmachus restores the Hebrew idiom here, reading παρὰ τοὺς υἱοὺς τῶν ἀνθρώπων.

---

22. Jeremias finds an indication of a shift from "servant" to "child" in *Martyrdom of Polycarp* 14.1, where God is described as ὁ τοῦ ἀγαπητοῦ καὶ εὐλογητοῦ παιδός σου Ἰησοῦ Χριστοῦ πατήρ (*TDNT*, 5:704). Compare *Didache* 9.2.3; 10.2.3.

23. παῖς clearly means "boy" or "child" in Matt 2:16; 17:18; 21:15; Luke 2:43; 8:51, 54; 9:42; John 4:51; Acts 20:12; "servant" in Matt 14:2; Luke 7:7; 12:45. Matthew's version of the story of the (so-called) centurion's servant uses παῖς throughout (Matt 8:6, 8, 13), which should perhaps be translated "child"; Luke's δοῦλος removes the ambiguity (Luke 7:2, 10).

24. Aquila seeks to convey the force of the hiphil by coining a new verb, reading ἐπιστημονισθήσεται here.

25. Thus Aquila, Symmachus, and Theodotion here read ὑψωθήσεται καὶ ἐπαρθήσεται καὶ μετεωρισθήσεται.

26. W. Zimmerli sees evidence here that the translator understands the Servant as a future messianic figure (*TDNT*, 5.666-67).

- 52:15 οὕτως θαυμάσονται ἔθνη πολλὰ ἐπ' αὐτῷ, καὶ συνέξουσιν βασιλεῖς τὸ στόμα αὐτῶν. ὅτι οἷς οὐκ ἀνηγγέλη περὶ αὐτοῦ ὄψονται, καὶ οἳ οὐκ ἀκηκόασιν συνήσουσιν.

θαυμάσονται is synonymous with ἐκστήσονται (v. 14). The translator seems here to guess at the meaning of the Hebrew יזה, evidently from נזה, "sprinkle" (cf. Lev 5:9; Num 8:7; Aquila and Theodotion read ῥαντίσει; Jerome, *asperget*).[27] ἐπ' αὐτῷ (= עליו) is connected not to "kings shall shut their mouths [at him]," as probably in MT, but to "thus many nations/Gentiles will be amazed [at him]." In v. 15b, "those to whom it was not announced concerning him" (οἷς οὐκ ἀνηγγέλη περὶ αὐτοῦ) replaces "that which was not told them" (אשר לא ספר להם). In the same way, "those who have not heard" replaces "what they did not hear." In the Greek, the emphasis lies on the potential addressees rather than the potential message. περὶ αὐτοῦ (in place of להם) must be seen as a further reference to the servant/child, following ἐπ' αὐτῷ in v. 15a. Future tenses (ὄψονται, συνήσουσιν) replace Hebrew perfects (התבננו, ראו). As we shall see, these modifications are all exploited in Paul's citation of this passage in Rom 15:21.

- 53:1 κύριε, τίς ἐπίστευσεν τῇ ἀκοῇ ἡμῶν; καὶ ὁ βραχίων κυρίου τίνι ἀπεκαλύφθη;

κύριε is lacking in the Hebrew. Its insertion means that the questions are addressed to God, who is still, however, referred to in the third person. This made it possible for Christian trinitarian theology to find here a distinction within the one divine lordship (cf. Gen 19:24; Ps 110:1).[28] The insertion heightens the sense that Isa 53:1 marks a new start and is not in direct continuity with 52:13-15.

- 53:2 ἀνηγγείλαμεν ἐναντίον αὐτοῦ ὡς παιδίον, ὡς ῥίζα ἐν γῇ διψώσῃ, οὐκ ἔστιν εἶδος αὐτῷ οὐδὲ δόξα. καὶ εἴδομεν αὐτόν, καὶ οὐκ εἶχεν εἶδος οὐδὲ κάλλος.

---

27. RSV speculates similarly, reading "so shall he startle many nations" (corresponding to, "As many were astonished at him . . . ," v. 14). Jobes and Silva point out that "the translator of Isaiah . . . often harmonizes his text to the context, especially if parallelism is involved" (*Invitation to the Septuagint*, 217). This is probably what has happened here.

28. So Tertullian: *brachium enim tuum, non domini dixisset, si non dominum patrem et dominum filium intellegi vellet* (*adv. Prax.* 13).

ἀνηγγείλαμεν can be connected to ἀκοῇ in the previous verse, but it is difficult to understand in the present context. J. Ziegler suggests emending to ἀνέτειλε μέν, which might correspond more closely to the Hebrew ויעל ("and he grew up"). But ἀνατέλλειν is not used (in the LXX or elsewhere) of the growing up of children; it does not elsewhere translate עלה; and there is no parallel elsewhere to the ἀνέτειλε μέν construction.²⁹ παιδίον is a possible rendering of יונק (from ינק "suck"; cf. Deut 32:25; Ps 8:3); but in this context the reference is probably to a young plant (a sense attested elsewhere for יונקת, cf. Job 8:16; Hos 14:7; Symmachus reads καὶ ἀνέβη ὡς κλάδος ἐνώπιον αὐτοῦ). In the Hebrew, two *waw*-clauses (ונראהו, ונחמדהו) should probably have a final sense: "he had no form or comeliness *that we should look at him*, and no beauty *that we should desire him*" (RSV); οὐκ εἶδος αὐτῷ οὐδὲ ἀξίωμα ἵνα ἰδῶμεν αὐτὸν οὐδὲ θεωρία ἵνα ἐπιθυμήσωμεν αὐτόν (Symmachus). The Septuagint seems to intend οὐδὲ κάλλος as a rendering of the second *waw*-clause³⁰ and ignores the final sense of the first one. The result is a new sentence: "And we saw him, and he had neither form nor beauty." תאר and מראה are both rendered as εἶδος.

- 53:3 ἀλλὰ τὸ εἶδος αὐτοῦ ἄτιμον ἐκλεῖπον παρὰ πάντας ἀνθρώπους, ἄνθρωπος ἐν πληγῇ ὢν καὶ εἰδὼς φέρειν μαλακίαν, ὅτι ἀπέστραπται τὸ πρόσωπον αὐτοῦ, ἠτιμάσθη καὶ οὐκ ἐλογίσθη.

The paraphrastic ἀλλὰ τὸ εἶδος αὐτοῦ ἄτιμον represents the Hebrew נבזה ("he was despised," pointed as a participle in MT), and results in an unnecessary repetition of what has already been said about the servant/child's appearance (compare the use of εἶδος in 52:14; 53:2 [x2]; Symmachus reads ἐξουδενώμενος). ἐκλεῖπον παρὰ πάντας ἀνθρώπους renders the difficult חדל אישים ("lacking [of] men"?) and might be translated, "found wanting with all men." The servant/child is ἄνθρωπος ἐν πληγῇ ὢν καὶ εἰδὼς φέρειν μαλακίαν, a slightly paraphrastic translation of איש מכאבות וידוע חלי in comparison to later renderings (e.g., Symmachus: ἀνὴρ ἐπίπονος καὶ γνωστὸς νόσῳ). In the remainder of the verse, active verb forms in the He-

---

29. But see Ziegler's defense of this emendation (*Isaias*, 99), citing instances elsewhere in Isaiah where the manuscript tradition confuses the two verbs.
30. Jobes and Silva suspect here "an attempt to make sense of a clause [the translator] did not fully understand" (*Invitation to the Septuagint*, 220).

brew ("as one who turns the face from us," "we esteemed him not") are assimilated to the passive נבזה.

- 53:4 οὗτος τὰς ἁμαρτίας ἡμῶν φέρει καὶ περὶ ἡμῶν ὀδυνᾶται, καὶ ἡμεῖς ἐλογισάμεθα αὐτὸν εἶναι ἐν πόνῳ καὶ ἐν πληγῇ καὶ ἐν κακώσει.

οὗτος here corresponds to the emphatic הוא, but no equivalent is provided for אכן ("surely"), with which this verse opens. The translator thus loses the antithesis between what is now perceived to be the case and a previous perception now seen to be erroneous (cf. Symmachus: ὄντως . . . ἡμεῖς δέ . . .). In the previous verse the translator rendered חלי appropriately as μαλακία ("sickness"); here, however, he offers τὰς ἁμαρτίας ἡμῶν for חלינו, influenced presumably by references to "our sins" and "our trangressions" in vv. 5, 6. Thus the servant/child here "bears our sins" — language that (in conjunction with similar language in v. 12) will later prove significant for early Christian reflection on the death of Christ (1 Pet 2:24; Polycarp, *Phil* 8.1; cf. Heb 9:28). Still more significant is the free rendering of ומכאבינו סבלם ("and our blows he bore [them]") as περὶ ἡμῶν ὀδυνᾶται ("he suffered for us"): as we shall see, περὶ ἡμῶν here underlies the Pauline ὑπὲρ ἡμῶν formula. The two parallel statements are more accurately rendered by Symmachus: ὄντως τὰς νόσους ἡμῶν αὐτὸς ἀνέλαβεν καὶ τοὺς πόνους ὑπεμείνεν.[31] The three ἐν-phrases represent Hebrew passive participles, with the reference to God (מכה אלהים) omitted from the second one.

- 53:5 αὐτὸς δὲ ἐτραυματίσθη διὰ τὰς ἁμαρτίας ἡμῶν καὶ μεμαλάκισται διὰ τὰς ἀνομίας ἡμῶν. παιδεία εἰρήνης ἡμῶν ἐπ' αὐτόν, τῷ μώλωπι αὐτοῦ ἡμεῖς ἰάθημεν.

The phrases διὰ τὰς ἁμαρτίας ἡμῶν and διὰ τὰς ἀνομίας ἡμῶν occur in this order in Vaticanus, 1 Clement, and Justin, but are transposed in Barnabas, Alexandrinus, and Sinaiticus (followed by Rahlfs and Ziegler). The Hebrew equivalents are מפשענו and מעונתינו. The first-plural pronouns have influenced Paul's διὰ τὰ παραπτώματα ἡμῶν (Rom 4:25), although its primary source is Isa 53:12 (see below).

---

31. Symmachus according to Eusebius; Aquila according to 86, a ninth- or tenth-century manuscript that contains several inferior readings here. Compare the translation offered in Matt 8:17: αὐτὸς τὰς ἀσθενείας ἡμῶν ἔλαβεν καὶ τὰς νόσους ἐβάστασεν.

Mistranslation and the Death of Christ

- 53:6 πάντες ὡς πρόβατα ἐπλανήθημεν, ἄνθρωπος τῇ ὁδῷ αὐτοῦ ἐπλανήθη. καὶ κύριος παρέδωκεν αὐτὸν ταῖς ἁμαρτίαις ἡμῶν.

In v. 6a, the awkward repetition of the verb loses the balance achieved by the Hebrew verbs, תעינו and פנינו. In the second half of the verse, the translator freely paraphrases the Hebrew ויהוה הפגיע בו את עון כלנו ("and YHWH has extended to him the transgression of us all"); compare Symmachus, κύριος δὲ καταντῆσαι ἐποίησεν εἰς αὐτὸν τὴν ἀνομίαν πάντων ἡμῶν. παραδίδοναι recurs twice in v. 12, where it translates הערה ("he poured out") and הפגיע (there, "he made intercession").³² The verb form here corresponds to Rom 8:32, as the verb form in v. 12 corresponds to Rom 4:25.

- 53:7 καὶ αὐτὸς διὰ τὸ κεκακῶσθαι οὐκ ἀνοίγει τὸ στόμα. ὡς πρόβατον ἐπὶ σφαγὴν ἤχθη καὶ ὡς ἀμνὸς ἐναντίον τοῦ κείροντος αὐτὸν ἄφωνος οὕτως οὐκ ἀνοίγει τὸ στόμα αὐτοῦ.

The Hebrew reads, נגש והוא נענה ("he was oppressed and he was afflicted"). The translator provides no equivalent for the first term, but appropriately subordinates the opening clause ("he on account of illtreatment") to "opens not his mouth." This text is probably associated by Luke with Jesus' silence at his trial before Herod (cf. Acts 8:32; Luke 23:9-10).

- 53:8 ἐν τῇ ταπεινώσει ἡ κρίσις αὐτοῦ ἤρθη. τὴν γενεὰν αὐτοῦ τίς διηγήσεται; ὅτι αἴρεται ἀπο τῆς γῆς ἡ ζωὴ αὐτοῦ. ἀπὸ τῶν ἀνομιῶν τοῦ λαοῦ μου ἤχθη εἰς θάνατον.

At the opening of v. 8, MT reads מעצר וממשפט לקח ("by oppression and judgment he was taken away," perhaps meaning "by a perversion of justice he was taken away" [NRSV]). The translator has introduced the idea of "humiliation" and made "justice" or "judgment" the subject of ἤρθη, in place of the servant/child. In the question that follows, ישוחח should per-

---

32. As Jobes and Silva note, "the strong Hebrew expression 'the Lord has struck him with the iniquity of us all' is softened by means of the verb παραδίδωμι, a term that this translator uses at various times when he needs to get out of a difficulty" (*Invitation to the Septuagint*, 223).

227

haps be translated "consider": "His generation who will consider?" which could be an expression of outrage at the servant's treatment by his contemporaries. In its Greek form the question reads, "His generation who will recount [διηγήσεται]?" thus prompting the reader to understand τὴν γενεὰν αὐτοῦ as some kind of event. Thus this question could come to serve as testimony to the mystery of the Son's generation from the Father.[33]

In the ὅτι-statement, a Hebrew verb referring to the servant (נגזר "he was cut off") is again given another application, here to "his life." Thus, "he was cut off from the land of the living [מארץ חיים]" becomes "his life was removed from the land/earth." Luke, whose citation from vv. 7-8 ends at this point, may see here a reference to the ascension (Acts 8:33). Also to be noted is the Septuagint's clear reference to the servant/child's death: ἤχθη εἰς θάνατον represents the difficult נגע למו ("a blow to him" [?]): the translator either read למות in his exemplar (so *BHS*) or, more likely, decided that this is what למו must mean. ἤχθη is derived from v. 7: as a sheep was led to slaughter, so the servant/child "was led to death."

- 53:9 καὶ δώσω τοὺς πονηροὺς ἀντὶ τῆς ταφῆς αὐτοῦ καὶ τοὺς πλουσίους ἀντὶ τοῦ θανάτου αὐτοῦ. ὅτι ἀνομίαν οὐκ ἐποίησεν, οὐδὲ εὑρέθη δόλος ἐν τῷ στόματι αὐτοῦ.

MT here reads ויתן את רשעים קברו ואת עשיר במתיו ("and he gave his grave with the wicked and with the rich man in his deaths"). In the Septuagint, the statement becomes a divine oracle with a future reference (δώσω for ויתן). The translator takes את not as a preposition ("with") but as the marker of the definite object — although neither רשעים nor עשיר has the definite article. He must therefore insert another preposition to coordinate the first pair of substantives (קברו/רשעים) and selects ἀντί, giving a sense still more obscure than the Hebrew: "I will give the wicked in place of his tomb," or perhaps, "I will exchange the wicked for his tomb." Is this supposed to be a statement in which God promises to avenge the death of his servant/child?[34] ἀντί is repeated in the second half of the sentence: ". . . and the rich in place of his death." The unexpected Hebrew singular עשיר and

---

33. Irenaeus, *Adv. haer.* 2.28.5, in opposition to the Valentinian genealogy of the aeons. Later this text is cited on both sides of the Arian debate: see Athanasius, *Exp. fid.* 1, *De syn.* 28; Theodoret, *Hist. eccl.* 1.3. Other writers (e.g., Justin, Gregory Thaumaturgus) find here a reference to the incarnation.

34. So Zimmerli, *TDNT*, 5:677.

plural מתיו are emended, so that τοὺς πλουσίους corresponds to τοὺς πονηρούς, and ἀντὶ τοῦ θανάτου αὐτοῦ to ἀντὶ τῆς ταφῆς αὐτοῦ. The selection of ὅτι ("for") for the concessive עַל ("though") turns the statement that follows into an explanation of the previous divine action ("I will give"), rather than highlighting the inappropriateness of a human action (MT: "he gave," but perhaps read with 1QIsaiah[a]: "they gave"). ἀνομία represents חמס ("violence"); and εὑρέθη has no equivalent in the Hebrew.

- 53:10a-b καὶ κύριος βούλεται καθαρίσαι αὐτὸν τῆς πληγῆς. ἐὰν δῶτε περὶ ἁμαρτίας, ἡ ψυχὴ ὑμῶν ὄψεται σπέρμα μακρόβιον . . .

The translator here transforms a negative statement into a positive one. MT reads ויהוה חפץ דכאו החלי ("and YHWH wills to bruise him, he has made [him] sick[?]"). The translator takes החלי not as a verb but as a noun with the article; the substantive חלי has already occurred in v. 3 (ידוע חלי "acquainted with sickness") and v. 4 (חלינו "our sicknesses"). Its rendering as τῆς πληγῆς alludes to v. 3 (ἄνθρωπος ἐν πληγῇ ὤν) and v. 4 (ἐν πόνῳ καὶ ἐν πληγῇ καὶ ἐν κακώσει). καθαρίσαι αὐτόν represents דכאו ("to bruise him"), although the translator is aware that דכא normally has a negative sense: in v. 5 the participle מדכא was translated μεμαλάκισται ("he has been weakened").[35] "And the Lord wills to cleanse him of his wound": this is the first indication of the servant's vindication. In contrast, Symmachus reads: κύριος ἠθέλησεν ἀλοῆσαι αὐτὸν ἐν τῷ τραυματισμῷ ("The Lord willed to smite him in his wound"). Like the earlier translator, however, Symmachus agrees that החלי is to be construed as a substantive with article, not as a verb.

In v. 10b, MT comprises a subordinate clause (אם תשים אשם נפשו "if you offer as an offering his soul"), followed by three coordinated statements about the servant: "(1) he will see [his] seed, (2) he will lengthen [his] days, and (3) the will of YHWH shall prosper in his hand." The translator reduces these to a single statement. He assumes that "his soul" does not belong to the subordinate clause but is the subject of "will see," and he also assimilates it to the second-plural δῶτε: "If you make a sin offering, *your* soul will see. . . ." σπέρμα μακρόβιον understands יאריך ימים ("he

---

35. I. Seeligmann suggests that in v. 10 the translator may have confused this verb with זכה "to cleanse" (reading ז for ד) or (more likely) with its Aramaic equivalent דכא (*The Septuagint Version of Isaiah: A Discussion of Its Problems* [Leiden: Brill, 1948], 50).

will lengthen [his] days") as an adjective ("long of days") qualifying "seed." The translator attaches the concluding *waw*-clause to v. 11, rewriting it as he does so. Symmachus again gives a more accurate rendering of the Hebrew: καὶ θέλημα κυρίου ἐν χειρὶ αὐτοῦ εὐοδωθήσεται.

- 53:10c-11 . . . καὶ βούλεται κύριος ἀφελεῖν ἀπὸ τοῦ πόνου τῆς ψυχῆς αὐτοῦ, δεῖξαι αὐτῷ φῶς καὶ πλάσαι τῇ συνέσει, δικαιῶσαι δίκαιον εὖ δουλεύοντα πολλοῖς καὶ τὰς ἁμαρτίας αὐτῶν αὐτὸς ἀνοίσει.

If the statement that "the will of YHWH will prosper in his hand (וחפץ יהוה בידו יצלח)" concludes v. 10, the following verse would open with the difficult phrase, "From the distress of his soul he shall see . . . (מעמל נפשו יראה)." RSV suggests here: "He shall see the fruit of the travail of his soul . . ." The Greek translator assumes that חפץ at the end of v. 10 is a verb rather than a substantive and translates it as at the beginning of v. 10: καὶ βούλεται κύριος (rather than Symmachus's καὶ θέλημα κυρίου). This creates difficulties with the following phrase (בידו יצלח), which the translator solves by way of a connection with "from the distress of his soul" in v. 11. "The Lord wills . . . from the distress of his soul": what is missing from this sentence is clearly the idea of *removal*. Hence ἀφελεῖν is inserted, although it is entirely unrelated to בידו יצלח: "And the Lord willed to remove the distress of his soul. . . ." The translator may have surmised that צלח was just a variant spelling of שלח ("send"), and that "in his hand he sent from" (בידו שלח/צ מ-) must be a Hebrew idiom meaning "to remove."

Remarkably, these manipulations of the text produce a stronger and more lucid statement about the servant's vindication than anything in the Hebrew. This statement is based on the decision to render four Hebrew finite verbs (יצדק, ישבע, יראה, ויצלח) as infinitives dependent on βούλεται (ἀφελεῖν, δεῖξαι, πλάσαι, δικαιῶσαι). The Lord wills to remove, to show, to form, and to justify. The evidence of 1QIsaiah[a, b] and 4QIsaiah[d] suggests that the translator may well have found יראה אור ("he shall see light") in his exemplar, and not just יראה (MT). Reading in his exemplar that "the Lord wills, . . . he [the servant] will see light," the translator assumes a *purposive* relationship between the two verbs: hence, "The Lord wills . . . , to show him light." By analogy with this, ישבע בדעתו ("he will be satisfied in his knowledge") is traced back to the divine will to form the servant in understanding (πλάσαι τῇ συνέσει); and יצדיק צדיק (incorrectly understood

Mistranslation and the Death of Christ

to mean "he will justify the righteous one . . .") is understood similarly (δικαιῶσαι δίκαιον). The righteous one is characterized as εὖ δουλεύοντα πολλοῖς, on the assumption that עבדי לרבים is a distinct semantic unit in which עבדי must somehow function as a participle. Thus, the probable sense of the Hebrew ("The righteous one, my servant, will justify many") is replaced in the Greek by "the Lord wills . . . to justify the righteous one who serves many well." The Hebrew לרבים (but not the Greek πολλοῖς) is apparently echoed in the Markan Last Supper narrative, where Jesus' blood is said to be poured out ὑπὲρ πολλῶν (Mark 14:24).

- 53:12 διὰ τοῦτο αὐτὸς κληρονομήσει πολλοὺς καὶ τῶν ἰσχυρῶν μεριεῖ σκῦλα, ἀνθ' ὧν παρεδόθη εἰς θάνατον ἡ ψυχὴ αὐτοῦ, καὶ ἐν τοῖς ἀνόμοις ἐλογίσθη. καὶ αὐτὸς ἁμαρτίας πολλῶν ἀνήνεγκεν καὶ διὰ τὰς ἁμαρτίας αὐτῶν παρεδόθη.

Here, αὐτὸς κληρονομήσει πολλοὺς renders the Hebrew אחלק לו ברבים ("I will give him a share with the many"). ἀνθ' ὧν παρεδόθη εἰς θάνατον ἡ ψυχὴ αὐτοῦ renders הערה למות נפשו ("he poured out his soul to death"). The verb form παρεδόθη recurs at the end of the verse, where καὶ διὰ τὰς ἁμαρτίας αὐτῶν παρεδόθη translates ולפשעים יפגיע ("and he interceded for transgressors"). The concluding statements about the Servant in relation to the sins of others are respectively echoed in Heb 9:28 (εἰς τὸ πολλῶν ἀνενεγκεῖν ἁμαρτίας) and Rom 4:25 (ὃς παρεδόθη διὰ τὰ παραπτώματα ἡμῶν).

The preceding analysis has highlighted a considerable number of cases in which the translation technique is, to say the least, eccentric — and was perceived as such by later translators such as Symmachus, whose rendering is normally much closer to the plain sense of the Hebrew. If, on some occasions, the Hebrew does not have a "plain sense" and allows for a number of possible translations, elsewhere this is clearly not the case. Whether we prefer to speak of "free translation," or "mistranslation," or a combination of the two, the Septuagintal translator goes his own way, producing a text whose semantic content overlaps with the original Hebrew but by no means coincides with it. What is striking is that it is often precisely the points of non-overlap and non-coincidence that proved important for Paul and other early Christian readers.

In the following translation of the Fourth Servant Song in Greek, italics represent the most significant deviations from the probable underlying Hebrew. Underlining represents points at which Paul either explicitly cites material from this passage or draws upon its lexical resources in order to interpret the death of Christ in its saving significance. It is notable how often these coincide.

> 52:13 Behold, my servant shall understand, and shall be exalted and glorified greatly.
> 14 Just as many *will be* astonished at you — so disreputable *shall be your* appearance among men and *your* glory among men —
> 15 so shall many nations [Gentiles] *be amazed at him,* and kings shall shut their mouth. For <u>those to whom</u> it was not announced <u>concerning him shall</u> see, and *those who* have not heard *will* understand.
> 53:1 <u>Lord, who believed our report?</u> And the arm of the Lord, to whom was it revealed?
> 2 *We announced* before him [one] like a *child,* like a root in thirsty ground, having no appearance or glory. *And* we saw him, and he had *neither* appearance *nor beauty.*
> 3 *But his appearance was dishonourable,* found wanting with all men, a man stricken and knowing [what it is] to bear sickness. *For* his face was turned away, he was dishonored and he was not esteemed.
> 4 This one bears our *sins* and *suffers for us,* and we considered him to be in distress and *misfortune* and oppression.
> 5 But he was wounded <u>on account of our sins</u>, and was weakened on account of our transgressions. The discipline of our peace was upon him, by his wound we were healed.
> 6 All of us have strayed like sheep, each one *strayed* to his own way. And the Lord *gave him up* to our sins.
> 7 And he opens not his mouth on account of ill-treatment. As a sheep is led to the slaughter and as a lamb before its shearer is silent, so he does not open his mouth.
> 8 *In [his] humiliation his judgment was taken away.* Who shall tell of his generation? *For removed from the earth is his life.* By the transgressions of my people *he was led to death.*
> 9 And *I will* give the wicked *in place of* his tomb, and the rich *in place of* his death. *For* he committed no *transgression,* nor was deceit found in his mouth.

10 And the Lord wills *to cleanse him of his wound*. If *you* [pl.] offer a sin-offering, *your* soul will see *a long-lived posterity*. And the Lord wills to remove
11 the distress of his soul, *to show him* light *and to form [him] in understanding, to justify the righteous one who serves many well;* and he will bear their sins.
12 Therefore he shall *inherit many,* and shall share the spoils of the strong, because his soul <u>*was delivered up*</u> to death, and he was reckoned among the lawless. And he bore the sins of many, <u>*and was given up on account of their sins*</u>.

From one perspective, Isaiah 53 in Greek is a seriously flawed representative of the Hebrew original. From another perspective, it can be seen as supplanting that Hebrew original, functioning directly as scripture in Greek-speaking Jewish and Christian communities with no possibility but also no need of recourse to the Hebrew. Thus it is this text that survives in multiple copies, whereas the more accurate translation of Symmachus must be laboriously reconstructed from scattered fragments of evidence. If the Greek text is at some points less lucid than the Hebrew, at other points it is more so — notably in its testimony to the Servant's death and vindication. If each of its "mistranslations" represents the loss of an original semantic content, its place is always taken by a new semantic content, or at least by a semantic *potential* waiting to be realized. Ironically, it is precisely the deviations from the Hebrew that establish this as an independent text in its own right, not as a mere local representative of a distant foreign original. Without recognizing them as such, it was precisely in the deviations that early Christians first glimpsed the possibility of a positive soteriological interpretation of the death of Christ. In the light of such momentous discoveries as this, it is unsurprising that the Septuagint could be viewed as an inspired text in its own right.

Paul, the Servant and the Septuagint

On two occasions, Paul cites material from the Fourth Servant Song (Isa 52:15 = Rom 15:21; Isa 53:1 = Rom 10:16). In addition, at least one probable allusion has been noted (Isa 53:12 = Rom 4:25). There is also a third way in which Paul and other early Christian writers draw on scripture.[36] Citation explicitly refers back to the scriptural text. Allusion does so implicitly; in a strong allusion, the reader or hearer must recognize the reference to the underlying text in order to grasp the full force of the new statement. Yet it is also possible for scripture to function even without this explicit or implicit backward reference. A scriptural text can serve as a lexical and semantic resource or reservoir from which terms, phrases, or concepts can be freely drawn and adapted to new uses. Fully embedded in their new contexts, they do not draw attention to their scriptural origin; and yet the scriptural impact on the new context may be at least as profound here as in the case of citations and allusions. In the case of Isaiah 53, the claims that Christ died "for us" or "for our sins," that he was "given up" and that he "humbled himself," and that all this took place for the benefit of "the many" are all apparently derived from this chapter. These claims are Pauline, but they may also be traced back to the common tradition of Hellenistic Christianity. An obvious locus for such a tradition is the church at Antioch, where Isaiah in its Septuagintal form was presumably familiar, and where Paul himself would have participated in the early process of tradition formation.[37]

Before pursuing this early use of Isaiah 53 any further, there is a preliminary matter to be discussed. It is currently debated whether Paul's citations retain links with their original scriptural contexts, or whether they are wholly integrated into their new contexts.[38] This debate is relevant here because Paul's citations from the Fourth Servant Song both relate to Christian mission, and it might be argued that they need not entail any identification of the servant with Christ.[39] To refute that argument, it must be

---

36. Richard Hays proposes "echo" as a third mode of Pauline intertextuality: "Quotation, allusion, and echo may be seen as points along a spectrum of intertextual reference, moving from the explicit to the subliminal" (*Echoes of Scripture in the Letters of Paul* [New Haven and London: Yale University Press, 1989], 23). For Hays, "allusion" implies authorial intention and readerly recognition, whereas "echo" lacks these associations and is thus less historically circumscribed (p. 29). My own third mode of Pauline intertextuality is also concerned with the "subliminal" but is broadly historical in orientation.

37. For the importance of Paul's links with the church at Antioch, see N. Taylor, *Paul, Antioch and Jerusalem: A Study in Relationships and Authority in Earliest Christianity* (JSNTSup 66; Sheffield: Sheffield Academic Press, 1992), 88-110 and passim.

38. For examples of the respective views, see Hays, *Echoes of Scripture*, in which "echoes" frequently derive from the wider contexts of texts Paul cites; and C. Tuckett, "Paul, Scripture and Ethics: Some Reflections," *NTS* 46 (2000): 403-24.

39. According to Morna Hooker, the quotation from Isa 53:1 "does not mean that the

shown that the two citations retain links with the scriptural story of the servant from which they have been extracted.

In the first case, Paul uses his citation to confirm the assertion that "not all believed the gospel" and to establish the link between faith and hearing:

> But not all believed the gospel. For Isaiah says, "Lord, who believed our report [τίς ἐπίστευσεν τῇ ἀκοῇ ἡμῶν]?" So faith comes from hearing [ἡ πίστις ἐξ ἀκοῆς], and hearing through the word of Christ. (Rom 10:16-17, citing Isa 53:1)

In the second citation, Paul says that his ambition is

> to preach the gospel where Christ is not named, lest I should build on another's foundation; but, as it is written, "Those to whom it was not announced concerning him shall see, and those who have not heard will understand." (Rom 15:20-21, citing Isa 52:15)

The two citations form a contrasting pair. In Isaiah, the second passage (Isa 52:15) directly precedes the first (Isa 53:1). According to Paul, they both articulate the divine intention for Christian mission: its worldwide scope, which includes all who are currently still ignorant of Christ, and, conversely, the intractable fact that, when the gospel is preached, "not all" believe. Contrary to the usual view, there is nothing to suggest that Paul relates Isa 53:1 specifically to "Jewish unbelief."[40] The question is whether the two citations entail an identification of the servant/child with Christ, or whether their original context is irrelevant to the new context to which Paul relocates them.

The citation of Isa 53:1 immediately follows a citation from the same context (Isa 52:7, in the abbreviated and modified form: "How timely are the feet of those who announce good things!" [Rom 10:15]). Elsewhere, Paul cites four further passages from this immediate context (Isa 52:5, 11, 15; 54:1). For our present purposes, it is important to highlight both the

---

rest of this chapter was in St Paul's mind"; similarly, in the case of Isa 52:15, "there is no indication that he has in mind anything but this one verse" (*Jesus and the Servant: The Influence of the Servant Concept of Deutero-Isaiah in the New Testament* [London: SPCK, 1959], 117).

40. On this see my *Paul, Judaism and the Gentiles: Beyond the New Perspective* (2nd ed.; Grand Rapids: Eerdmans, 2007), 331-32.

concentration of material drawn from this section of Isaiah and the modifications apparently introduced by Paul himself.⁴¹ The fact that Paul cites no fewer than six texts from Isa 52:5–54:1 suggests that each one is cited with some awareness of its original context. As we shall also note, Paul (like other early Christian writers) takes particular care to reproduce the exact Septuagintal wording in the immediate vicinity of the Fourth Servant Song (Isa 52:15; 53:1; 54:1).

Isaiah 52:5

<u>δι' ὑμᾶς</u> διὰ παντὸς <u>τὸ ὄνομά</u> μου <u>βλασφειμεῖται ἐν τοῖς ἔθνεσι</u>. (Isa 52:5 LXX)

<u>τὸ γὰρ ὄνομα</u> τοῦ θεοῦ <u>δι' ὑμᾶς βλασφειμεῖται ἐν τοῖς ἔθνεσιν</u>, καθὼς γέγραπται. (Rom 2:24)

Paul abbreviates slightly (omitting διὰ παντός), transposes the first two clauses, and replaces μου with θεοῦ. γάρ serves to introduce the citation, although, unusually, a fuller citation formula is also added at the end.⁴²

Isaiah 52:7

πάρειμι ὡς ὥρα ἐπὶ τῶν ὀρέων, ὡς πόδες εὐαγγελιζομένου ἀκοὴν εἰρήνης, ὡς εὐαγγελιζόμενος ἀγαθά, ὅτι ἀκουστὴν ποιήσω τὴν σωτηρίαν σου λέγων Σιων βασιλεύσει σου ὁ Θεός.

(I am present as the spring upon the mountains, as the feet of one announcing a message of peace, as one announcing good things, for I will make your salvation heard, saying to Zion: your God shall reign.)

Paul abbreviates the citation and appears to correct it in light of the Hebrew:

---

41. For Paul's use of Isaiah as a whole, see the table in J. R. Wagner, *Heralds of the Good News: Isaiah and Paul "in Concert" in the Letter to the Romans* (Leiden: Brill, 2002), 342-43.

42. For detailed analysis, see Stanley, *Paul and the Language of Scripture*, 84-86.

Mistranslation and the Death of Christ

How will they preach unless they are sent? As it is written: How timely are the feet of those who announce good things [ὡς ὡραῖοι οἱ πόδες τῶν εὐαγγελιζομένων τὰ ἀγαθά]! (Rom 10:15)

How pleasant upon the mountains are the feet of the one who announces a message of peace, who announces good . . . (Isa 52:7 MT)

Paul omits the references to the mountains and to the announcement of the message of peace, but restores MT's "how . . ." (מה), which LXX connects to the preceding הנני, producing the phrase πάρειμι ὡς ("I am present as"), which determines the rest of the statement. Paul's ὡραῖοι may be compared to Aquila's ὡραιωθήσαν.[43] The plural εὐαγγελιζομένων introduces a new deviation from the Hebrew, however.[44]

Isaiah 52:11

ἐξέλθατε ἐκεῖθεν καὶ ἀκαθάρτου μὴ ἅπτεσθε, ἐξέλθατε ἐκ μέσου αὐτῆς, ἀφωρίσθητε, οἱ φέροντες τὰ σκεύη κυρίου. (Isa 52:11)

διὸ ἐξέλθατε ἐκ μέσου αὐτῶν καὶ ἀφωρίσθητε, λέγει κύριος, καὶ ἀκαθάρτου μὴ ἅπτεσθε. (2 Cor 6:17)

In the Pauline version, ἐξέλθατε ἐκεῖθεν is omitted, and καὶ ἀκαθάρτου μὴ ἅπτεσθε and ἐξέλθατε ἐκ μέσου αὐτῆς, ἀφωρίσθητε are transposed. διό and καί are added to the new opening phrase, and αὐτῆς is changed to αὐτῶν, assimilating the passage to its new context. λέγει κύριος is inserted, as in the citation of Isa 28:11-12 in 1 Cor 14:21 (which, however, deviates sharply from the LXX).[45]

---

43. See D.-A. Koch, *Die Schrift als Zeuge des Evangeliums: Untersuchungen zur Verwendung und zum Verständnis der Schrift bei Paulus* (BHTh; Tübingen: Mohr-Siebeck, 1986), 67. Eusebius preserves a reading purporting to derive from Theodotion and remarkably similar to Paul's; Koch rightly discounts this (p. 66 n.).

44. See further Stanley, *Paul and the Language of Scripture*, 134-41; Wagner, *Heralds of the Good News*, 170-74.

45. For discussion of the question whether 2 Cor 6:14–7:1 is a Pauline or non-Pauline interpolation, see V. P. Furnish, *II Corinthians: A New Translation with Introduction and Commentary* (AB; New York: Doubleday, 1984), 371-83. Furnish concludes that "the passage

Isaiah 52:15

οὕτως θαυμάσονται ἔθνη πολλὰ ἐπ' αὐτῷ, καὶ συνέχουσιν βασιλεῖς τὸ στόμα αὐτῶν. ὅτι <u>οἷς οὐκ ἀνηγγέλη περὶ αὐτοῦ ὄψονται, καὶ οἳ οὐκ ἀκηκόασιν συνήσουσιν</u>. (LXX)

... οὕτως φιλοτιμούμενον εὐαγγελίζεσθαι οὐχ ὅπου ὠνομάσθη Χριστός, ἵνα μὴ ἐπ' ἀλλότριον θεμέλιον οἰκοδομῶ, ἀλλὰ καθὼς γέγραπται, <u>οἷς οὐκ ἀνηγγέλη περὶ αὐτοῦ ὄψονται, καὶ οἳ οὐκ ἀκηκόασιν συνήσουσιν</u>. (Rom 15:20-21)

In a citation that coincides exactly with the Septuagint, Paul speaks of his future ambitions for his Gentile mission (cf. Rom 15:16). This application to the Gentiles has surely been suggested by ἔθνη πολλά (Isa 52:15a), even though Paul does not cite this. Here, at least, a Pauline citation remains dependent on its original context.[46] At two points Paul is here dependent on Septuagintal "mistranslation." First, "that which was not told them" (MT) is rendered as "Those to whom it was not told *about him*." In the original context, the reference is to the Servant. In its new context, the reference is to Christ, since "about him" is dependent on "not where Christ has [already] been named." Paul here clearly identifies Christ with the Servant.[47] Second, a distinction is drawn in the Greek between present ignorance ("those to whom it was not told...," "those who have not heard...") and future knowledge ("... shall see," "... shall understand"). In Paul's interpretation, the transformation is to be occasioned by his own mission to places where Christ is not yet named. In contrast, the Hebrew speaks of a miraculous realization that has already taken place without any human agency: "For what was not told them they have seen, and what they did not hear they have understood." At both points, Paul's argument is dependent on the Greek rewording.

---

is of non-Pauline composition, but was incorporated by the apostle himself as he wrote this letter" (p. 383). However, the citation of Isa 52:11 is fully in line with Pauline citational practice elsewhere.

46. So Wagner, *Heralds of the Good News*, 333-34.

47. Dunn's claim that Paul sees himself as the Servant overlooks the dual reference of περὶ αὐτοῦ to the Servant and to Christ, and thus to Christ *as* the Servant, the Servant *as* Christ (*Romans 9-16*, 865-66).

Isaiah 53:1

κύριε, τίς ἐπίστευσεν τῇ ἀκοῇ ἡμῶν; καὶ ὁ βραχίων κυρίου τίνι ἀπεκαλύφθη; (LXX)

κύριε, τίς ἐπίστευσεν τῇ ἀκοῇ ἡμῶν; (Rom 10:16)

As with Isa 52:15 (Rom 15:21), Paul's wording is identical to that of the Septuagint or Old Greek. The whole verse is cited in John 12:38, again in its exact Septuagintal form; contrast the free rendering of Isa 6:10 LXX that follows in John 12:40.

Isaiah 54:1

Εὐφράνθητι, στεῖρα ἡ οὐ τίκτουσα, ῥῆξον καὶ βόησον, ἡ οὐκ ὠδίνουσα, ὅτι πολλὰ τὰ τέκνα τῆς ἐρήμου μᾶλλον ἢ τῆς ἐχούσης τὸν ἄνδρα. (LXX)

γέγραπται γάρ, εὐφράνθητι, στεῖρα ἡ οὐ τίκτουσα, ῥῆξον καὶ βόησον, ἡ οὐκ ὠδίνουσα, ὅτι πολλὰ τὰ τέκνα τῆς ἐρήμου μᾶλλον ἢ τῆς ἐχούσης τὸν ἄνδρα. (Gal 4:27)

Paul's exact reproduction of Isa 54:1 LXX suggests a pattern. Passages at the beginning and end of the Fourth Servant Song are cited in their precise Septuagintal form (Isa 52:15; 53:1; 54:1). In contrast, passages cited from earlier in Isaiah 52 are subject to expansion (v. 11), abbreviation (vv. 5, 7), transposition (vv. 5, 11), adaptation (v. 11), and emendation (v. 7). Similar phenomena may be found in Paul's other Isaiah citations in Romans: conflation (Rom 9:33 = Isa 28:16 + 8:14; Rom 11:26-27 = Isa 59:20-21 + 27:9; Rom 14:11 = Isa 45:23 + 49:18); abbreviation (Rom 15:12 = Isa 11:10); transposition (Rom 10:20-21 = Isa 65:1-2); and adaptation (Rom 3:15-17 = Isa 59:7-8; Rom 9:27-28 = Isa 10:22-23).[48] Apart from the three cases already

---

48. See the detailed discussion in Stanley, *Paul and the Language of Scripture*, 113-25, 144-47, 166-71, 176-79, 183. Koch offers the following typology for Paul's modifications: "Abänderung der Wortfolge; Abänderung von Person, Numerus, Genus, Tempus und Modus; Auslassungen; Zufügungen; Austausch von Zitatteilen durch eigene Formulierungen;

noted, it is only in Rom 9:29 that Paul exactly reproduces a text from Isaiah LXX (Isa 1:9). Yet, with the partial exception of the Isa 52:7 citation, Paul generally seems to presuppose a text corresponding closely to the Septuagint.[49] Most modifications to this text are manifestly his own. Paul's Isaiah citations contribute to the textual criticism of the Septuagint mainly by confirming the essential reliability of the later manuscripts.[50]

Several conclusions follow from this analysis of the relevant Pauline Isaiah citations.

1. Of the twelve verses between Isa 52:5 and 53:1, five are cited by Paul (52:5, 7, 11, 15; 53:1). On one occasion, two of these are cited together (Rom 10:15-16 = Isa 52:7; 53:1). On another occasion, the use to which Paul puts a text is clearly derived from its original context (Rom 15:21 = Isa 52:15). There are thematic unities in Paul's readings of these texts and of Isa 54:1. Three are applied to positive or negative aspects of Christian mission (Isa 52:7, 15; 53:1). The other three are addressed to the people of God in its old or new forms (52:5, 11; 54:1). In the face of these observations, it is hard to maintain that Paul's citations sever links with the original scriptural context.

2. Paul's reading of Isa 52:15 demonstrates that he can identify the servant with Christ. The significance of this point will become clearer as we uncover the intertextual links that bind Isaiah 53 to Pauline soteriological discourse.

3. It is striking that, at the beginning of the Fourth Servant Song, Paul abandons his habit of free citation and begins to quote texts verba-

---

Austausch von Zitatteilen durch Formulierungen aus anderen Schriftstellen (Mischzitate)" (*Die Schrift als Zeuge des Evangeliums*, VIII-IX).

49. The texts surveyed here do not bear out Koch's conclusion, "dass der von Paulus vorausgesetzte LXX-Text bereits eine hebräisierende Überarbeitung erfahren hat" (*Die Schrift als Zeuge des Evangeliums*, 78).

50. Contrast Timothy Lim's claim that "[t]extual variety and pluriformity characterized the scriptural scrolls that [Paul] consulted" (*Holy Scripture in the Qumran Commentaries and Pauline Letters* [Oxford: Clarendon Press, 1997], 160). Lim argues that a Pauline citation can be said to be "septuagintal" only if it agrees with the Greek *at places where the Greek diverges from the Hebrew* (pp. 140-42). On this criterion, a citation that corresponds exactly to Isa 54:1 LXX would not be "septuagintal," since the Greek here renders the Hebrew with unusual accuracy. But that is to overlook the fact that there may be any number of equally accurate ways to translate a passage of Hebrew into Greek. If Paul (a) cites a text that accurately renders the Hebrew, and (b) cites it in precisely its Septuagintal wording, then he is citing the Septuagint.

tim. As we have already seen, early Christian writers in general were unusually concerned with verbal precision in their citations from this passage, to such an extent that these can be regarded as broadly reliable for text-critical purposes. This concern for verbal accuracy reflects the very great significance that Greek-speaking Christians ascribed to this text; the Pauline citations seem to establish a trend in this respect. They are also compatible with the hypothesis that Paul had at some point intensively studied this text in its Septuagintal form. This hypothesis is suggested by the terminology he employs in speaking of the death of Christ in its saving significance: as we shall now see, much of this terminology is drawn from Isaiah 53.

The Servant and the Death of Christ: Isaiah 53 LXX as Lexical Resource

There are at least four points where Pauline language about the death of Christ is decisively influenced by Isaiah 53 LXX. According to Paul, Christ died "for us," or "for our sins." He was "given up" by God, but it can also be said that he "humbled himself." At each point, Isaiah 53 provides Paul with lexical and semantic resources that enable him to present the death of Christ not primarily as a human act of rebellion (cf. 1 Thess 2:14-16; 1 Cor 2:6-8)[51] but as the saving act of God. It is through Isaiah 53 that the soteriological significance of Jesus' death initially comes to light.

These connections with Isaiah 53 have been proposed before, but they have not always proved persuasive.[52] In the discussion that follows, several reasons for reopening this issue will come to light. In particular, I shall argue that formulae relating to Christ's death (ὑπὲρ ἡμῶν, ὑπὲρ τῶν ἁμαρτιῶν ἡμῶν) must be traced back to Isaiah 53 LXX *even though* they do not exactly reproduce its wording and cannot be regarded as "allusions."

---

51. The ἄρχοντες τοῦ αἰῶνος τούτου in 1 Cor 2:6, 8 are probably human rather than demonic (so G. Fee, *The First Epistle to the Corinthians* [NICNT; Grand Rapids: Eerdmans, 1987], 103-104). Paul's terminology is perhaps influenced by Ps 2:2, which tells how οἱ ἄρχοντες were gathered together κατὰ τοῦ κυρίου καὶ κατὰ τοῦ Χριστοῦ αὐτοῦ. This passage is applied to the crucifixion in Acts 4:25-28. It would be a mistake to read the later conceptuality of Colossians or Ephesians back into 1 Corinthians.

52. See Hooker, *Jesus and the Servant*, 116-23.

FRANCIS WATSON

Christ Died "for Us"

Paul's ὑπὲρ ἡμῶν formula is apparently derived from Isa 53:4 LXX, ". . . and he suffered for us [καὶ περὶ ἡμῶν ὀδυνᾶται]." It occurs in the following passages:

> . . . ὅτι ἔτι ἁμαρτωλῶν ὄντων ἡμῶν Χριστὸς <u>ὑπὲρ ἡμῶν</u> ἀπέθανεν (Rom 5:8)
> . . . ἀλλὰ <u>ὑπὲρ ἡμῶν</u> πάντων παρέδωκεν αὐτόν . . . (Rom 8:32)
> . . . τὸν μὴ γνόντα ἁμαρτίαν <u>ὑπὲρ ἡμῶν</u> ἁμαρτίαν ἐποίησεν (2 Cor 5:21)
> . . . γενόμενος <u>ὑπὲρ ἡμῶν</u> κατάρα . . . (Gal 3:13)

Variants of this phrase occur in the following passages:

> . . . ἔτι κατὰ καιρὸν <u>ὑπὲρ ἀσεβῶν</u> ἀπέθανεν . . . (Rom 5:6)
> . . . ἐκεῖνον . . . <u>ὑπὲρ οὗ</u> Χριστὸς ἀπέθανεν (Rom 14:15)
> . . . τοῦτό μού ἐστιν τὸ σῶμα τὸ <u>ὑπὲρ ὑμῶν</u> . . . (1 Cor 11:24)
> . . . κρίναντας τοῦτο, ὅτι εἷς <u>ὑπὲρ πάντων</u> ἀπέθανεν . . . (2 Cor 5:14, cf. v. 15)
> . . . τοῦ ἀγαπήσαντός με καὶ παραδόντος ἑαυτὸν <u>ὑπὲρ ἐμοῦ</u> (Gal 2:20)

While the Isaianic περὶ ἡμῶν must mean "for us" or "for our sake," Paul's substitution of ὑπέρ for περί makes the vicarious nature of Christ's sufferings still clearer. That Paul has the Isaianic phrase in mind is evident from a passage in his earliest extant letter, in which περὶ ἡμῶν is apparently what he originally wrote:

> . . . through our Lord Jesus Christ, who died <u>for us</u> [τοῦ ἀποθανόντος περὶ ἡμῶν] so that whether we wake or sleep we shall live with him. (1 Thess 5:10)
> περὶ ἡμῶν ℵ* B 33; ὑπὲρ ἡμῶν P³⁰ ℵ² A D F G etc.

Here, a shift from περί to ὑπέρ would represent a scribal assimilation to normal Pauline usage: περί therefore qualifies as the harder reading. A similar shift is evident in 1 Cor 1:13 ("Was Paul crucified for you?"), where περὶ ὑμῶν is read by P⁴⁶ B D*; and in Gal 1:4 (". . . who gave himself for our sins"), where περὶ τῶν ἁμαρτιῶν ἡμῶν is read by P⁴⁶ ℵ* A D F G etc. (ὑπέρ: P⁵¹ ℵ¹ B H). The survival of περί in P⁴⁶ (1 Cor 1:13; Gal 1:4) suggests that it may also have been attested in 1 Thess 5:10, where there is a lacuna.[53] In twice replacing περί by ὑπέρ (1 Thess 5:10; Gal 1:4), the correctors of Sinaiticus seem to represent the tendency of the textual tradition as a whole.

According to Isa 53:4 MT, the servant "bore our sicknesses" [חלינו] and "carried our blows" [מכאבינו]. Three ancient Greek translations of this text are extant:

οὗτος τὰς ἁμαρτίας ἡμῶν φέρει καὶ περὶ ἡμῶν ὀδυνᾶται (LXX)
αὐτὸς τὰς ἀσθενείας ἡμῶν ἔλαβεν καὶ τὰς νόσους ἐβάστασεν (Matt 8:17)
ὄντως τὰς νόσους ἡμῶν αὐτὸς ἀνέλαβεν καὶ τοὺς πόνους ὑπέμεινεν (Symmachus)

It is the translation that deviates most clearly from the Hebrew that memorably encapsulates the Servant's significance in the statement: "He suffered for us." Paul ignores the verb: the "for us" formula and its variants are accompanied by a range of verbs (and not just by ἀπέθανεν). While Paul can cite the formula in its original form (περὶ ἡμῶν: 1 Thess 5:10; cf. 1 Cor 1:13), he prefers a preposition that underlines its vicarious connotations. Despite this adaptation, however, the formula remains dependent on Isaiah 53 LXX.[54] Without this text, there would be no basis for the claim that what took place in Christ's death took place "for us."

If Paul's "for us" is Isaianic, it is possible that τὸν μὴ γνόντα ἁμαρτίαν ὑπὲρ ἡμῶν ἁμαρτίαν ἐποίησεν (2 Cor 5:21) is also influenced by ἀνομίαν οὐκ ἐποίησεν (Isa 53:9).[55] If so, then Isa 53:9 is the source of the belief that Jesus suffered sinlessly, and indeed that his entire life was sinless (cf. 1 Pet 2:22-23). It was the one who committed no sin who suffered for us.

---

53. The hypothesis that περί is original to these three texts would be falsified if it could be shown that either P⁴⁶ or ℵ* is elsewhere in the habit of replacing ὑπέρ with περί. A survey of fifteen Pauline occurrences of ὑπέρ with the genitive, all extant in P⁴⁶, gives no evidence of any such tendency (Rom 8:31; 9:3; 15:8, 9; 16:4; 1 Cor 4:6; 10:30; 15:29; 2 Cor 1:11; 12:10; Eph 5:2, 20; Phil 1:7; Col 1:7, 24).

54. Against Jeremias, *TDNT*, 5:710.

55. So Furnish, *II Corinthians*, 340.

The Death of the Servant "for Our Sins"

Unlike Hebrews and 1 Peter, Paul does not adopt the language of "bearing sin" (Isa 53:4, 11, 12), but he does draw on prepositional phrases connecting the Servant's suffering with "our" or "their" sins:

αὐτὸς δὲ ἐτραυματίσθη <u>διὰ τὰς ἁμαρτίας ἡμῶν</u> καὶ μεμαλάκισται <u>διὰ τὰς ἀνομίας ἡμῶν</u> (Isa 53:5)
... καὶ <u>διὰ τὰς ἁμαρτίας αὐτῶν</u> παρεδόθη (Isa 53:12)

The term ἁμαρτία occurs seven times in Isaiah 53 LXX (vv. 4, 5, 6, 10, 11, 12 [x2]), ἀνομία three times (vv. 5, 8, 9).[56] These figures represent a standardizing of the more diverse Hebrew vocabulary: ἁμαρτία is used to translate חלי (v. 4), עון (vv. 5, 6, 11), אשם (v. 10: περὶ ἁμαρτίας),[57] חטא (v. 12), and פשע (v. 12); ἀνομία translates עון (v. 5), פשע (v. 8), and חמס (v. 9). In Isaiah 53 LXX more clearly than in MT, the Servant's vocation is related to "sin."

In Rom 4:25, it is said of "Jesus our Lord" that he was "handed over on account of our trespasses" (παρεδόθη διὰ τὰ παραπτώματα ἡμῶν). The verb form is drawn from Isa 53:12 (on which see below), and διὰ τὰ παραπτώματα ἡμῶν betrays the influence of διὰ τὰς ἁμαρτίας ἡμῶν and διὰ τὰς ἀνομίας ἡμῶν (v. 5; cf. v. 12). Paul here prefers παράπτωμα to ἁμαρτία or ἀνομία; this term occurs nine times in Romans, six of them in 5:12-21. Paul here is neither citing nor alluding; rather, he is adapting Isaianic conceptuality to his own purposes, but without drawing attention to his source.

In Rom 4:25, Paul retains the Isaianic preposition but replaces the noun. Elsewhere he adopts the opposite procedure, retaining ἁμαρτία (pl.) from the Isaianic prepositional clauses but varying the preposition:

... τοῦ δόντος ἑαυτὸν <u>περὶ τῶν ἁμαρτιῶν ἡμῶν</u> (Gal 1:4: for the text, see above)
... Χριστὸς ἀπέθανεν <u>ὑπὲρ τῶν ἁμαρτιῶν ἡμῶν</u> κατὰ τὰς γραφάς (1 Cor 15:3).

---

56. The figures would be six and four respectively if ἀνομίας were read in place of ἁμαρτίας at the end of v. 12.

57. It is not clear that ἐὰν δῶτε περὶ ἁμαρτίας (Isa 53:10) underlies Paul's use of περὶ ἁμαρτίας in Rom 8:3. The second plural δῶτε makes a christological application difficult.

Mistranslation and the Death of Christ

The constant element in the three passages (Rom 4:25; Gal 1:4; 1 Cor 15:3) is the pronoun ἡμῶν; the preposition and the noun may or may not coincide with the Isaianic exemplar.[58] Yet, in their slightly differing terminology, the three passages are saying the same thing. 1 Cor 15:3 is especially significant in its claim (1) that scripture is the source of the early Christian insight into the saving significance of Jesus' death; and (2) that this is the view of the early church as a whole, rather than being unique to Paul (cf. v. 11).

The "Giving Up" of the Servant

The LXX translator has recourse to the verb παραδίδοναι on three occasions:

> καὶ κύριος <u>παρέδωκεν</u> αὐτὸν ταῖς ἁμαρτίαις ἡμῶν (Isa 53:6). MT: "And YHWH has caused all of our transgression to meet him [הפגיע בו]."
>
> ἀνθ' ὧν <u>παρεδόθη</u> εἰς θάνατον ἡ ψυχὴ αὐτοῦ . . . καὶ διὰ τὰς ἁμαρτίας αὐτῶν <u>παρεδόθη</u> (Isa 53:12). MT: "He poured out [הערה] his soul unto death . . . , and he interceded [יפגיע] for transgressors."

Paul's use of παραδίδοναι in connection with the death of Christ is influenced by both active and passive usages in Isaiah 53:

> ὃς <u>παρεδόθη διὰ</u> τὰ παραπτώματα ἡμῶν καὶ ἠγέρθη διὰ τὴν δικαίωσιν ἡμῶν (Rom 4:25)
>
> ἐν τῇ νυκτὶ ᾗ <u>παρεδίδετο</u> . . . (1 Cor 11:23)
>
> ὅς γε τοῦ ἰδίου υἱοῦ οὐκ ἐφείσατο ἀλλὰ ὑπὲρ ἡμῶν πάντων <u>παρέδωκεν αὐτόν</u> (Rom 8:32)

---

58. In 1 Cor 15:3 the reference to Isaiah 53 is not independent of the LXX, as J. Jeremias claims, appealing to the absence of the Pauline ὑπέρ (*The Eucharistic Words of Jesus* [trans. N. Perrin; London: SCM Press, 1966], 103). The change in the wording does not affect the dependence. Incidentally, there is no sign of ὑπέρ in later translations of Isaiah 53. In v. 5, Aquila reads καὶ αὐτὸς βεβηλωμένος ἀπὸ ἀθεσμίων ἡμῶν, συντετριμμένος ἀπὸ τῶν ἀνομίων ἡμῶν (ἀπό = -מ). In v. 12, Symmachus reads καὶ τοῖς ἀθετοῦσιν ἀντέστη.

Exact correspondences with the verb forms παρέδωκεν and παρεδόθη in Isa 53:6, 12 should be noted; indeed, in each case Paul also reproduces the word following the verb (αὐτόν, διά).[59] In 1 Cor 11:23, παρεδίδετο should be translated "given up," not "betrayed," since the reference is probably to God's action rather than Judas's. In these Pauline statements as in Isaiah 53 LXX, the verb serves to highlight the divine causality at work in the Servant's death. Also to be noted is the possible dependence of Rom 4:25b on Isa 53:10-11, βούλεται κύριος ... δικαιῶσαι δίκαιον εὖ δουλεύοντα πολλοῖς. For πολλοί (Isa 53:11, 12 [x2]), see Rom 5:15 (x2), 19 (x2).

The "Humiliation" of the Servant

In Isa 53:8 LXX, we are told that ἐν τῇ ταπεινώσει ἡ κρίσις αὐτοῦ ἤρθη (MT: "By oppression and judgment he was taken away"). It is possible that this statement underlies Paul's ἐταπείνωσεν ἑαυτόν (Phil 2:8), where the reference is to the self-humiliation of the human Jesus in subjecting himself to the way of the cross. Yet possible connections between the Philippian Christ-hymn and Isaiah 53 are more persuasive if we suppose an influence from whatever prior translations or revisions underlie the later work attributed to Aquila, Symmachus, and Theodotion.[60] In v. 4, both Aquila and Symmachus state that the Servant was reckoned to be πεπληγότα ὑπὸ [τοῦ] θεοῦ καὶ τεταπεινωμένον (the final word here is also attested for Theodotion). This may further support the suggestion that Paul's ἐταπείνωσεν ἑαυτόν is formulated under the influence of Isaiah 53. Having humbled himself, Christ became ὑπήκοος μέχρι θάνατον (Phil 2:8). ὑπήκοος could derive from Isa 53:8, where Symmachus may have read: προσήχθη καὶ αὐτὸς ὑπήκουσεν καὶ

---

59. These correspondences are overlooked by Hooker, who argues that, for Paul as for Mark, παραδίδωμι is "the natural word to use, and it is impossible to link it with any particular Old Testament passage" (*Jesus and the Servant*, 122).

60. The traditional view is that "the Septuagint" (understood as a singular entity) was essentially complete by the time Ben Sira was translated into Greek (late second century BCE); that the translations of Aquila, Theodotion, and Symmachus belong to the second century CE; and that no significant translation took place during the intervening period. This simple picture is called into question by the demonstration that the Daniel translation ascribed to Theodotion is probably pre-Christian, and by the discovery of a Greek Minor Prophets manuscript (8HebXIIgr), differing from the LXX and dating back perhaps to the late first century BCE. See S. Jellicoe, *The Septuagint and Modern Study* (Oxford: Oxford University Press, 1974), 74-99.

οὐκ ἤνοιξεν τὸ στόμα αὐτοῦ.⁶¹ μέχρι θάνατον may derive from εἰς θάνατον (Isa 53:8, 12). According to Phil 2:7, Jesus took upon himself "the form of a servant" (μορφὴν δούλου) in his incarnation. The παῖς of the Fourth Servant Song is a "slave" as well as a "child," since he can be described in Isa 53:11 as "the righteous one who serves many well" (δίκαιον εὖ δουλεύοντα πολλοῖς). But Paul's μορφὴ δούλου may also reflect non-Septuagintal translation possibilities. At 52:13, Aquila and Symmachus both read δοῦλος μου rather than παῖς μου. In 52:14, Aquila reads ὅρασις αὐτοῦ καὶ μορφὴ αὐτοῦ for LXX's τὸ εἶδός σου καὶ ἡ δόξα σου; in 53:2, οὐ μορφὴ αὐτῷ καὶ οὐ διαπρεπεία for LXX's οὐκ εἶχεν εἶδος οὐδὲ κάλλος (Symmachus here retains εἶδος). It is also plausible that Paul's ἑαυτὸν ἐκένωσεν (Phil 2:7a) derives from נפשו ... הערה (Isa 53:12: "he poured out his soul"), although unfortunately none of the later translations is extant at this point.⁶²

In addition to his explicit citations, then, Paul draws on a range of material from Isaiah 53 LXX and may also be aware of other translation possibilities. The most important Septuagintal passages are as follows (again, underlining = Pauline use; italics = mistranslation):

οὗτος τὰς *ἁμαρτίας* ἡμῶν φέρει καὶ <u>περὶ ἡμῶν</u> *ὀδυνᾶται* (Isa 53:4; cf. 1 Thess 5:10; Rom 5:8; 8:32; 2 Cor 5:21; Gal 3:13)

αὐτὸς δὲ ἐτραυματίσθη <u>διὰ τὰς ἁμαρτίας ἡμῶν</u> καὶ μεμαλάκισται διὰ τὰς ἀνομίας ἡμῶν (Isa 53:5; cf. Rom 4:25; 1 Cor 15:3; Gal 1:4)

καὶ <u>κύριος παρέδωκεν αὐτὸν</u> ταῖς ἁμαρτίαις ἡμῶν (Isa 53:6; cf. Rom 4:25; 8:32; 1 Cor 11:23)

ἐν τῇ <u>ταπεινώσει</u> ἡ κρίσις αὐτοῦ ἤρθη ... ἀπὸ τῶν ἀνομιῶν τοῦ λαοῦ μου *ἤχθη <u>εἰς θάνατον</u>* (Isa 53:8; cf. Phil 2:8)

ὅτι *ἀνομίαν* οὐκ ἐποίησεν, οὐδὲ εὑρέθη δόλος ἐν τῷ στόματι αὐτοῦ (Isa 53:9; cf. 2 Cor 5:21)

βούλεται κύριος ... <u>δικαιῶσαι δίκαιον εὖ δουλεύοντα πολλοῖς</u> (Isa 53:10-11; cf. Rom 4:25; 5:15, 19; Phil 2:7)

ἀνθ' ὧν <u>παρεδόθη εἰς θάνατον</u> ἡ ψυχὴ αὐτοῦ, καὶ ἐν τοῖς ἀνόμοις ἐλογίσθη. καὶ αὐτὸς ἁμαρτίας <u>πολλῶν</u> ἀνήνεγκεν καὶ <u>διὰ τὰς ἁμαρτίας</u> αὐτῶν <u>παρεδόθη</u> (Isa 53:12; cf. Rom 4:25; 5:15, 19; 1 Cor 15:3; Gal 1:4; Phil 2:7)

---

61. ὑπήκουσεν is attested by Eusebius; 86 reads ἤκουσεν here and is supported by Jerome (*audiens non aperuit os suum*, attributed to Symmachus and Theodotion).

62. See J. Jeremias, "Zu Phil 2:7: Ἑαυτὸν ἐκένωσεν," *NovT* 6 (1963): 182-88.

To these we may add a possible awareness of alternative translations such as the following:

Ἰδοὺ συνήσει ὁ <u>δοῦλος</u> μου (Isa 52:13, Aquila, Symmachus; cf. Phil 2:7)
ὅρασις αὐτοῦ καὶ <u>μορφὴ</u> αὐτοῦ (Isa 52:14, Aquila; cf. Phil 2:7)
οὐ <u>μορφὴ</u> αὐτῷ καὶ οὐ διαπρεπεία (Isa 53:2, Aquila; cf. Phil 2:7)
πεπλήγοτα ὑπὸ τοῦ θεοῦ καὶ <u>τεταπεινωμένον</u> (Isa 53:4, Aquila, Symmachus; cf. Phil 2:8)
προσήχθη καὶ αὐτὸς <u>ὑπήκουσεν</u> καὶ οὐκ ἤνοιξεν τὸ στόμα αὐτοῦ (Isa 53:8, Symmachus [?]; cf. Phil 2:8)

If these connections are plausible, then Paul can be shown to have cited or drawn upon a wide range of material from the Fourth Servant Song. Whether his use of this material was mediated through "pre-Pauline tradition" is doubtful, since its use cannot be reliably traced back behind the Greek-speaking community at Antioch, with which Paul was associated from an early period.[63] Christians in Antioch were presumably more likely to study Isaiah in Greek than were Christians in Jerusalem.[64] If Paul was aware of other translation possibilities, these may conceivably have been mediated through Jerusalem-based Christians who read Hebrew; but that is speculation. It is more plausible to imagine Paul himself as a participant in the early processes of tradition formation at Antioch, in which crucial decisions were taken on the basis of Isaiah 53 LXX about how Jesus' death was to be understood. As a result of this early preoccupation with this text, traditional formulae were preserved — but rarely if ever elaborated — in Pauline statements dating from some years later.[65]

---

63. Contra Jeremias, *TDNT*, 5:706.

64. 1 Cor 15:3-5 would demonstrate that the entire early church understood the death of Jesus on the basis of Isaiah 53 LXX only if Paul here quotes a fixed formula verbatim. In spite of the arguments of Jeremias (*The Eucharistic Words of Jesus*, 101-103), this seems unlikely.

65. This suggests an answer to the question raised by Richard Hays, why Paul does not more explicitly identify Jesus with the Suffering Servant of Isaiah 53 (*Echoes of Scripture*, 63). Isaiah 53 was foundational to Paul's thinking and language about the death of Christ, and its foundational status is evident from the traditional terminology derived from it.

Conclusion

Owing to its "mistranslations" (i.e., its substitutions, emendations, additions, paraphrases, and so on), Isaiah 53 LXX deviates considerably from its Hebrew exemplar. These "mistranslations" are fundamental to the Pauline and early Christian appropriation of this chapter, which provided not only material for citation but — still more importantly — crucial semantic resources for the development of a positive, soteriological understanding of the death of Christ. It is mistranslation that makes it possible to affirm that Christ died for us, or that he died for our sins.

Mistranslation is the substitution of one semantic potential for another — of (for example) "he suffered for us" for "he bore our blows." Mistranslation highlights the dual relationship of the new text to the original, characterized at the same time by dependence and by autonomy. From one perspective, "he suffered for us" is a mistranslation; from another, its new semantic potential exists not to be corrected but to be realized. If a translation represents the original, it also displaces it and becomes itself an original. For Greek-speaking Christians, Isaiah 53 LXX *is* scripture, in the fullest and most direct sense. Along with the texts from the Psalms that shape the Gospel passion narratives, this passage provides the essential hermeneutical grid or lens through which the death of Jesus is interpreted. The death of Jesus is, as it were, *textualized*. The historical and political factors operative in this event are either subsumed into a scriptural framework (passion narratives: Psalms 22, 69, etc.), or altogether suppressed by it (Paul: Isaiah 53). Thus, in most of the Pauline passages, the sole agents in this event are God and God's Servant/Son. All others play the part of the onlookers who, in the Fourth Servant Song, retell the story of the Servant and confess the momentous divine saving act that has taken place therein, in spite of all appearances to the contrary. The event of Jesus' death is truly understood only as it is reinscribed within the scriptural text. To confess that "Christ died for our sins according to the scriptures" is *not* to acknowledge that (as a matter of fact) Christ died for our sins, and that (helpfully for apologetic purposes) scripture provides subsequent confirmation of something we already know. To confess that "Christ died for our sins . . ." is to confess an already textualized event that would become quite another event if detached from its textual matrix.

That, at least, would seem to be the implication of ". . . according to the scriptures." The event must be reinscribed within scripture; scripture must rewrite the event. And "scripture" here is the text in its Old Greek form, in which it is written not that the Servant bore our sicknesses but that he was delivered up for us and for our sins.

On Probabilities, Possibilities, and Pretexts: Fostering a Hermeneutics of Sobriety, Sympathy, and Imagination in an Impressionistic and Suspicious Age

Edith M. Humphrey

The Challenges

To present a successful paper in biblical studies during the course of a "Learned Society" meeting, it is important to surf the newest wave of approach or method. The promising new biblical scholar will seize one of these new trends, but play her hand out in a fresh way, or apply the template to an unexpected text, with startling results. Better still, she will come up with a new synthetic approach that putatively handles the text or texts better than other methods have done. Or she will perform a clever metanarrative on the current approaches, disclosing their strengths and exposing their weaknesses.

We all have done it, I suspect; and frequently what happens is that we end up illumining not the text, nor the theology that the text expresses, but our own cleverness. This is a syndrome that comes easily to scholars who find themselves in a context of multiple approaches, methods, and perspectives, and a context that also celebrates this diversity. Indeed, we were perilously close to the edge during the colloquium that gave rise to this volume, in which each of us has been engaged to "showcase" his or her "particular approach and expertise." I am not exempt — though I am, at this point, pushing back at the assignment, rather than embracing it. For I may find myself in the ironic position of that would-be saint who conquered pride, only to be heralded as he went down the street by a hundred little demons, all calling out, "Make way for the holy man...." Again, one doesn't want to be too cynical about the current climate. It is true that biblical interpretation has been enriched by the wealth of literary, rhetorical, and sociological approaches throughout the past fifty years. The diversity of lenses, however, has yielded two unfortunate results: first, the impression that any commentator must join the hermeneutical playground by approving or finding yet another thing to "do" with the text; second, the suspicion that today's reader may without guilt subvert or use the text, since we can never be sure of authorial intent, anyway, and the current emphasis is on deconstruction and the readerly imagination.

Both a general critique and a specifically Christian critique may aptly be brought to bear on these trends. First, the ancients wrote and read, and human beings still write and read today, either because they know they are not alone or to learn that they are not alone. Writing and reading are means of communication, or better still, communion. Even those with a totally solipsistic view of writing — "I write to express myself" — discover that in the act of writing they have understood more fully what they meant to say. Consider the undergraduate who doesn't want to write an essay in order to prove to the professor that she has mastered the material: "I know all this stuff. Why do I have to spend time putting it down in a pretty format?" Amazingly, if she is a true student, and not simply a mechanic of words, she finds that in starting to "write it up" she encounters difficulties or possibilities that she had only inchoately intuited. She converses with the subject matter, struggling with it and with herself, and a deeper understanding is reached.

Homo loquens/audiens Becomes *Homo scriptans/legens*

But more commonly those who read and write have assumed that this is a means by which author and readers communicate with each other. Even the great mystics, like St. Teresa of Avila, wrote down intensely personal moments because they thought these would be of help to others, as well as of help to themselves. Solidarity with others and communion were the stuff of their humanity. Moreover, reading widely helps the naïve to verify the maxim of Terence: *Homo sum: humani nil a me alienum puto* ("I consider nothing human alien to myself"). Reading expands our world, extends our horizons; or, to put this less subjectively, it clears our eyes to see the expansive nature of the world that is *there*, and to discover that those things which appear strange are connected to us in an unexpected manner.

Thus I am optimistic enough to believe that the written word is a means of communication and, beyond that, may become a means of intimate communion between author and readers, between one culture and another, and between various readers of a single text. Despite our critical understanding of the difficulties concerning "knowing" and the acknowledged distance between the "knower" and the "known," we still assume that communication goes on. The proliferation of conferences and diverse means of communication in this post-Kantian age testifies to our intransigence on this score. When we think soberly, and not simply speculatively, we must admit that we believe in communication, and indeed that we want to hear and speak with each other. *Homo sapiens* is quite properly *homo loquens* and *homo audiens* and so becomes *homo scriptans* and *homo legens*.

Yet it is also clear that true communication — much less communion — does not always occur serendipitously or automatically. Our nature is such that we must approach the task of speaking, hearing, reading, or writing in such a way that these are not futile. Our own age, marked by the questions of epistemology and jaded by the vicissitudes of time, soberly has stressed the distance between ourselves and the object of knowledge, the alien quality of the world of the text, the more remote world of its elusive author, and the necessity for a hermeneutics of suspicion. These insights, and this stance, have been salutary. Yet they have also afflicted us with a curious amnesia surrounding the very reasons why we read and write. What happens if, in full awareness of these difficulties, but with a newly recovered realism concerning the human propensity for communication, we move on from talk of distance and suspicion and foster instead a hermeneutics of sympathy, all the while aiming for an active (but not eccentric) imagination in the reading process?

Let me stress that this is nothing new. I am seeking to recover an approach to reading that has been assumed by many in the past, implicit in the human activity of communication, and explicit in the Christian idea of revelation. That is, the phenomenon of literary artifacts springs from the human sense that "we are not alone"; the long-time discussion of "genre" in literature assumes that, with an understanding of shared conventions, different readers can read a text with some common understanding. The biblical texts, however, while partaking of this world, go beyond this yearning for communication and this contractual idea of exchanged knowledge. Indeed, they embody and interpret the quest for communication in terms of the belief that God has forged a covenant with his people and that God is in the process of gathering them into one communion. The restlessness of our hearts, expressed in the search for human communication, finds its *telos* in communion with God, and so with each other — these bonds are forged by the One known to us as Logos and Love embodied. That Christians acknowledge and respond to the many and diverse ways by which God has spoken is central to their identity. Conviction that God reveals both verbally conscribed truths and his very self is thus foundational to our approach to Scripture.

This means that the stance of the Christian reader and communicator of the sacred text is to be marked both by a commonsense approach to the biblical literature and by a holy attentiveness. We should be alert to both the anticipated and the astonishing, seeking the obvious "meaning(s)" of a text but also prepared to allow the text, and the Spirit who guides our reading, freedom. We may well be moved beyond articulated insights about God and reality into a more mysterious realm of communion with God himself and into a vision of reality that we do not normally recognize. The text, as an example of its particular genre and with its centripetal aspects, presents us with strong probabilities of meaning, many of which can be transmitted propositionally and clearly; yet we have also to deal with the centrifugal aspect of communication, by which there is a mysterious remainder beyond the signaled message(s), an impetus that directs our imaginations to worship and to wonder. As we read, probabilities and possibilities of meaning engage us — for the text and God are *there*. The weight of these should prevent us from fastening upon texts as pretexts for our own fond ideas and ideologies. Yet even our pre-understandings are not useless, for we bring them to the text in conversation. However, to allow pretexts to preclude surprises means that we render the text mute, or at least muzzle it. The "neptic" (or watchful) reader knows that she reads the text as part of a faithful community, and she is prepared instead for the text, and its divine Author, to read and search her and her community. If the reader does not adopt this identity of solidarity or practice this vulnerability, dialogue may well devolve into a barren (and boring) soliloquy, in which the reader finds in the text exactly what she puts there.

Let's fill this out by means of a consideration of three very different types of texts — a "purple" passage from one of Paul's polemical epistles, a climactic narrative from the Fourth Gospel, and a vision that is found in the very centre of Apocalypse.

Directive Rhetoric Suggests a Story (Romans 8:12-29)

Romans 8 commends itself to us as a luminous chapter in a heavily rhetorical epistle. It is a passage that combines parenesis with hope, adding the necessary "so what?" to Paul's argument for a righteous God, but moving beyond this to embrace a cosmic vision. We begin our reading at v. 12: "So then, brothers [and sisters], we are debtors not to the flesh. . . . For all who are led by the Spirit of God are the sons of God."

What's that? Do I detect a wail of alarm, of outrage? Why use this exclusivist term "sons of God" when Paul is clearly addressing the entire community? Here is where our hermeneutic of sympathy and vulnerability must come firmly into play. For there are other points where Paul does use the word *tekna* (children) for the Christian community, even in this very passage (cf. 8:21). But that is not the chosen term at 8:12; rather, Paul appears to select the term *huioi theou* advisedly. For by it, and in conjunction with the phrase "led by the Spirit of God," he is surely directing our imaginations to that anointed "Son of God" who after the paradigmatic baptism was led by the Spirit into the place of testing (cf. Luke 4:1). Paul's theme from this point on in ch. 8 will be that of suffering and the purpose of suffering in God's plan for the cosmos. The gospel story[1] discloses Jesus as Son of God, or Messiah, in his humble baptism, when the heavens were "apocalypsed" and the Spirit descended upon him (Mark 1:10), and when he then went on to stand firm in temptation; so Paul looks for the great moment when Jesus' followers, led by the Spirit throughout the vicissi-

---

1. Those who do not think that Paul was privy to any summary story of Jesus' life and ministry may find the connection astonishing. Obviously Paul did not have our Gospels to hand; however, it is unlikely that he knew nothing about key moments in Jesus' life, particularly those moments that would have been connected with early church practice (such as baptism). The debate concerning Paul's knowledge of traditions later contained in our Gospels is ongoing, and this is not the place to pursue this question. However, it is salutary to consider that the epistles do not represent Paul's initial proclamation to the communities he addresses, but letters that presuppose some previous knowledge. This is not the only place that an allusion to a specific moment in Jesus' life or teaching may be detected.

tudes of this painful life, will be disclosed ("apocalypsed," 8:19) as little "sons of God" — for they have been, like Jesus, anointed by the Spirit. To "translate" this little phrase into the correct language of our day ("children" rather than "sons") too hastily is to miss Paul's deepest point in the passage: our suffering is parallel to that of the Sufferer *par excellence,* and our anointing is informed by his anointing. The illustrious translators of the NRSV have unfortunately silenced the overtones of this passage, along with a similar argument in Gal 4:4-7: unsatisfied with removing "Son of Man" from the Old Testament, they have removed "sons of God" from the purview of the New Testament reader as well. The text has been flattened and our imaginative wings clipped.

Yet there is an offense in this text for every reader — not simply for the politically correct, but for the anxious dogmatist as well. For as the passage begins with a putatively "exclusivist" image for redeemed humanity, so does it end with a bracingly untraditional image for God: "Likewise, the Spirit helps us in our weakness, for we do not know how to pray as we ought, but that very Spirit intercedes with wordless groanings" (8:26). Paul has set before us the picture of a suffering (*sustenazō,* 8:22) and tormented creation, "in travail" (*sunōdinō,* 8:22) for a new birth, with redeemed humanity groaning inwardly as well, involved in the process. We are groaning inwardly (*en heautois stenazomen,* 8:23), for it is the Holy Spirit that gives voice to our labor cries (*stenagmois alalētois,* 8:26), a kind of midwife to the birthing process. Indeed, it is the Holy Spirit who is giving birth, for we simply are "waiting," says Paul, while the Spirit does the work of God, bringing to fruition what God has begun.

While Paul uses no feminine pronoun in sketching this picture, the activity of the Holy Spirit is poignantly depicted by means of female imagery. In this passage the sovereign God has identified so closely with the creation that the Spirit is understood to be deeply immanent — indwelling, comforting, giving voice to the inchoate cries of creation and the confused distress of our own human plight. The trope of end-time "labor" issuing in the new age is, of course, a traditional one in eschatological passages. For example, the anonymous seer of 4 Ezra, a rough contemporary of Paul, presents in his tenth chapter a visionary woman figure who, in her cry of pain, is transformed into the heavenly Jerusalem. Similarly, Paul exploits the story of the fall and suggests that we are in the process of having the primal "curse" undone. His language in 8:21-22 reminds us of the double penalty upon humanity — the intransigence of the soil and the pain of fertility. What is remarkable here is that God's own self takes on the pain of that double curse, so that in the end the new birth will be disclosed in joy, and the creation will be again in a state of *shalom*. For the traditionalist who is wary of female imagery for God, this may be an uncomfortable picture — are we back to an animism, reverting to a worldview in which creator is indistinguishable from creation? Hardly. For Paul has already established, at this point in his argument to the Romans, a robust view of the sovereignty and purposeful action of God. Yet here his language is evocative of a great mystery — that God, in these last days, has taken to working from the inside of the created order, and not simply from above. What Paul sketches in Romans 8 is schematically stated in Eph 4:9-11: "The ascending One is the very same as the descending one . . . that this One might fill all things . . . and give gifts to humanity." Later, the patristic theologians were to use the language of assumption and indwelling: by the Incarnation God has assumed human nature; by Pentecost, God has filled his people and, indeed, the entire cosmos.

Both those who are "revisionally" minded and those who are traditionally minded are brought up short in their reading of Romans 8. For the passage is bookended by startling language and by potential offenses; oblivious of party loyalties, it speaks in its very own voice. Our imaginations can be informed by these nuances only if we do not drown out these uncomfortable notes by our twenty-first-century shibboleths and anxieties. Yet within the passage, there is something that confirms our worldview — though this perspective was not immediately apparent to many ancients! Past readings of the term *ktisis* (or, in the Vulgate, *creatura*) tended to fasten upon the *human* creation and seemed unable to leap to the full scope of Paul's vision.[2] That is, whether blinkered by an anthropocentric view of the world or misled by Paul's specific reference to the resurrection ("redemption of our body"), they tended to assume that the section was concerned only with the resurrection of human beings, and not with the renewal, the bringing to birth, of a new creation. Though, by ecclesial temperament, I am happy to give great weight to the interpretations of ancients such as St. Augustine and St. John Chrysostom, here seems to be a

---

2. See, for example, Augustine, "On Romans 8:18-24," in *St. Augustine: Eighty-Three Different Questions* (trans. D. L. Mosher; The Fathers of the Church: A New Translation; Washington, DC: The Catholic University of America Press, 1977), 149-57; and John Chrysostom, "Homily XIV on Romans," in *Library of the Fathers of the Holy Catholic Church Anterior to the Division of the East and West 7* (Oxford: John Henry Parker, 1941), 244-47.

case in which the ancient church needs the contemporary church. In our readings of the Scriptures, members of the church enter into fruitful and corrective discussion with each other. For Paul, in speaking of the *ktisis*, "subjected against its will," is surely referring to the entire created order that by the primal fall has been plunged into a cycle of corruption and death. And it is creation "herself" who is personified here, eagerly awaiting the revelation of what redeemed humanity has become — true "anointed ones," true "sons of God." For just as the death of human bodies has meant shame for the world, so the redemption of our body will mean glory for the new creation.

The creation waits, and we wait: God does the work through the Spirit, and yet, wonder of wonders, we participate in this! Though still hampered by "hardship, distress, and nakedness" we are, in Christ, relearning that "bridge" position for which we were made: following the firstborn, as members of a large family, we are fulfilling, through prayer, the priest-like role that God gave to humanity at the beginning of days — even to the extent that, like the Son, we may be "accounted sheep to be slaughtered" (8:36). So, then, the chapter confirms not only the importance of the human body but the importance of God's entire creation. This speaks a word of affirmation to our own society, according to which physicality and ecology are utterly significant. Nature is not to be considered as a mere backdrop for our human exploits, but as the beloved creation of God, given to us to nurture, though we have marred her by our self-centered ingratitude. Could it be that, in the light of God's new calling to *theōsis* — our participation in the inheritance (8:17), glory (5:2; 8:21), and even form (*summorphos*, 8:29) of the Son — the corollary of our transformation might be the "humanization" of (at least some of) the created order? Though such speculation is admittedly fanciful, an opening is provided in the text through Paul's personification of *ktisis*, which sparks an intriguing centrifugal musing.

John 20:11-31: Narrative Instructs and Suggests Mystery

We began by examining a passage of instruction and ended up in the midst of a suggestive (or, some might say, tendentious) story. As we turn to our example from the Gospel, we discover that narrative also carries instruction, while transporting the reader by tantalizing details that remain obstinately mysterious. The Fourth Gospel comes to its first dramatic conclusion in that mystifying passage where the risen Jesus meets Mary Magdalene the sorrowing and Thomas the skeptic. Scholars have struggled for centuries over Jesus' admonition that she not touch him (20:17) since he has not yet gone up to the Father, when this is followed two vignettes later by his invitation to Thomas to do this very thing (20:27).[3]

However such questions are answered, the Easter morning and evening scenarios provide examples of those who have been surprised by joy, and they clearly articulate the intimate bond that has, by the crucifixion and resurrection, been established between the disciples and God. This intimacy is both suggested by the narrative and declared in the embedded speech. Mary is addressed in tenderness, with attention to her distress, and called by name, thus being brought to a joyful point of recognition. Thomas is challenged by his very own words of *défi* and then inspired to name Jesus "my Lord and my God!" On the level of verbal instruction, Mary is told to deliver a message to the entire company of believers: "Go to my brothers [and sisters] and tell them, 'I am ascending to my Father and your Father, to my God and your God" (20:17). On the same level, Thomas is included in the verbal blessing "Shalom," told not to doubt but to believe, and entrusted with a benediction that concerns those of the household of faith who are not even yet part of the great story: "Blessed are those who have not seen and yet have come to believe" (20:29).

So, then, the narratival and verbal cues lead the attentive reader to understand that a new communion has been established between God and those who are in communion with Jesus, and that this new situation embraces others who are not part of the written story. Indeed, the ideal reader is led to find himself or herself in the narrative through the benediction of Thomas. Jesus' Easter blessing spills over the pages of the Gospel and into real life. Again, we note that Jesus both names the beloved and by his light brings even the most cautious member of the community to name him in intimacy. In case the narrative is not clear enough, the narrator caps off the sequence by naming its specific purpose: "that you may believe that Jesus is the Christ, the Son of God, and that through believing you may have life *in his name*" (20:31).

---

3. Some have harmonized the passages by nuancing the differences between *haptō* (translated as "cling to") and the verbs used in instructing Thomas. The most natural reading of his injunction to Mary is, however, that she not handle him, for the time being.

Clearly the overall thrust of the narrative is not in the first place to lead the reader into the realms of speculation but to confirm the message and function of the entire Gospel. Yet there are details in the text that cry out to be recognized. Is it significant that Jesus appeared first to Mary, a woman, and crowned that intimacy by speaking her name and commissioning her? Surely it is largely by means of this passage that Mary Magdalene has accrued such importance in the Christian tradition, East and West, for centuries: she has fired the imagination of penitent, liturgist, egalitarian, and misogynist. Thus tradition has pointed to this climax of the Fourth Gospel, honoring Mary Magdalene with the title "apostle to the apostles," or even "equal to the apostles," and chanting in rapture that, in obedience to Jesus, she "threw away the ancestral curse, elatedly saying to the apostles 'death is overthrown!'"[4]

Contemporary exegetes have naturally read a more pressing agenda into this episode, contrasting Mary's first sight of the risen Jesus with the more conservative rehearsal of Peter as the first seer and berating an ecclesial tradition, beginning with Luke (who supposedly favors Peter), that has taken away Mary's birthright. So Ann Graham Brock, who begins with the premise that "New Testament scholarship has uncovered aspects of many patriarchal tendencies within certain branches of early Christianity and their attempts to suppress the significance of women's leadership roles, especially that of Mary Magdalene."[5] Yet careful examination of such analyses shows that the premises too easily dictate the results. Sober thought about the distance between our culture and the first-century world should prevent us from supposing that the Gospel itself carries such a message. Brock, seeking clues of struggle and power relations, and preoccupied with the question of status, cannot read Luke or the Fourth Gospel in their own terms. For neither Gospel is primarily concerned with the status of women or the establishment of male apostles as the guarantors of orthodoxy or of church structure: they seek to place Jesus in the central position.

Yet sensitivity to the details of the Gospel suggests that the appearance to Mary holds some deep significance. It is surely telling that Jesus' first sign is done in the presence of a woman and in such a manner as to

---

4. See Tone 4 of the Troparia ("hymns of the day") for Sundays, "Divine Liturgy of St. John Chrysostom," in *The Great Book of Needs* I (South Canaan, PA: St. Tikhon's Seminary Press, 1998).

5. A. G. Brock, *Mary Magdalene: The First Apostle and the Struggle for Authority* (HTS 51; Cambridge: Harvard University Press, 2003), 13.

bless the married state, while Jesus' final act is first perceived by a woman (20:15) in a garden and signifies the renewal of all things. In Genesis God seeks Adam: "where are you?" In John, the woman seeks one who is her teacher, but who will be rightly addressed as "Lord and God." Just as the Fourth Gospel begins with allusions to Genesis, so it ends with intimations of the new creation: "that you may have life in his name."

Again, why does Jesus permit Thomas (though Thomas does not avail himself of the permission) what is forbidden to Mary Magdalene? Is this a different kind of touching, or does the difference signal two distinct moments in salvation history? For example, does the author of the Fourth Gospel envisage a two-step crossing of boundaries: up and back from the realm of the dead; up and forward to a glorified corporeal existence? If so, then the second step occurs off-stage, with Jesus returning to visit his bemused disciples, in scenes where he is both recognizable but altered. Though the Fourth Gospel does not include, with Luke-Acts, a narrative of the ascension, it seems unlikely (as some have suggested) that in John the resurrection and ascension have been conflated. The risen Jesus' final words to the "Beloved" disciple and the narratival warning regarding the meaning of these words (21:22-23) demonstrate a conviction that the resurrection appearances have come to an end: the return to the Father is complete, and the community now is waiting for Jesus to "come" for them. This expectation of a return, coupled with the constant references to Jesus "in the bosom of the Father," "returning whence he came," "departing so that the Paraclete can come" all point to a Johannine knowledge of a final ascent tradition as separate from the resurrection appearances. The actual ascension, along with Jesus' baptism, the transfiguration, and the institution of the Lord's Supper, remain unnarrated in the Fourth Gospel but everywhere make their mark. It is hard to conceive of an ideal reader for this text who does not already have these narratives fixed as part of his or her mental furniture. What remains mysterious for us is the particular process of resurrection that the readership may have understood along with this author, and its temporal or logical connection with the ascension and the giving of the Spirit.

The theologically minded, following this centrifugal "spin," may well find themselves asking questions with regard to such matters. What is the relationship between Jesus' crucified hour of "glory," the unnarrated scene when the "dead hear his voice," the resurrection morning, the unnarrated ascension, and the giving of the Spirit? Why is it "better for Jesus to leave" so that "the Spirit can come"? In what sense are the physical seers and the non-apostles "blessed" and what does this mean for ecclesiology? One can hardly say that the text explicitly invites such questions — yet, far from forbidding them, its allusive nature issues a kind of invitation. The note is sounded, indeed, from an earlier point of the Gospel, where Jesus cries out, "He who believes in me . . . out of his belly shall flow rivers of living water," and where the evangelist comments, "He spoke this concerning the Spirit, whom those who believe in him would receive: for the Holy Spirit was not yet [given], because Jesus was not yet glorified" (7:38-39). So, then, the narrative instructs believing readers in an indirect manner, drawing them into the narrative and evoking many more possibilities of interpretation than those found in more directive texts. In this way, the Fourth Gospel may be likened to an icon, which by its perspective *enfolds* would-be observers, giving them the sense of being in the scene, rather than simply observing it. Because readers must actively collude with the text, it is possible that they may misread from time to time: it is not always clear where we are dealing with probabilities, over against merely pursuing possibilities. This does not mean, however, that any so-called "reading of the text" actually reads *the text*. The cues of the narrative, as directed by embedded propositions and conclusions, as suggested by repetition and poignant symbolism, are still patent to the attentive reader.

Revelation 11-12: Vision Fires the Imagination While Confirming Theology

We turn finally to the most evocative text, which is symbolic and open by its very genre — the Apocalypse of Jesus to John. Chapters 11 and 12, though divided by some exegetes in terms of putative structure of the book, each pursue certain motifs by which they are firmly linked. One of these is the fate of their heroes — the two witnesses in ch. 11 and the Messiah child in ch. 12. Chapter 12 has puzzled numerous commentators, since the Messiah child is assumed (taken up) without an intervening death — an event that defies the normal presentation of Jesus' life, since a few select biblical heroes are *assumed* as a reward for righteousness, but Jesus *ascends* after victory over a complete death. John, of course, is well acquainted with the slain and *resurrected* Lamb: "the standing having-been-slaughtered Lamb" dominates ch. 5 and the ensuing seal sequence. The actions of ch. 11

are equally bizarre, but few today experience them that way since we do not share the same cultural background as the original readers. Here an informed and careful study helps us to discern the astonishing scenario that John creates. For the two witnesses — whether Enoch and Elijah, Moses and Elijah, or a paradigmatic priest and king from the prophecy of Zechariah — are figures who are traditionally associated with assumption. Their assumptions are not here narrated, however, though we might have expected an assumption scene, followed by a vision of what they will do when they return on the last day from their reserved pause in heaven in order to fill their eschatological role. What *is* underscored is not assumption, but martyrdom and resurrection, followed by ascension. The one who died, rose, and ascended is pictured in ch. 12 as assumed; the ones who in legend were assumed here take on the role of witnesses who die, rise, and ascend.

Let us begin with the vision of the child. Assumption language surrounds the entire chapter, even while it frames a central declaration that heightens the actions of casting down and dying. Our eye begins by looking up to the heavenlies, where we see enacted a divine drama. As we look up, we see the standoff between the woman and the dragon, and the male child is snatched *(harpazō)* away to God and the throne, while the woman flees (12:1-6). In the second scene, the archenemy and his minions are thrown down (vv. 7-9): this is celebrated in the proclamation of vv. 10-12, where Satan's downfall is linked to the death of the Lamb and the martyrs' witness, and where joy is envisaged in heaven, coupled with woe on earth. We cut back to the contest between the woman and the dragon and learn that she is helped by being given two great divine wings to fly away — yet she flies not to heaven like Icarus, not to the promised land like Israel, but to the wilderness where she must endure more suffering (vv. 13-17). Motion is vigorous: up to heaven, down to earth, down into death, up to heaven, down to earth, "up" to the wilderness.

The seer, it seems, knows the apocalyptic techniques so well that he can play with them. It seems he is also current with the grammar of assumption, so that he can use this trope in a subversive manner. Here is a sophisticated and almost playful (though ultimately serious) application of assumption language, whereby John wages his theopolitical warfare. As in the rest of the Apocalypse, the visionary turns the tables on imperial power, initially seeming to adopt the perspective uncritically, then exposing it as inadequate. In the words of Harry O. Maier, "Rehearsing in order to reverse, enthroning so as to decrown, setting up only to knock down, Revelation unmasks the masquerade of tyrannical political power and urges its hearers to walk a more costly way."[6] So John wields his weapons of reversal in an unexpected direction. You want an emperor? You want a king who will rule all the nations? You want a human being who is invincible? You want a man so bound for greatness that his end is apotheosis? Well, it isn't Caesar! Here is that one who will rule the nations with iron! This mere child is the one, a humble figure who is the Ruler of right. If anyone has the power to escape death, it is this one! If any is worthy of apotheosis, it is this one! We watch as this promised child is taken up to the very throne of God.

Yet, we have already met this person under another figure in the initial heavenly vision, where One stands in the midst of the throne and simultaneously in the midst of the elders (*en mesō tou thronou kai en mesō tōn presbyterōn*, 5:6). The Lion who has the throne by birthright also stands as a Lamb amidst his suffering people; he is the standing slaughtered Lamb. So, too, in ch. 12. For in the *vision* the child is assumed without dying, and thus is presented as the candidate *par excellence* for special divine protection and honorific status; but in the *oracle* (12:10-12) that interprets the vision, we hear not of an apotheosized child nor of a king who rules by iron. Instead, the loud voice from heaven proclaims the Lamb who has conquered by his blood, whose rule of vulnerability is shared by those who hold to the testimony of Jesus. The child's greatness is revealed not in his iron rule or mighty departure to the heavenlies, but in his death. It is his humiliation and *not* his exaltation that issues in the Dragon's downfall. Like child, like mother: her wings to fly take her to her own time of tribulation, and not to a land of milk and honey (Exod 19:4; Deut 32:10-14). Her time of "preparation" is that same "time, times and half time" in which the beast is permitted to exercise terror (13:5) and in which the two witnesses prophesy in sackcloth (11:3). Exaltation is dependent upon holding to the testimony, though the whole is governed by divine protection (i.e., "help" comes to the beleaguered woman from heaven and from the created earth).

We consider now the mysterious two witnesses of ch. 11, also figured as olive trees and lampstands. These two are protected by divine fire, and

---

6. H. O. Maier, *Apocalypse Recalled: The Book of Revelation after Christendom* (Minneapolis: Fortress Press, 2002), 199.

they also have authority to cause drought, to turn water into blood, and to strike the earth with plagues. The description of their Mosaic and prophetic authority (11:5-6) is juxtaposed with the ensuing scene (11:7-10) in which they are overcome and martyred, then corporally shamed in that typological place corresponding to Rome, Jerusalem, Sodom, and Egypt (11:7). They die, a spectacle to the people and a cause of joy to their enemies. They then rise to a true resurrection (11:11), not simply a revival: they are animated by the very *pneuma* of God and they stand (active voice *estēsan*), striking those who observe the scene with terror. Their resurrection is an epiphany; so too is their exaltation. Invited by God, *"anabate!"* they ascend on the cloud of heaven, while enemies look on (11:12). Here we note both similarities and differences with the ascension accounts of Jesus in Luke and Acts: the cloud imagery, common to Hellenistic and Hebrew exaltation, is present in both; John adopts while Luke avoids the usual Hellenistic term for ascent *(anabasis)* in order to protect the story of Jesus from pagan overtones. John the seer is more adventuresome! How is it that he can use frank exaltation language for these two human martyrs? It is because in their entire pattern of life they have called attention to the pattern of the Lamb: they are arch-witnesses, if you like. What is remarkable about them is that they *die* even though they have been given "power" to avoid death. In dying like the one whom they are patterning, they then follow in the upward movement — resurrection and ascension. But the ascensions are possible only because the victory has already been accomplished, in the "city where also their Lord was crucified." They are not important, ultimately, because of their great status, but because they number with the "servants, the prophets and saints and all who fear the name, both small and great" (11:18) whom God will reward.

Let us consider the rhythm of the vision. John is first given a rod to measure the worshipers of God (11:1). All that follows seems to be the result of John's measurement: we see the two great witnesses, with all the prowess that they have been given; we behold their death, how they follow in the footsteps of the crucified One; we see their humiliation, then their resurrection and exaltation, and then the judgment. The measurement of the saints is qualitative and quantitative: all who assume the pattern of Jesus are included. John, it seems, has a visionary offence for every reader. The visionary images adopted and undermined in ch. 12 take their aim most directly at the imperial ideal, that is, the Greco-Roman ideas of power. Yet the Hebrew version of dominion is also subtly challenged in the embedded reference to the child who "will rule with a rod of iron." This Lamb conquers by sacrifice. The visionary images adopted in ch. 11 come more directly from the Hebrew Bible and parabiblical traditions — patriarchal and national heroes are evoked and are given heroic characteristics readily appreciated by one conversant with these narratives. But all this power — power to inflict plague, power to transform water into blood, power even to die — is beside the point. Their true worth lies in their willingness to follow in the pattern of the dying and now standing Lamb. Moreover, this is no honor peculiar to *them* — God will reward all his servants, whether "small" or "great." In this chapter is implied the dynamic of 22:8-9, the insistence that all is leveled before God. The narrative of the two witnesses challenges most directly the eschatological traditions of privilege afforded the "greats" of the Hebrew Bible, but it also collaterally damages the Greco-Roman values, because of the overtones of Greco-Roman assumption imagery and the conflation of Jerusalem with Rome (11:8). Yet, as is convenient with symbolic imagery, John has his cake and eats it too. The sympathetic reader of these two visions in chs. 11 and 12 is led imaginatively to honor the two witnesses and the child, by a direct connection with Hebrew Bible and Greco-Roman narratives of power. Then, this direct use of the imagery is dissolved before our eyes as we find all heroes leveled before one who will not be a hero in their terms. Both the direct and the inverse connections are made by the responsive reader: we experience, as we so often do with John, a sense of vertigo.

The sympathetic and attentive reader will not kick against the directive pricks of this narrative. Rather, he or she will *notice* the strange dynamics of the narrative visions, *receive* the surprises of the narrative, *work imaginatively* with the author, and so *forge* the suggested connections with the biblical and legendary material. To read in this way means that the reader must indeed *allow* the imaginative vertigo to set in, so that we experience, as did John, the disorientation of the visionary world. We are to undergo a conversion of the imagination. Embedded amidst the visions are the directions, corrections, and tensions offered by embedded oracles and propositions — we must accept these, even when they seem to contradict the visions. So we learn that the two witnesses ascend only because they follow in the train of the Risen-Ascended One; so we intuit that the Anointed One, though worthy of assumption and safekeeping by the Father, has been shockingly given over to death — yet he lives.

Because we are drawn into the imaginative work of the seer, we become a part of the world of the text and understand our solidarity with the Messiah. By this vision, we don't simply learn "esoteric dope" about God's purposes; we discover that we are enfolded in them. Yet even here, even in the most "open" of texts, the text never becomes our own property. We cannot, if we remain attentive, do whatever we want with the imagery. There may be many possibilities open to the attentive and imaginative reader of the Apocalypse, but to style the book as a sample of "fantasy" literature, as does, for example, Tina Pippin,[7] and to marry ideology to this approach is to create a new work, and to turn this breathtaking vision into a nightmare. So Pippin sees in ch. 12 the kidnapping of the child from a desolate woman (rather than a sign of victory when the child is taken on high); so she labels the entrance into the New Jerusalem at the climax of the vision a gang rape of a helpless bride by 144,000 males. Assuming that the text is violent, this would-be reader does improbable violence to the text.

Robust Theological Conversation and the Scriptural Text

We move to our tentative conclusions, after having considered what a sober yet imaginative approach might look like when reading three very different kinds of texts. What I have sketched in this paper is not a new method, but an approach. I have been intent on reversing the most common academic stance adopted toward the scriptural text today, the mode of "suspicion," forging in its place "a hermeneutics of sympathy." I have also called for a twofold watchfulness — a watchfulness of the mind, which will mean that we read with sobriety, heeding the directions of the text, and a watchfulness of the imagination, which means that we will, with anticipation, heed and follow the openings that the text presents to us.

Though the three selections are different, coming from a letter, a Gospel, and an apocalypse, they share a visionary or revelatory quality, for they fasten upon God's action of re-creation, assumption, and resurrection. The poetic nature of these passages may mean that we find here more "scope for imagination" than in other biblical pieces; yet close attention to the first two texts, with their centrifugal impulse, has shown that they re-

---

7. T. Pippin, *Death and Desire: The Rhetoric of Gender in the Apocalypse of John* (Louisville: Westminster John Knox Press, 1992).

tain an integrity and a means of directing the willing reader. Hard-case scenarios can remove blinkers, accentuate the obvious, and direct us to what we have previously overlooked. Even in the most extreme case of the Apocalypse, we have seen that a relatively "open" genre may shape our reading through the sights and sounds related by the seer, through the interpretation of the mediating angel, and through the intrusion of the implied author. The Apocalypse has been disdained by many and so left unread; for the exuberant reader, the challenge is to retain a certain sobriety.

For it is certainly the case that such texts can fire the imagination, causing our hearts to respond to what our minds have already received. In speaking of the visionary book of Revelation, Michael Wilcock explains that the narrative presents itself as an "intensive" rather than an "extensive" theological work, coloring in what we have learned elsewhere in the Scriptures. In a similar vein, the Eastern Orthodox biblical scholar Stylianopoulos[8] impresses upon the student that the whole of Scripture has not simply a historical, a literary, and a theological level, but also works transformationally on those who will read with the *heart*. If he is correct, then we see, in an extreme form in the book of Revelation, a characteristic shared by the whole of Scripture — Scripture functions, among other roles, as an icon, a living picture through which we meet the One who is the Word.

So Wilcock describes John's vision in these terms:

> The conviction that Revelation really is meant to *reveal* truth, and not to obscure it, and that its treasures really do lie on the surface if one looks for them in the right light, is by no means the same as a belief that its meaning will be spelt out for us verbally, with logic and precision. Of course God does not despise verbal communication; after all, "the Word" was the name he gave to his own Son. But his words, his declarations, and arguments and reasonings, have all been spoken by the time he brings John to Patmos. What he has in store for his last unveiling is a word of a different sort: an acted word, a word dramatized, painted, set to music — a word you can see and feel and taste. In fact, it is a sacrament.
>
> It is no use reading Revelation as though it were a Paul-type theological treatise in a slightly different idiom, or a Luke-style history pro-

---

8. T. G. Stylianopoulos, *The New Testament: An Orthodox Perspective* (Scripture, Tradition, Hermeneutics 1; Brookline, MA: Holy Cross Press, 1999).

jected into the future. You might as well analyse the rainbow — or the wine of communion or the water of baptism. Logical analysis is not what they are for. They are meant to be used and enjoyed.

We . . . of all people, should understand this. We live in a post-literate age, which, tiring of words, is beginning to talk again in pictures. So television replaces radio, and the noun "image" comes back into use with a dozen connotations. Well, God knew about it long ago and when his children have had enough of reciting systematic theology, he gives them a gorgeous picture-book to look at, which is in a different way just as educational.

Pictures, potent images of Christian truth, to use as we use the sacraments — that is what we are given in Revelation. . . . It is the images that stick. John's pages are studded with them . . . that our imagination, as well as our mind, should grasp the key concepts of the faith. So, till the bridegroom returns — till the city descends from the sky, and the day of the wedding-feast dawns — we do this, in remembrance of him.[9]

Thus, reading the end of the Book first, beginning with a place where angels and wise scholars have mostly feared to tread, I have learned something about the nature of the whole Scriptures. This is consonant, I should add, with my experience of theology and the church. As I was nurtured academically in the "hard school" of apocalypses, so I was nurtured spiritually in the "hard school" of a para-church movement, the Salvation Army, which seems to be in the process of becoming more ecclesial. I learned there that even self-consciously non-ecclesial communities of faith have an implicit ecclesiology. Similarly, there is no simple "reading of the Bible," for we all read within a tradition, despite protestations of *sola scriptura*. Thus, as will already be apparent, I am concerned to read the Scriptures both in terms of what we can know about their original context and in terms of the historical and worldwide traditions of the entire church. I want, without apology, to read the texts as a part of a deep and living Tradition.

As I read in this manner, I am confirmed in the conviction that Scripture offers more to us than entertaining and culturally contextualized narratives, more than theological and ethical propositions, more than re-

---

9. M. Wilcock, *The Message of Revelation: I Saw Heaven Opened* (Downers Grove, IL: InterVarsity Press, 1975), 24-25.

vealed gnosis about who we are in this world. But Scripture does not offer *less* than these things. (Such an assurance is intended to mollify those who, like Timothy Ward, express discomfort with regard to the model of Scripture as an icon.[10]) That is to say, we must read the Scriptures as literature, as theology and ethic, and as revelation of truth. In the end, however, God gives us far more — by means of the Scripture, he gives us, if we will receive, himself.

So the words instruct, and form, and fire the imagination — they act at the same time as an icon of the Word himself, drawing us beyond all these good things to the source and *telos* of all Good. And so my foundational aim has been to do nothing particularly novel here. As a literary analyst, I have called attention to imagery, to the actors, to the actions, to repetition of words; as one interested in rhetoric and history, I have heeded the explicit and implicit polemic, the echoes to other texts, and the subtle and more directive cues in the text. With wonder, I have noted that the centripetal aspects of these texts are fairly clear, and I have suggested where the centrifugal dynamics might lead us to intriguing discussion and even speculation. The one dynamic may, of course, be confused with the other; yet we are reading here in community, and so there is a safeguard built into our process, as we study and converse with each other.

In all this, we take seriously the command reiterated by our Lord, "love the Lord your God [and so also God's written Word!] with all your heart, soul, and mind." In fostering this deep love, and following where this leads, we learn how the biblical text can and must contribute to our most bracing and robust theological conversations.

---

10. T. Ward, "The Bible, Its Truth and How It Works," in *Fanning the Flame: Bible, Cross and Mission — Meeting the Challenge in a Changing World* (ed. P. D. Gardner, C. J. H. Wright, and C. Green; Grand Rapids: Zondervan, 2003), 17-42.

An Intertextual Reading of Moral Freedom in the Analects and Galatians

K. K. Yeo

I was asked to offer an interpretation of the New Testament text that can contribute to a robust theological conversation across the globe. In order to demonstrate a theologico-cultural translation of Paul's theology in light of Confucian ethics, I, as a Chinese Christian, will read the Analects and Galatians intertextually. I will say something about the kind of intertextual reading I employ, then proceed with the intertextuality between Confucius and Paul on the themes of human nature and moral freedom. For Chinese Christians, both the Analects and Galatians are scriptures (no doubt privileging the Bible over the Four Books of the Confucian canon); both texts are authoritative and meaningful to their ethical and religious lives. Inevitably, interpreters read from their social locations, bringing with them presuppositions and their cultural texts that are both limiting and creative to the biblical text. A faithful translation is not simply a historical recovery of what the text meant, but a creative engagement with the text that allows it to continue speaking to modern readers.

In times past, much has been made of the precise explication of a text (exegesis), with warnings against reading into the text what is not there (eisegesis). The classic distinction between "exegesis" (objective reading,

---

I am grateful to the Henry Luce Foundation and the Association of Theological Schools for granting me the Henry Luce III Fellowship, enabling me to research the intertextuality of the Analects and Galatians. This essay is a part of that writing project. Unless otherwise noted, all translations of the biblical texts and the Analects are my own.

historical meaning out from the text) and "eisegesis" (subjective reading, meaning into the text) may not be helpful once we move to an intertextual reading. At best the "exegesis/eisegesis" concern might be a construct that assumes scholars can transcend their culture and detach themselves from their own time and place, yet be able to become immersed in the past and know it with certainty. At worst, the "exegesis/eisegesis" differentiation is a scholarly fear of living in partial knowledge, the insecurity of shared ownership of any text, or the alienation of self from the *network of texts* with which we all work.[1] I am here assuming that a purely objective reading of Confucius and Paul that transcends culture is unrealizable. The language of Confucius (fifth-century BCE Chinese) and Paul (first-century CE Greek) is not always clear, and our knowledge of their worlds is limited. But these assumptions do not lead us to despair; we need to be all the more diligent in seeking understanding — and doing so by means of intersubjective and intertextual reading.

Intersubjectivity and Intertextual Reading, Galatians 3:8

The term "intertextuality" was coined by Julia Kristeva to indicate that a "text" — be it a person, an interpretation, a reading, an object — exists not in a closed system of its own but in interrelation with other "texts" that preceded it or coexist with it through quotations, references, allusions, and other influences of various kinds.[2] This intersubjective influence conveyed through the medium of a "text" is clearly seen in "various cultural discourses,"[3] because "the text is a tissue of quotations drawn

---

    1. The presuppositions of exegetes are conditioned by their language and culture. Exegesis based on grammatical analysis is often deemed to render the most objective reading of the biblical text. However, interpreters of the Bible using the same philological and grammatical reading may offer diverse meanings of the same text. For we understand grammar and history not according to objective and abstract principles but in relation to our subjective, partial, and changing assumptions about language and history. Thus even a grammatical reading is not without subjective input. Words become archaic, their referents unknown. Some texts contain words found nowhere else and require an educated guess as to their meaning.

    2. J. Kristeva, "Word, Dialogue and Novel," in *The Kristeva Reader* (ed. T. Moi; New York: Columbia University Press, 1986), 34.

    3. J. Culler, *On Deconstruction: Theory and Criticism after Structuralism* (Ithaca, NY: Cornell University Press, 1982), 32.

An Intertextual Reading of Moral Freedom in the Analects and Galatians

from innumerable centers of culture."[4] Both axes of intertextuality — via the writer (who is also the first reader) and his or her readers (who co-produce the meaning of the text) — require a dialog with the text in the production of meaning.

This *reproductive and productive* process of reading allows the text/writer and reader/interpretation to be intersubjective. A text not only carries meaning but also allows, and even requires, the reader to create meaning in the act of reading. Similarly, readers not only interpret texts but also are being read by texts — that is, their own stories are made meaningful (whether positively or negatively) by the texts themselves. Because understanding and reading are processes that are reproductive and productive, a writer cannot have an absolute control on the meaning of a text or limit its meanings to his or her own original intention. The authority of interpretation does not reside in the text itself or in the first writer alone but is to be found also in the interactive process of the text, involving both the writer and the reader, which I have previously called "rhetorical interaction."[5] In his letter to the Galatians, Paul himself carries out a "rhetorical interaction" with the scriptures as he engages two historically separate events, namely, Abraham and Christ. Paul proposes what the scriptures say: "The scripture preproclaimed (προευηγγελίσατο) the gospel to Abraham that 'all the Gentiles will be blessed in you'" (Gal 3:8). Paul contends that the gospel that comes through Abraham to all Gentiles (nations) is a gospel "beforehand," which is to say that it "preaches the gospel by anticipation" (it does not mean, "preaching a preliminary gospel").[6] Paul can say the scripture proclaims the gospel in advance[7] because of his christological interpretation — though the Old Testament texts can be read non-christologically as well.[8] This point is significant to our work here because

---

4. R. Barthes, *Image, Music, Text* (New York: Hill & Wang, 1977), 146.

5. Yeo Khiok-khng (K. K.), *Rhetorical Interaction in 1 Corinthians 8 and 10: A Formal Analysis with Its Preliminary Implications to a Chinese Cross-cultural Hermeneutic* (Leiden: Brill, 1995), 15-49.

6. A. T. Hanson, *Studies in Paul's Technique and Theology* (London: SPCK, 1974), 64. Cf. F. F. Bruce, "The Curse of the Law," in *Paul and Paulinism: Essays in Honour of C. K. Barrett* (ed. M. D. Hooker and S. G. Wilson; London: SPCK, 1982), 33.

7. The word is found only here in the New Testament.

8. Gal 3:9 draws out the implications of the scriptural proof in verse 8: "So then, those who are of faith are blessed with Abraham who had faith" (RSV). The relationship between the old people of God and the new people of God could be understood in terms of Abraham and Christ. Paul understands the original promise as made to include all humankind, and he

it locates the indigenization of the gospel of Christ within the cultural language of Confucianism although historically the Christ event happened centuries after Confucius (and Abraham). My purpose is not to argue that a certain "proto-gospel of Christ" existed in the Analects; this kind of historical argument is unnecessary. I prefer to use Paul's Christ-hermeneutics in reading history backward from Christ (ca. first century CE) to Abraham (1800 BCE) to Confucius (ca. 550 BCE) and to claim this is simply a valid hermeneutical move.

This essay is therefore a manifesto or *apologia* for a theological translation of Chinese Christians. It seeks to articulate how it is possible to maintain a Chinese identity *and* a Christian identity concomitantly without capitulating to some western or other cultural model of Christian identity. To be a Chinese Christian is to adopt a distinctive, unique identity that owes much to both traditions but is *sui generis*. Confucius and Paul converge across a surprisingly broad front. Yet, the Christ of the Cross completes or extends what is merely implicit or absent in Confucius; and Confucius amplifies various elements of Christian faith (e.g., community, virtues) that are underplayed in individual, western Christianity. To demonstrate a Chinese Christian intertextual reading of the Analects and the epistle to the Galatians, we will look at the theme of moral freedom and human nature.

Moral Freedom and Human Nature

The goal of Confucius's and Paul's ethics is to envision a society where freedom might be achieved for all. This vision assumes that human beings are created equally and for freedom, with subtle differences between Confucius's view and Paul's.

---

sees its fulfillment in the mission to the Gentiles. The promise to Abraham is a pre-announcement of the gospel that God would set right the Gentiles by their faith. From this it follows ("as" in Gal 3:9) that those persons who have trusted God are blessed as Abraham was blessed.

An Intertextual Reading of Moral Freedom in the Analects and Galatians

Human Nature and Moral Weakness

Confucius's View

Confucius understands that all human beings are born with a similar nature; "nurture" shapes their potentiality differently (Analects 6:19; 17:2). The contrast Confucius makes between *jun-zi* (best moral self) and *xiao-ren* (immature moral self) (4:11, 16, 24; 13:7, 23, 25, 26, 37; 14:6; 15:24; 16:8) indicates that, in his mind, whereas all human beings are endowed with the same inclination toward goodness, the environment and habituation may cause some to give in to weakness, while others learn to overcome it and to do good. Because those characterized by *xiao-ren* (immature moral self) fail to habituate themselves in virtue, they are incapable of making moral choices; they live in bondage. Those characterized by *jun-zi* (best moral self) persist in cultivation of virtue; therefore they have resources to make correct moral decisions and live in freedom.

Confucius believes in education and learning, and he believes that morality can be taught. Confucius sees the equality of human beings as (1) the equality of the possibility for actualizing oneself, and (2) the equality of the value of the human being-qua-human being.[9] Confucius believes that human nature is not morally weak. Analects 5:10 and 6:12 are good texts to support this view. In Analects 5:10 we read,

> Zai Yu [a disciple of Confucius] slept during the day. The Master said: "Rotten wood is beyond carving; a dung-and-mud wall is beyond plastering. As for Yu, what is the use of reprimanding him?" The Master said: "At first, my attitude toward men was to hear their words and believe in their deeds. Now my attitude toward men is to hear their words and observe their deeds. It was due to Yu that I have changed this."[10]

Even though these two sayings of Confucius are found in one verse, they were probably said in two different settings. In any case, we can see that

---

9. Hsieh Yu-Wei, "The Status of the Individual in Chinese Ethics," in *The Chinese Mind: Essentials of Chinese Philosophy and Culture* (ed. C. A. Moore; Honolulu: University of Hawaii Press, 1967), 310.

10. Huang Chi-chung, *The Analects of Confucius* (New York: Oxford University Press, 1997), 74.

Confucius's judgment of Zai Yu has changed. First he chastises Zai Yu and says that he is beyond teaching and reforming. But in the second saying Confucius declares that he is now more careful in passing judgment, waiting until after he has heard the person's words and seen his or her works.

In the second text, Analects 6:12, Ran Qiu (a disciple of Confucius) responds to Confucius, "It is not that your way does not commend itself to me, but that it demands powers I do not possess." The Master replies, "He whose strength gives out collapses during the course of the way/journey; but you deliberately draw the line" (6:12).[11] Is virtue for Confucius then (a) *knowing* what is right and doing it or (b) *a moral force* that causes one to do the right and good thing? In the former case, Zai Yu claims to know his moral obligations but lacks the moral force to fulfill them. The problem with Zai Yu is that he does nothing (such as to seek instruction) for his moral "weakness." He claims not to possess the proper moral will. However, Confucius claims that virtue, such as benevolence, is not far away. Confucius says, "If I want benevolence, then benevolence is here!" (Analects 7:30).

Confucius understands that human beings are born equal, with the same potential of becoming the best moral self. He also assumes that *tian* (Heaven) endows all with the resource to become benevolent, the highest virtue that characterizes moral freedom. Even though the path to moral perfection is difficult, education by means of virtue cultivation will overcome moral weaknesses. However, Paul is not as hopeful as Confucius regarding human endeavor as the way to achieve moral freedom and perfection.

Paul's View

Paul has a different understanding of moral weakness and the "moral self" because his understanding of God differs from Confucius's understanding of *tian* (Heaven). Unlike Confucius's natural anthropology (*tian's* endowment of equal potential on all to become their best moral self), Paul has a spiritual anthropology. Without God's Spirit, Paul sees human beings incapable of achieving moral freedom, since the binding force of the "evil age" (Gal 1:4) and sin render human beings helpless. Without God's Spirit, people are incapable of being freely human, of being virtuous, of doing good,

---

11. My translation.

of loving God and their neighbor. In Gal 6:7-8 Paul addresses the ethical life and its consequences: "Do not be deceived; God is not mocked, for whatever a person sows, this he will also reap. The one who sows to his own flesh will reap corruption from the flesh, and the one who sows to the Spirit will reap eternal life from the Spirit." The exhortation is directed to the members of the Galatian community, to live authentically with themselves, with God, and with the Spirit.[12] The natural principle of sowing and harvesting applies to the religious and moral life as well: sowing in the flesh produces corruption, and sowing in the Spirit produces the fruit of the Spirit, which is eternal life.

The contrast between the flesh and the Spirit was noted previously in the epistle to speak of the two powers under which a person lives (Gal 4). The phrase "in his own flesh" (Gal 6:8, εἰς τὴν σάρκα ἑαυτοῦ) here is odd. It may refer to circumcision — not the act of being circumcised but to what "circumcision" signifies, that is, membership in the people of God. This makes sense when it is read in the context of "corruption of the flesh" and "eternal life from the Spirit." In other words, he who depends on circumcision to maintain his status as a member of God's people will end up in death; he who depends on the Spirit to do so will receive eternal life. The sowing and reaping imagery suggests the natural cycle of cause and effect; the point here is not one's *effort* but rather the *realm* to which one intentionally submits and in which one walks and lives.

The contrast between "corruption" (φθοράν) and "eternal life" (ζωὴν αἰώνιον) suggests mortality and resurrected life, respectively (Gal 6:8).[13] If so, this point advances Paul's argument that the *new life in Christ* ushers in the new age of salvation for both Jews and Gentiles, a sign of which is the endowment of the eschatological Spirit. The Spirit will in turn unite Jews and Gentiles as God's faithful, bear its fruit to guide and empower the community, and finally grant resurrected life to them. In contrast to "sowing to the Spirit" (εἰς τὸ πνεῦμα), sowing to circumcision ("his own flesh") brings forth corruption (Gal 6:8), partly because the realm of circumcision/the law is a realm without the Spirit ("works of the flesh" in Gal 5:19). Even though the play on the word "flesh" (circumcision and human existence without the Spirit) may be confusing, Paul has already shown

---

12. It is self-deceiving to think one can outwit God. God cannot be "mocked" (μυκτηρίζεται), i.e., "treated with contempt."

13. See 1 Cor 15:42, 50; Rom 2:7; 5:21; 6:22-23.

through an allegorical interpretation in Gal 4:21-31 that those born "according to flesh" (implied "without the Spirit") are also those who want to hold to circumcision and the law as a sign of the flesh. It is not circumcision per se that Paul objects to, nor its role in Judaism; it is rather circumcision as a requirement for membership in the people of God when Christ has shown that faith together with the Spirit — not works of the law — brings about that membership. In the age of Christ, "works of the flesh," namely, the existence prescribed by circumcision and the law, are morally invalid for the people of God because the Spirit of God now in the eschatological age is the giver of new life and virtue to a new and inclusive community.

Paul's understanding of the existence in the flesh emphasizes that it is without the Spirit. Betz explains the consequence of the works of the flesh:

> Previously Paul had associated "flesh" with circumcision and "the works of the flesh," but in 6:8 he goes further. "Sowing into the flesh" is done by obedience to the Jewish Torah, a move which would result in missing salvation altogether (cf. 5:2-12). But the same harvest can be reaped by letting the "works of the flesh" flourish (cf. 5:19-21). A life thus corrupted by the "flesh" cannot "inherit the Kingdom of God" (5:21). In this sense "sowing into the flesh" means . . . the very opposite of "crucifying the flesh" (5:24). In either case, the end will be "eternal annihilation."[14]

The consequence for those under the law, holding to circumcision, and born without the promise of the Spirit is slavery. In terms of moral life, existence without the Spirit results in "fornication, immorality, licentiousness, idolatry, sorcery, enmity, strife, jealousy, anger, selfishness, dissension, factions, envy, drunkenness, carousing, and things like these" (Gal 5:19-21). "Works of the flesh" denotes the consequence of living under the power of sin and not in the realm of the Spirit. Paul's idea of freedom in the Spirit is unique, one not shared by Confucius's ethical belief that all can live a life of freedom if they attend to self-cultivation.

---

14. H. D. Betz, *Galatians: A Commentary on Paul's Letter to the Churches in Galatia* (Philadelphia: Fortress Press, 1979), 308-9.

An Intertextual Reading of Moral Freedom in the Analects and Galatians

Moral Freedom

People of God in the Life of the Spirit: Positive and Negative Freedom

Freedom in Galatians is about freedom from the constraint (negative freedom) of evil and sin, and the freedom to live fully for the community (positive freedom). Gal 5:1-6 defines for its Gentile readers the new reality of freedom for which Christ redeemed them. The God who calls them has a goal for them: ἐπ' ἐλευθερίᾳ ("to freedom"), i.e., *freedom from* the burden of circumcision, the curse of the law, the bondage of sin, and *freedom for* life in the Spirit, that is, the blessings and righteousness in Christ, as well as guidance from and dependence on the Spirit. God's creation of a new humanity (Jews and Gentiles) in Christ is the work of the Spirit for the sake of the freedom of all.

The danger facing the Christians in Galatia was that they would misunderstand the freedom in Christ as the license to do whatever they pleased. Paul warns the readers what not to do and what to do with their new freedom: "Only do not let your freedom become an opportunity for the flesh, but through love be slaves to one another" (Gal 5:13b-c). It is significant to note that, despite the spiritual anthropology of Paul, he does share an ethical view similar to that of Confucius in the sense that Paul also employs a lot of imperatives in Galatians 5–6. We might not want to call fruit of the Spirit "virtue," but Paul is giving the Galatian Christians imperatives.

Paul speaks first of a negative freedom and gives a negative imperative. The purpose of God giving freedom to believers was not to allow "the flesh" to become a sprouting ground of sin. As used in Gal 5:1-26 the word "flesh" has the negative connotation of life without the Spirit and in opposition to the realm of the Spirit. The word "flesh" in the negative imperatives in Gal 5:13 ("Do not use your opportunity for the flesh") and 5:16 ("Do not gratify the desires of the flesh") is not a purely anthropological term in the neutral sense. "Flesh" and the "desires of the flesh" refer to neither the carnal aspect of human existence nor the "unredeemed" portions of a human body. Rather, "flesh" is understood in terms of the negative and enslaving power of sin and evil. The human propensity is to live without dependence on God or other people, thus under the negative power of sin and death. The self-centeredness of human beings can be wrongly perceived as freedom, yet it only results in the intensification of the power of sin. For Paul there is no such state as freedom independent of sin or God; there is only either a realm under God or sin. Human existence is dependent on either one, and the consequences are righteousness and freedom under the realm of God, and sin and bondage under the realm of sin. Those who think they can be free independently are actually allowing sin to control their lives; sin will dominate their creaturely existence.

Second, Paul speaks of a positive freedom and gives a positive imperative. In Paul's thought, freedom by definition cannot be used for its own ends. To overcome the negative freedom, Paul has a distinctly spiritual understanding of freedom.[15] Human existence without the guidance of the Spirit is at best self-gratifying and self-absorbing, at worst self-binding and self-destructive. The role of the Spirit is essential in guiding and energizing those who are in Christ, enabling them to live a life of freedom in service to one another; this spiritual freedom occupies Paul's thought in Gal 5:13-26. Those who walk according to the Spirit comprise the community "in Christ."[16] The positive imperative of Paul is that the Galatians should "walk by the Spirit" (5:16).[17] Here the "Spirit" refers to God's Spirit, which was promised as the eschatological gift for Jews and Gentiles. The role of the Spirit is to bring forth the new community, characterized by their love, the consequence of which is the fruit of the Spirit. The Spirit guides the community of Christ to live in freedom to love God and one another; the Spirit not only overcomes the controlling power of the flesh but also binds the community in freedom.

Third, Paul speaks of the moral choice between Spirit and flesh. The reason for the incompatibility of Spirit and flesh lies in their opposing nature: "For the desires of the flesh are against the Spirit, and the Spirit is against the flesh" (5:17a). These two powers have directly opposite functions: the Spirit of God liberates, saves, empowers, guides, and grants life and righteousness; the desires of the flesh control, deprive, limit, confuse,

---

15. The theme of the Spirit is introduced in Gal 3:2-5. Paul discusses the role of the Spirit in 3:14; 4:6, 29, as well as 5:16-18, 22, 25; 6:1, 8.

16. On the apocalyptic macrocosmic and microcosmic explanation of Paul's anthropology in Gal 5:16-17 (and Rom 7:14-15), see D. E. Aune, "Zwei Modelle der menschlichen Natur bei Paulus," *Theologische Quartalschrift* 176 (1996): 28-39.

17. In parallel to Jewish thought, in which those under the law walk *(hālak)* by the law (Lev 26:3; Deut 5:33; 11:22; 26:17; 28:9; Pss 1:1-2; 81:13; 86:11). So walking is a metaphor that points to the practice of life or to one's lifestyle.

and kill. Therefore, these two spheres or powers cannot coexist in any community of faith.

Since the Spirit and the flesh represent two different realms or powers, Paul argues that the Galatians cannot assume they can do whatever they want (5:17b), either running back and forth between the realms of the Spirit and the flesh or thinking they can live without both. The Galatians must choose the Spirit,[18] for not choosing the Spirit is by default an existence in the flesh.

Following the Spirit toward Freedom of Community

The communal context of freedom is basic to the teachings of both Confucius and Paul. We have seen that Confucius's teaching of *jun-zi* (best moral self) and *xiao-ren* (immature moral self) has to do with one's virtuous life that builds up the community. For Paul the relational ethics of loving those in the body of Christ and the spiritual ethics of following the Spirit have their consequences on the freedom of a community.

We have seen in the last section that the result of the dominion of the flesh is self-centeredness and therefore divisiveness in a community. However, the realm of the Spirit is life and freedom for the community. Those who identify with the crucified Messiah gain freedom from the power of bondage, sin, and evil: "Those who belong to Christ have crucified the flesh with its passions and desires" (Gal 5:24).[19] Paul asks the Galatian readers to follow the Spirit and not to do anything that would divide the community: "If we live by the Spirit let us also follow the Spirit. Let us not be conceited, provoking one another, being envious of one another" (5:25-26).

Living in the realm of the Spirit means that believers have to be obedient to the Spirit's leading as believers walk (περιπατεῖτε) in the Spirit. There is no need to be conceited, to provoke one another, or to be envious of others. The promise of blessings to the heirs of Abraham eliminates any need for jealousy or boasting. The presence of God's Spirit in the life of the faithful eliminates strife and dissension in the community. What is meant by "walking in the Spirit" is seen in the two words περιπατεῖτε and στοιχῶμεν, used respectively in Gal 5:16 and 5:25. The former has the sense of letting the

---

18. Similarly F. J. Matera, *Galatians* (SP; Collegeville: Liturgical Press, 1992), 200, 207.

19. In Rom 6:6 Paul's language is that the "old self" (ὁ παλαιὸς ἡμῶν ἄνθρωπος) was crucified with Christ.

Spirit direct or control;[20] the latter conveys Paul's desire that the community of faith keep in step with the leading of the Spirit.[21] Paul is exhorting the believers to constantly make the decision to yield themselves to the Spirit. The preservation of unity within a diverse community (Jews and Gentiles) could only be realized as those who believe in God realize the truth of living (ζῶμεν) in relation by the effectual power of God's Spirit.

The Spirit in Paul's Ethics Gives Us Insights into Confucius

This discussion of Paul's ethics enables us to see the one major weak point in the ethics of Confucius. Confucius's silence concerning human finitude and the power of sin may be due to naive assumptions about human reality. It may be this ignorance that led his ethics to a form of moralism. Even with a charitable reading of Confucius's creative *tian* (Heaven) cosmology and the dynamic of *ren* (benevolence) in renewing old traditions, his ethic does not give enough warning of the darkness and evil inherent in the principalities and powers. Paul's theological ethics, specifically that of the Spirit and the flesh, can correct this weakness in Confucian ethics.

However, Confucius's advocacy of becoming fully human through discipline is a helpful lens for reading Paul's theology. We will use the Confucian idea of "fully human" as best moral self *(jun-zi)* or benevolent person *(ren ren)* to read Paul's ethics of freedom for others, namely, "through love become slaves to one another" (5:13, διὰ τῆς ἀγάπης δουλεύετε ἀλλήλοις).

The Freedom to Become Human

Freedom is understood by both Paul and Confucius as directed toward others; once others are free, one will be free as well. This is especially true for Confucian ethics, which believes that freedom of others and oneself is

---

20. περιπατεῖτε in Gal 5:16 is used in a figurative sense to refer to how one lives or conducts one's life. In the instance here, "to live one's life" or "to walk in the Spirit" is to "let your conduct be directed by the Spirit." Since the verb is a present active indicative, it has the meaning of continuously allowing the Spirit to control or to direct (5:18 ἄγεσθε) the various activities of one's life.

21. The word στοιχῶμεν in 5:25 implies a more rigid meaning of "moving in a definite line." H. N. Ridderbos, *The Epistle of Paul to the Churches of Galatia* (Grand Rapids: Eerdmans, 1953), 210 n. 24: "as in military formations or in dancing."

freedom of all to be fully human. We will look to Confucius's articulation of this relational ethics and in turn use it to read Paul's understanding of "freedom to serve."

Freedom, Goodness, and Benevolence

Freedom in Confucian ethics has to do with choosing goodness and benevolence *(ren)*, particularly that of the community. As Hsieh Yu-Wei writes, "The freedom advocated in Confucian ethics is the freedom to do good or the freedom to choose what is good. It is ethical freedom of choice."[22] In the Analects, Confucius says that "when I walk alone with two others, they may serve me as my teachers. Choose what is good and follow it, but avoid what is evil" (Analects 7:21). "If you set your mind on *ren*, you will be free from evil" (Analects 4:4). These indicate that all one has to do in freedom is within the limit of goodness. In Confucian thought, choosing good means to choose *ren* because *ren* is the principle of the good. In the Analects, "Yen Yüan asked about *ren*. The Master said, 'To subdue one's self and return to propriety *(li)* is *ren*. If a person can for one day subdue himself and return to propriety *(li)*, all under Heaven will ascribe *ren* to him. Is the practice of *ren* from a person himself, or is it from others?'" (Analects 12:1). Cheng Chung-Ying writes,

> once one can do right things without reliance on outside authority, one may be said to achieve moral autonomy and moral maturity. This inner transformation with larger and deeper moral freedom and social responsibility speaks to Confucius's notion of "self-cultivation" *(xiuji)* of virtues one finds originating from oneself.[23]

The freedom of an ideal person lies in his or her realization that he or she is free to be fully human, to be a sage in an open and unhindered way. Moral freedom is about building the common good of the community. The *jun-zi* (best humanity or best moral self) is an ecumenical person and not a sectarian (Analects 2:14).

22. Hsieh Yu-Wei, "Status of the Individual," 310.
23. Cheng Chung-ying, "Confucian Onto-Hermeneutics: Morality and Ontology," *Journal of Chinese Philosophy* 27 (2000): 35.

To Be Fully Human via Differentiation and Socialization

In the Confucian worldview, the complex interrelationship of human affairs speaks of becoming fully human through the processes of differentiation and socialization. Individuation and personhood actualization take place in dyadic social relations that make all fully human.[24]

The Confucian notion of the human being is essentially that of a social person who learns the science and art of adjusting to the world.[25] Confucius sees liberal education not only as book learning but also as ritual practices that reinforce the interaction of the self with the larger community (from self, to family, to society, to the nation, to the world). That constant reinforcement serves as a process of self-cultivation when it is practiced in the spirit of loyalty, reverence, brotherhood, discipleship, and so forth.

Human beings authenticate one another's existence. One becomes fully human not by detaching oneself from the world but by making sincere attempts to harmonize one's relationship with others. With regard to the social aspect of self-cultivation in the process of becoming fully human, Confucius says, "Virtue does not exist in isolation; there must be neighbors" (Analects 4:25).[26] "In order to establish oneself, one helps others to establish themselves; in order to enlarge oneself, one helps others to enlarge themselves" (Analects 6:28).

Human beings are transformed by participation with others in ceremonies that are communal. That is the mandate of Heaven, that all may live in righteousness and orderliness in relation to others as a society of sacredness. To be a *ren ren* (a loving person) is to express and to participate in the holy as a dimension of human existence. Fingarette writes, "Human life in its entirety finally appears as one vast, spontaneous and Holy Rite:

---

24. Tu Wei-ming observes this Confucian understanding of selfhood cultivation in the grid of the social dyad. Tu argues that "a social dyad is not a fixed entity, but a dynamic interaction involving a rich and ever-changing texture of human-relatedness woven by the constant participation of other significant dyadic relationships." Tu Wei-ming, *Confucian Thought: Selfhood as Creative Transformation* (Albany: State University of New York Press, 1985), 237.

25. M. Weber, *The Religion of China: Confucianism and Taoism* (trans. H. H. Gerth; Glencoe: Free Press, 1951), 235.

26. Cf. H. Fingarette, *Confucius — The Secular as Sacred* (New York: Harper and Row, 1972), 42.

the community of man."²⁷ To be a *ren ren* is to be courteous, diligent, loyal, brave, broad, kind (Analects 13:19; 14:5; 17:6) as actualized in public.

On the same concern of social self, we now turn to Paul: in his debate with the Judaizers in Galatia, Paul argues similarly for the significance of community over individuality, specifically for his concern for the inclusion of Gentiles as members of God's elect. He also argues for the necessity of differentiation between Jews and Gentiles in socialization (coexistence), for in Christ there will always be a place for the uniqueness of different ethnicities, yet in unity and equality.

Being Fully Human as Social Selves with Moral Obligation toward Others

Social Self and Moral Obligation

Ren ren as social self means that relationship with others constitutes who a person is as a human being. A person cannot be "fully human" by himself or herself. The best self *(jun-zi)* can be achieved only by extending a helping hand to others. To be *ren ren* or *jun-zi* is to relate to others virtuously, knowing that who one is depends intricately on who others are. Consequently, hurting others also means hurting oneself. In a world of violence and war, no one is the winner. In family quarrels or gang feuds, every member diminishes his or her "best self," becoming less than human.

The existence and freedom of the Confucian ideal person lie in his or her moral will to be such a person and to help others to be their best selves. In other words, the notion of freedom here speaks of an obligation one has toward others. For all are bound to one another to be human: in edifying others, one edifies oneself; in being racist toward others, one diminishes one's own dignity as a human being; in not forgiving others, one binds oneself; in granting others peace, one is in fuller communion with others. Fingarette expresses this idea differently but well: "My life is not a means to maintaining the relationship; the relationship is my life, not something external to it that I serve. Each such relationship that I live, if it is indeed an

---

27. Fingarette, *Confucius*, 17. Cf. Analects 3:17; 4:5, 6, 8. For a different interpretation of *ren* and *li* in Confucius's thought, see Fung Yu-lan, *Short History of Chinese Philosophy* (ed. D. Bodde; New York: Macmillan, 1948), 72, 94; and Tu, *Confucian Thought*, 81-92.

authentically humanizing relationship, constitutes my life as being by that much and in that respect a more fully human life."[28]

This is not to say that an ideal person does good to others only for the sake of his or her own benefit. Though such hope is surely there, doing good to others is not for selfish reasons, but for the sake of benevolence and fulfilling one's humanity. Since humans are social beings and life is public, the excellent person finds his or her home in being benevolent *(ren)*. The Master said: "The benevolent man [*ren zhe*] is attracted to benevolence [*ren*] because he feels at home in it" (Analects 4:2).[29]

Human beings are unavoidably social. Society begins with one's relationship with one's parents and extends to one's relationship with the global village. This is the social context where *li* (propriety) and *ren* (benevolence) manifest themselves in concrete ways. On one occasion when Confucius had a dialogue with his disciples he asked them on what they had set their hearts (ambition in Chinese). Zi Lu (a disciple of Confucius) said that he would like to share his carriage, horses, clothes, and furs with his friends, and even if they were worn and torn when returned he would have no regrets. Another disciple, Yen Yuan, said that he would never boast of his goodness and never parade his achievements. Zi Lu then asked his Master the same question. Confucius replied, "I wish to comfort the old, be truthful to friends, and cherish the young" (Analects 5:26).[30]

Freedom to Serve

The moral obligation toward others is not of the choosing of an autonomous self. To be human is to live in a social context, constantly aware of the dynamic of one's relationship with oneself, with others, and with things.[31] During a period of desolation and abandonment, Confucius rhetorically defended his need to associate with people of the world, rather than to run away with the birds and beasts (Analects 18:6). Rosemont clarifies for us how the modern understanding of the autonomous self cannot understand the Confucian social self:

---

28. H. Fingarette, "The Music of Humanity in the Conversations (Analects) of Confucius," *Journal of Chinese Philosophy* 10, no. 4 (1983): 339.

29. D. C. Lau, *Confucius: The Analects* (Harmondsworth: Penguin Books, 1979), 29.

30. Huang, *Analects*, 78.

31. H. Rosemont Jr., "On Confucian Civility," in *Civility* (ed. L. S. Rouner; Notre Dame: University of Notre Dame Press, 2000), 189.

An Intertextual Reading of Moral Freedom in the Analects and Galatians

The Confucian self is not a free, autonomous individual, but is to be seen relationally: I am a son, husband, father, teacher, student, friend, colleague, neighbor, and more. I live, rather than "play" these roles, and when all of them have been specified, and their interrelationships made manifest, then I have been fairly thoroughly individuated, but with very little left over with which to piece together a free, autonomous individual. . . . In order to be a friend, neighbor, or lover, for example, I must have a friend, neighbor, or lover. Other persons are not merely accidental or incidental to my goal of fully developing as a human being; they are essential to it. Indeed, they confer unique personhood on me, for to the extent that I define myself as a teacher, students are necessary to my life, not incidental to it.[32]

Unlike our modern thinking of the autonomous self and equal rights for autonomous selves, the communities envisioned by Confucius and Paul do not include the freedom to choose one's parents, siblings, relatives, or socio-historical contexts. Even one's friends and enemies present themselves at the crossroads of life without the exercise of one's will. In Confucian teaching, however, there is a strong sense of moral choice — that is, there is a virtuous way to be related to other people, whether parents or strangers. Likewise, for Paul there is a freedom inherent in being human in the presence of the other. While Confucius sees the rationale for moral obligation to others as an ethical one, Paul sees the reason for relating virtuously to others as a christological one. In his letter to the Galatians Paul points out that the communal life of freedom in the Spirit requires guidance from the law of love. The positive end of Christ giving freedom to humanity is "through love [becoming] slaves to one another" (Gal 5:13c, NRSV). The freedom given to believers is to be used to "serve as slaves to one another"? The word δουλεύετε is literally translated as "to be enslaved to," not "to serve." The term "slave" has a pejorative connotation; thus a more neutral term, "to serve," is used here. But Paul's point of setting "serving as slaves to others" in the context of freedom and bondage is noteworthy. The word δουλεύετε occurs in 4:8, 9, 25, also suggesting the meaning of enslavement. Paul probably is making a play on words such as "freedom" and "enslavement" to make the point that there is no freedom outside slavery either to sin or to righteousness, either to the law or to Christ.

---

32. Rosemont, "On Confucian Civility," 189.

But the realm of righteousness, of being in Christ, and the blessings it gives constitute maximum freedom. The paradox of Pauline theology, of freedom and slavery, is that the one who seeks to be served by others in order to justify his or her freedom will eventually live in bondage, while the one who is free will seek to be "a slave" to others — a slave not in bondage but in *free will to love.*

Paul frequently uses the term "'slave' of Christ" to designate himself and the believer (1 Cor 7:22; Rom 12:11; 14:4, 18). The metaphor has Old Testament roots in the reference to slaves of Yahweh, referring to Jewish leaders such as Moses, David, and Isaiah, thus connoting a position of prestige, privilege, and honor (see Deut 34:5; Josh 1:1; Judg 2:8; 2 Kgs 18:12; Isa 42:19). This meaning is used by Paul (Rom 1:1; Phil 1:1) in addition to the meaning of obedience as of a slave to a master (1 Cor 3:5; 2 Cor 2:14; 3:6; 4:5). For Paul, since the new existence in Christ and in the Spirit is different from being "in the flesh" or "under the law," he understands "law of love" (6:2) and the new obedience of being a "slave of Christ" as freedom to love and to serve.

In light of the Christ event, Paul identifies himself as one honored to be a "slave" (δοῦλος, cf. Rom 1:1; Phil 1:1), living in the new realm of the righteousness of God and serving the living God in the obedience of faith. It is in serving Christ as Lord that Paul believes human beings can find the freedom that leads to righteousness. The truth of the gospel is best expressed in this paradoxical metaphor of faith as a slavery that brings freedom. It thereby points to the fact that Gentiles can enjoy full membership in the people of God without taking up nomistic services ("works of the law").

Both in Pauline theology and in Confucian ethics, the mutual indebtedness of love is the guarantee of communal freedom. Confucius believes that *li* (ritual propriety) is grounded in *ren* (love), and together both are perceived to be the agents of freedom for the community. Similarly, Paul points out that the communal life of freedom in the Spirit requires guidance from the law of Christ, which is the law of love (Gal 6:2; 5:14; see also Rom 13:10).

Freedom, Death, and the Human Story of Mutual Indebtedness

The theological interest of this essay is to search for moral freedom in a world of violence; the path to that hope is found in the realization that mutual indebtedness constitutes the essence of being human. While Confucius has the understanding of social self and best moral self, Paul deliberately uses the metaphor of "slave" (δοῦλος) to speak of human freedom. Paul deliberately uses "slave" as a self-reference in relation to God as "master" (κύριος) because, although the imperial/cultural language of slavery denotes bondage, the theological language of the Cross transforms its negative connotations and renders it the proper definition of freedom. Paul uses the traditional language of slavery and infuses it with new meaning — that is, the God-Christian paradigm for the master-slave relationship is about a master who has absolute power, yet surrenders it on the Cross for the sake of love. In this Christian reinterpretation, a slave is one living not in bondage but in freedom to love and in joy to serve. The language of the Cross makes all fully human so that the human story does not end in violence and despair. Thus the ethics of both Confucius and Paul affirm that our human story is threaded with love, that we are born to be free, free to be of service to others. The modern idea of the autonomous self independent of others is a dangerous concept. The question is not whether we can or cannot be autonomous selves; the question is, once we are, are we still human?

A Latin American Rereading of Romans 7

Elsa Tamez

The Bible in Latin America is read in several distinct ways. One is the traditional fundamentalist manner, another is the a-critical repetition of foreign biblical studies from the First World, and the last is the contextual reading of the Bible. The newest is the contextual reading or, as it is most commonly called, "the rereading of the Bible in the light of reality." My study will be done within this hermeneutical framework.

Biblical rereading arose in the 1970s within a general rethinking of various disciplines in the light of their own reality beginning in the 1950s, especially in sociology and education.[1] For the first time in the South of the Americas, Latin American theories appeared that were not an echo of the output from the countries of the North. Freire, Fanon, Rulfo, García Márquez, and others were the actors in this stage, begun five decades ago.[2]

Today philosophy and psychology are being rethought within this

---

1. The name varies depending upon the country. In some places it is called "popular reading of the Bible," in others, "pastoral reading"; it is also common to hear it called "communitarian reading of the Bible." The name "contextual reading" came from outside Latin America.

2. In sociology, the theory of dependency; in pedagogy, the pedagogy of the oppressed; and in literature, the creation of a world narrated with their own codes and styles that are understood in the light of the real world.

Translation by Gloria Kinsler.

same framework.[3] We are not saying that this contribution is unique and only from Latin America. The majority of the exponents recognize in their writings that they have been influenced by distinct thinkers outside of Latin America.

Theology and rereading of the Bible from a Latin American perspective gained greater resonance in the 1970s. Gustavo Gutiérrez is known for having pioneered this way of doing theology with his book *A Theology of Liberation*. Carlos Mesters and Severino Croato, Catholics, and Milton Schwantes, a Protestant, are also pioneers in the Latin American rereading of the Bible. This biblical rereading is done in an ecumenical context; the majority of the participants are Catholic because Latin America is a continent with a high percentage of Catholics.

The Catholics discovered the Bible with the opening given by the Second Vatican Council, and since then there has been a great awakening in biblical studies. Today they are the ones who most develop the rereadings through courses, workshops, and networks in each country and at the regional level, although generally the advisors are Protestant and Catholic.

What Is a Biblical Rereading?

Allow me to repeat here the definition that I gave at the Triennial Translation Workshop meeting in Brazil in 2003:

> A rereading is a new reading of the text in which another network of meanings is constructed distinct from an earlier reading. The newness is due to the elements that appear in the construction process of the new network or structure of meanings. The elements can be, for example, new archeological or linguistic discoveries or the application of new literary methods. In the case of a Latin American rereading, it is repeatedly new because the elements found in reading and rereading the text are directly related to "from where the text is read," "who is reading it," "when," and "why." In other words, it is the reader's placement (social, cultural, racial, gender, economic), perspective, histori-

---

3. In October of 2005 the first Latin American Congress on Psychology of Liberation was held in Costa Rica. Prior to that there had already been various conferences on Latin American philosophy of liberation with the leadership of Enrique Dussel.

cal and utopian options that condition the reading, and, for that reason, the permanent production of new readings.

All exegetical methods that the reader commands and that the text can resist can be used, but these questions will always be considered fundamental. It is from there that the "epistemological rupture" is affirmed, exactly at the starting point. The idea, the discourse, the reading of the Bible is not elaborated independent of reality. The lived reality helps in understanding the Scriptures, and the Scriptures help in understanding the lived reality.[4]

I believe that within a wide sector — both popular and academic — in Latin America there is now a cognitive framework that permits doing biblical rereading in a natural way, almost unconsciously.

It needs to be said that the influence of Hans-Georg Gadamer and Paul Ricoeur regarding the reservoir of meaning and added meaning is strong, and it is used consciously among Latin American biblical scholars.[5] This is because the fundamental preoccupation is in front of the text, the effect of the text on today's recipients. That is to say, if in the analysis of the text one goes behind the text to reconstruct the situation (using historical-critical or sociological methods), this serves to enrich the meaning in front of the text. If the analysis in one moment concentrates on the composition of the discourse (using literary structuralism or even rhetorical or pragmatic methods), it is also to enrich those persons or communities who confront the Bible today.

The seventh chapter of Romans has been a headache for many biblical scholars, who have written abundant and varied materials about it without coming to any agreement. For ordinary readers the text is a mystery difficult to understand. For various experts in Romans, Paul's critique of the law, understood as the Torah, becomes delicate because of the fear of being accused as anti-Semitic. For an important circle of Latin American scholars, Paul's critique of the law (νόμος) is fundamental in today's discussion of the Rule of Law.[6] In Latin America the text challenges us to read

---

4. In this sense, I think it is very important to consider the history of the effects of the text *(Wirkungsgeschichte)* as part of the comprehension of the text, agreeing with U. Luz, *Matthew in History: Interpretation, Influence and Effects* (Minneapolis: Fortress Press, 1994).

5. See S. Croato, *Biblical Hermeneutics: Toward a Theory of Reading as the Production of Meaning* (Maryknoll, NY: Orbis Books, 1987).

6. See Consultation of "Economists and Theologians on Subject, Law and the Rule of Law," Costa Rica, December 2004.

from a contextual perspective. The pastoral challenge is: What does the text say today to Latin American readers in light of their experience with the law?

Beyond the Mosaic Law

From the outset it is important to show to which law Paul is alluding. It seems to us that the law in Romans 7 does not refer only to the Torah. The Torah is present in an oblique form throughout the text, but the text cannot be reduced to that. It is very probable that Paul has the Torah in mind when he uses the term "commandment" (7:8), and when he refers to the law as "holy, just and good" in 7:12; he also has the Torah in mind when he refers to νόμος as holy law (7:12). Nevertheless, it is more confusing when he speaks of the law of the mind (νοῦς, 7:23), the law of God (7:22, 25), the law of sin (7:23ff.), and the law of the members (7:23).

Michael Winger, in his study of the law in Paul, affirms that the apostle is conscious of a wide range of meanings in his use of the term "law." According to Winger, we must distinguish between the meaning and the reference, because that is what permits one to recognize when it refers specifically to the Jewish law or to other uses of νόμος in Paul's world. According to Winger, in the Greco-Roman world the term νόμος has a variety of meanings, from the law (νόμος) of a city or town to the law (νόμος) as custom or tradition; it can even mean force.[7]

Obviously, the Mosaic law is not absent in our text; nevertheless, we believe that, to be able to show the limitations of this law due to the theological debate of Paul's time (the inclusion of Gentiles in the faith of Jesus Christ independent from the law of circumcision), Paul understands the term in an abstract way in order to treat it in generic terms, which includes positive, natural law and any logic that can be perceived as law. Therefore he speaks of the law of the members, of the mind, of sin, and of God. In other texts he speaks of the law of the Spirit.

---

7. M. Winger, *By What Law? The Meaning of Nomos in the Letters of Paul* (Atlanta: Scholars Press, 1992), 4.

ELSA TAMEZ

The Literary Context

The literary context also helps us understand the text. Romans 7 forms part of the block of chs. 5–8. I would like to take a look at my own personal adaptation of a section of the *Structure of the Greek Text in Romans* by Phillip Rolland.[8] The headings are mine.

> **Theme of the Section:** The Challenge to Live as Resurrected (5:1–8:39)
> **Antithesis:**
> A. The multitude of the descendants of Adam (5:1-21)
>   B. The slavery of "old men and women" (6:1–7:6)
>   C. The power of sin — legitimized by law — kills (7:7-25)
> **Thesis**
>   C'. The Power of the Spirit — God's gift — gives life (8:1-11)
>   B'. The freedom of the sons and daughters of God (8:12-21)
> A'. The firstborn of a multitude of brothers and sisters (8:22-30)
> **Conclusion:** Hymn to God's love (8:31-39)

The chiastic structure shows the importance of considering the whole section so as not to see in the apostle a profound anthropological pessimism. The rhetorical strategy here is to carry the antithesis to the climax, "Who will rescue me from this body of death?" (C), to immediately develop the good news of the Spirit who raises mortal bodies (8:11).

By seeing the placement of ch. 7 in its relation to the previous chapter and that which follows, we find that ch. 7 is in close relationship with ch. 6, which speaks of being dead to sin in order to live a new life (6:4) and being free from sin to bear fruit for God (6:22). Chapter 8 emphasizes the gift of God's Spirit poured out in hearts so that human beings will be capable of bearing fruit, free from the law and sin. Then ch. 7, which we are analyzing, describes the problem of the law (all kinds of law), especially its vulnerability in its complicity with sin. What is important to Paul, then, is not to condemn the law but to show another way to live that is more fruitful.

---

8. P. Rolland, *Epître aux Romains: Texte grec structure* (Rome: IBP, 1980).

A Latin American Rereading of Romans 7

Rom 7:1-7 is a transition that unites the former discussion about dying to sin and rising to bear fruit.

Rereading Romans 7:7-25

In Rom 7:7-25 Paul presents two points of clarification with respect to three fundamental aspects: the law, sin, and the self. The first point deals with sin and the law and the second with sin and the human being. In our rereading we are going to concentrate only on these two points.

Romans 7:7-13: Sin and the Law

Verses 7:1-13 underline a relation between sin and law, which has disastrous and fatal results for human beings. It leads to an annihilation of the self's conscience, being supplanted by the law:

> 8 But sin, seizing an opportunity in the commandment, produced in me all kinds of covetousness. Apart from the law sin lies dead. 9 I was once alive apart from the law, but when the commandment came, sin revived, 10 and I died, and the very commandment that promised life proved to be death to me. 11 For sin, seizing an opportunity in the commandment, deceived me and through it killed me. . . . 13 It was sin, working death in me through what is good, in order that sin might be shown to be sin, and through the commandment might become sinful beyond measure.

The first impression upon reading this Pauline discourse is that it is dense, almost incomprehensible, and seems to have little to do with concrete reality. Nevertheless, everyday life can shed light to help us understand it. A key to entering into the sense of the text is to observe a concrete context in which the excluded experience the law. I am going to describe some very common examples, everyday examples, from where I live.

The Ruiz family has to leave their rented house because they cannot comply with the contract. For two months they have not been able to pay the rent. The factory in which Señor Ruiz was working went broke and dismissed the employees without their benefits.

Let's analyze this: "The Ruiz family has to leave their rented house because they cannot comply with the contract. For two months they have not been able to pay." Up to here everything is fine. It is good that there is a law that regulates the renting of houses. If not, there would be no stability for the renter (who could be thrown out any minute) or for the landlord (who could be swindled by the renter). Nevertheless, the problem with the law comes when there is no money to pay the rent. This has to do with the economic system: the factory goes broke, which leads to dismissal without benefits. The result is the following: the Ruiz family obeyed the law and are left in the street because they have no family who can take them in.

> A young Nicaraguan living in Costa Rica, Tomás, who works in construction, is met by a policeman in the street one Saturday after work. Because his papers are not in order and he does not have a work permit, he is given the option of being deported or of giving the policeman 3,000 colones (less than $10). Tomás can't find work in his own country and gives him the money. The policeman now can buy notebooks for his daughter.

Let's analyze: It is good to have immigration laws, but many like Tomás do not qualify for them; Tomás cannot survive in his own country and needs to look for life in another country. The country Tomás chooses needs cheap labor, and the lack of documentation is ignored in construction projects. The police have a miserable salary and blackmail the undocumented to get a pittance. They know the laws and can manipulate them in their favor. The result: Tomás breaks the law by giving the bribe to the policeman because he needs the work.

There are thousands of cases like these where classism, racism, and sexism are present. The examples reflect the common relationship of many people to the law in our Latin American societies. If each case were analyzed, one would observe that the law is good and should exist. It is good that there are contracts for renters, that there are labor laws, and that thieves are jailed. The function of laws, as we all know, is to provide order and to give the possibility of living together. Nevertheless, according to experience, this happens only at the level of what should be. At the level of actual being, that is to say within the reality of a sinful system, compliance with the law does nothing but bring to light the inter-human injustice of the sinful system.

It was sin, working death in me through what is good, in order that sin might be shown to be sin, and through the commandment might become sinful beyond measure. (7:13b)

It is easy to detect behind the text a social order constructed according to certain interests. This order also has a logic: a law, "the law of sin." The legal and normative law becomes impotent in its task to do justice. In the same way, it can be manipulated.[9]

The examples above do not imply that there are no positive experiences with the law. Take for an example the right of pregnant women to have four months off with no loss of salary during that time. But, again, thanks to this good law, women who might potentially become pregnant cannot find work easily. The system, in order to function, needs institutions, and these need norms, but the system, the institutions, the norms or laws become complicit, even without meaning to do so, in covering up injustice. We could say the same when speaking of prejudicial cultural habits.

This sinful system is what, in my understanding, Paul in Romans calls sin (ἁμαρτία) in the singular; it is structural sin constructed by the unjust practices of human beings. In Pauline terms, it is "all ungodliness and wickedness of those who by their wickedness suppress the truth." It is against this that God reveals God's wrath, says Rom 1:18.

Human beings remain subjugated as slaves under this sinful power. Sin needs the law to hide its wickedness with legitimacy. This is the way sin is committed without consciousness of guilt. Jesus of Nazareth was condemned unjustly by Roman law in complicity with Jewish justice. A crime was hidden by the laws of that time.

We can ask ourselves: Is this rereading in front of the text supported by a reading behind the text? I believe that a study of the law in Paul must investigate the apostle's experience with the law.[10] I don't think it is too

---

9. It is not surprising that in cases of assassinations, thanks to a "good" lawyer, the murderer goes free. Today, a good lawyer is one who defends his client well independently of his or her guilt.

10. P. Garnsey (*Social Status and Legal Privilege in the Roman Empire* [Oxford: Clarendon Press, 1970]) and A. N. Sherwin-White (*Roman Society and Roman Law in the New Testament* [Oxford: Oxford University Press, 1963]) give us an idea about how Roman law worked in the first century. See also E. Tamez, *Amnesty of Grace: Justification by Faith from a Latin American Perspective* (Nashville: Abingdon Press, 1993).

foolish to say that much of Paul's criticism of the law comes out of his own experience with the law, be that Roman or Jewish. Let's remember that he suffered flagellation, the forty minus one, under the Jews as well as the Romans. We find written in the book of Acts his experience in prison and with the tribunals. It is worth stopping a bit to look at this experience of Paul, the missionary, with the law.

In Philippi, a Roman colony, the magistrates sent Paul and Silas to be flogged naked in public and jailed them afterward without any trial. They were accused of disturbing the city, of being Jewish, and of preaching customs that the Romans could not accept and practice. That was not the original motive, of course; it was an economic issue, but that was useless before the law. According to the book of Acts, Paul and Silas had Roman citizenship, and it was totally illegal to flog and jail Roman citizens without a trial. Because of this, when the magistrates were informed, they asked Paul and Silas to leave the city (Acts 16:16-38).

In Thessalonica the accusers were the Jews. The real problem was religious, but this didn't matter before the law, so the official accusation was, "they are turning the world upside down, acting contrary to the decrees of the emperor, saying there is another king named Jesus." The arrested believers paid bail and were released (Acts 17:1-8). In Ephesus a similar event happened, but this time it occurred because of the sale of small silver statues of the goddess Artemis.

The last eight chapters in the book of Acts are dedicated to the narration of Paul's experience with the Roman and Sanhedrin laws. It was a very negative experience, beginning with his arrest and flogging without a trial. He was thought to be an Egyptian terrorist (21:38). Felix waited for Paul to give him a bribe and did not free him (24:26). After two years of his accusers being unable to verify his guilt, he should have been released, according to Roman law, but according to the narrator of Acts the governor left him in jail in order to ingratiate himself with the local people (24:27). Paul's appeal to the emperor did not help; rather, this point of Roman law that favored Roman citizens was turned against him. When the governor and Bernice wanted to free him, they felt tied by their own law: "Agrippa said to Festus, 'This man could have been set free if he had not appealed to the emperor'" (26:32).

It is striking that this biblical writer, a Jew of the Diaspora, the one who wrote most about the law, was imprisoned and experienced repeated conflicts with the law. Let's return to our text in Romans.

A Latin American Rereading of Romans 7

In the section we are considering, 7:7-13, Paul emphasizes the distance between the law and sin. The law is not sin in itself ("What should we say? That law is sin? By no means!" 7:7). In 7:12 he even says that the law is holy and that the commandment is holy, just, and good. The law or commandment is intended to give life (7:10); of this Paul has no doubt.

Nevertheless, for Paul, the world of evil, of structural sin or sinful systems, is only known through the functioning of the law.

> I was once alive apart from the law, but when the commandment came, sin revived and I died, and the very commandment that promised life proved to be death to me. For sin, seizing an opportunity in the commandment, deceived me and through it killed me. (Rom 7:9-11)

The examples cited above, we repeat, allow us to see behind the text a sinful system that clearly shows its face when attempting to follow the law.

This is because the legalistic functioning of all law today does not allow for considerations of mercy about a particular situation; therefore, in following the law injustices are committed, despite those who carry out the law. The Ruiz family is thrown out onto the street in compliance with the justice of the law because they could not pay the rent. Nobody can blame the law or those who carry it out. There is no consciousness of guilt because it is done legally. The fundamental problem is the whole sinful system that needs the law to affirm and legitimate itself. Without the law, says Paul, sin is dead (7:8), that is, it cannot function to show its legality. The law ties the hands of those who would desire that cases which apply the weight of the law take a more just course. Franz Hinkelammert, theologian-economist of Costa Rica, affirms in his study of the Gospel of John that in the observance of the law sin is committed when the law is followed legalistically without considering first the life of its subjects.[11]

What is important, then, are the subjects. Paul writes in terms of himself, but he deals with the real bodily life of the subjects. The law must subordinate itself to this criterion. Jesus expresses this with very simple and illuminating words: "The Sabbath was made for humankind, and not humankind for the Sabbath."

In Rom 7:9-11 the alienation of the self appears with the appearance of the law, which takes the place of the self (". . . but when the command-

---

11. F. Hinkelammert, *El Grito del Sujeto* (San José: DEI, 1999).

ment came, sin revived and I died"). The self, the human conscience that discerns, dies when the law functions, because it doesn't follow differing criteria according to the real situation of persons, but applies universal legal opinions valid in every time, place, and situation. It is here where the sinful system or sin gets its strength. The law inevitably is converted into a mechanism utilized by sin. It is in this sense that sin takes advantage of the law and human discernment has no place. This is why that which is human dies. There is no room for human interference. We know that the origin of the law is rooted in disorder and violence. The task of the law is to bring order and do justice; nevertheless, when the rigor of the law is applied, it resorts to violence to bring order. The jurists Austin Sarat and Thomas R. Kerns analyze this problem as something intrinsic to the law.[12]

The situation becomes grave in the extreme when there is complicity between a violent sinful system and the application of the laws (including their institutions, traditions, and cultural habits). Both logics (the law and sin) unite to reinforce each other and produce death.

We could ask ourselves, what becomes of the subjects, the individuals? Aren't they complicit? Can the problem simply be reduced to sin and the law as logic or rationalities independent of persons?

Romans 7:14-24: Sin and the Self

Romans 7:14-24 goes on to underline precisely the other type of relation: sin and the human condition of the self. This relationship also has disastrous results, producing human trauma.

In the previous paragraphs we learned that when the law is followed blindly the self is eliminated. This would mean that the conscience of the subject, distinct from the law, can function with discernment and can orient itself by the criterion of inter-human well-being. But the case is not so simple, even when Paul says with nostalgia that he once lived apart from the law (7:9)!

If the case were so simple, and human beings were always good, there would be no need for laws to regulate our living together. Individual

---

12. See Austin Sarat and Thomas R. Kerns, *Law's Violence* (Ann Arbor: University of Michigan Press, 1995). Franz Kafka shows it brutally in his novella-length story *In the Penal Colony* (1919).

consciences would be enough to prevent people from entering into injustices and violence. Therefore Paul himself makes us see in these texts the complexity of the problem. For him, the human condition is fragile, and human hearts can harbor greed and egoism.[13] The tension between life and death is present in everything and in everyone. There are not some good and others bad. That is why sin, the sinful system of society, not only absorbs the law but also attracts very human desires toward greed and egoism (ἐπιθυμία). Many honest persons suddenly find themselves involved in corruption. We remember that in Romans 1–3 it was greed and egoism that began the construction of structural sin, with people practicing all kinds of injustices (ἀδικίαι) and covering them up with religious and philosophical rationalizations. It is this that Paul called "practices of ungodliness and injustice that suppress the truth in injustice" (1:18). He refers to these practices as "sin" (ἁμαρτία) in the singular only beginning in Rom 3:9. It is a personified and enslaving power.

However, Paul wants to make clear that the problem is neither the law itself nor the person, but sin (ἁμαρτία). Paul presents a tragic dilemma in human beings: their conscience, their minds (νοῦς), are separated from their practice, and their wants are separated from their actions. This does not mean an alienated conscience being replaced by the law, but a conscience that knows what it wants and that is oriented by the good but ends up by doing bad, which it doesn't want to do, being motivated by sin. This reality is described as a human tragedy. Paul repeats it four times:

> For we know that the law is spiritual; but I am of the flesh, sold into slavery under sin. I do not understand my own actions. For I do not do what I want, but I do the very thing I hate. (Rom 7:14-15)

> For I know that nothing good dwells within me, that is, in my flesh. I can will what is right, but I cannot do it. For I do not do the good I

---

13. It is interesting to compare this Pauline thought on the human condition with the náhuatl thought. In náhuatl philosophy the sages have the task to "humanize the wants" of the humans. According to Léon Portilla, in náhuatl "person" is the tradition of the diffraction of the "countenance and heart." The human being is born without countenance, and it is through the work of the sages and the experience of life that one begins acquiring countenance, that is, personality. With the heart, which signifies movement and dynamism, it is the task of the sages to "humanize the wants" of the heart. See M. León Portilla, *La filosofía náhaut* (México: UNAM, 1979), 228-29.

want, but the evil I do not want is what I do. Now if I do what I do not want, it is no longer I that do it, but sin that dwells within me. (7:18-20)

So I find it to be a law that when I want to do what is good, evil lies close at hand. For I delight in the law of God in my inmost self, but I see in my members another law at war with the law of my mind, making me captive to the law of sin that dwells in my members. (7:21-23)

So then, with my mind I am a slave to the law of God, but with my flesh I am a slave to the law of sin. . . . Wretched man that I am! Who will rescue me from this body of death? (7:25b, 24)

Two things stand out in these texts: (1) the tension and distance between wanting to do good and the working of evil as the final result of the intention; and (2) the reality of sin (ἁμαρτία) as the cause of this incoherence. This seems to be an abstract description, but in reality Paul is drawing on everyday reality. It can be read from different levels, some superficial and others more complex.

In the examples we can mention from our everyday reality, all the persons do wrong things through necessity, but none of them have the intention of doing wrong. Certainly they wouldn't break the law if they were living in a just, humane, and nonviolent world. Let's look at this example of something that happens every day.

> Maria Luisa became a prostitute a few days ago. She is the mother of three young children, and her husband has abandoned her. She could not find work anywhere, and, because her children need to eat, she decided to follow the way of her friend who is in a similar situation. She hates her work; she says she feels used and dirty when she returns home. She spends a lot of time bathing. According to the law, she should not work as a prostitute "without permission," so she works clandestinely. She does not will to have this kind of life. Applying the words of Paul, we could say "she does what she does not want to do and what she wants to do is out of her reach." The problem, then, is the unjust environment in which she lives — in other words, sin, not only structural sin but the sin that invades her as a person: in order to survive Maria Luisa does that which harms her and is against her will.

A Latin American Rereading of Romans 7

On another level, we observe the officials who are obligated to follow the law and, with sorrow, give the sentence: to jail the poor person who robs, to throw onto the street families who cannot pay the rent, to persecute the prostitute, etc. Many times they discern that they are clearly committing an injustice when applying the law, but they feel tied by the law and see no other alternative but to follow the law or lose their job. What they want to do they don't do and what they do they don't want to do. They are puppets of the system and its laws, to their great sorrow.

> Roberto, an Afro-Caribbean, is accused of stealing a purse and goes to jail. He denies that he stole any purse. In any case he is put into prison. The purse reappears, and Marcos, a Mestizo, is taken to the court. During the interrogation he confesses that he had to steal because he needed money for his sister who is very sick. He says that he would never have been able to forgive himself if she had died. Marcos realizes that he should not have taken the purse, but he could find no alternative. Roberto is freed, and he leaves the jail furious. He feels racism. The police feel compassion for Marcos but still send him to jail.

Finally, we have those persons whose human fragility becomes an accomplice of the law and of sin. Their lifestyle in society is such that, although these persons have a clear conscience and don't want to do what they do, their greed and egoism form an alliance with the powerful logic of the corrupt system. They feel impotent to go against the current because they know that their personal interests will be affected and they will lose out. Their status will diminish, or they will be destroyed. Therefore, they are willing to participate in the practice of injustice.

> Pedro is a distinguished business administrator. The business evades paying taxes and fires the workers without paying benefits. Pedro has to fix the accounts in such a way that the state control will not be suspicious. Pedro feels uncomfortable having to do these things, but he does them because he wants to be promoted so as to buy a house with a pool.

We have, then, a real dilemma in the human condition that lives within a sinful system. The drama is accentuated by the rhetorical style and by the concentric structure of the text.[14] Certainly the situation is dramatic.

In summary, in Rom 7:7-13 we read of structural sin and the vulnerability of the law, all types of laws. The law is good, but on uniting with sin it becomes a deadly weapon alienating the human conscience. In Rom 7:14-24 we read of the relation of sin to human vulnerability. Sin takes advantage of human weakness so that the person does the wrong that he or she does not want to do. When sin, the law, and human vulnerability come together, a human tragedy is created with no way out. Therefore, for Paul, there must be a liberation from the law, sin, and death. So in Romans 8 he speaks of the newness of the Spirit as a way toward new horizons within inter-human relations and relations with God — not contractual relations, but relations of grace and friendship.

It seems to us that, through a contextual reading, Paul's critique of the law is an important contribution to understand the crisis of civilization in which we now live, not only in Latin America but in the whole world.

And because the pastoral dimension is important for Latin American biblical scholars, I cannot finish this essay without saying that I, like Paul, give thanks to God for the revelation of God's justice and grace. Paul in his discourse challenges us to incarnate God's justice and grace, making it effective in our lives, communities, and societies.

---

14. In the three sections of Romans 1–11 Paul gives a negative climax, then immediately presents a very positive answer. See Rolland, *Epître aux Romains*.

Theology and Luke 16:19-31

To Squeeze the Universe into a Ball — Playing Fast and Loose with Lazarus?

Edith M. Humphrey

In T. S. Eliot's "The Love Song of J. Alfred Prufrock," the speaker asks if it would be worth it, "after the cups, the marmalade, the tea," to proclaim "I am Lazarus, . . . Come back to tell you all," only to have the listener respond, "That is not what I meant at all."

We have had much talk, not of the "marmalade and tea" type, but of the type characterized by careful analysis, distinctions, and contextual probing of Luke 16:19-31. Indeed, in my major contribution to this symposium ("On Probabilities, Possibilities, and Pretexts") I have made a plea for a sober contextual reading of Scriptures, even of texts that seem to present more "openings" for speculation than many. Yet our common text — the parable of Lazarus and Dives — has provided grist for the imaginative mill of many an artist, including notables such as Chaucer, Shakespeare, Milton, Boswell, Thomas Hardy, Melville, and T. S. Eliot, as we have seen in the phrases just quoted. Among those of this symposium whose questions have centered upon the demonstrable meaning of the text (however established), I find myself tempted to push at the "openings" that our parable provides, even while echoing Prufrock, "Do I dare/Disturb the universe? . . . And should I then presume?/And how should I begin?"

And so, anticipating the retort, "That is not what Luke (or Jesus) meant, not what he meant at all," I would direct us to read the parable through the eyes of some of these artists. Though at times this exercise may illuminate the artist and his context more than the pericope, we may also by it grasp the extensive potential of the parabolic genre, as seen in this curious example of Luke 16:19-31. In following this method, we flout, with Blomberg,[1] the received critical opinion that parable, by its nature, must have only one main point.[2] After all, it seems that we must be responsive to the peculiar shape of this passage, which sports, in its received form, at least a double climax and provides plenty of "openings" for the fertile imagination.

We begin with a seventeenth-century author whose mindset does not eschew the most obvious "message" of the parable — that of justice and righteous reversal. Richard Crashaw expostulates, in "Upon Lazarus his Teares,"

> RICH *Lazarus!* richer in those Gems, thy Teares,
> Than *Dives* in the Roabes he weares:
> He scornes them now, but o, they'l sute full well
> With th' Purple he must weare in Hell.[3]

This stanza epitomizes the motif that our parable shares with the Gospel of Luke in general, celebrated from the beginning in Mary's song, expounded in the Sermon on the Plain, and emphasized in much of Luke's special material concerning wealth and poverty. Our parable goes beyond the common theme of "death the great leveler," found in various traditional stories;[4] the grammar of the parable suggests a reversal of fortunes, without explicitly commenting on the respective morality or immorality of Lazarus and Dives. So it is that the passive, suffering, longing castaway, who has actions performed upon him ("cast" at the gate, dogs licking wounds, angels carrying him away) is transformed in the second scene into a blissful companion of Abraham. An earlier English poet, Langland, indeed played up

---

1. Craig Blomberg, *Interpreting the Parables* (Downers Grove, IL: InterVarsity Press, 1990).

2. A. Jülicher, *Die Gleichnisrede Jesu* (2 vols.; Tübingen: J. C. B. Mohr, 1988-89), followed by Jeremias, Dodd, and a host of others.

3. "Upon Lazarus his Teares," in *The Complete Poetry of Richard Crashaw* (ed. G. W. Williams; New York: New York University Press, 1972), 18.

4. I remain agnostic concerning the reason for parallels with the Si-Osiris folktale, the various Judaic versions represented by *y. Sanh.* 23c; *y. Hag.* 77d (Gressman et al.), and Lucian's dialogues entitled *Gallus* and *Cataplus* (Hock). Some have argued for a direct or indirect connection with these stories, which may simply share a common framework and motif.

this moment of the narrative in his *Piers Plowman* reference to Lazarus "amonges patriarkes and profetes pleyende togyderes" in Abraham's lap.[5] In the English imagination, the final state of Lazarus takes on overtones of intimacy with God's notable children, a deep reversal of his first state "among the dogs" (animals associated in the ancient world with the rejected Gentiles). The parable's reversal is stunningly re-sketched by Crashaw, well-known poetic master of contrasts. No longer powerless, Lazarus indeed appears as one who might have the power to go on an errand of mercy. By contrast, the rich man, formerly joyful, active, and satisfied, is demoted to a passive position of longing. The parable articulates this reversal without moralizing or explanation in the authoritative statement of father Abraham: "Child, remember that during your lifetime you received your goods, and Lazarus likewise bad things; but now he is comforted here, and you are in agony." Crashaw, with his inimitable turn of phrase, captures the dominant "shock" of the parable — that Lazarus is rich, that tears are gems, and that purple is a premonition of judgment. "Blessed are the poor" provides its outrage beyond the first-century context into the seventeenth century.

Yet this picture is questioned by a voice closer to our own time. Melville, with his flair for the eccentric, fills in the sketch of Lazarus and "old Dives" in his description of "The Spouter Inn," assaulted by wind and cold, and managed (ominously) by the proprietor "Coffin."[6] With wry playfulness, he contrasts "poor Lazarus" who braves the wind Euroclydon (cf. *Eurakylōn*, Acts 27:14), his teeth "chattering . . . against the curbstone for his pillow," with the presumptuous rich man inside the building "in his red silken wrapper" who would have "a redder one afterwards." Melville uses the reversal theme in sheer irony, for from his modernist perspective there is no real "afterwards": "[t]he universe is finished; the copestone is on, and the chips were carted off a million years ago." Humankind may marvel at

---

5. *Piers Plowman*, B. 16.252-71. For a critical e-version of the B text (and others) of *Piers Plowman*, see the University of Virginia website: http://etext.lib.virginia.edu/toc/modeng/public/LanPier.html.

6. *Moby-Dick,* chapter 12. During the symposium, William A. Allen helpfully suggested that Melville was most probably influenced in the choice of the name Coffin by the Essex whaling disaster, in which a young man, Coffin, was chosen by lot and (willingly) killed as the situation among the few remaining on the boat grew desperate. The entire lurid story is told by Nathaniel Philbrick in his novel *In the Heart of the Sea: The Tragedy of the Whaleship "Essex"* (New York: Penguin Books, 2000).

the inequities of life and may remark sadly that Dives, for all his riches, has a frozen heart — yet there is no real comfort to be had in a hope of an eschatological reversal, for the cosmos itself tolerates social inequity. Melville's narrator Ishmael, despite his biblical namesake, questions whether there is indeed a "God who hears": so we are sent back to the parable to read again.

Though most interpreters of the parable have not followed Melville in his rejection of eschatological theodicy, typically they have also not been content to allow the story's "reversal" to go unexplained in terms of ethics or theology. That is, most have not agreed with Richard Bauckham that "it is a parable concerned with the single issue of wealth and poverty."[7] (Here I should remark that Bauckham's reading is salutary for those who would emasculate the parable by insisting that it speaks only of "greed" and not of "wealth" — as though human beings could parse that difference with ease!) This being said, it is still, for the most part, Bauckham *contra mundum*. Most have not agreed with him that "what is not stated is not relevant"[8] — if by "stated" we mean *explicitly proposed* as an explanation for the reversal. In harmony with the narrative method observed in Auerbach's *Mimesis*, the action and speech of this sparse and unpsychologized parable carry much weight. Thus, readers from the second to the twenty-first century have noted and found significance in the following details: the parable's context following a difficult story concerning the proper use of wealth and "eternal tents"; the fact that Lazarus is named; the meaning of his name; the apt place of "one who has been helped" in the bosom of the patriarch of faith; the proximity of Lazarus to the rich man's house and gaze; the rich man's indifference; his overly modest request simply to have relief, and not a change in estate; his postmortem assumption that Lazarus is a mere servant, indeed, one who must "come down" to him; the atypical mercilessness of Abraham (who had mercy on Sodom); the implication that Dives, like his brothers, will not hear Moses and the prophets; the impossibility of persuading such, even by extraordinary means; and the confirmation of that dynamic in the Johannine story of another Lazarus, where neither his resuscitation nor even the resurrection of Jesus is convincing to those who will not repent.

---

7. R. Bauckham, "The Rich Man and Lazarus: The Parable and the Parallels," *NTS* 37 (1991): 233.

8. Bauckham, "The Rich Man and Lazarus," 233.

The story, then, has not usually been read in terms of a bare reversal. Instead, readers have found in such details *reasons* for the reversal, beyond the mere rebalancing of the scales, and implications of the eschatological reversal for Christian action and belief. Let us take as typical the commentary of John Bunyan, whose "Interpreter" explains Abraham's gnomic dictum in Luke 16:25 by means of an allegory concerning the brothers "Patience" and "Passion."[9]

Bunyan's Interpreter does not dwell simply upon the profligacy of Passion and the quietness of Patience. To this is added Passion's devaluation of "all the divine testimonies of the good of the world to come" (cf. Luke 17:20) and his scornful treatment of Patience. These touches, plus the apt intertext of 2 Cor 4:18 regarding the value of things unseen, are consonant with the context of the parable as a diptych with that of the unjust steward. Eyebrows may be raised, however, at the *Schadenfreude* depicted by the Interpreter, and found also in some earlier "readings," though not even intimated in the parable itself: "Patience will have to laugh at Passion because he had his best things last."

Surely it is reaction to such readings that led the Canadian William Wilfred Campbell to pen his demurring lyric entitled *Lazarus*,[10] in which compunction disturbs the well-earned rest of the righteous. In this poem the newly deceased Lazarus speaks with the patriarch, exclaiming that he cannot rest in Abraham's bosom because of the "cry from some fierce, anguished breast . . . like dream-waked infant wailing for the light." The plaintiff cry of the lost distracts him from the seraphic song and causes him to exclaim, "This is no heaven until that hell doth die!" Certainly Campbell has here framed a counter-story, one resistant to the possible implications of the parable. The pious may be irritated by his audacity in correcting a dominical parable. The scholarly may remark that his poem is beside the point, since the Lazarus parable is not intended to give us any information concerning the next world: it is neither for nor against Purgatory, neither for nor against the possibility of postmortem repentance. Yet Campbell's lyrics serve as an accent, reminding us that this parable is fixed within a canon, where there are passages suggesting that, against all odds,

---

9. John Bunyan, *The Pilgrim's Progress* (Baltimore: Penguin, 1965), 62-63.

10. From "Later Canadian Poems," edited by J. E. Wetherell. See http://mailserver.pts.edu/exchange/humphrey/Drafts/RE:%20Essay%20on%20Lazarus.EML/1_text.htm#_ftnref1 and http://www.uwo.ca/english/canadianpoetry/confederation/later_cdn_poems/william_wilfred_campbell.htm. This poem accessed December 12, 2008.

even the greedy, even the profligate and hard of heart, have repented. Campbell's hero is described as making the long descent to hell, a descent of mercy still in progress, in search of those crying for mercy. As the quester descends, for a very long time on his journey, and urged by the love of Christ, he approaches those lost in anguish, while behind him he hears "a glorious shout." Is this the shout of those who hope to see the quest successful? Perhaps it is the jubilation of the angels, because the lost are being sought? Or perhaps we are even to imagine the exclamation of a compassionate Jesus, "Well done, thou good and faithful servant!"

Of course, the theological question remains: is Campbell trying to square the circle? Is there something left to rescue in that one who calls for mercy but will not repent? Or is this in the nature of the gospel itself, that, by trampling down death by death, "what is impossible" has been made "possible" (18:27)? Milton, in his *Paradise Lost*, juxtaposes the impassable gulf between hell and paradise with the demonically conceived bridge that Death and Sin together forge between earth and hell:

> But lest the difficulty of passing back
> Stay his [Satan's] return perhaps over this Gulf
> Impassable, Impervious, let us try
> Advent'rous work, yet to thy power and mine
> Not unagreeable, to found a path
> Over this Main from Hell to that new World
> Where Satan now prevails, a Monument
> Of merit high to all th'infernal Host,
> Easing thir passage hence, for intercourse,
> Or transmigration, as thir lot shall lead. (X.252-61)

In *Paradise Lost*, Satan's minions can forge a way between Hell and earth to celebrate Satan's power, allowing not simply for communication but for emigration. Luke's Gospel proclaims that there is a more significant crossway, that monument of perfect merit, by which the law and the prophets have been fulfilled. Seen within the context of Luke-Acts as a whole, the final interchange of the parable is utterly significant. With deftness, the closing phrase intimates the One who will join the ranks of the suffering, not to be "abandoned in Hades" but to rise,[11] providing that wit-

---

11. The textual conundrum in this text is vigorously debated. We here prefer the reading

ness by which "repentance and forgiveness of sins" may be proclaimed to all the nations. In the end, though the parable may not be directed in the first place toward speculation regarding the ultimate question of life after death, contemplation upon the mundane matters of money and self-centeredness leads us, with the Gospel writer, to celebrate the one by whom resurrection has been accomplished, and repentance made possible for those who *are* persuaded. By this pragmatic parable, we are provided with a microcosm, "the world squeezed into a ball" (as T. S. Eliot puts it), and asked to consider what Patrick Reardon has called "the apocalyptic perspective" — "more is going on than seems to be going on."[12]

---

anastē, not only for textual reasons, but because of the power of the crescendo thus afforded the story, where Dives' less precise *poreuthē* is strengthened in the final more explicit reference to resurrection. Not only would a visitation from the dead prove useless to those who will not heed the prophetic and Mosaic witness, but even a resurrection will not be convincing.

12. P. Reardon, *The Trial of Job: Orthodox Christian Reflections on the Book of Job* (Ben Lomond, CA: Conciliar Press, 2005).

A Confucianist, Cross-cultural Translation of Luke 16:19-31: Ethics, Eschatology, and Scripture

K. K. Yeo

Language is metaphorical; therefore, translation requires interpretation.[1] Translation involves finding the right words in the target language, expressing the dynamic equivalence of the text, and communicating the theology of the text to the intended audience. Translation is not just word for word; it is also an indigenous interpretation of the biblical text.[2] A cultural interpretation of a biblical text unleashes its divine utterance as it overcomes cultural barriers and transcends the literary limitations of the text.[3] This intertextual and cross-cultural interpretation is rhetorical (involving audience interaction), hermeneutical (interpreting meaning of meaningfulness), and theological (inscribing the narrative of God in the lives of the readers).[4] This method of translation creates a living encounter between the meaningful world of the text and the life world of an interpreter, thus making the text "sacred."[5]

---

1. See K. K. Yeo, *Rhetorical Interaction in 1 Corinthians 8 and 10: A Formal Analysis with Its Implications for a Chinese, Cross-cultural Hermeneutic* (Leiden: Brill, 1995), 31-37.

2. See K. K. Yeo, "Navigating Romans Through Cultures," in *Navigating Romans Through Cultures: Challenging Readings by Charting a New Course* (ed. K. K. Yeo; New York: T&T Clark International, 2004), 1-7.

3. See K. K. Yeo, "Culture and Intersubjectivity as Criteria of Negotiating Meanings in Cross-cultural Interpretations," in *The Meanings We Choose* (ed. C. H. Cosgrove; Edinburgh: T&T Clark International, 2004), 99-100.

4. Yeo, *Rhetorical Interaction*, 67-74.

5. P. Ricoeur, *Figuring the Sacred: Religion, Narrative, and Imagination* (ed. M. I. Wallace; trans. David Pellauer; Minneapolis: Fortress, 1995), 68-72.

A Confucianist, Cross-cultural Translation of Luke 16:19-31

Ethics

Reading Luke 16:19-31 as an example, Chinese readers or translators of Confucianist persuasion recognize that the text contains moral lessons based on a fictional story of a nameless (his name is "Dives" according to an ancient Latin text) rich (πλούσιος) man (and his brothers) who feasted extravagantly (εὐφραινόμενος λαμπρῶς) every day; a poor (πτωχός) man named Lazarus (equivalent of the Hebrew name Eliezer, meaning "God's help"), who longed to be filled with mercy; and Abraham, who is the common father of all and who gathered his kind in his bosom (κόλπος). The names of the characters may sound alien to Chinese readers, but the moral lessons sound familiar. In particular, one lesson stands out: one's ethical responsibility in this life is to be a moral person who relates to and empathizes with others *(jun-zi)* in love *(ren ren)*. In the Lukan text, the rich man is selfish and does not care for others. In the language of the Confucian ethic, he is less than human himself — he is worse than the dogs, who at least would lick the sores of Lazarus (assuming that the licking of dogs has partial healing). The rich man does not relate to others while he is alive; consequently, he is fated for Hades (ᾅδη). Hades or the underworld is the dwelling place of those less than human. Hades is dark and painful because there is neither human nor divine love.

The Lukan text seems to emphasize life now and life after death. While the Confucianist worldview understands the fluidity of the world here and the world after death (thus ancestor reverence),[6] it does not advocate ethical life in this world in order to escape punishment in the afterworld. Thus, Chinese translation of this text ought not to highlight fear of the afterlife as the motivation for good works in this life; neither is there an indication in the Lukan text that fear is the motivation of morality and piety. Consistent with the Torah whose intention for the covenant people is for them to love God and to love their neighbor, Confucius taught that to be a holy person *(sheng ren)* is to engage in self-cultivation in relation to others. Confucian ethics emphasizes that only in relation to others can one become human.[7] To translate the Lukan text in Confucianist language, the

---

6. See K. K. Yeo, "The Rhetorical Hermeneutic of 1 Corinthians 8 and Chinese Ancestor Worship," *BI* 2, no. 3 (1994): 298-311; idem, *Ancestor Worship: Rhetorical and Cross-Cultural Hermeneutical Response* [Chinese] (Hong Kong: Chinese Christian Literature Council, 1996).

7. See my chapter "An Intertextual Reading of Moral Freedom in the Analects and

rich man is less than human (in his life on earth and in the life after his death) because he does not know how to relate to others, especially the poor and the needy. His "suffering pain" (ὀδυνᾶσαι) in the next world can be understood as his insistence on living by himself. He chokes himself to death by his own wealth. In the Chinese view of the underworld, he is the *gui* (evil ghost) — rather than a *shen* (god or divine being) or *xian* (angelic being) — because he does not have morality, and he is an egoistic individual. As a consequence of dehumanizing himself, he will spend the next life in torment as less than human. He will yearn for human fellowship and will thirst for love in his self-disintegration, but in Hades there will be neither human beings to accompany him nor dogs to lick him. Selfishness is a form of self-destruction. In contrast to the rich man, Abraham and the poor man become gods *(shen)* or angels *(xian)* in the mythological worldview of Chinese readers. *Shen* and *xian* are virtuous people whose (full) humanity is elevated to partake of divinity. They are blessed in the next world to protect and help people on earth.

Eschatology

"There is a great chasm . . . and no one can cross" (Luke 16:26, μεταξὺ ἡμῶν καὶ ὑμῶν χάσμα μέγα ἐστήρικται . . . μηδὲ ἐκεῖθεν πρὸς ἡμᾶς διαπερῶσιν) between this life and the next, yet the readers are privileged to cross over from this life to the next. The rich man, his brothers, and Lazarus cannot overcome the chasm, but Abraham and the rich man are able to communicate between their worlds. These are literary constructs based on the author's power to decide whether this life and the next are fluid. Premodern worldviews generally affirm the fluidity of time and space. However, there is a difference between Confucius's understanding of time and the New Testament's. Confucius's worldview is cyclical,[8] and he invests his ethic in the present. If we do not know life now, we cannot speculate about death and the afterlife (Analects 11:11). Thus, the Confucian ethic invests in self-cultivation in this world. There is no eschatology in Confucianism. How-

---

Galatians," pp. 271-89 in this volume. See also K. K. Yeo, *What Has Jerusalem to Do with Beijing? Biblical Interpretation from a Chinese Perspective* (Harrisburg: Trinity Press International, 1998), 152-59. Cf. Analects 4:25; 6:28.

8. K. K. Yeo, "Messianic Predestination in Romans 8 and Classical Confucianism," in *Navigating Romans Through Cultures*, 285-89.

ever, the eschatological framework of the Lukan narrative also requires accountability for our ethical life. The Lukan text portrays the eschatological reversal of comfort and pain, of abundance and lacking, of the giving and withholding of mercy (ἔλεος) for the rich man and Lazarus. Whether in a cyclical or eschatological worldview, both Confucianism and the Lukan texts believe in moral accountability. The eschatological worldview of Luke grants hope to the innocent poor and judgment to the oppressive rich, and enhances the Confucian worldview with a prophetic challenge.

Scriptures

Lastly, the statement that the brothers of the rich man "have Moses and the prophets" (Luke 16:29, ἔχουσι Μωϋσέα καὶ τοὺς προφήτας) suggests that the law and prophetic tradition of the Jewish canon is adequate for people to live according to God's will. In the same way, Chinese Christians may assume that the Four Books of the Confucian canon give clear guidelines for readers to live as human beings. The prophetic wisdom of every culture is sufficient "to bear witness" (16:28, διαμαρτύρηται) for one to become a responsible self in giving mercy to others. Jewish tradition has Moses and the prophets (16:29); Chinese tradition has Confucius and the moralists. Thus, the understanding of "love your neighbor" — the neighbor as one near us and different from us — whether in the Old Testament or the Four Books, is a common law of life across cultures and religions. Those "who do this [law] will live" (10:28, τοῦτο ποίει καὶ ζήσῃ). The essence of this law of love and life cultivates us to become fully human. We love others not because we are superior, but because our humanity is realized in its fullness as we love them.

Though each culture or religion is adequate in giving its law of life, a cross-cultural reading of sacred texts is necessary, not only because it expresses ideas across places, times, and languages, but also because it "resurrects new life" beyond monocultural text. The Lukan admission that "If they do not listen to Moses and the prophets, neither will they be convinced even if someone rises from the dead" (16:31) suggests a rupture of the author's intention. Abraham did not allow Lazarus to "rise from the dead" to warn the brothers of the rich man, yet the author of the Lukan text has warned the readers what Lazarus would say. The literary and hermeneutical construct of Luke dictates that Scripture points to and is fulfilled in Christ (cf. Luke 24:13-35). Depending on the textual traditions of the ancient or modern readers, the story of Abraham, Lazarus, and the rich man will have a different intertextual relationship with readers — in my case with Confucian texts. Luke 16:19-31 drives readers back to the world of the sacred texts, be that of "Moses and the prophets" (16:29) or of Jesus, the One who rises "from the dead" (16:30, 31). Death is unable to heal the sin-sick world. Only the scriptural narrative of Christ has the power to inscribe a new story of salvation.[9] The Scripture will always shed light on our human need, for it points to Christ's story always, that "all flesh shall see the salvation of God" (3:6).

---

9. See K. K. Yeo, ed., *Lucan Wisdom: A Literary and Theological Reading of Luke* [Chinese] (Hong Kong: Excellence, 1995).

A Rereading of Luke 16:19-31

Elsa Tamez

Many times in Latin America there is no clear separation between reality and fiction. Our world is not very different from the narrated world called *magical realism* in literature.[1] Examples include the world of *Pedro Páramo* (by the Mexican novelist, Juan Rulfo), which shows the world of the dead as if they were alive; or the world pictured by Colombian author Gabriel García Márquez in *One Hundred Years of Solitude;* or the fictional worlds of Alejo Carpentier, Miguel Angel Asturias, and many other authors of our Latin American or Caribbean stories. For example, a description of bags full of human skulls could appear in the "magical realism" of one of our literary works and also in the lives of the people who have suffered under dictators. Much of our literature speaks of the dead as if they were alive and of the living as if they were dead. This reflects our reality. And this is the reference that will help me to interpret this text.

In Luke 16:19-31, I see two scenes with the same reality: One occurs in the everyday life of the living and the other in the world of the dead. Both realities are horrible, and they are very much alike. The biggest difference is in the people, nothing more. Both realities show in an eerie, unsettling way that the division between the living and the dead is not that great.

This text is deeper than the traditional interpretations of prizes and punishments. It speaks of a reality presented on two planes. If the first

---

1. Gabriel García Márquez pointed this out in his acceptance speech when he received the Nobel Prize in literature.

scene did not exist, neither would the second one. The second scene is the result of the first. Consequently, the entire text is an invitation to reject the two-dimensionally drawn reality, transforming the first scene.

First Scene

In the first scene, we have two people who are exactly opposite: one rich and one poor. The rich man is dressed luxuriously, in purple and in linen, two materials that indicate power, status, and wealth. The poor man is depicted as being afflicted with disease. The text states: "he was covered in sores." The eyes of the narrator of the parable are not drawn to the clothes of the poor man, but rather to what he sees immediately, which is the weeping, pustule-covered skin. The rich man went through life enjoying fine food and drink — as the narrator says, "celebrating splendid parties" (εὐφραινόμενος λαμπρῶς). This indicates that he must have had a large house in order to receive his invited guests, which the parable indicates that he did on a daily basis (καθ' ἡμέραν). Surely he must have had a great fortune. The wealthy of ancient times reinforced their power status through banquets. The rich man in the parable was made visible through the many people who entered the door of his dining room. The poor man, on the other hand, did not have a house. He was an indigent who sat in the doorway of the rich man, the text says "lying flat," "prostrate" (ἐβέβλητο) against the door. He chose the door because he wanted others to see him. He wanted to be a person. His very body is a prophetic word that denounces social inequality. Those who are invited to the banquet must walk right past this outcast. But they do nothing. They don't see him. Or if they do see him they only view him with great indifference or even scorn. The only ones who do take notice of him are not people, but the dogs that come to lick his sores. These are not the "man's best friend" kind of dogs. No, the text wants to paint a scene of nausea and profound inhumanity. So the dogs come and lick the sores. The dogs of those times were a filthy animal, and here the parable wants to take to the extreme the existence of a non-person in the unequal society that is on display. While one is being visited by distinguished persons in order to eat the delicacies offered at the banquet, the other is being visited by dogs that lick the sores of his very body. The sores are the banquet for the dogs. And Lazarus, just like the dogs, dreamed of eating the crumbs that fell from the table of the rich man.

Usually, during the composition of a story, there is a mechanism built in for creating compassion in the readers. The poor man should fill the reader with pity, and the reader should identify with the poor man. However, for a Central American, this scene doesn't have to create pity in order to provoke solidarity. The scene risks being completely rejected, because, as well as provoking anger at the egotism and indifference of the rich man, it also causes nausea at the lack of dignity of the poor man. The two attitudes, that of the rich and that of the poor, should fill the reader with nausea as well as rage and rejection. In this sense, the text, through these two opposites (the rich man and the poor man), represents two simultaneous messages: a prophetic denouncement of inequality, and at the same time a call for the poor to maintain their dignity.

Now in the same text we find indications of this call to dignity. Notice that in the parable of the rich man and Lazarus, the poor man has a name. The text calls him by his name, Lazarus. This was unusual. The poor men and women whom Jesus healed had no names. They were called by their illnesses — the man with the withered hand, the woman who could not stop bleeding, the man who was born blind, etc. Curiously, in this parable we find a poor person who has a name, and it is the person who is the most miserable of all the poor who appear in the stories and parables. His name, Lazarus, is the same one as the brother of Martha and Mary, whom Jesus resurrected. This is very significant. The name Lazarus is associated with many things: resurrection, life, friendship, family meals. Jesus gave this poor man lying in the street the name Lazarus, so that he could raise him up like Lazarus. A life that is spent waiting for the crumbs off the table is like that of a dead person, a nobody. The text chose to call him by his name and thus give a fundamental recognition to this being who was invisible to the wealthy. The rich man, in contrast, did not receive a name; he was left anonymous.

Second Scene

The narrator also describes the second scene very dramatically. This second scene is in danger of being rejected. The scene is pathetic, as is the first one, but longer. In the second scene, in contrast to the first, there is movement, or, to say it better, dialogue that calls for actions. The situation seems inverted. The one who is reclining at the banquet table at the bosom of

Abraham is now Lazarus; he is passive, as in the first scene, not speaking (is he also indifferent as the rich man was in the first scene?). Now Lazarus, who was not noticed by the rich man in the first scene, is seen in the second: "In Hades, being tormented, he lifted his eyes and saw Abraham far away with Lazarus at his bosom" (v. 23). The rich man is not called rich, as he stopped being rich when he entered the world of the dead. The tongue of the ex-rich man appears in place of that of the dogs. The ex-rich man calls, pleading that Lazarus come and soothe his torments with a dampened fingertip. But his petition is denied, and he is reminded of his indifference to the poor man before his death. The narrator inverts the situation, saying: "you received your good things, now there is no comfort." It is impossible to overcome the barriers that separate the two: "between them there is an abyss that keeps them apart." The first scene did not speak of a chasm that separated the rich man and Lazarus. Nevertheless, it is there; it is a barrier symbolized by the act of a stratified, egotistic society against solidarity. This barrier, unlike that of the abyss of Hades, can be surmounted through a change in attitude working toward solidarity. The abyss of the second scene is defined because of where it is; even if they want to, those on one side of the abyss cannot be compassionate, nor can those on the other side escape the torments.

The ex-rich man has a very important thought. He wants to change the situation in real everyday life so that this unrealistic, unchangeable life doesn't repeat itself. He believes that if he cannot escape the torments, perhaps his family still can. He asks Abraham to send Lazarus back to the world of the living to warn his people. But this petition is also denied. (They already had Moses and the prophets to show them the just way.) The narrator is skeptical with respect to the everyday life of the wealthy. If they won't listen to the Scriptures, then someone raised from the dead won't be able to convince them either. That is to say, they had the poor right in front of them, at their very door, and they were not capable of understanding the Scriptures that speak of the love of God for the non-person.

Implications

We have here two scenes, similar and touching, of a reality. The scenes beg to be rejected. Neither one nor the other should exist; they are both sick worlds that crave to be healed, saved, transformed. But this is only possible through the reality of everyday life, by interfering in the first scene. This is because the second scene, that of Hades, depends on the first, or refers back to the first. It is the other side of the first. If the first scene didn't exist, the second one would not either. The first scene must be changed, that of the reality of daily life, in order to erase the second one. Reality cannot be changed from the world of the dead. In the parable, the rich man wants to change the second scene, but he cannot (Lazarus cannot pass over to the other side where the ex-rich man is in order to moisten his finger to put on the ex-rich man's tongue). The rich man also wants to change the first scene in the sense that he wants Lazarus to be sent to warn his family, his five brothers. But he can't do this either (Abraham does not believe that resuscitating Lazarus will change the rich family). In other words, the parable shows that everything is played out in the real world . . . this world. To leave it for later is already too late for both oneself and one's descendants. The teaching of the parable, we understand, is that we have the Scriptures and the prophets, and they have the power to transform and convert. If they cannot do it, neither can a man who is raised from the dead (Luke 16:31).

The two scenes, presented as mirror images, invite us to change the path of the real world. Abraham rejects three times the petition of the rich man. But the second scene invites us not to enjoy vengeance against the rich man (Abraham calls him "child"), but rather to see that only here on earth can the abyss between the rich and the poor be overcome.

The central message of the parable in its time, the time of Luke, was that the people already know the Scriptures (Moses and the prophets). This should be enough to transform people and make them come together to help the poor and confront their needs. If the writings do not do it, neither will a dead man brought to life do it.

The message for us Christians who have the Scriptures is this: How can we understand them but not have the capacity to see these scenes as a mirror of our actual world? To have the Scriptures is not only to understand them, but also to commit ourselves to live according to them.

PART 4
TEXT, TRANSLATION, AND THEOLOGY

Quo vadis? From Whence to Where in New Testament Text Criticism and Translation

Richard N. Longenecker

Scholarly study of the New Testament has come a long way, especially during the past two centuries. This is true with respect to all of the disciplines that constitute the macro-agenda for a scholarly understanding of the New Testament. But it is particularly true with regard to matters of text and translation. Both of these important areas of scholarly concern involve issues of great complexity and deserve extensive treatment. Here, however, we must confine ourselves to a few brief comments in highlighting some of the major advances and challenges in these two areas of New Testament study.

In what follows, I would like to do three things with regard to each of these New Testament disciplines of text and translation: first, to set out something of an overview of the high points and advances, yet also the limitations and deficiencies, of the past; second, to speak of where New Testament scholarship seems to be today; and, finally, to identify some of the challenges that New Testament scholars face as we seek to move forward. Time and space being limited, our treatment must necessarily be severely constricted. Nonetheless, it is hoped that what is presented will be helpful in viewing the broader picture and gaining perspective.

Text

It is impossible in only a few paragraphs to spell out in any detail what has transpired in the scholarly study of the New Testament's textual tradition.

That has been done most adequately by Kurt and Barbara Aland in their *Der Text des Neuen Testaments* of 1983, with a second revised edition in 1988 (both editions have been translated into English and published in 1987 and 1989 respectively).[1] Yet certain phenomena, events, scholars, and advances need to be identified here in order to provide some consciousness of what has taken place in the past, where we are today, and what challenges lie before us for the future. At risk of oversimplification, it may be said that three periods stand out as being especially important in the history of the New Testament text: (1) the patristic period, (2) the Reformation period, and (3) the modern critical period.

The Patristic Period

The patristic period, which may be dated from Clement of Rome in the late first century to Jerome and Augustine in the mid-fifth century, is, of course, of primary importance in any study of the New Testament text. It is necessary, however, not to treat the textual tradition of patristic times in any monolithic fashion. Two phases need to be distinguished: (1) a time when various Christian communities possessed their own favored "apostolic" writings and textual traditions were developing with some degree of freedom, which can be dated from the late-first or early-second century through to the middle of the third century, and (2) a time following the official Roman persecution of Christianity that was instituted in 250-260 by Decius (who reigned 249-251), Valerius (who reigned 253-260), and the tetrarchy that ruled during the two years between them, and then was reinstituted in 303 by Diocletianus (who reigned 284-305), with those imperial policies dramatically reversed by Constantine (who reigned 306-337) after his conversion to Christianity in 313. It was during this latter phase when Christians — both when suffering persecution and then when enjoying acceptance and peace — came to realize that they needed to standardize their New Testament writings, a time that can be dated from the last quarter of the third century through to the end of the fifth century.

---

1. K. Aland and B. Aland, *The Text of the New Testament: An Introduction to the Critical Editions and to the Theory and Practice of Modern Textual Criticism* (trans. E. F. Rhodes; Leiden: Brill; Grand Rapids: Eerdmans, 1987; 2nd ed., 1989).

Quo vadis? *From Whence to Where in Text Criticism and Translation*

That a diversity of text forms existed during the earlier phase, that is, during the first two centuries of the Christian era, is attested (1) by variant readings in the Old Latin, the Old Syriac, and certain Coptic versions that may be presumed to have incorporated some earlier readings, (2) by variations in the biblical texts quoted by such early Greek church fathers as Irenaeus and Origen (even though their writings were preserved by the Western church only in Latin translations), and (3) by differences in the text forms of the New Testament papyri, which were found among other papyrus materials in the Fayyum district of Egypt over a century ago. More allusively, early textual diversity is also suggested by what can be known about Marcion's text of Luke's Gospel and ten of the Pauline letters (Marcion's so-called *Apostolikon* or "Apostolic Writings"), as reported mainly by Tertullian and Origen, which readings seem not to have been unique to Marcion but were evidently accepted as well among certain other groups of early Christians.

Some of the more obvious examples of diverse textual traditions during these first two Christian centuries have to do with: (1) the inclusion or omission of the negative οὐδέ in Gal 2:5 ("we did *not* give in to them for a moment, so that the truth of the gospel might remain with you"), with Irenaeus and Tertullian quoting this passage as though the negative was omitted in their circles; (2) the inclusion or omission of chs. 15–16 in Paul's letter to the Romans; (3) the inclusion and placement of the doxology of Rom 16:25-27, whether after 14:23, after 15:33, after 16:23/24, after both 14:23 and 15:33, after both 14:23 and 16:23/24, or omitted entirely; (4) the inclusion or omission of ἐν ʹΡώμῃ ("at Rome") in Rom 1:7 and 15; (5) the inclusion or omission of ἐν ʹΕφέσῳ ("at Ephesus") in Eph 1:1; (6) the plural αἱ διαθῆκαι ("the covenants") or the singular ἡ διαθήκη ("the covenant") in Rom 9:4; (7) the accusative plural αὐτούς ("them") or the dative plural αὐτοῖς ("to them") in Heb 8:8; and (8) the reading of the Greek substantival passive participle at the beginning of Rom 1:4 — that is, whether it appeared in Greek as τοῦ ὁρισθέντος ("the one appointed" or "designated") or as τοῦ προορισθέντος ("the one predestined"), as suggested by the Latin *praedestinatus* that is to be found in the Old Latin, Jerome's Vulgate, and many Latin writers (though Origen, as preserved in Rufinus's abridged Latin version of his Romans commentary, insisted that the true reading is *destinatus*, "designated," and not *praedestinatus*, "predestined"). Each of these cases (and more, of course, could be cited) reflects a particular theological dispute that occurred during the first two centuries of the Christian era — with each of them also giving evidence of a text that was somewhat fluid before the "families" of texts (or, at least, before the Byzantine family of texts) became standardized. And a number of these textual variants continue to influence and support some of those same theologies today.

It was, however, during the latter part of the third century and throughout the fourth century — in response to both persecution by antagonistic emperors and then later acceptance and the restoration of peace by Constantine — that the major text types or "families" came into existence. For under Roman persecution there was not only a systematic destruction of Christian churches and Christian centers but also public burnings of Christian writings and texts, with a resultant widespread scarcity of New Testament manuscripts; whereas during the age of Constantine there was a rapid growth of Christianity, with the resultant need for a large number of New Testament texts.

The Reformation Period

The end of the fifteenth century and the entire sixteenth century constituted a time of intense interest in the Bible, with Christians being challenged by the Renaissance (which began in the fourteenth century in Italy) and motivated by the Protestant Reformation (which took definitive form in the early sixteenth century in Germany) to return to their biblical roots. With respect to the text of the New Testament, the most important scholar of the day was Desiderius Erasmus of Rotterdam (1469-1536), the religious humanist, who was trained as a Roman Catholic theologian but worked principally as a Latin and Greek linguist. He was a highly significant figure throughout Europe, becoming even professor of divinity at Cambridge University in England from 1509 to 1514.

Erasmus is best known today for having produced, based on only four or five twelfth- to thirteenth-century Byzantine manuscripts, a critical Greek text of the New Testament (or *Novum Instrumentum*), which was comparable in many ways to what in the seventeenth century came to be called the "received text" *(Textus Receptus)*, with accompanying textual notes and Latin translation. In his day, however, Erasmus was more applauded — though also often criticized — as a paraphraser of the New Testament, appropriating a method used by the Greek rhetorician Quintilian (late first century A.D.) and the Latin rhetorician Themistius (fourth century A.D.) on writings of classical authors and applying it to the contents of the New Testament. For to paraphrase a text was to improve its clarity, and so to facilitate its translation from one language to another.

Erasmus's Greek text quickly became the basis for some of the most important New Testament commentaries of the sixteenth century — not only those by Protestants but also some of those written by Roman Catholics. Martin Luther in his lectures on Romans, for example, while working basically from the Basel edition of the Vulgate of 1509 and Faber Stapulensis's Latin edition of the Epistles of St. Paul of 1512 and 1515 (especially for the first eight chapters of Romans), often corrected the Vulgate (particularly in chs. 9–16) by reference to the first edition of Erasmus's Greek New Testament, which was published and became available to him early in 1516. And Thomas de Vio (surnamed "Cajetan"), the Roman Catholic bishop of Gaeta — who was a scholastic theologian of great stature and influence, and who in 1518 had presided as the papal legate in the examination of Luther at Augsburg — devoted himself during the latter years of his life (in 1525-34) entirely to the writing of biblical commentaries (first on the Psalms, then on the Gospels, the Acts, and the letters of the New Testament, and finally on the Pentateuch, Joshua, Proverbs, Ecclesiastes, and Isaiah 1–3). But he got into trouble with his ecclesiastical superiors when writing his New Testament commentaries because (1) he departed from the Latin text of the Vulgate, using instead the critical editions of the Greek prepared by Erasmus and Faber, and (2) he sounded, at times, too much like Luther, at least to those who claimed to be his judges.

Erasmus's Greek text also became the basis for Luther's German translation of the New Testament (his so-called *Septembertestament*, because it was published in September of 1522), which, in turn, was incorporated into his complete German Bible of 1546. And Erasmus's Greek text was the text for William Tyndale's very important English translation of the New Testament that he began to publish in 1525 while in exile, which was, in turn, the prototype for such lesser English translations as the Great Bible of 1539, the Geneva Bible of the 1550s, and the Bishops' Bible of 1568 — with Tyndale's translation, together with many of these lesser English versions, culminating in the King James Version of 1611.

RICHARD N. LONGENECKER

The Modern Critical Period

The modern period of New Testament textual criticism may be somewhat difficult to characterize, simply because we are all a part of it and much too close to developments to be objective in our evaluations. Nonetheless, at least three phases of this period, which dates from about the mid nineteenth century to today (and will undoubtedly continue), can be identified: (1) a time when a number of important early Greek uncial manuscripts of the Bible became known to the scholarly world, when judgments regarding the text of the New Testament were based primarily on external manuscript evidence alone, and when relations between the Greek texts and their "families" were fairly well "established"; (2) a time when internal data also became important in textual criticism; and (3) a time when papyrus texts of the New Testament were discovered and then later seen to be of great importance in the identification of early traits and features in the textual traditions of the second and third centuries, before efforts were made to standardize the New Testament text and the main "families" of texts were formed in the third and fourth centuries.

Phase One

The primary impetus for the first phase of modern textual criticism was (1) the coming to light of the contents of Codex Vaticanus (B, 03), which had been housed in the Vatican library since at least the end of the fifteenth century and whose text Vatican authorities finally allowed to become known in the mid nineteenth century, and (2) the recovery of Codex Sinaiticus (ℵ, 01), which Konstantin von Tischendorf of Leipzig discovered in 1844 amid piles of waste paper in the monastery of St. Catherine on Mount Sinai and arranged in 1859 to be moved to St. Petersburg (with the Russian government later selling it to the British Museum, where it resides today). Earlier, in 1830, the Berlin philologist Karl Lachmann (1793-1851), who was the first scholar to make a decisive break with the *Textus Receptus*, had called for New Testament scholarship to go "back to the text of the early fourth-century church." But now with the Greek New Testament texts of Codex Vaticanus and Codex Sinaiticus, Tischendorf (1815-1877) — who had been sponsored by Czar Nicholas I to search for ancient biblical materials, and who had also found in his extensive travels some twenty-one other uncial manuscripts — was able, supported by the writings of Samuel P. Tregelles (1813-1875), to provide evidence for earlier and more reliable readings than those provided by the *Textus Receptus*.

Inspired by the "discoveries" (or, more properly, the "recoveries") of Vaticanus and Sinaiticus, and building on the challenge of Lachmann (in 1831 and 1842 to 1850) and the studies of Tischendorf (during 1841 to 1872) and Tregelles (during 1857 to 1879), Brooke F. Westcott (1825-1901) and Fenton J. A. Hort (1828-1892) set out in 1863 to establish the text of the Greek New Testament on a more critically assured basis. Hort seems to have been the one who was principally responsible for the original conception and early development of the theory of "family" relations between the ancient Greek texts, whereas Westcott took the lead in applying that theory in practice. On all points, however, they worked in close collaboration. And in 1881 they published the results of their labors in *The New Testament in the Original Greek*, with those results having a profound effect on all New Testament study thereafter.

As a result of the work of Westcott and Hort, most scholars today recognize three basic types or "families" of texts (or, perhaps, four, if we include a distinctly "Caesarean" family) in the textual tradition of the Greek New Testament, with various subtypes and combinations of these families identified as well. The earliest and probably primary family is the "Alexandrian" text, or what Westcott and Hort called the "Neutral" text because it appears to have not been contaminated by later scribal changes (i.e., as evidenced in the Byzantine and "Western" textual traditions). It was prominent in the region of Alexandria, hence its name. But it was also used in various churches throughout the eastern part of the Roman empire. A second type is the bilingual Greek-Latin text that has often been called the "Western" text, which may have had roots among certain Christians as early as the mid-second century and was used dominantly in western portions of the empire. A third is the "Byzantine" text, which has also been called the "Syrian" or "Antiochene" text because it is thought to have originated in the late third century at Antioch of Syria. This third family of texts has also been called the "Koine" ("common") text — or, today, often the "Majority Text" — simply because, being represented by a few uncials and the great bulk of minuscule manuscripts from the ninth through the fifteenth centuries, it is numerically most prevalent. It is also called the "Received Text" since it is generally comparable to the Greek text worked out by Erasmus (1469-1536) in the early sixteenth century, with that text then developed on a somewhat broader basis in the seventeenth century and called the *Textus Receptus*.

RICHARD N. LONGENECKER

Phase Two

The inauguration of phase two of the modern critical period of New Testament textual criticism must be credited to Martin Dibelius (1883-1947), Rudolf Bultmann (1884-1976), and Karl Ludwig Schmidt (1891-1956). None of these scholars was a text critic in the strict sense of that term — though, of course, all three worked extensively with the New Testament text and made numerous pronouncements about it. More important for New Testament textual criticism, however, is the fact that in their advocacy and development of *Formgeschichte* and the *formgeschichtliche Methode* (which expression and method they undoubtedly picked up from Eduard Norden's 1913 *Agnostos Theos: Untersuchungen zur Formgeschichte religiöser Rede*), Martin Dibelius, Rudolf Bultmann, and Karl Schmidt, who worked independently but along very similar lines, highlighted in their writings (beginning in 1919 and continuing throughout the mid-twentieth century) the redactional activities of the New Testament evangelists in their composition of the Gospels (also, as with Dibelius, in the composition of Acts).

What we as English-speaking scholars today call "form criticism" and "redaction criticism" has been used in a wide diversity of ways, both destructively and constructively. This has been true not only with respect to the traditions that underlie the New Testament generally, but also with reference to the composition of our canonical Gospels and Acts. And much has transpired in the development of these scholarly New Testament disciplines since their inauguration. Yet it must be stated that what Dibelius, Bultmann, and Schmidt did for text-critical studies — as well as what many others have done in these areas, whatever their various motivations and however they have proceeded — has been to lay emphasis on the necessity of always taking into consideration the internal features of an author's purpose, compositional habits, expressional patterns, and theology, as well as the external factors having to do with textual "families" and manuscripts, when making text-critical judgments. And it is this insight and understanding that has become more and more important in modern text-critical studies — whether it be called "form" or "redaction" criticism with respect to the canonical Gospels and Acts, "epistolary" or "rhetorical" analysis when dealing with the New Testament letters, or "narrative theology" as underlying everything written.

Quo vadis? *From Whence to Where in Text Criticism and Translation*

Phase Three

Discoveries during the 1890s of New Testament koine Greek papyrus manuscripts and portions among the many non-literary papyri found in the Fayyum region of Egypt, as well as continuing identifications of further New Testament papyrus texts, have been a boon in all sorts of ways for New Testament study. With respect to matters regarding text criticism, these papyrus materials of whole and partial texts (which today number a total of 116 relatively whole manuscripts and very brief portions of New Testament Greek texts) have always been brought into the text-critical data bank of New Testament scholarship as they have become known and studied — though usually only in a somewhat subsidiary fashion and often only in something of a supporting role.

Of late, however, a thorough reevaluation of the textual history of the New Testament has been inaugurated by Kurt and Barbara Aland and their associates at the Institute for New Testament Textual Research, Münster, Germany. It is a reevaluation that builds on the work of Westcott and Hort with respect to the family relations of the uncial and minuscule manuscripts, and so seeks to spell out with greater clarity the Greek textual traditions of the fourth through the fifteenth centuries. More importantly, it attempts to clarify the textual situation of the second and third centuries — principally by reference to data drawn from the New Testament papyri that can be dated to those centuries and from later biblical papyrus texts that continue some of those particular traits and features. So the Alands' reevaluation of the New Testament's textual history — which in many ways is not just a reevaluation, but more like a revolution — lays primary emphasis on the earlier papyrus New Testament materials and only then seeks to show how what is found in those earlier texts was continued, developed, adjusted, or omitted in the later families of texts.

What the Alands' reevaluation does that is revolutionary is to begin with the extant papyrus New Testament texts that stem from the second and third centuries (or, at least, that reflect texts of that time), attempting always to interpret them in their historical and sociological contexts, and then to seek to understand how those textual traditions were used in the families of texts that came about during the third and fourth centuries and continued on through to the fifteenth century — rather than the other way around of first studying the relations and features of the later textual families and then inferring from them what must have been the situation before. So in its layout of a critical apparatus, the papyri are cited first, then the uncials, then the minuscules, followed by evidence drawn from the versions, church fathers, and lectionaries — as can be seen in the twenty-seventh edition of the *Nestle-Aland* critical Greek text (NA^{27}) and the fourth edition of the United Bible Societies' *Greek New Testament* (UBS^4), both of which were published in 1993 and both of which have been thoroughly revised to reflect the Alands' reevaluation of the New Testament's early textual history.

As a result of the work of Kurt and Barbara Aland and their colleagues, the textual variants of every New Testament passage in both NA^{27} and UBS^4 have experienced a complete review — often with different significances seen in the data from what had been previously proposed, different arrangements of the evidence made, and different conclusions drawn with respect to particular variants. Their work, in fact, is of the nature of a revolution that gives promise of opening up new vistas for our understanding of the textual history of the second and third centuries of Christendom, which takes us back to an earlier time before attempts were made to standardize the New Testament's text and before the families of texts were formed.

Challenges for the Future

What, then, can be said regarding the challenges of today that have an impact on the future of New Testament text criticism? The past course of debate during the patristic period and the past course of investigation during the Reformation period have not always been the most helpful, largely because (1) the most important codices and texts were not in hand, and even much of what was then at hand was not used, (2) methods for the interpretation of the textual data had not been developed, and (3) tools for handling the vast amount of material were not available. As Christians who respect tradition, we honor our forebears — but we are not required always to agree with them.

In the last two centuries, however, we have been blessed with new discoveries of immense relevance for the establishment of the New Testament text — principally, (1) the recoveries of Codex Vaticanus (from Vatican restraints) and Codex Sinaiticus (from St. Catherine's monastery on Mount Sinai), together with the coming to light of a number of other uncial Greek biblical manuscripts, and (2) the unearthing of 116 (to date) Greek New Testament papyri (from the Fayyum district of Egypt), some relatively intact and others only fragmentary. Further, we have gained immensely from the work of a number of scholars who have proposed various methodologies for the use of these materials in order to understand more adequately the textual history of the Greek text of the New Testament — with some of these proposals only demonstrating the "dead end" quality of some methods and approaches, but others setting out a basis for and pointing the way toward real advances. Obviously, being so close temporally and in our sympathies to certain major text-critical endeavors of the past century and a half, it is difficult to be entirely objective. Nonetheless, I believe that among those scholars who have provided a basis for and pointed the way toward real advances in New Testament textual criticism have been principally B. F. Westcott and F. J. A. Hort in the latter part of the nineteenth century and Kurt and Barbara Aland more recently in our own day. In addition, during the past few decades we have been provided with computer tools to enable us to handle more adequately and much more rapidly the vast amount of textual data at our disposal.

Our challenge today, therefore, is to build on what has gone before and so to move more productively into the future. That will involve not only (1) further analyses of the large body of uncial and minuscule manuscripts dating from the fourth through the fifteenth centuries, and (2) further studies of the purpose or purposes, compositional habits, expressional patterns, and theology of each of the New Testament writers, but also (3) particular attention to the text of the Greek New Testament during the second and third centuries, with that attention being mainly directed to the New Testament papyri from Egypt, quotations of the New Testament by the early church fathers, translations of the Greek New Testament in the earliest Latin, Syriac, and Coptic versions that derive from early Greek texts, and compilations of New Testament texts in the earliest church lectionaries.

Translation

Integrally related to text criticism is biblical translation. For not only have translations of the New Testament been motivated by (1) a desire to preach and teach the Christian gospel, (2) a perceived need to get back to the roots of the Christian religion, especially in light of external ideologies that oppose the Christian message or internal theologies that threaten its dissolution, and (3) the realization that receptor languages are always changing with the passing of time; but also there has been a heightened interest in biblical translation wherever there has arisen a widespread consensus that the text of the Bible, whether Old Testament or New (or both), has become more firmly established. Each of these factors has played its part in all of the three principal periods set out above, and so each needs to be spoken about briefly here.

The Patristic Period

During the first century and a half of Christendom, while many regional languages existed throughout the Roman empire, the world language was Greek — not only in the East but also in the West. Thus all of the New Testament was written in koine Greek (the vernacular language of the day), which was spoken and understood by almost everyone throughout the empire. About 180, however, the situation began to change. For in western regions of the empire, Latin was not just the official language of the state but also became dominant among the people; while in eastern regions, Syriac and Coptic began to claim equal vernacular status with Greek. Christians, therefore, found it necessary to translate their New Testament into Latin, Syriac, and Coptic. And so in the late second and early third centuries there appeared the first editions of the Old Latin, Old Syriac, and early Coptic New Testament.

This phenomenon of vernacular translation became intensified during the latter part of the third century and throughout the fourth and fifth centuries when (1) Christianity was rapidly expanding and (2) Christians came to realize that they needed to standardize their New Testament writings. So because of the expansion of Christianity — that is, for external reasons — it became necessary not only to perfect the existing Greek, Latin, Syriac, and Coptic versions of the New Testament so that people might better understand the Christian gospel, but also to produce Armenian, Gothic, Georgian, and Ethiopic translations for those living at the extremes of the empire so that the people in those regions might also have the "Good News" of the Christian message in their own language. Also because of the major text types or "families" of texts that were then being formed in the main centers of Christendom during these centuries — that is, for internal reasons — Christians felt compelled to be constantly perfecting their translations so as to bring them more into conformity to what they believed had been originally written.

Further, in the Roman church a very troubling translation problem had arisen. For with so many different editions of the Old Latin, and with some of them influencing other Latin translations, the situation had gotten so out of control that at many places in the various Latin Bibles, particularly in the Gospels, no two Latin translations agreed. In the latter part of the fourth century, therefore, Pope Damasus (366-384) undertook to remedy such an intolerable situation. So he commissioned the young, erudite scholar Eusebius Sofronius Hieronymus (347-420) — that is, Jerome as he is known in French and English, who was born at Stridon in Dalmatia (northern Italy), brought up in a wealthy Christian home, and well educated at Rome in grammar and rhetoric — to produce a uniform and dependable revision of the Latin Bible based on the best available Latin and Greek texts.

In preparation for his revision of the Latin New Testament, Jerome took up residence in two major eastern cities of the Roman empire, that is, in Antioch of Syria during 374-379 and then in Constantinople during 379-382, where he learned Greek and studied the works of the eastern church fathers. In his revision of the Latin New Testament he rejected the so-called Western Text, principally because of its harmonization of passages in the Gospels. Rather, he based his translation on (1) what he thought to be relatively good Latin versions and (2) what is now known as the Alexandrian family of Greek texts, that is, Codex Vaticanus (B, 03) and Codex Sinaiticus (ℵ, 01) — though without rejecting textual data from what was later identified as Greek Byzantine materials, particularly from the Byzantine readings for the Gospels that were later incorporated into Codex Alexandrinus (A, 02). In 384 Jerome presented his translation of the four Gospels to Pope Damasus, just before the pontiff's death; and in 405 he presented the translation of his completed Latin Bible, including both Testaments.

Jerome's translation at first met with violent opposition in the Roman Catholic Church, though by the eighth and ninth centuries it was at least respected along with the many other Old Latin translations. Eventually, however, it prevailed, simply because of its intrinsic worth vis-à-vis the Old Latin translations. By the end of the Middle Ages it became accepted as the standard translation of the Roman Catholic Church and was given the name Vulgate, which signifies (as does the word κοινή in Greek) "vernacular speech" or "a translation for the common people."

The Reformation Period

The sixteenth century was also a time of great translation fervor. For the western world, Latin had become the sole language of the church and the only proper language of scholarship, and people were expected simply to fall into line. But Luther's emphases on (1) the importance of Scripture vis-à-vis church tradition and (2) the need for the people to be able to understand the Scriptures for themselves, coupled with (3) the widespread acceptance of Erasmus's new edition of the New Testament Greek text (even though based only on four or five late Byzantine texts), provided fresh impetus for the translation of the New Testament (as well as, of course, for the translation of the whole Bible) into the vernacular speech of the people.

In September 1522 Luther published his famous German New Testament, which became known as the *Septembertestament* because of its month of publication (later incorporated into his complete German Bible of 1546). In 1525 the English Lutheran William Tyndale, while in exile in Germany, began to publish his important translation of the New Testament, which was not only generally faithful to the "received" Greek text of his day but also fluent and idiomatic in its English expression; in 1539 Miles Coverdale, who had earlier worked with Tyndale in exile, published his English translation of the New Testament, which became part of what was called "The Great Bible"; in 1557-60 English Calvinists, dubbed "Puritans" and exiled in Geneva, published "The Geneva Bible," with marginal notes; in 1568 "The Bishop's Bible" was published, which was a revision of "The Great Bible" done by a group of English bishops directed by Matthew Parker, the Archbishop of Canterbury; and in 1611 the King James Version of the Bible, which was heavily indebted to Tyndale's translation and done over a period of seven years (from 1604 to 1611) by six groups of scholars (two from Westminster, two from Cambridge, and two from Oxford), was published.

All of these Protestant translations in their rendering of the New Testament were based on Erasmus's Greek text, which had been "established" on the basis of four or five late Byzantine manuscripts. Somewhat comparable in the world of Roman Catholicism was the Rheims English translation of the New Testament in 1582, which, when joined with the English translation of the Old Testament, became the Douay-Rheims Bible in 1609 — but this translation was based principally on the Latin Vulgate, and so it reflected the Greek text only to the extent that Jerome himself had used textual materials later codifed in codices Vaticanus, Sinaiticus, and Alexandrinus.

The Modern Critical Period

Translation of Scripture, and particularly the translation of the New Testament, has been prominent whenever the following five factors (or, at least, most of them) have been joined: (1) a desire to reach out to people who live in other cultures and who speak other languages; (2) a need to get back to the roots of the Christian religion, especially in light of external ideologies that oppose the Christian message and/or internal theologies that are perceived to threaten its dissolution; (3) the "establishment" of a more adequate Greek text on which to base contemporary, vernacular translations; (4) the availability of new linguistic data, which makes possible a better understanding of what is written in the biblical texts; and (5) a recognition that receptor languages are constantly in the process of change. And all of these factors have converged in the modern critical period, thereby giving rise to a spate of vernacular translations of the Bible generally and of the New Testament in particular.

The first of these factors (i.e., "the need to reach out to people in other cultures with other languages") was certainly present in the patristic period — as witness the early editions of the Old Latin and Old Syriac and the first Coptic translations, which were then followed by Armenian, Gothic, Georgian, and Ethiopic translations. It was present, as well, in the Reformation period — as witness Luther's *Septembertestament*, which inspired many other Germanic and English versions. And with the rise of the Christian missionary movement in the nineteenth century and the continuance of that missionary thrust in many quarters of the church today, this factor of missionary outreach has given new urgency to the translation of the Christian Scriptures.

Likewise, the second factor (i.e., "the need to get back to the roots of the Christian religion, especially in light of external ideologies that oppose the Christian message and/or internal theologies that are perceived to threaten its dissolution") has always played a part in motivating fresh translations during the patristic and Reformation periods. And it continues to motivate many, if not all, of the present-day translations of the Bible. Such a motivation can be seen quite clearly, for example, in the very first words of the "Editor's Foreword" in the Jerusalem Bible:

> The form and nature of this edition of the Holy Bible have been determined by two of the principal dangers facing the Christian religion today. The first is the reduction of Christianity to the status of a relic — affectionately regarded, it is true, but considered irrelevant to our times. The second is its rejection as a mythology, born and cherished in emotion with nothing at all to say to the mind.[2]

Just as important, however, and particularly relevant for our purpose here, is the third of the above mentioned factors (i.e., "the 'establishment' of a more adequate Greek text on which to base contemporary, vernacular translations"). This was an important factor in the third and fourth centuries with the standardization of the church's Greek texts and the formation of the major textual families. For an "established" text gave rise to the revision of existing vernacular translations and served to promote the production of further translations. Likewise, it was very significant in the sixteenth century with the publication of Erasmus's "critically established" Greek New Testament, which had a profound effect on all New Testament translations from Luther's *Septembertestament* of 1522 to the King James Version of 1611. And it has certainly been a factor in the modern critical period, first, as based on the work of Westcott and Hort, in the establishment of the text from the fourth century onward, but also through the work of Kurt and Barbara Aland and their associates in focusing attention on the textual traditions of the second and third centuries. In fact, this latter reevaluation of the church's earliest textual history gives promise of being even more important than the former in its influence on all future translations of the New Testament.

Factors 4 and 5 (i.e., "the availability of new linguistic data" and "a recognition that receptor languages are constantly in the process of

---

2. A. Jones, ed., *The Jerusalem Bible* (London: Darton, Longman & Todd; New York: Doubleday, 1966), v. (Translation of *La Bible de Jérusalem* [Paris: Cerf, 1961].)

change") may not always have motivated earlier translators as they do today — though it may be argued that the better translators of earlier days were aware of such matters. But today it must be said that the presence of new linguistic data has certainly motivated and had a profound effect on all modern biblical translations — in particular, the cognate linguistic data from the Ras Shamra (Ugaritic) tablets and the Dead Sea Scrolls in our understanding of the Old Testament and the new linguistic data from the Greek biblical papyri and the Nag Hammadi texts in our understanding of the New Testament. Further, translators today have become more highly sensitized than before to the constantly changing nature of their receptor languages, with structural changes in these languages occurring more and more rapidly, vocabulary taking on a diversity of meanings (sometimes even different meanings), foreign words and expressions being imported, new idioms created, and subtle nuances elusively moving about.

In addition, during the present period of biblical scholarship, Bible translation has become a major academic discipline. All biblical exegetes and all translators of biblical texts have shared, to some degree, in the development of the science and art of Bible translation. And there have been many linguistic theorists who have made significant contributions to the discipline. But it is undoubtedly Eugene A. Nida (born in 1914 and now retired in Brussels, Belgium) who has been most significant in leading the way toward a better understanding of effective Bible translation and has been most influential in inaugurating what may rightly be called a "revolution" in the field of Bible translation.

Building on his studies in linguistics and anthropology at the University of California at Los Angeles, the University of Southern California, and the University of Michigan — and working closely with the Summer Institute of Linguistics, which is the alter ego of Wycliffe Bible Translators — Nida developed a meaning-based approach to Bible translation. His theory lays emphasis on "dynamic" or "functional" equivalence in biblical translation, rather than what has been called "literal," "formal," "semantic," "grammatical," "linguistic," "textual," "word," or "pragmatic" equivalence. And in his work with the American Bible Society and the United Bible Societies from 1943 to his retirement in 1980, as well as in his extensive travels, tireless teaching, numerous writings, and many students, Nida has had a profound impact on all Bible translations today, both in the western world and throughout the third world — and both, it must be said, on those who agree with him in his understanding of what kind of "equivalence" is appropriate in the translation of biblical texts and on those who differ, thereby engendering a very profitable discussion on this most crucial matter.

Challenges for the Future

While as Christians we believe it to be vitally important, the translation of the Bible is hardly an easy task (which statement may quite rightly be viewed as the understatement of the year by those involved in biblical translation). It requires (1) the best "critically established" texts, (2) expertise in the languages of the Bible, as well as at least some ability in cognate languages, (3) sensitivity to the culture, ethos, particular emphases, and overall intent of the various biblical writers, (4) an understanding of the receptor language, which must include all sorts of indigenous linguistic, cultural, and anthropological factors, (5) a native fluency of expression in the receptor language, and (6) ultimate dependence on the God who inspired the original writers to also illuminate the present translators. Translation of the Bible is not just a transference of words. Rather, it is both a science, with all of the expertise, diligence, and care required in a science, *and* an art, with all of the intuitive, visionary, and expressional factors expected of an artist. Further, it requires diligence and fortitude — not only in the actual work of translation but also in responding to criticism. For the history of Bible translation has been one of rejection — at times of exile, occasionally even of martyrdom. Seldom, unless authorized by a king for his own political purposes, have biblical translators or their translations been widely honored.

Nonetheless, we live today in exciting times with respect to the translation of the Bible. Advances (1) in our understanding of the New Testament's earliest textual history, (2) in our comprehension of the linguistic data of both the Old and the New Testaments, and (3) in our perceptions of how to most effectively translate Scripture into the many vernacular languages of the day — all of this gives promise for a far better day in the future. What we cannot allow, however, is for any translation of the Bible (whether of the western world or of the so-called Third World) to become so honored and so revered that it becomes, in effect, a fossilized relic of the past, and therefore, with the inevitable changes that occur in every receptor language, fails to communicate to people today or in the future. That is what took place with respect to the two greatest translations of western Christendom, the Latin Vulgate and the old English King James Version. But that history must not be allowed to repeat itself.

Our commitment as Christian translators of the Bible is not to the preservation of any one particular translation (not even to the NRSV or the NIV). Rather, ours is a commitment (1) to God and his purposes in our world, (2) to the gospel ("Good News") that is inscripturated in the Bible, and (3) to productions of vernacular and contemporary translations of the Bible in a manner that appropriately represents the Christian message and is able to be understood and appreciated by all people in their various cultures and circumstances. Thus the challenge for New Testament scholars today is to move forward in the work of biblical translation on the basis of all of the present-day advances in biblical scholarship, constantly reaching out to new areas and constantly revising past endeavors — as God gives us wit and energy, coupled with his grace and enablement.

Conclusion

Quo vadis? in the title of this essay is an obvious play on the question of Peter to Jesus in John 13:36: "Lord, where are you going?" In 1896 the Polish novelist Henryk Sienkiewicz used that Latin expression as the title for his pseudo-historical novel about the love of a Roman army officer for a young Christian woman of ancient Rome, with not-too-veiled analogies being drawn to the political situation of his beloved Poland under Russian subjugation. And I have extended that usage as a pretext for discussing "From Whence to Where?" in the history of New Testament textual criticism and translation.

Like every human enterprise, the interpretation of the New Testament is a story of disparate data, diverse perspectives, and frequent false starts, which have sometimes resulted in rather wayward conclusions — but it is also a story of new discoveries, heroic endeavors, at times an emerging consensus, and certain important scholarly advances in understanding that have proven helpful for the present and give promise for the future. As confessing Christians we believe that the New Testament writings, together with those of the Old Testament, possess revelatory value from God (without here attempting to delineate either the nature or the extent of that revelation). Further, we affirm ultimate dependence on the

Spirit of God to interpret and apply that revelation in an adequate fashion for life and thought today (without here attempting to spell out any particular theory about the nature of God's Spirit or the way in which he works). Yet, as Christian scholars, we are also aware (1) that the biblical writings are rooted in history, with respect to both their content and their composition, and so are subject, in large measure, to our current human canons of historical and literary investigation for their interpretation, (2) that our contemporary understandings of the biblical writings have not come about *de novo*, but are influenced by past interpretations and conditioned by present perspectives, and (3) that what is held in our day regarding the text, translation, and interpretation of the New Testament will have repercussions for the study of these materials in the future, as well as for what will be believed in the future about the gospel that is proclaimed in them.

Like children raised in a loving but sometimes dysfunctional family — one that was never perfect, but one that usually attempted to do its best in various situations and under varied circumstances — we as New Testament scholars have had a goodly heritage, though also a somewhat checkered history. We must respect and honor those who have gone before us, even when disagreeing with them. For we "stand on the shoulders" of those who have preceded us. Nonetheless, profiting from both their advances and their mistakes, we need to move beyond our predecessors by the judicious use of new textual data, new historical insights, new methods for organizing the material available into a comprehensible whole, and new appreciations of the tasks of communication that have become available to us during the past 150 years — and so, under the direction of God's Spirit, be better able to fulfill our calling as New Testament scholars in the body of Christ and the family of God.

Index of Modern Authors

Agamben, G., 158
Aland, B., 4, 15, 19, 20, 26-29, 31-33, 35, 49, 52-56, 58-60, 328
Aland, K., 4, 14, 15, 20, 28, 30-35, 48, 49, 52, 54, 57, 65, 103, 104, 106, 107, 109, 328
Allen, W. A., 309
Attridge, H., 168, 175
Aune, D. E., 88, 280
Auwers, J.-M., 148, 149

Badiou, A., 158
Baker, M., 129, 135
Barclay, J. M. G., 157
Barrett, C. K., 179
Barrett, D., 62
Barthélemy, D., 218
Barthes, R., 273
Bassnett, S., 5, 139
Bauckham, R., 310
Beker, J. C., 162
Betz, H. D., 158, 278
Biber, D., 185
Black, M., 15
Blomberg, C., 308
Botha, P. J. J., 158
Boyer, F., 148

Bratcher, R. G., 117
Brault, J., 149
Brenner, A., 119
Brock, A. G., 260
Broman Olsen, M., 187
Brower, R., 117
Brown, R., 81, 83
Bruce, F. F., 2, 78, 117, 273
Bunyan, J., 311

Campbell, W. W., 311
Caragounis, C. C., 29
Carson, D. A., 118, 119, 125
Catford, J. C., 122, 128-30, 132
Cheng Chung-ying, 283
Chesterman, A., 186
Chomsky, N., 126
Clarke, K. D., 39
Clines, D. J. A., 148
Collinge, N. E., 2
Collins, C. J., 123
Colwell, E. C., 53, 103
Comfort, P., 62, 63, 66, 67, 76, 77, 79, 112, 113
Conrad, S., 185
Coste, J., 172
Courtés, J., 162

347

INDEX OF MODERN AUTHORS

Cranfield, C. E. B., 220
Crashaw, R., 308
Crisp, S., 120
Croato, S., 291, 292
Croy, N. C., 171
Culioli, A., 130
Culler, J., 272
Cullmann, O., 217

David, C., 149
Delay, F., 148
Depussé, M., 149, 151, 152
deSilva, D. A., 173
Diab, M., 187
Dunn, J. D. G., 220, 238

Echenoz, J., 149
Ehrman, B. D., 3, 79
Epp, E. J., 52, 73
Ewert, D., 2, 117

Farstad, A. L., 3, 30, 96, 123
Fee, G., 65, 77, 83, 241
Fingarette, H., 284-86
Fitzgerald, J. T., 174
Fitzmyer, J., 221
Fung Yu-lan, 285
Furnish, V. P., 237, 238, 243

Gadamer, H. G., 150, 292
Gamble, H. Y., 25
Garnsey, P., 297
Gaventa, B. R., 157, 161
Genette, G., 160
Gheorghita, R., 179
Gignac, A., 139, 149, 153, 154, 156, 158, 160
Goodacre, M., 29, 33
Gourgues, M., 149
Green, J. B., 202
Greimas, A. J., 162
Grelot, P., 149
Grenfell, B., 76
Grice, P., 135

Grobel, K., 112
Grudem, W., 122, 127
Gueunier, N., 149, 151
Guthrie, G. H., 177
Gutiérrez, G., 291
Gutt, E. A., 136

Haenchen, E., 65
Hafemann, S., 7
Hanson, A. T., 273
Harris, J. R., 60
Hasel, G., 6
Hatim, B., 132, 133, 139
Hays, R. B., 159, 234, 248
Head, P. W., 53, 103
Hermans, T., 138
Hester, J. D., 158
Hinkelammert, F., 299
Hodges, Z. C., 3, 30, 96
Holmes, M. W., 3
Hooker, M., 234, 235, 241, 246
Hort, F. J. A., 71-74, 86, 333
Hoskier, H. C., 47
Hsieh Yu-Wei, 275, 283
Huang Chi-chung, 275, 286
Hunston, S., 185
Hunt, A., 76
Hurley, R., 205

Jacquier, E., 27, 51
Jakobson, R., 2
Jeanrond, W. G., 154
Jellicoe, S., 246
Jeremias, J., 220, 223, 243, 245, 247, 248
Jobes, K. H., 222, 224, 225, 227
Johansson, S., 186
Johnson, L. T., 167, 168, 177, 205
Jones, A., 342
Jülicher, A., 308
Juen, A., 155
Junack, K., 28

Kafka, F., 300
Karavidopoulos, J., 15

Index of Modern Authors

Kennedy, G., 185
Kenyon, F., 64, 65
Kerns, T. R., 300
King, K. L., 19, 24
Knox, R. A., 167, 168
Koch, D.-A., 237, 239, 240
Köster, B., 15, 49
Koester, C. R., 168
Koptak, P. E., 161
Kraftchick, S. J., 7
Kress, G., 129
Kristeva, J., 272
Kubo, S., 117

Lacocque, A., 156
Lake, K., 56
Lançon, P., 149
Langland, W., 309
Lassave, P., 151, 154
Lau, D. C., 286
León-Portilla, M., 301
Lim, T., 140
Longacre, R. E., 121
Longenecker, B. W., 160, 163, 165
Louw, J. P., 196
Luz, U., 292

Maier, H. O., 264
Marrow, S. B., 178
Marshall, I. H., 72, 73, 203
Martini, C. M., 15
Martyn, L., 156, 158, 162, 163
Mason, I., 132, 133, 139
Matera, F. J., 281
McEnery, T., 185
Melville, H., 309
Menken, M. J. J., 221
Meslée, V. M. La, 149
Mesters, C., 291
Metzger, B. M., 1-3, 15, 29, 34, 39, 71, 83, 87, 106, 113, 117
Meyer, C. F., 185
Milik, J. T., 218
Min, K. S., 20

Mink, G., 17, 21, 22, 28, 49-51
Mitchell, A. C., 178
Mojola, A. O., 122, 136, 137, 139, 141
Moore, S. D., 154
Morris, L., 86
Müller, M., 217
Munday, J., 5, 122, 129, 137, 139
Myers, C. D., Jr., 7

Nanos, M. D., 156, 157
Nestle, Eb., 15
Nestle, Er., 15
Newmark, P., 129
Nida, E. A., 2, 5, 117, 118, 123, 125-28, 139-41, 168, 196
Norden, E., 334

O'Donnell, M. B., 119, 185, 191, 197
Ollenburger, B. C., 7
Olohan, M., 186
O'Neill, J. C., 105
Orlinsky, H. M., 117

Panier, L., 163, 164
Parker, D. C., 51, 57
Parry, D. W., 218
Parvis, M. M., 57, 59
Patte, D., 162
Pfitzner, V. C., 171
Philbrick, N., 309
Phillips, J. B., 142
Pierpont, W. G., 3, 30, 96
Pippin, T., 267
Porter, C. L., 52, 64, 81
Porter, S. E., 2, 117, 118, 120, 123, 126, 127, 132, 187, 188, 191, 197
Porter, W. J., 118
Prévost, J.-P., 148

Qimron, E., 218

Racine, J.-F., 55
Rahlfs, A., 222
Reardon, P., 313

INDEX OF MODERN AUTHORS

Reppen, R., 185
Resnik, P., 187
Reumann, J., 7
Ricoeur, P., 154-56, 292, 314
Ridderbos, H. N., 282
Robbins, V. K., 169
Robinson, M. A., 3, 30, 32, 96, 103
Rolland, P., 294, 304
Rosemont, H., Jr., 286, 287
Royse, J. R., 53, 56, 103, 107
Ryken, L., 122

Sarat, A., 300
Schneiders, S. M., 150
Schroeger, F., 177
Schwantes, M., 291
Scrivener, F. H. A., 3
Seeligmann, I., 229
Seifrid, M., 157
Sevin, M., 148
Sherwin-White, A. N., 297
Silva, M., 222, 224, 225, 227
Soden, H. F. von, 30, 97, 100
Specht, W., 117
Sperber, D., 134-36
Stanley, C. R., 220, 236, 237, 239
Statham, N., 125
Stine, P. C., 118
Störig, H. J., 1, 117
Streeter, B. H., 59
Sturz, H. A., 55
Stylianopoulos, T. G., 268

Taber, C. R., 5, 126, 127
Talbert, C. H., 172
Tamez, E., 291, 292, 297
Taubes, J., 158
Taylor, N., 234
Thériault, J.-Y., 149
Tischendorf, C. von, 30
Tregelles, S. P., 30
Trivedi, H., 5, 139
Trobisch, D., 31, 98

Tu Wei-ming, 284, 285
Tuckett, C., 234
Turner, N., 102

Ulrich, E., 218

van der Kooij, A., 219
van Henten, J. W., 119
Venard, O.-T., 149
Venuti, L., 5, 139-41, 144
Via, D. O., 6
Vööbus, A., 15

Wachtel, K., 28, 35
Wagner, J. R., 236-38
Wallace, D. B., 3, 79
Ward, T., 270
Warren, W., 65
Watson, F., 235
Watt, J. M., 140
Weber, M., 284
Weima, J., 86
Wendland, E., 122, 136, 137, 139, 141
Weren, W., 27
Westcott, B. F., 71-74, 86, 117, 333
Wikgren, A., 15, 86
Wilcock, M., 268, 269
Wilson, A., 185
Wilson, D., 134-36
Wilt, T., 5
Winger, M., 293
Wisse, F., 29, 54
Witherington, B., III, 154
Wright, N. T., 217

Yeo Khiok-khng, 273, 314-16, 318
Youtie, H. C., 58, 59

Ziegler, J., 219, 222, 225
Zimmerli, W., 223, 228
Zizek, S., 158
Zlateva, P., 5, 141
Zuntz, G., 55, 58, 64-66, 83, 85

Index of Ancient Sources

OLD TESTAMENT

Genesis
3:6	223
19:24	224
32:22-32	150
35:3	174
42:21	174

Exodus
4:31	174
6:25	113
19:4	264

Leviticus
5:9	224
26:3	281

Numbers
8:7	224
25:7	113
25:11	113

Deuteronomy
4:29	174
5:33	281
11:22	281
26:17	281
28:9	281
32:10-14	264
32:25	225
32:35	177
32:36	177
34:5	288

Joshua
1:1	288

Judges
2:8	288

1 Samuel
17:50	167

2 Kings
18:12	288

Job
8:16	225

Psalms
1:1-2	281
2:2	241
2:7	68
8:3	225
22	249
39	178
69	249
81:13	281
86:11	281
94:7-11	178
110:1	224
135:14	177

Isaiah
1:9	240
6:10	239
7:14	216
8:14	239
9:1-2	79, 80
9:2	79
10:22-23	239
11:10	239
26:20	179
27:9	239
28:11-12	237
28:16	239
41:8	222

INDEX OF ANCIENT SOURCES

41:9	222	53:2	219, 222, 224, 225, 248	**Habakkuk**	
41:20	223			2:3-4	179
42:1-4	220	53:3	218, 225, 229	2:4	180
42:1	68, 222	53:4	221, 226, 229, 242-44, 247		
42:3-4	219			**NEW TESTAMENT**	
42:19	288	53:5	221, 226, 229, 244, 245, 247		
43:10	222			**Matthew**	
44:1	222	53:6-7	219	2:16	223
44:2	222	53:6	218, 220, 221, 226, 227, 244-47	3:2	180
44:18	223			3:17	68
44:21	222	53:7-8	221, 228	5:11	174
44:26	222	53:7	220, 221, 227	6:6	109
45:4	222	53:8	218, 219, 227, 244, 246, 247	8:6	223
45:23	239			8:8	223
49:1	165	53:9	218, 228, 243, 244, 247	8:13	60, 223
49:6	222			8:17	221, 222, 226, 243
49:18	239	53:10-12	233		
50:10	222	53:10-11	246, 247	12:18-21	220
51:12	223	53:10	218, 230, 244	13:21	174
52	239	53:10a-b	229	14:2	223
52:5-54:1	236	53:10b	229	15:27	94, 106, 107
52:5	235, 236, 239, 240	53:10c-11	230	16:21	60
		53:11-12	219	17:18	223
52:7	235-37, 239, 240	53:11	218-20, 230, 244, 246	19:29	43, 60
52:10-54:6	220			20:23	60
52:11	235, 237-40	53:12	218, 221, 222, 226, 227, 231, 233, 244-47	20:31	60
52:13-53:12	215, 218, 222			21:15	223
52:13-53:9	232			21:28	60
52:13-15	224	53:14	224	21:42	67
52:13	222, 247, 248	54:1	235, 236, 239, 240	21:44	66
52:14	218, 220, 223-25, 247, 248			24:9	174
		59:7-8	239	24:38	60
52:15a	238	59:20-21	239	25:21	176
52:15	218-20, 224, 233, 235, 236, 238-40	65:1-2	239	26:39	70, 71
		66:18-19	219	27:24	60
53	215, 218-22, 233, 234, 240, 241, 243-49			27:32	104
		Jeremiah		27:44	174
		1:5	165	27:46	60
53:1-12	220				
53:1-3	219	**Hosea**		**Mark**	
53:1	220, 223, 224, 233-36, 239, 240	14:7	225	1:10	255
				1:11	68

Index of Ancient Sources

3:7	60	8:2	104	16:19-23	202, 203, 205
3:31	60	8:3	176	16:19-21	188, 191, 204
5:22	104	8:35	60	16:19-20	127, 131
5:26	69	8:43	69	16:19	104, 105, 112, 113,
6:22	60	8:51	223		194, 197, 211
6:23	60	8:54	223	16:20	93, 95, 97, 103,
6:33	60	9:42	223		105, 107, 112, 194,
6:41	60	9:48	99, 100		195, 202
7:28	107	9:51	209	16:21	94, 95, 103, 105,
10:17-31	25	10:28	317		194, 197, 201, 202
10:35	60	10:29-37	206	16:22-25	112
11:3	38, 39, 60	10:38	105	16:22-24	189, 192
12:36	60	10:39	60	16:22-23	204
12:44	69	10:41	60	16:22	101, 109, 194, 201
14:24	231	11:11	60	16:23	103, 108, 194-96,
14:72	60	11:13	98		201, 202, 205,
15:28	221	11:21	176		322
15:32	174	12:15	176	16:24-31	202-4
		12:40	98	16:24	194-96, 202, 205
Luke		12:45	223	16:25-26	189, 192
1:3	208	12:54	60	16:25	103, 109, 194-97,
1:5	105	13:8	102		311
1:14	176	13:14	98	16:26	100, 103, 109,
1:51-53	203	13:27	60		194, 197, 202, 316
2:43	223	13:35	60	16:27-28	190, 192
3:6	318	14:2	104	16:27	98, 194, 195, 202
3:11	102	15:1-2	210	16:28	205, 317
3:32	60	15:2	176	16:29-31	190, 193
3:34	109	15:3-32	210	16:29	97, 101, 103, 109,
3:37	60	15:11-32	206, 208		110, 194, 197, 317,
4:1	255	15:20	100		318
5:27	105	16:1-13	210	16:30	194, 195, 197,
5:39	102	16:1	104, 105		202, 318
6:4	60	16:6	60	16:31	97, 98, 108, 194,
6:20	208	16:7	102		195, 197, 211, 317,
6:21	99	16:14-31	210		318, 323
6:22	174	16:14-18	210	17:1	210
6:24	208	16:14	210, 211	17:16	100
6:26	60, 99	16:15	211	17:20	311
7:2	223	16:17	210	17:23	38, 40, 46
7:10	223	16:19-31	93, 187, 188, 197,	17:33	181
7:19	180		200, 206, 207,	19	194
8:1–9:50	209		307, 315, 318, 319	19:22	102

353

INDEX OF ANCIENT SOURCES

19:42	109	7:46	40	3:13	223		
20:17-18	67	7:52	78, 79	3:26	223		
21:11	60	7:53–8:11	75, 77, 88	4:25-28	241		
21:38	78	8:7	60	4:25	223		
21:43	67	8:9	60	4:27	223		
22:17	60	8:12-20	79	4:30	223		
22:30	60	8:12	79, 80	4:32	176		
22:37	221, 222	8:15-30	78	5:1	105		
22:41	70	9:4	35, 38	5:34	105		
22:43-45	70	9:5	35	7	98		
22:43-44	70, 72	9:38-39a	80, 81, 88	7:17-50	209		
23:9-10	227	10:7	60	7:17	108		
23:32	221	12:16	223	8–12	98		
23:33	73	12:23	223	8:9	105		
23:34	72, 88	12:32	223	8:32	220, 227		
24	66	12:34	223	8:33	228		
24:3	73, 74	12:38	220, 223, 239	8:37	81		
24:6	73, 74	13:2	60	9:11	105		
24:12	73, 74	13:26	60	9:12	105		
24:13-35	318	13:31	223	9:33	105		
24:36	73, 74, 102	13:36	345	9:36	105		
24:39	60	14:10	60	10:1	105		
24:40	73, 74	16:18	60	10:19	60		
24:50	38, 60	16:20	176	11:4	208		
24:51	73, 74	16:23	38, 60	11:19	174		
24:52	73, 74	17:11	60	11:28	105		
24:53	78	18:1	38, 60	12:13	105		
		18:31	60	13	98		
John		20:11-31	257	13:14	60		
1:9	180	20:15	259	13:33	68		
1:18	74	20:17	60, 258	15:4	60		
1:23	81	20:29	258	16:12	37, 40, 51		
1:34	75	20:31	258	16:14	105		
3:14	223	21:4	60	16:16-38	298		
3:31	180	21:16	60	16:22	108		
4:51	223	21:17	60	17:1-8	298		
5:2	38, 41, 60	21:22-23	259	17:34	105		
6:14	180	21:24	60	18:2	105		
6:23	60			18:7	60, 105		
7:36	78	**Acts**		18:24	105		
7:38-39	262	1:14	60	19:24	105		
7:39	60, 223	2:7	44, 60	19:29	173		
7:40-52	79	2:41–5:42	211	19:31	173		

20:9	105	6:1–7:6	294	8:26	256
20:12	223	6	294	8:29	257
20:24	60	6:4	294	8:31	243
20:28	181	6:6	281	8:32	227, 242, 245, 247
21:12	105	6:19	147		
21:38	298	6:22-23	277	8:36	257
23:15	98	6:22	294	9:3	243
23:30	60	7	293, 294	9:4	329
24:26	298	7:1-13	295	9:27-28	239
24:27	298	7:1-7	295	9:29	240
26:32	298	7:7-25	294, 295	9:33	239
27:1	105	7:7-13	295, 299, 304	10:15-16	240
27:8	38, 60	7:7	299	10:15	235, 237
27:14	309	7:8-13	295	10:16-17	235
		7:8	293	10:16	220, 233, 239
Romans		7:9-11	299	10:20-21	239
1–11	304	7:9	300	11:26-27	239
1–3	301	7:10	299	12:11	288
1:1	288	7:12	293, 299	13	31
1:4	329	7:13b	297	13:10	288
1:7	84, 329	7:14-24	300	14:4	288
1:15	329	7:14-15	301	14:11	239
1:17	179	7:18-20	302	14:15	242
1:18	301	7:21-23	302	14:18	288
2:7	277	7:22	293	14:23	329
2:16	45, 60	7:23	293	15–16	329
2:24	236	7:24	147, 302	15:3	174
3:9	301	7:25	293	15:8	243
3:15-17	239	7:25b	302	15:9	243
4:25	226, 227, 231, 233, 244, 245, 247	8	304	15:12	239
		8:1-11	294	15:13	176
		8:3	244	15:16	238
4:25b	246	8:11	60, 294	15:20-21	235, 238
5–8	294	8:12-29	255	15:21	220, 224, 233, 239, 240
5:1–8:39	294	8:12-21	294		
5:1-21	294	8:12	255	15:33	329
5:2	257	8:17	257	16:2	176
5:3	174	8:19	256	16:4	243
5:6	242	8:21-22	256	16:23	329
5:8	242	8:21	255, 257	16:24	329
5:15	246, 247	8:22-30	294	16:25-27	329
5:19	246, 247	8:22	256		
5:21	277	8:23	256		

INDEX OF ANCIENT SOURCES

1 Corinthians

Ref	Page
1-2	83
1:2	83, 84
1:13	242, 243
2:1	82, 83
2:6-8	241
2:6	241
2:7-8	83
2:7	83
2:8	241
2:10	83
3:5	288
4:6	243
4:9	173
7:22	288
10:9	60
10:30	243
11:23	245-47
11:24	242
12:10	60
14:21	237
14:34	60
15:3-5	248
15:3	244, 245, 247
15:29	243
15:42	277
15:50	277
15:54	60

2 Corinthians

Ref	Page
1:1	84
1:4	174
1:11	243
1:12	60
2:14	288
3:6	288
4:5	288
4:18	311
5:3	38, 60
5:14	242
5:15	242
5:21	242, 243, 247
6:2	288
6:14-7:1	237
6:17	237
7:4	176
12:10	243

Galatians

Ref	Page
1-2	165
1	148, 157, 158, 160
1:1	159, 162-64
1:3	159
1:4	161, 164, 242-45, 247, 276
1:6-12	147
1:6	158, 159
1:7	159
1:8-9	158
1:8	159, 162, 163
1:9	158, 159
1:10	159, 161, 163
1:12	163
1:13-15	161
1:14	165
1:15	159, 164
1:16	161, 163, 165
1:17	159
1:20	158
1:23-24	161
2	148, 157, 158, 160
2:2	159
2:5	159, 329
2:6	159
2:7	159
2:9	159
2:12	159
2:14b-21	161
2:14	159
2:17	159
2:20	161, 164, 242
3:1	158, 159
3:2-5	280
3:2	158, 159
3:3	159
3:5	159
3:6-4:7	164
3:8	272, 273
3:9	273, 274
3:11	179
3:13	242, 247
3:14	154, 159, 280
3:15	158
3:16	159
3:17	158, 159
3:18	159
3:19-20	162, 163
3:19	159, 163
3:20	163
3:21	159, 162
3:22	159
3:28	159, 164
3:29	159
4	277
4:1	158
4:4-7	256
4:4	164
4:5	159
4:6	280
4:8	287
4:9	159, 287
4:11	158
4:12	161
4:14	159
4:15	159
4:16	159
4:20	158
4:21-31	164, 278
4:21	159
4:23	159
4:25	287
4:26	164, 239
4:29	280
4:30	159
5-6	164, 279
5:1-26	279
5:1-6	279
5:2-12	278
5:2	158

Index of Ancient Sources

5:4	159	1:11	176	8:6	179
5:7	159	1:24	243	8:8	329
5:11	159			9:15	179
5:13-26	280	**Philemon**		9:28	180, 226
5:13	279	6	60	10:7	172, 178
5:13b-c	279			10:10	178
5:13c	287	**1 Thessalonians**		10:25	177, 179
5:14	288	1:6	176	10:26-31	169, 177
5:16-18	280	2:3-6	87	10:26-30	181
5:16	158, 279-82	2:7-8	87	10:26	170
5:17a	280	2:7	85	10:30	178, 179
5:17b	281	2:11	86	10:31	178
5:19-21	278	2:14-16	241	10:32-39	169, 178
5:22	176, 280	2:17	86	10:32	170
5:24	278	2:19	176	10:33	172, 173, 176
5:25-26	281	5:10	243, 247	10:34	172
5:25	280-82			10:35-36	179
6:1	158, 280	**1 Timothy**		10:37-38	179
6:2	288	2:9	60	10:37	179
6:7-8	277	3:13	181	10:38	179
6:8	277, 278, 280	3:15	175	11:1-40	169, 173, 177
6:14	159			11:4	180
6:18	159	**Hebrews**		11:9	178
		1:1	178	11:13	178
Ephesians		1:5	68	11:16	177
1:1	83, 329	2:7-9	173	11:17	178
1:14	181	2:10	172	11:26	174
4:9-11	256	2:14	175	11:33	178
5:2	243	3:6	61, 178	11:35	176
5:8-14	170	4:1	179	11:39	179
5:20	243	4:7	178	11:40	179
6:4	170	4:12-13	168	12:1-4	171
		4:12	181	12:1-2	173
Philippians		4:16	178	12:1	173
1:1	288	5:5	68	12:2-3	178
1:7	243	5:7-9	172	12:2	173, 176
2:7	247, 248	5:7	172	12:3	181
2:7a	247	5:11-14	172	12:5-13	171, 172
2:8	246-48	6:12	179	12:11	176
2:29	176	6:15	179	13	31
		6:17	179	13:3	175
Colossians		6:19	181	13:14	177
1:7	243	7:6	179	13:17	181

357

INDEX OF ANCIENT SOURCES

13:18	175	1:8	61	14:18	61
13:21	60			18:19	60
		Jude		18:21	61
James		5	48, 60	19:17	61
1:2	176	15	48, 61	19:20	61
1:22	29	18	48	20:11	38
2:3	29, 48, 60	22-23	47, 48	21:4	60
2:4	29			21:16	60
4:14	48, 60	**Revelation**		22:6	267
		1:20	61	22:8-9	266
1 Peter		3:7	60		
1-2	48	4:4	60		
1:6	29	5	262	**EARLY CHRISTIAN**	
1:16	29	5:6	60, 264	**LITERATURE**	
2:5	48, 60	5:12	264		
2:9	181	5:13	60	**1 Clement**	
2:22-23	243	6:8	46, 60	16	220
2:24	221, 226	6:11	60	16.3-14	220
2:25	29, 221	7:1	61	16.3	220
3:18	40	7:9	61	16.7-9	220
4:14	174	9:12	61	16.12	220
4:16	29	9:20	60		
5:9	48, 60	11–12	262	**Athanasius**	
5:10	29	11	262, 266	*Exp. fid.*	
		11:1	265	1	228
2 Peter		11:3	264		
2:6	29	11:5-6	265	*De syn.*	
2:11	29	11:7-10	265	28	228
2:15	29	11:7	265		
3:6	29	11:11	265	**Barnabas**	
3:10	29, 51	11:12	265	5.2	221
3:16	29	11:18	61, 265		
3:18	29	12	262, 265	**Clement of Alexandria**	
		12:1-6	263	*Strom.*	
1 John		12:7-9	263	1.22	216
1:7	29	12:10-12	263, 264		
3:1	48, 61	12:13-17	263	**Epiphanius**	
3:19	48, 60	13	31	*Ancoratus*	
5:10	29	13:5	264	31.4-5	71
5:18	29	13:8	61		
		13:15	60	**Eusebius**	
2 John		13:18	87	*Ecclesiastical History*	
1:12	60	14:8	61	3.39.17	78

Irenaeus			SECOND TEMPLE		4QIsaiah[b]	
Adv. haer.			LITERATURE		fr. 39: Isa 53:11-12	218
2.28.5		228				
3.21.1-3		216	Josephus		4QIsaiah[c]	
			Ant.		fr. 37-39: Isa 52:13–53:3,	
Justin			12.103-9	216	6-8	218
1 Apol.			20.214	176		
31		216			4QIsaiah[d]	
			Letter of Aristeas		fr. 11 ii: Isa 53:8-12	218
Dial.			257	176		
13		220	302	216	CLASSICAL	
13.2-9		220	308-11	216	LITERATURE	
13.3		220				
13.4		220	Philo		Aristotle	
13.5		220	*Life of Moses*		*Nicomachean Ethics*	
13.6		220	2.37-40	216	8	174
13.7		220			9	174
13.8		220	Testament of Judah			
			23.3	176	Herodotus	
Martyrdom of Polycarp					*Persian War*	
14.1		223			6.67	173
			RABBINIC			
Polycarp			LITERATURE		Xenophon	
Philippians			*y. Sanh.*		*Memorabilia*	
8.1		226	23c	308	2.3.14	176
Ps-Justin			*y. Hag.*		EASTERN	
Coh. ad Graec.			77d	308	LITERATURE	
13		216				
					Confucius	
Theodoret			QUMRAN		*Analects*	
Hist. eccl.			LITERATURE		2:14	283
i.3		228			3:17	285
			1QIsaiah[a]		4:2	286
			col. XLIV	218	4:4	283
APOCRYPHAL					4:5	285
LITERATURE			1QpHab		4:6	285
			7.14–8.1	179	4:8	285
4 Maccabees			8.13	176	4:11	275
13:23		175	12.1-15	176	4:16	275
					4:24	275

INDEX OF ANCIENT SOURCES

4:25	284, 316	11:11	316	14:5	285
5:10	275	12:1	283	14:6	275
5:26	286	13:7	275	15:24	275
6:12	275, 276	13:19	285	16:8	275
6:19	275	13:23	275	17:2	275
6:28	284, 316	13:25	275	17:6	285
7:21	283	13:26	275	18:6	286
7:30	276	13:37	275		

www.ingramcontent.com/pod-product-compliance
Lightning Source LLC
Chambersburg PA
CBHW021816300426
44114CB00009BA/197